Macintosh upgrade

Upgrade cost	New Mac	Mac upgrade A	Mac upgrade B
CPU			
RAM			
Accelerator			
Floppy			
Hard disk			
Backup			
Monitor			
I/O cards			
Printer			
Network cards			
Communication cards			
Subtotal hardware			
Software			
Buying			
Other			
Subtotal other			
Total			

Upgrade Your Macintosh® and Save a Bundle

Bob Brant

FIRST EDITION
FIRST PRINTING

© 1991 by **Bob Brant**.
Published by Windcrest Books, an imprint of TAB Books.
TAB Books is a division of McGraw-Hill, Inc.
The name "Windcrest" is a registered trademark of TAB Books.

Library of Congress Cataloging-in-Publication Data

Brant, Bob.
    Upgrade your Macintosh and save a bundle / by Bob Brant.
        p.   cm.
    Includes bibliographical references and index.
    ISBN 0-8306-7770-4   ISBN 0-8306-3770-2 (pbk.)
    1. Macintosh (Computer) 2. Microcomputers—Upgrading. I. Title.
TK7889.M33B73 1991
621.39'16—dc20   91-16522
                                                  CIP

TAB Books offers software for sale. For information and a catalog, please contact TAB Software Department, Blue Ridge Summit, PA 17294-0850.

Acquisitions Editor: Ron Powers
Book Editor: John W. Bottomley
Production: Katherine G. Brown
Book Design: Jaclyn J. Boone
Paperbound Cover: Sandra Blair Design, Harrisburg, PA   EL1

Contents

Acknowledgments

This book is dedicated to Steven Jobs and the other incredible members of the original Apple Macintosh[1] team whose vision, perseverance, and skills made it possible to introduce a better computer for "The Rest of Us;" and to John Scully whose vision carried the Macintosh forward and made it an everyday reality in corporate America. Credit must also respectfully be given to the resident geniuses at Xerox Palo Alto Research Center for their STAR system, the forerunner of the Lisa (the parent to the Macintosh), even though it was not allowed to evolve to its full potential there; to the whiz kids over at Atari and Commodore who have shown Apple, on more than one occasion, how a good idea can be "colored" and improved upon; to the individuals on the late Don Esteridge's IBM PC Boca Raton "dream team" who took an Apple idea, re-innovated it, and changed the face of the earth forever; and finally, to the hard working individuals at Apple, and all the third-party vendors—both software and hardware—for continuously pushing the "outside of the envelope" as Chuck Yeager would say. Their hard work, dedication, and commitment to the Apple Macintosh ideal constantly changes the shape and destiny of computing for the rest of us . . . always for the better!

Special thanks are due to Darwin Gross, author, musician, way-shower to many, and the most humble, creative genius, anyone could ever have the good fortune to meet, for the continuing inspiration.

---

[1] This book presumes you are already familiar, at least in passing, with Apple Computer, Inc., and the Apple Macintosh computer. If you want additional information, contact any authorized Apple Dealer or Apple Computer, Inc., 20525 Mariani Ave., Cupertino, CA 95014, (408) 996-1010. Apple, the Apple logo, and Macintosh are registered trademarks of Apple Computer, Inc.

Warm thanks and appreciation to my wife, Bonnie Brant, for challenging the ideas, proofreading and ensuring my written expression fell somewhat within the confines of the English language; and to my mother, Mary Brant, for first sparking my interest in books, writing, and life.

Thanks and appreciation also go out to Ron Powers, Stephen Moore, Kimberly Martin, Carol Nelson, Melissa Adams, and many other hard-working folks at TAB and Osborne who "proved" to me that publishing industry workloads are every bit as demanding as those in the electronics industry.

Thanks must also be extended to Kate Paisley of Apple Computer, Inc., Public Relations, for connecting me with the various Apple people and departments to fulfill the requirements of this book.

Similar thanks must also be extended to numerous individuals at third-party vendors for making this book possible and for keeping the flame of the Macintosh idea burning brightly.

Preface

Change is the key word in the 1990s. You know this; the media in all its forms bombards you with this fact daily. It applies particularly well to your computer needs. Whatever computer you have today, a better one will be available tomorrow. You will want this computer. In fact, you will need it. This is the message your salivary glands and other body sensory apparatus will deliver to you after looking at the slick color photos in the marketing brochure.

Enter this book. It offers you a rational and money-saving alternative to buying each new computer model as it is announced. Treat it as you would a friend or business associate—as a great sounding board for your new ideas—but you have to make the final decision yourself.

In the beginning

The book you now hold in your hands builds on a successful heritage. It owes its life to Ron Powers, the acquisitions director at TAB/Windcrest. Ron reasoned that if you can upgrade your DOS PC[1] and save a bundle, then you can certainly do the same thing for your Macintosh.

Ron is right of course—you can save a bundle. This book tells how you can do it in two ways, either to upgrade the model you have or to be smarter about the model

---

[1] Aubrey Pilgrim's *Upgrade Your IBM Compatible and Save a Bundle* (Windcrest 1990) and *Build Your Own 80486 and Save a Bundle* (Windcrest 1991), and earlier books in the series do an excellent job in this area.

you get. Third-party vendors make the tools that allow even the earliest of the Mac models to be upgraded to screaming 68030 versions that are equal in speed and performance to Apple's newest models and compatible with the latest Macintosh software—all for a fraction of the cost of buying a new machine. Beyond that, if you buy the right Macintosh model at the right time from the right source at the right price, you can also save a bundle.

Your input and feedback

Feedback from readers of my previous book, *Build Your Own Macintosh and Save a Bundle* (Windcrest 1990), proved that in upgrading or building your Mac, you are dealing with a rapidly changing field and information set and you really have to hustle just to keep up with it.[2] In fact, a newsletter has grown up to serve just that purpose.[3]

Like the physics principle you read about in your school days, the Heisenberg Uncertainty Principle (the light you are looking with alters what you are looking at), if you take a given field or set of data and look at it from a different point of view or level of awareness, it changes the results you get.

I am amazed to see how many new wrinkles, twists, shortcuts, and original ideas emerge when Mac enthusiasts from all over the world collectively put their attention on a particular niche area. I expect to see the same—even more so—from this book because of its wider appeal. I look forward to your letters.

May the Force be with you

Time is definitely on your side. Macintosh computer parts are less expensive today than they were a year ago. A used Mac will always be less expensive than buying a new one. With five million Apple Macintoshes in the world, a substantial market in used Macintoshes and equipment has emerged within the last few years that only strengthens and reinforces Apple's new Macintosh sales. These trends, combined with ever more efficient marketing and distribution channels, will continue to serve your interests in the future. You are only seeing the tip of the iceberg today. More hardware and software options will be available in the future, and they will cost less as time goes on.

We are all individuals, and each person's concept of the Macintosh will always be different from the next person's. I continue to hold the vision that the highest purpose of the better computer for "The Rest of Us" will best be served by each person "custom-tailoring" a Macintosh to meet his or her own unique needs, and that there will always be new, different, and better ways to do this. Starting with

---

[2] My other book offers an alternative cost saving idea: Start with an Apple Macintosh logic board and put a board in a box to save a bundle.

[3] The newsletter focus is on upgrading your own Mac or assembling one from catalog parts to fit your unique needs. It is available from Brant Associates, P.O. Box 68708, Portland, OR 97268.

the platform that Apple has provided, whether staying outside the box or going within, you cannot help but benefit from what these chapters provide.

It has been said that nothing is stronger than an idea whose time has come. If that is true, then you are about to embark on a voyage of expanding information and knowledge from which there is no turning back. The corporate management at Apple and third-party Macintosh vendors should be pleased because this cannot help but sell more Apple Macintosh computers—both new and used. Knowledge is power, and all I have done here is to move the pivot point a little closer to you, the user.

Who I am

I am a full-time Macintosh consultant who provides both software and hardware solutions for a wide range of business clients. In 1983, as Operations Manager for a publishing firm in Northern California, I became "hooked" by having one of the first $10,000 Apple Lisa systems on my desk. My initial Macintosh introduction followed a short time later, and several years in various sales and management capacities with Businessland, Nynex, Microage, and a regional reseller in the northwest honed my experience. Prior to that, a combined 10 years with DEC and Data General in the minicomputer industry with a B.S.E.E. from the University of Denver and credits toward M.S.E.E. and M.B.A. degrees gave me my frame of reference.

Introduction

"**If you don't know** where you are going, you will probably end up someplace else" is how Yogi Berra of the New York Yankees baseball team put it many years ago. So a brief overview of this book is in order before you get started—its organization and purpose, who should use it, how you should use it, its chapter contents, and some helpful starting hints.

Organization and purpose

I presume if you are reading this book, you are either a Macintosh owner now or planning to become one. If you are a DOS PC owner and have picked this book up out of curiosity, to build your knowledge base, or because of a future need, rest assured that I will spend little time pontificating about the virtues of the Macintosh versus a DOS PC—this book should offer you a genuine and objective service.

I am not pushing the Macintosh. My own computer consulting business has introduced me to both gung-ho DOS PC and gung-ho Macintosh users, each group offering compelling reasons for their own viewpoint. While I can pass on either solution to a client, sometimes both working together is the answer. At this time, the Macintosh alternative is more attractive than ever to today's first time users in both price and performance.

It's actually far easier to upgrade any model Macintosh than it is to do the equivalent in the DOS PC world. No DIP switch settings to worry about, fewer cables to connect, no complicated software to load, and no BAT files to create. Also, formatting your hard disk is a breeze compared to a DOS PC. Although the concepts are similar, this book will not help you to upgrade your 8086/8-, 80286-, 80386-, or 80486-based computer. Some excellent books are already available to help you do just that. Aubrey Pilgrim's *Upgrade Your IBM Compatible and Save a Bundle* (Windcrest 1990), *Build Your Own 80486 and Save a Bundle* (Windcrest 1991), and earlier books in the series do an excellent job in this area.

Philosophy, options, process

Why upgrade your Mac? It's easy to do. Whatever generation of Macintosh you own, all of them are readily expandable today. No matter how old your Macintosh is, you shouldn't consider it obsolete until you have looked at your circumstances. This book will help you do that.

Much information has been made available on upgrading your Macintosh computer, but no source has gathered it together into one place. This is what you now hold in your hand. This book will answer your questions in the three areas of:

- Philosophy—Why should you upgrade your Macintosh?
- Options—How can you make the best choices in Apple and third-party upgrades?
- Process—How do you upgrade the Macintosh you currently own?

No attempt has been made to present all the options, because the actual products used in upgrading can change so quickly that the book would be out of date by the time it returned from the printers. This task is performed extremely well by the excellent weekly and monthly magazines in addition to quarterly product guides that service the Macintosh community. See chapter 18 for the complete list.

This book will, however, give you a foundation and the tools you can use over and over in the future. What is the best solution to fit your needs? You still have to make that decision. You hold in your hands a road map and guidelines to assist you.

Low-end focus

While anybody can buy an outstanding Macintosh setup for $100,000 and an almost outstanding setup for $10,000, the average person, department, or business is not interested in making this type of investment. This book is aimed at the lower end of the budget spectrum. Consequently, a lot of neat high-end parts have been left out, but ongoing discussions in the Macintosh publications just mentioned will keep you posted on developments. There is literally no upper end to Macintosh. I've focused on the budget-conscious group, because it is possible to do a lot if you know what you are doing. This book will definitely help you.

The key steps pointed out by Kenny Rogers in his "Gambler" song—hold, fold, walk away, and run—are sometimes the most appropriate alternatives to consider when buying or upgrading your Macintosh.

Being neither a hardware nor a software genius myself, these chapters have deliberately been kept simple. But nifty technical things have been done, and I have found some of them. Because the ideas are not mine and I do believe in giving credit where it is due, you will notice the abundance of notes informing you where to look.

Who should use this book

Whether you are a first-time Macintosh buyer or a Mac owner, reading *Upgrade Your Macintosh and Save a Bundle* will show you why upgrading your Mac or buying a used one might be a good idea for you and the reasons why with very few exceptions it will always cost less than buying a new Macintosh.

How you should use this book

This book is not a technical manual with detailed schematics and board-level engineering details. The instructions, photographs, and illustrations assist you in doing the upgrades in the shortest possible time so that you might enjoy the fruits of your labor—a higher performing Mac that has saved you a bundle without buying a new one.

The book also gives you the actual thought processes you should consider—guidelines, tradeoffs, and finally the step-by-step, illustrated instructions for upgrading any Mac from a Mac 128 to a Mac IIfx, including the new Classic, LC, and IIsi models. For example, you will learn how to expand memory, add a floppy or hard disk drive, change to a bigger display, speed up your Mac with an accelerator card, install an expansion chassis, and other upgrade options. Sources are mentioned at the end of each option chapter to make it easier for you to get started and order your own parts.

We live in a rapidly changing world, so the specific product/company information on these pages will change. This process of change is relentless, like the grass growing in your yard in the summertime. Expect that when you go through the process outlined here that prices, products, companies, or all three will have changed. I can almost guarantee it sight unseen.

You will be able to use the how-you-do-it information for a long time. Plus, you will add to it over time as your own experience grows. The bottom line is that you should use the sources and references mentioned in the chapters to research and investigate your own best solution. Consider specific products shown only as a starting point of departure.

Chapter overview

Figure I-1 shows the complete chapter lineup and contents overview. Chapters 1 through 5 cover the philosophy, chapters 6 through 11 offer the options, and chapters 12 through 18 cover the process.

- Chapter 1 discusses why you should consider upgrading. Money savings are a big reason, but not the only one. This chapter also presents why you might not want to upgrade and how you can buy new and still save money. Several factors affecting the upgrading vs. buying decision are illustrated.

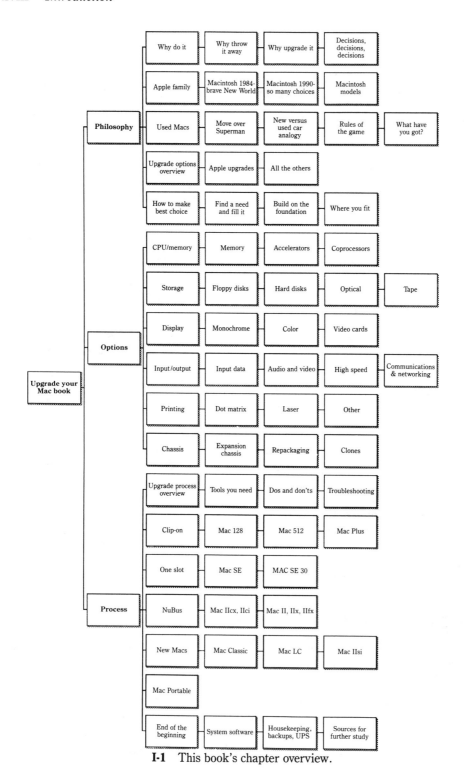

I-1 This book's chapter overview.

- Chapter 2 gives you a brief historical overview of all fourteen Mac models and examines the Apple Macintosh Family models vs. the discontinued Mac models. Five classifications of Mac models are introduced to simplify discussion throughout the remainder of this book, and the models within each class are discussed in more detail.
- Chapter 3 discusses used Macs, how they can help you, the market, the sources, the strategies, and the pros and cons of using them.
- Chapter 4 overviews the upgrade options available to you. It discusses the Apple upgrades, and then gives an overview of the upgrade options discussed in the following chapters concerning memory/CPU, storage, display, input/output, printing, and chassis option products you might find useful.
- Chapter 5 discusses the how you expand/upgrade/buy another Mac process and the elements that go into it in detail. This chapter focuses on the thought process you should be using, and applies them to several Macintosh system designs giving you practical tools, worksheets, and questions you can use.
- Chapter 6 discusses memory and CPU upgrade options. It also covers the pros and cons of memory upgrades, SIMMs and their continuing price decline, the benefits of accelerator boards, and coprocessors.
- Chapter 7 discusses short-term, working, and long-term storage options. The pros and cons of floppy disks, hard disks and their continuing price decline, and optical disks and tape products are also examined here.
- Chapter 8 discusses display options and examines monochrome and color monitors, including how to choose the best one and the right video card for you. Specific recommendations are made for each category.
- Chapter 9 discusses input/output options and explores input data, audio and video, processing and control, communications, and networking alternatives. Specific recommendations are made for each category.
- Chapter 10 discusses dot matrix, laser, and other printer alternatives. This chapter examines some of the products available now and makes spcific recommendations for each category.
- Chapter 11 discusses what Mac expansion chassis and repackaging options do for you, and what clones might do to you.
- Chapter 12 overviews the upgrade installation process—the subject of the remaining chapters—and discusses the tools you need, *do*s and *don't*s, and troubleshooting guidelines.
- Chapter 13 goes through an illustrated disassembly of the clip-on Macintosh models and how you add various option upgrades.
- Chapter 14 goes through an illustrated disassembly of the one-slot Macintosh models and how you add various option upgrades.
- Chapter 15 goes through an illustrated disassembly of the NuBus Macintosh models and how you add various option upgrades.
- Chapter 16 goes through an illustrated disassembly of the three new Macintosh models and how you add various option upgrades.
- Chapter 17 goes through an illustrated how you open the Portable Macintosh and how to install modem, memory, and other upgrades.

- Chapter 18 briefly explores Apple System Software, reviews housekeeping tips including the importance of backups and why you should have a UPS (uninterruptible power supply), and presents sources for increasing your Macintosh knowledge base on an ongoing basis.

You can do it

Upgrading seems difficult only because there are so many choices. This book has already done the difficult work. With a little guidance, you can certainly do things yourself and save money in the process. Anyone who has ever assembled a component stereo system or attached a video recorder to a TV set can probably handle any Macintosh upgrading.

When you finish reading *Upgrade Your Macintosh and Save a Bundle*, you will know how to upgrade your Mac or when to get another one, how much it will cost, where to get the parts, and how to install them. This knowledge can save you big bucks. Those with more experience might just want to jump directly into a chapter that interests you, or you might read it from cover to cover with a bag of munchies at your side.

Chapter 1
Why upgrade your Macintosh

Don't do it. Don't throw away your Macintosh, unless you absolutely must. Besides, just looking at Fig. 1-1 is enough to make you sad.

You have probably heard the saying, "If it ain't broke, don't fix it," many times. Nowhere is this more true than with your Macintosh. If you own one of the early vintage Macs, chances are by now you are well into your second power supply. Chances are equally likely you have never had to replace anything else. The floppy disk, monitor, keyboard, mouse, and hard disk (probably in an external case)—the electromechanical parts that wear out over time—are all original vintage issue. The fact is that these parts are likely to give many more years of service before they need replacement, depending on your usage of them. The logic board, the "heart" of your Macintosh, is likely to last far beyond that because it is all solid-state electronics—it has no moving parts to wear out. Its only demise occurs if you drop it, fry it, freeze it, or zap it; sudden shocks, excessive heat or cold, and static electricity are its only enemies, not old age.

1-1 Don't throw your Macintosh away . . . upgrade it.

Why throw it away

Someone told me years ago that if the automobile had kept up with the computer in rate of change and increase in price performance, your top-of-the-line Cadillac would get 1,000,000 miles per gallon and cost $2.50. Today, the results would be even better. As one writer put it, "Had your car's fuel efficiency improved at this rate over the same 31-year life of the integrated circuit, you would have a lifetime supply of gas on your first fillup!"[1]

Think about it for a moment. Some of the functions accomplished on the mainframe computers of the 1960s that occupied a room and required raised floors, heavy-duty electrical service, and special air conditioning[2] can today be accomplished faster on your pocket calculator—certainly on a full-function notebook computer you can carry in your briefcase—and definitely on your Macintosh!

Why then do people get rid of their old Macs? It's called "perceived obsolescence" or "conspicuous consumption," or, if you are in a larger organization, "industry standards," or just plain "keeping up with the Joneses." Whatever term you use, it is the process by which perfectly functioning current models are traded in for new ones. Whether you are talking about automobiles, stereo systems, kitchen appliances, or toys, the process is universal and an integral part of our advanced industrialized society. In its simplest form, the marketing departments of all companies create "images" when advertising their new products. These images cause you to salivate over their newest, shiny-smooth model somewhat bypassing your higher brain functions of reason. You buy the newest model. Then you figure out what to do with the old model you have. Next year the process repeats itself.

What is another reason people get rid of their old Macs? The new Mac model does more at the same price. Microcomputers in general and Macintoshes in particular differ from automobiles, stereo systems, kitchen appliances, and toys in this one important area of price versus performance. The Macintosh computer on your desk today does more work than the computers that filled a room 20 years ago, and costs far less. The productivity improvement with other products has not been as dramatic; if there has been an improvement, chances are it too is computer-related. Part of the fabric of our computer industry is that new machines are announced each year that deliver improved performance at the same price.

The original Mac 128 in 1984 came with 128K RAM, 400K internal floppy, internal 9″ monitor, keyboard, and mouse, and cost $2495—and you paid full list through a dealer to get one. The Mac LC comes with 2Mb RAM, 40Mb internal hard disk, 1.4Mb internal floppy, 12″ RGB Color Monitor, keyboard, and mouse for the same $2495. Almost any Apple dealer would be happy to give you this discount and make the sale.

First, the good news

No matter what kind of Macintosh you now own, it is a sure bet that you would like to extend its capability in some way. The good news for all Macintosh owners is that the world is beating a path to your doorstep. No matter what you are doing with your Mac today, some third-party vendor is probably working on a way to help your Macintosh do that function better, faster, and cheaper.

---

[1] Patrick Gelsinger, "Smaller Is Bigger," *CIO*, November 1990, p. 110.

[2] Nico Krohn, "IBM's Five-Chip 370 Processor Could Lead to Desktop Mainframes," *Infoworld*, 2/19/90, p. 5. Who would have thought it possible only a few short years ago?

Now, the bad news

The Macintosh you are currently using, whether you bought it new, used, or built it yourself (my other book shows you how), is worth less upon resale today than what you paid for it, and in the future will be worth far less than you paid for it, guaranteed. Apple, in order to promote its newest models, must offer you a better, faster, and/or cheaper Macintosh than the one you now own in order to make you reach in your pocket and pull out the money to buy a new Mac. Of course, when Apple introduces this model, it makes the one you own worth less—simple, just like used car prices decline from year to year when the new models are introduced.

If you own a Macintosh now, any Macintosh, you are an automatic participant in this game—willing or not. For example, on October 15, 1990, Apple introduced its new Classic models replacing the SE models and removed the SE models from its price list. Your Macintosh SE was automatically worth $500 less after dinner than it was before breakfast time.

What this means to you

Accept your lot in life graciously. Know that with whatever Macintosh you are now using or plan to use, it is virtually certain that a slicker, faster, cheaper, or lighter one will be developed in the future. Just as new models roll off the Detroit auto assembly lines each year, the marketplace in its quest for better price/performance (and Apple's stockholders!) demand continued Macintosh improvement and innovation. Still more intense innovation is demanded of the third-party vendors, whose product cycles are even shorter than Apple's.

You, the astute Macintosh user, are the real beneficiary of this change because you can work it to your advantage. Just as you wouldn't necessarily buy a new auto each year, it isn't necessary to always buy the latest Macintosh model either. You can add enhancements to the Macintosh model you own to get the maximum value out of it, and save your big outlays for those times when there have been major changes made to the Macintosh product line. Keeping in mind, of course, the XIVth corollary of Murphy's Law, that loosely translated states, "Never buy serial number 0001 of anything—wait for others to test the new and improved model to verify that it is improved and continues to work after it is new."

Why upgrade it

There are many good reasons to upgrade and money is only one of them. Expand or upgrade the Macintosh you already have, and:

- Enjoy more capability. Want greater price/performance? Easy. Add a more powerful, faster CPU, memory, hard disk, floppy disk, or monitor to the Macintosh you already own.
- Save money. Adding any or all of these options is still less than the cost of buying a more powerful Macintosh. Buying a new Mac model every time one is announced is expensive.

- Buy time. Extend the useful life of your Macintosh. No matter what generation of Macintosh you have, don't consider it obsolete. All of them are readily expandable today via one means or another. Defer the need to make a much larger investment in a new Macintosh. Add the options you need only when you need them and spread your investment out over time.
- Keep what you already have and are comfortable with. If you have grown accustomed to and prefer your present keyboard, mouse, and screen, why change anything? Add a little more horsepower under the hood and enjoy the same performance as the newest top-of-the-line Mac models.
- Keep control of what you are using and for which you have stockpiled parts (and developed labor skills). This is a corollary of the previous user-oriented item that applies to the systems manager in a larger organization. An upgrade is usually a far better use of your company's investment in 20, 200, or 2000 Mac Plus machines and in-house repair talent.[3]
- Do it quickly and painlessly. Let your fingers do the walking through any one of the Macintosh magazines or trade publications, compare offers, make your decision, and the upgrade of your choice will be in your hands in a day or two via expedited carrier.

On the other hand

Then why doesn't everyone just go out and buy upgrades rather than new Macs? Sometimes the best solution is not to, and you are better off buying a more powerful Macintosh. In this case, you can still save a bundle if you:

- Buy at a discount. There are many Macintosh channels available to help you today, particularly if you live in a large city. Apple dealers in large cities must be fiercely competitive. Give them your business, but help yourself out and don't be afraid to haggle on price. Mail order is another attractive source. The back pages of *MacUser, Macworld,* and *MacWEEK* magazines are filled with ads offering the latest in Mac hardware at a discounted price.
- Buy used. The pages of *MacUser, Macworld,* and *MacWEEK* magazines are also filled with ads from used Mac hardware dealers.
- Buy in volume. Whether through your company, your business, a local user group, a group of business associates, or your club, you will do even better if you make your purchases in volume. When you start talking 3, 5, or 10 machines and up, Apple dealer or mail order, you really get the attention of the salesperson on the other end who is usually commissioned. That person, to secure his or her fee, then becomes your "inside" salesperson.

---

[3] Emily Kay, "Setting up an in-house repair shop," *MacWEEK*, 7/31/90, p. 48. The article shows how in-house repair shops enable managers to save money and keep control. Its remarks also apply to in-house upgrades. Also see: Emily Kay, "Old Macs applied to new uses," *MacWEEK*, 1/23/90, p. 26. This article discusses how companies save money by first upgrading, then turning over older Macs to less sophisticated users.

- Buy "right." If you buy the latest model just after it is introduced, you will always pay a premium price. If you can plan your purchase or purchases to occur a little later in the cycle you can pocket significant savings.

Expand or upgrade the model you have or buy a new machine—if you are smart about the what, when, and how you do any of these, you can come out way ahead. This book can help you. It covers your decision-making criteria, upgrade products, and actual hands-on information for installing upgrades in any Macintosh model.

Decisions, decisions, decisions

Let's take a closer look at some of the economic factors or cost justification reasons that would influence your decision to upgrade or purchase.

Your present Macintosh is declining in value

In Fig. 1-2, the first vertical bar (A) represents how much you paid for the Macintosh you already own. You know this price exactly. Depending on when you bought your Mac and whether you are in business or purchased it for your own use, this price has been written off, amortized, justified, already expended, etc. You get the idea. The point is your original investment was made and has already been dealt with. It's history. Any decision you make today has to be justified by today's realities and has to stand on its merits using today's facts. Never let yourself get boxed in by past decisions. It might be a better decision for you to throw away an investment in a roomful of Mac 128s and buy new machines, but it might not. Let today's facts decide.

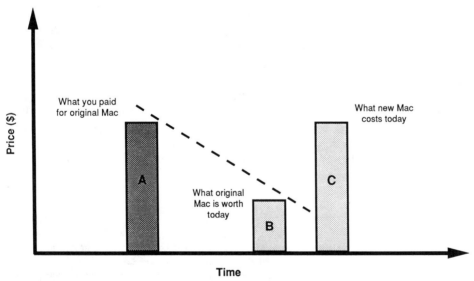

1-2 Comparison of Mac costs over time.

One fact remains—regardless of the model you bought, when you bought it, or the price you paid—it is worth less today. This is denoted by the second bar (B) in Fig. 1-2. Until you sell it, you don't know this price exactly because it is determined by when, where, and how you sell it, and who you sell it to. You can get a good idea by looking at what other models similar to yours are going for in any of the excellent publications that service the Macintosh community (see chapter 18 for the complete list). Check your local classified ads (particularly if you live in a larger city) and talk to a few of the larger used Macintosh resellers. In any event, it will be less. Of course, there are no absolutes in life. While your vintage Mac 128 is worth little today, it might be a priceless artifact when they recover it from a time capsule only 50 years from now. Maybe another good reason not to throw it away!

New Macintosh models offer increased price performance

Another fact is that any new Mac you buy today will deliver more performance for the same price compared to the Mac you purchased several years ago; recall the earlier example of the Mac LC versus the Mac 128. The third bar (C) in Fig. 1-2 is the cost of a new Macintosh you purchase today.

Examine Fig. 1-2 for a moment. Your three alternatives at this point are to:

- Keep what you have and purchase a new Mac for price C. This is the most expensive alternative, but it gets you a new cost depreciation basis if you use the Mac in your business, and you have the latest and greatest in hardware to run your programs on.
- Sell what you have for price B and purchase a new Mac for price C. Your total investment is C minus B. The best of both worlds, this alternative gives you the benefits of a new Mac at the lowest out-of-pocket cost. On the other hand, you have to go through the time and effort to sell your old Mac and this could disrupt or impact your current work duties.
- Keep what you have and do nothing. The least expensive alternative is possibly the least productive alternative.

Do you have any other alternatives? Absolutely!

Upgrading the Mac you have requires lower cost outlay

Regardless of the Mac you have, upgrading it will cost less than buying a new "equivalent" model. Your upgraded Macintosh can even deliver greater performance than the equivalent new Mac model, and you can still save money! Figure 1-3 makes my point in picture form. No matter what you spent originally—amount A is history now—your upgrade cost U today is going to be less than the cost C of buying a new Mac. Maybe I should be conservative here and say "usually." Obviously, you can find circumstances where a new Mac is less expensive. Then your solution is simple—buy the new Mac. However, sometimes the upgrade cost will be substantially less.

If you thought I was "talking through my hat" in Fig. 1-3, Fig. 1-4 delivers the crusher. Figure 1-4 shows the actual models and price tradeoffs that you'll look at

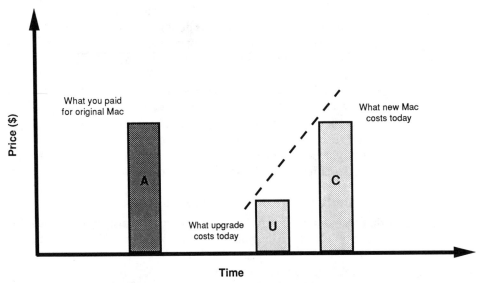

1-3 Upgraded versus new Mac costs over time.

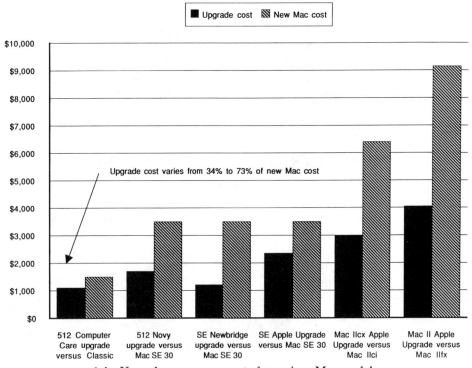

1-4 Upgrade versus new costs for various Mac models.

in detail in chapter 5. (If you're not a believer, take a look now!) Notice that upgrade costs vary from 34% to 73% of new Mac costs. The latest Apple price reductions of March 1991 are included in the figures to give the new purchase prices the best possible advantage!

Upgrading your Mac has a quick payback

Mac upgrades usually have a short payback period too. If you have a perfectly good working Mac and it just has a slower hard disk in it , what is it worth to you to lay out the $500 or so it might cost for a new one? Look at it in terms of a formula:

$$\frac{\text{cost of upgrade} \quad (\$)}{\text{your cost (\$/hour)} \times \text{time you save (hours/day)}} = \text{time to recover (days)}$$

Or for a hard disk that cost you $500 and saved you one hour per day and your burdened cost to the company including expenses is $20 per hour:

$$\frac{\$500}{(\$20/\text{hour} \times 1 \text{ hour/day})} = 25 \text{ days}$$

In other words, you recovered the cost of the upgrade in one month. That kind of puts it in perspective, doesn't it?

A used Mac plus an upgrade costs less than a new Mac

Let's say that you bought the Mac sold in the Fig. 1-2 example at price B. You can upgrade that Mac and still have it be less than the cost of a new one. In other words, B plus U is still less than C. An excellent example of this today is a used Mac II with the Apple IIfx upgrade still costs far less than a new Apple IIfx—even at street prices! You'll look at this and other examples in detail in chapter 5.

Water over the dam

Let me retrace my steps a bit. Don't fall into the trap of adding the price you originally paid for your Mac to the cost of an upgrade you are presently contemplating then comparing that figure to the cost of buying a new Mac.

After you bought your Mac, the price you paid for it is history, water over the dam as they say. What is it worth today? Is it worth what the price you are carrying on your books? Or is it worth the street price? Whose street price? Suppose your machine is in a lot better (or worse) shape? Are you selling it into the retail or wholesale channel? I could go on and on. You don't know what it's worth to you until you actually sell it. You don't need to consider the price you paid for your Mac originally in your current upgrade plans.

Focus on the "money in fist" aspects of the deal. What is your outlay or expenditure for the cost of various alternative upgrade strategies versus acquiring new equipment? You will usually find upgrade strategies pencil out better, sometimes far better, than buying new. In fact, you will find out you can really save a bundle! You'll look at how to check these figures in chapter 5.

Exceptions to the rule

Are there exceptions? Absolutely. There are exceptions to everything in life. Can you take your original vintage Mac 128 up to and beyond the capabilities of a Mac SE 30? You bet. Just add the appropriate accelerator board. Can you add color capability and extra slots to it? Yes, you can. Although you can do it, and it might still cost less than buying a new Mac, reasons other than just plain economic ones enter the picture at this point. Simply put, when you want to jump across several generations of Macintosh models and make major capability upgrades (color, more slots), you are usually better off buying the new Mac model with the capabilities you want. Chapter 5 will show you the reason.

Don't buy every new Mac model as it comes out. Buy a new model only when it introduces a major technological innovation or uniquely meets your application needs. To save the most, wait until later in its life cycle when its price has been reduced before buying this new model, or buy the Mac model that follows in that product line. Invariably, the price performance of the follow-on Mac is usually better and its initial price is usually lower. In either event, nothing stops you from buying your new Mac in a "smart" way and also saving a bundle.

In a nutshell

Here are the key points you have learned in this chapter.

- Your present Macintosh model is losing its value.
- New Macintosh models must offer increased price performance for you to buy them. They must do more and cost less than the previous models offered in order to sell.
- Third-party vendor add-ons to your Macintosh can increase its performance and extend its functional lifetime indefinitely.
- By upgrading the Mac you already own, you can: enjoy more capability and greater price/performance via a faster or bigger CPU, memory, hard disk, floppy disk, or monitor; spread your investment out over time by adding these options only as you need them; defer the time to make an investment commitment to a new Macintosh and extend the useful life of your present Macintosh; keep what you already have and are comfortable with and add only a little more horsepower under the hood to increase performance to equal the levels of newer Mac models; upgrade quickly and painlessly versus buying a new Macintosh; and last but not least, save money because adding upgrade options costs less than buying a more powerful Macintosh.
- Sometimes it is better to buy a new Macintosh model. Then you save money if you buy at a discount, buy used, buy in volume, or buy at the right time.
- You don't need to buy a new Macintosh until one offers you a step increase in technical capability or a unique match to your application needs. Then buy the new model or the next one introduced in the series.

Chapter 2
Apple Macintosh family overview

W hich is the best Mac for you? Within the Apple Macintosh family are 14 models to choose from. My goal is to sort these out and organize them for you. Along the way, you'll also see that not all Macs are created equal. Some are easier to expand than others. This chapter looks briefly at the features and prices of all the different Mac models ever made and then introduces a classification structure used throughout the rest of the book that makes it easier to look at and compare various Mac models with one another. I'll begin with a short Macintosh family history, a snapshot of the Mac models, and how they were introduced and evolved. Use Fig. 2-1 to help you keep the different models in perspective as I introduce them.

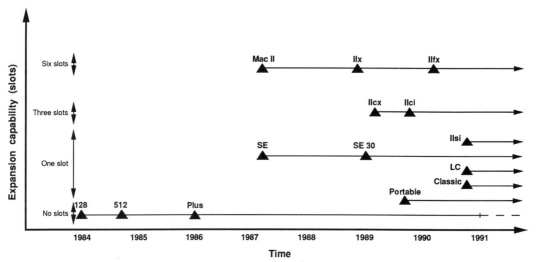

2-1   Mac family models grouped by slots and announcement date.

A short Apple Macintosh family history

More than any other computer that has ever been marketed, the Apple Macintosh has changed the face of the computer universe. It has placed computer power in the hands of non-computer people and enabled the accomplishing of regular business tasks far easier and much faster. Its reach now extends far beyond business to students, scientists, engineers, government workers, and nonprofit volunteers. In business, it is equally likely to be the tool of a large multi-national corporation's CEO as it is likely to be found assisting the starting entrepreneur working out of an office at home. Why has this happened?

Apple had a better idea. How else can you explain it?

Initially, the Macintosh was positioned squarely against IBM PCs and their clones. Now it is "the second standard." Why, despite its overwhelming disadvantage in numbers, price, and marketing when it was first introduced, has the Macintosh succeeded? Simple. The Macintosh has sold itself.

In company after company around the world, when PC users tried a Macintosh and then tried out the identical application on their DOS PC and later were asked to choose between a Macintosh and a DOS PC machine, if price was removed from the equation, they overwhelmingly chose the Macintosh. Study after study conducted in these corporations proved the Macintosh was easier to learn and easier to use.

This is why IBM and others are running, not walking, to copy the Apple Macintosh graphical user interface (GUI). Of course they can't make a "clone" copy of it. That would guarantee a lawsuit from Apple, a company with a long history of vigorously defending its legal rights. But they can write software that creates a shell around their existing DOS operating systems that appears to give the DOS PC machine a Macintosh-like "windows" and "icons" environment. Apple has clearly won the "what system software is best" argument with its Macintosh. Everybody is trying to copy it yet stay out of direct legal confrontation with Apple. Apple's only consolation is that imitation is still the sincerest form of flattery.

The open Macintosh

The first Macintosh was a "closed" Macintosh. You couldn't get "into" it, you had to attach whatever device you wanted to attach "onto" its connectors on the outside of the box. It was deliberately designed that way.

New or different uses for the Mac were discovered by virtually every owner. There was always a different application and use the Mac could be applied to if only you could get inside the box to improve its performance. Within a very short time, third-party vendors, driven by market needs, figured-out how to make it into an "open" Macintosh. Another common meaning for "open" computers are those with widely licensed hardware and system software. This is not what is being discussed here; the Apple Macintosh does not fit this criteria—today.

Ever since that time, every Macintosh has had the capability of being an open Macintosh. When Apple legitimized the process by offering "slots" on a later generation of Macintosh computers that third-party vendors could attach their option adapter cards to, the floodgates to Macintosh upgrade products were opened wide. The flow has never ceased. That is the reason I can even write this book. Let's see how that came to be.

Macintosh 1984

Although Apple introduced its revolutionary new Macintosh with a splash and its usual PR fanfare (few TV commercials have ever topped Apple's January 1984 "Brave New World" Super Bowl spot for pure impact), PC pundits and industry experts gave it little chance against the incumbent and dominant offerings of the IBM DOS PC and its compatibles. They were right, and they were wrong.

The experts were correct in seeing that the introductory model in the line, the Mac 128, was slow (a snail beside today's offerings!), its floppy disk drives were even slower, the 400K floppy media was usually too small to accommodate the task you wanted to do, the software was neat but primitive and limited, and frequent system crashes and error messages occurred for reasons you really couldn't fathom. It had no powerful spreadsheet, word processing, or database software.

The Mac 128 grows

The experts were wrong, on a massive scale, in their failure to foresee the impact the simplicity and elegance of the Macintosh interface would make once appropriate software and hardware tools were available. The Mac 128, with its easy-to-learn, easy-to-use graphical user interface, plus its physical transportability, accumulated loyal users in droves and sowed the seeds that would later make it a second standard next to the DOS PC.

The experts were wrong because they overlooked the heart of the Macintosh. The painfully learned lessons of the previous decade's computer makers were not lost on the engineers at Apple responsible for the Macintosh's architecture. DEC bootstrapped itself into being the second largest computer company after IBM by ensuring each successive product generation of its PDP-11 and later its VAX family of computers was upwardly compatible with the previous one, a superset of it but retaining basic instruction set compatibility with the previous model. By standardizing the Macintosh central processing unit (CPU) on the Motorola 68000 microprocessor chip family, Apple took advantage of Motorola's depth of experience with the upward compatibility lesson. Also, the 68000 chip was architecturally superior to the 8088 and 8086 chips then in use on DOS PC Machines with its:

- 32-bit versus 8-bit computation power.
- 4Mb versus 640K directly addressable memory.
- Ability to handle bit-mapped graphics with ease.

Apple's system software *System* and *Finder* built upon this foundation. Even today, virtually all software applications programs run on every Mac in the entire family, although obviously at reduced performance levels on earlier models. The same does not hold true in the DOS PC world. Software built for an 80386 DOS PC will not necessarily work on an 80286 PC and is highly unlikely to work on an 8088/8086 PC.

In addition, Apple imposed Macintosh software application programming standards that were nonexistent in the DOS PC world. Although it made programs harder for programmers to write, it made them easier for users to use. If a user learned the desktop, icons, windows, pull-down menus, and point and click mouse functions in one program, all of those learned skills were transportable to any other program. On the Macintosh, it was a *de facto* standard that all programs could communicate with all others. Text or graphics could be transferred between programs at the click of a mouse via the clipboard or scrapbook. The only way to transfer data on a DOS PC machine was to buy an integrated application that did this function for you, and then only text.

The graphics function was the real killer. The functionality of the 68000 chip plus the extra horsepower and memory addressability it had versus the 8088 made it possible for all the Macs from the 128 through today's latest models to offer bit-mapped graphics so each point on the screen could be addressed uniquely.[1] Not

---

[1] Doug Clapp, *Macintosh! Complete*, Softalk Books, 1984. Although the book is dated today, it still offers one of the best discussions on the Mac's graphical user interface.

only did this give the user a CRT screen that was now a friendly environment, a paper-white display with legible characters, but graphics information could be easily generated, manipulated and cut and pasted into text documents. Also, the font characteristics of any text information on the screen could be instantly altered at the click of a mouse or stroke of a key. This was an overwhelming advantage over the DOS PC environment of that time.

Mac becomes a Plus

A few short years later, in early 1986, Apple had bridged the gap. The Mac Plus model with more RAM, more ROM, faster 800K floppy drives, and a small controller system interface (SCSI) port that you could connect up to hard drives and other fast peripherals was a real computer platform. When combined with Microsoft's powerful new spreadsheet (Excel) and word processing (Word) software, and database software from Blythe (Omnis) or Odesta (Helix), you had a business computer the equal of anything you could get in the DOS PC world.

Apple's LaserWriter was the real advantage. This combination of a reliable contemporary laser printer mechanism from Cannon, Adobe's unique Postscript software, plus a powerful 68000-based computer under the hood with lots of ROM and RAM memory, and Apple's efficient and unique AppleTalk networking communication scheme really put the Apple Macintosh on the map.

When combined with the newly announced and unique PageMaker page-layout software from Aldus, Apple could offer true desktop publishing to the world for the first time. As this combination of products saved time, money, and literally gave any man or woman with a desk the ability to create finished camera-ready output ready to take to a printer, it created an explosion in demand for Apple Macintoshes as they were vastly superior to contemporary DOS PC products.

Mac SE and Mac II add clout

Critics were further silenced by two other introductions from Apple a short time later in early 1987. With the introduction of the Macintosh SE model, Apple offered a more powerful and efficient heir to the Mac Plus and, for the first time, legitimized the concept of an expansion slot. Although earlier models could be expanded by a clip-on adapter to their CPU chip, the single expansion slot offered an Apple-endorsed uniform expansion interface that soon spawned a burgeoning business in third-party option boards. The introduction of its flagship 16 MHz 68020 chip-powered Mac II model, which made color available on a Macintosh for the first time and whose six NuBus expansion slots gave users expansion capabilities beyond their wildest dreams, really put the Apple Macintosh on the desks of corporate America and companies around the world.

The Mac II was Apple's answer to the DOS PC. It looked like a PC, was expandable like a PC, but produced brilliant and crisp color video output on its high-resolution monitor, required no "fiddling" with DIP switches on its optional expansion cards because of its "smart" NuBus expansion slot architecture, and was unmatched by anything available on the DOS PC for some time when running its graphics software. Apple sold all the SEs and Mac IIs it could make.

Enter the 68030 Macs

Apple's next Macintosh announcement did not come for another 18 months. As increasingly sophisticated software applications found their way onto the Macintosh, the need for more power became apparent. The Mac IIx was quietly introduced in late 1988. Although cosmetically similar to the Mac II (only the ID logo on the case was different), the IIx was the first Macintosh model to utilize a 16 MHz Motorola 68030 chip. The IIx also introduced the new floppy disk high density (FDHD) superdrive whose floppy diskettes offered 1.4Mb of formatted storage capacity. In minicomputer parlance of earlier years, the IIx was a mid-life kicker product, a model that extended the capability of an existing product, and allowed Apple to offer power users a solution while other new products were being developed.

The Mac SE 30, introduced by Apple in early 1989, gave users the power of a 16 MHz Motorola 68030 chip in a Mac SE case. The SE 30, which shared a case back, power/video module, and CRT display tube with the SE model, was transportable, expandable, offered an FDHD floppy, eight SIMM slots (expansion to 32Mb using 4Mb SIMMs), support for color, and an over four-fold increase in performance. The bullies that kicked sand in Apple's face for their 128 Mac introduction were forced to deal with its SE 30 big brother five years later. The SE 30's performance on any software product appeared even more magnified because it only had to redraw its traditional Macintosh-sized screen. Nobody criticized the SE 30 for speed!

A few months later, Apple introduced one of its best-engineered products ever, the 16 MHz 68030-powered Macintosh IIcx. This model, shown on the cover, features snap-apart construction with only seven parts: logic board, power supply, floppy, drive bracket, speaker/bracket, case, and lid. The hard disk, in its own bracket, just snaps in. One screw holds the lid on; remove it and another screw holds the floppy bracket in place. You can have the rest of the unit disassembled in under two minutes from a standing start. It is a technician's dream to work on, but technicians rarely get the opportunity—very few ever come in for repair. The IIcx features only three NuBus expansion slots versus the six in the Mac II and Mac IIx models because Apple's ownership surveys had indicated that only rarely did Mac users utilize more than three slots. However, the Mac IIcx model delivered the full power of the Mac IIx model in a more compact, 14-pound case, a case that made it the lightest of all Mac models—even the soon to be announced Mac Portable.

Mac Portable

Speaking of the Apple Macintosh Portable, even though its critics panned it upon its release, the December 1989 *Computer Shopper* carried the headline, "Apple Mac Portable: Overdue, Overweight, Overpriced?" and similar criticism was offered in other trade publications, the fact is that a Mac Portable rarely appears in the used-equipment market because its owner is not likely to part with it. The overriding fact is that Apple optimized the Mac Portable to be . . . portable! It has outstanding power-saving features beginning with its low-power CMOS 16 MHz 68000 CPU chip. You can run it for 6 to 12 hours before its battery needs recharging. The Portable retains all the features a Mac user has grown accustomed to: keyboard (configurable), trackball (a mouse is optional), FDHD floppy, 40Mb hard drive (optional), plus a high contrast, active matrix LCD screen. Combined with the fact that it offered owners a roughly twice the performance improvement over an SE model in a portable package they could backpack into the woods or up to a mountaintop, then set up and use, it isn't difficult to understand why its owners love it.[2] In early 1991, Apple began offering only a 2Mb RAM 40Mb hard disk Mac Portable, bundled with a new backlit, active matrix LCD screen at a price $2300 lower than its initial announcement pricing.

High-performance Macs

In late 1989, Apple built on the success of its best-selling Mac IIcx model and introduced its bigger brother, the 25 MHz 68030-powered Macintosh IIci. The Mac IIci model shares everything with the IIcx, except its ID logo on the case and its logic board. The IIci logic board improves on the IIcx's, which was itself an objet d'art, by taking a quantum leap forward. Aesthetic engineering-wise, the IIci combines more functionality and higher performance with fewer chips and higher reliability than the IIcx. The first Macintosh family member to host Apple's newly designed 512K ROM, the IIci board also contains on-board video logic. The IIci has no need for a separate video adapter card to drive a high-resolution monochrome or 8-bit color monitor; its 80 nanosecond RAM SIMMs do double duty as video RAM, and it offers a 120-pin processor direct slot (PDS) that accommodates static RAM cache cards that boost its performance even higher. Its new ROM and architecture boost it to roughly twice the performance of the IIcx and even more if the cache card is added.

Apple's highest performance Macintosh to date, the Macintosh IIfx, was introduced in early 1990. A true engineering workstation class machine, Apple's Mac IIfx gave PC DOS critics little to cheer about, but something to worry about: The IIfx blew away IBM's 486 PS/2 Model 70 and Compaq's 33 MHz 80386 in an independent testing company's cross-platform software product benchmarks.[3] Versus its Macintosh predecessors, the Mac IIfx is two to four times faster than an SE 30 or IIcx and approximately 60% faster than a IIci. Everything on the Mac IIfx is optimized for speed. The IIfx 68030 CPU and 68882 math coprocessor both run at 40 Mhz; it has 32K of 25 nanosecond static RAM cache memory, a new DMA (Direct Memory Access) controller for SCSI devices, two new PICs (Peripheral Interface Controller) for controlling floppy disks, and ADB (Apple Desktop Bus) devices, a superset of the 512K ROM introduced in the Mac IIci; and it has special 64-pin wide RAM SIMMs supporting overlapped read/writes. To give all this capability room to grow, the Mac IIfx shares the case and power supply of the Mac II and IIx models, and like them, features six NuBus expansion slots.

---

[2] Ric Ford, "One Mac to go and hold the RAM," *MacWEEK*, 10/24/90, p. 44; John Rizzo, "Have Mac, Will Travel," *MacUser*, September 1990, p. 192.

[3] John Batelle, "IIfx puts Apple at head of performance pack," *MacWEEK*, 3/20/90, p. 1. National Software Testing Laboratories of Philadelphia, an independent organization, did the testing.

New Macs

The three most recent Apple Macintosh family additions—the Classic, LC, and Mac IIsi—although announced concurrently in mid-October 1990, present three totally new "design points."[4] Each model can be looked at as the initial model for a whole family of computers to follow it in that class. If the success of Apple's marketing efforts can be judged by early sales figures, then Apple has scored a bull's-eye beyond its wildest sales projections with these three new entries. Apple dealers had the merriest of Christmas selling seasons in late 1990. Enthusiastic consumers, attracted by the announcement of new models featuring Macintosh technology at lower prices, flocked to the stores. With the Classic models sold out and going to 60-day backlog, the LC's production not quite up to demand, and the IIsi's selling briskly, consumers bought up the rest of the line and whatever else was available.

Why were customers enthusiastic? The Mac Classic that defines the present low-end of the Macintosh family offers almost Mac SE performance in an almost SE look-alike package in its entry level model with 1Mb RAM, FDHD floppy drive, keyboard, and mouse at a list price of only $999! But the Apple Classic model bundled with 2Mb of RAM and 40Mb hard disk at a list price of $1499 quickly became the best seller.[5] Comparing IBM's entry level model in the PS/2 line, the model 25, or newest low-end entrant, the PS/1, to the Classic is strictly no contest. The 2/40 Classic runs any Mac business software on the market today with reasonable gusto, any software that runs on any of the high-end Macs, plus you can put it in an over-the-shoulder tote bag and take it with you anywhere.

When you look at the overall picture—software/hardware costs and the value of your own time—the Mac Classic gives you a higher return on your investment versus the lower-priced DOS PC clones because of the Macintosh software advantage (its ease of learning and ease of using), plus almost all the mainstream Mac software ever written runs on the lowest-priced Mac Classic! How do you like them Apples, Charlie?

The Mac LC was targeted at a slightly different audience.[6] Think of it as a fighting machine to protect Apple's tremendous installed base of Apple II machines in the kindergarten through twelfth grade market. It is packaged in a streamlined low-profile case and is the lightest of today's Mac models weighing in at only 8.5 pounds. It is perhaps the slickest of all the new Macs offering a 16 MHz 68020 chip CPU like the Mac II with on-board color video—no extra video card needed—and a completely redesigned higher reliability, lower chip count logic board featuring several new multifunction chips. Unlike the original Mac II, it is available with 2Mb of RAM, 40Mb hard disk, FDHD floppy drive, keyboard, and mouse at a list price of only $2499. It was intended to be used with either Apple's

---

[4] Daniel Farber and Henry Norr, "They're here: Classic, LC, and IIsi," *MacWEEK*, 10/16/90, p. 1.

[5] Ric Ford, "Hands on the new Macs: Meet the Classic," *MacWEEK*, 10/30/90, p. 1.

[6] Doug and Denise Green, "Inexpensive Color Makes LC The Mac II For The Rest of Us," *Infoworld*, 11/26/90, p. 96.

new $599 color or $299 monochrome monitor. Color is now available to any Mac user at a very attractive price.

The LC is specifically designed to accommodate the new Apple IIe card. With it, the Mac LC can run virtually all software developed for Apple IIe systems. Educational institutions, with their hefty 40% and up discount structure from Apple, now have an interesting choice to make: Do they buy low-priced DOS PC clones or do they get color, Mac II performance, the Macintosh software advantage from Apple, and protection of their existing Apple II investment at the same time?

Apple's continuing ownership surveys after the Mac IIcx introduction indicated that 75% of all Mac II owners used only one slot in their Mac II—for the video card. Apple incorporated this information into all later Mac IIs. The result is that Apple's newest Mac II, the 20 Mhz 68030-powered Mac IIsi screamer is able to deliver high-end performance at a mid-range price.[7] The reason is that the Mac IIsi features on-board color video combined with an innovative single high functionality expansion slot that can accommodate either NuBus or SE 30 PDS expansion cards. The Mac IIsi is approximately 30% faster than the IIcx (the machine it is intended to replace), and much faster in hard disk intensive applications, and yet is list priced at $1600 less—$3769 for the 2Mb RAM, 40Mb hard disk IIsi versus $5369 for the 1Mb RAM, 40Mb hard disk IIcx. The Mac IIsi also features the new Apple 512K ROM first introduced on the IIci, a new low-profile case using snap-apart construction techniques first introduced on the IIcx, and the lower chip count (higher reliability) featured on all the new Macintosh logic board designs. It is easy to see why corporate users began lining up in droves to get their hands on the new Mac IIsi.

Although receiving only moderate consideration in the press, the new on-board sound recording and sound playback features of the Mac LC and IIsi (both come with their own clever little microphone) is perhaps the most important new announcement. Actually, superior sound handling has been a benefit to Mac users since the first Mac, and sound recording and playback via third-party vendors since about 1988. Putting 8-bit digitizing hardware onto the Mac logic board makes a big difference. Apple spent considerable time in its live, satellite-relayed, closed-circuit-televised, new product roll-out on October 15, 1990 promoting the benefits of sound. (Star Trek jokes were rampant in the Mac user community after the announcement—the character Scotty talked into his Macintosh in the Star Trek IV movie.) All Macintosh users should at least be thinking about how sound can help them in their business; Apple obviously will be.[8]

To give you a better idea of the price performance relationship among the different Mac models, refer to Fig. 2-2. Notice five generations of products can be linked by common characteristics and introduction times (the Portable is not shown). Notice how superior the price performance of the new Macintosh "fifth generation" is compared to the other models.

---

[7] Ric Ford, "Hands on the new Macs: Meet the IIsi," *MacWEEK*, 10/30/90, p. 1.

[8] Raines Cohen, "October CPUs: A sound investment," *MacWEEK*, 9/11/90, p. 1.

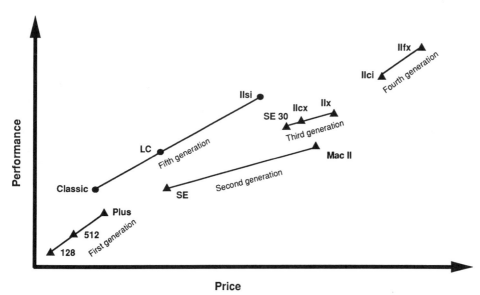

2-2   Mac family price performance; the Mac Portable is not shown.

Macintosh 1990

New, you can buy any Macintosh model Apple sells. In late 1990, that included 7 models. Used, you can buy any Macintosh model ever made. That adds 7 more. You have no fewer than 14 models to chose from. How do you chose the right Macintosh for you? That as well as how to upgrade/expand the Macintosh you have is answered by this book.

A new framework

Start by thinking of each Macintosh model in terms of how expandable it is. Remember how Fig. 2-1 showed the Macintosh models arranged by their expansibility versus their date of introduction? If you carry forward the thought of arranging the Macintosh models by their expansibility, notice how all the Mac models fall into four groups: six slots, three slots, one slot, and no slots. The one-slot group is larger than the rest and contains three subgroups: The original one-slot Macs, the new Macs (each having its own variation on the one-slot theme), and the Mac Portable. The six-slot and three-slot Macs have a common NuBus heritage; they differ only in the number of them, so they can be combined. If you arrange the Macintosh models by the grouping just described, the Mac family shown in Fig. 2-3 emerges with five distinct classifications:

- *Clip-on Macs*   This group includes the 128, 512 (or 512KE), and Mac Plus models. I've chosen to use the term *clip-on* Macs because this early category of Macs was not designed to be internally upgraded. They were a closed box. You were supposed to add upgrades by attaching to the outside of the box. The only real way that you can add expansion horsepower to this category of Macs was by "clipping on" or physically attaching something to the 68000 processor chip itself. Numerous third-party products are available that expand these Mac models in exactly this fashion.

- *One-slot Macs*   The Mac SE allowed expansion through its 96-pin expansion connector, the Mac SE 30 through its 120-pin PDS connector. Numerous third-party products are available to fit both these Mac models.
- *NuBus Macs*   The NuBus Macs come in six-slot (Mac II, IIx, and IIfx) and three-slot (Mac IIcx and IIci) versions. All follow the same rules for NuBus option card expansion, and numerous third-party products are available.
- *New Macs*   The new Macs are the Classic, LC, and IIsi models. All of these offer "one-slot" expansion, but each provides its own unique twist on the method.
- *Portable Mac*   The Mac Portable expansion is different again; it features a 96-pin expansion slot plus other slots for RAM, ROM, and modem. Many third-party products are available for it.

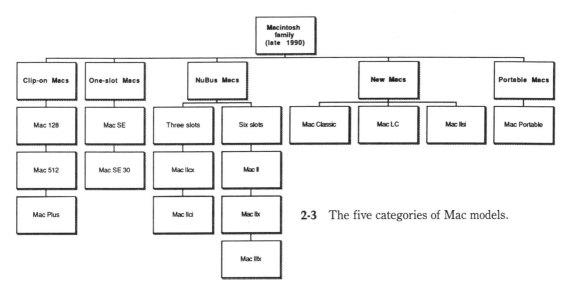

2-3   The five categories of Mac models.

Aha! it becomes clear

And it will become a lot clearer! Thinking of the Mac family in terms of these five categories has its advantages:

- It provides a framework for you to utilize in making your upgrade decisions.
- You're able to visualize the possible upgrades to your Macintosh better once you see the family it falls into.
- It's also useful to you in deciding what Macintosh model to select.

All upgrade options fall rather handily into this five-category framework. If it's a clip-on Mac upgrade, it'll work on all three clip-on Macs; if it's a NuBus upgrade, it will fit all the NuBus Macs; etc. Processor direct slot (PDS) upgrades for the SE

2-4 Apple advertisement for Mac family (late 1990).

and SE 30 are a special case, and upgrades for the Classic, LC, and IIsi all slightly different, and the same goes for Portable upgrades.

Now let's look at the actual models in the Mac family.

The Magnificent Seven

Figure 2-4 shows Apple's October 1990 advertisement that appeared in the major media throughout the Western world, positioning its three newest models with four existing ones and offering the strongest possible "cost-benefits" message covering all seven models. Let's take a closer look at these seven "current" members in the Apple Mac family (as of late 1990). Table 2-1 compares the seven family members in terms of memory/CPU, storage, display, and input/output, a framework I'll also be adopting for the remainder of the book (more on this later). Table 2-1 also offers the price comparisons.[9]

A few items should "jump" out at you after a brief study of Table 2-1:

- *CPU/memory* 2Mb is entry level across the board, except for the more powerful Mac IIci and Mac IIfx models that offer even more.
- *Storage* An FDHD floppy drive and 40Mb hard disk are also standard across the board except for the 80Mb hard disks offered in the Mac IIci and IIfx models.
- *Display* Except for the top-of-the-line Mac IIfx that just begs for all the biggest 24-bit color monitors you can connect up to it via custom display cards, the rest of the Mac lineup is self-sufficient. Either you have everything you need (with the Classic, SE 30, and Portable), or you just plug the monitor you want directly into your Mac (no extra video card required) (with the LC, IIsi, and IIci).
- *Input/output* All Macs have at least one or more slots of some kind. The newest Macs economize on ADB ports; the LC becomes the first and only Mac without an external floppy port; one SCSI and two serial ports are standard across the line; and the LC and Mac IIsi introduce 8-bit digital sound input and output to the family.

What can you discern when you step back and tie all these observations together? Apple starts you out with 2Mb RAM, 40Mb hard disk systems, minimum, across the line. It is serious about offering its customers hardware platforms that run its new System 7.0 software right out of the box. The four 68030 Macs will run it in all its glory, the 68020-based LC can do the same with the benefit of another chip, and the two 68000-based Macs can run it in reduced capability mode. Apple's CEO, John Scully, recently stated, he expects about 3 million Macs—a combination of new machines and the existing base—to be running System 7.0 in the next 12 months.[10]

---

[9] The Apple model lineup is from October 1990, but the prices are from Apple's March 1991 price list to give you the most recent and representative data.

[10] Daniel Farber, "Sculley plots '90s strategy," *MacWEEK*, 3/26/91, p. 1.

Table 2-1. Macintosh family (as of late 1990)

Macintosh Model	CPU/clock speed Base memory Maximum memory	Floppy storage Hard disk storage	Display type Display kind Display performance	Input/output slots I/O ports Sound	Price Model Type
Classic	68000-8 MHz 2Mb 4Mb	FDHD 40Mb	Integrated Mono 9-inch 512×342	Memory card slot 2 serial, SCSI, ADB, floppy Mono	$1499 (2/40)
SE 30	68030-16 MHz 2Mb 32Mb	FDHD 40Mb	Integrated Mono 9-inch 512×342	030 PDS 2 serial, SCSI, 2 ADB, floppy Stereo, 4 voice	$3498 (2/40)
Portable	68000-16 MHz 2Mb 9Mb	FDHD 40Mb	Integrated Mono 10-inch 640×400	PDS, ROM, RAM, Modem 2 serial, SCSI, ADB, floppy, video out Mono	$4199 (2/40)
LC	68020-16 MHz 2Mb 10Mb	FDHD 40Mb	On-board support For 8-bits@512×384 For 4-bits@640×480	020 PDS 2 serial, SCSI, ADB, video out Mono 8-bit input/output	$2798 (2/40)
IIsi	68030-20 MHz 2Mb 17Mb	FDHD 40Mb	On-board support For 8-bits@640×480 For 4-bits@640×870	030 PDS or NuBus 2 serial, SCSI, ADB, floppy, video out Stereo 8-bit input/output	$4197 (2/40)
IIci	68030-25 MHz 5Mb 32Mb	FDHD 80 Mb	On-board support For 8-bits@640×480 For 4-bits@640×870	3 NuBus slots, 1 cache slot 2 serial, SCSI, 2 ADB, floppy, video out Stereo, 4 voice	$6397 (5/80)
IIfx	68030-40 MHz 4Mb 32Mb	FDHD 80Mb	Via display card Up to 24 bits/pixel 16.8 million colors	6 NuBus slots, 1 PDS slot 2 serial, SCSI, 2 ADB, floppy Stereo, 4 voice	$8696 (4/80)

Table 2-2. Discontinued Macs (as of late 1990).

Macintosh Model	CPU/clock speed Base memory Maximum memory	Floppy storage Hard disk storage	Display type Display kind Display performance	Input/output slots I/O ports Sound	Price Model Type
128	68000-8 MHz 128K	400K	Integrated Mono 9-inch 512×342	No slots 2 serial, floppy, mouse, keyboard Mono	$200 used
512	68000-8 MHz 512K	400K	Integrated Mono 9-inch 512×342	No slots 2 serial, floppy, mouse, keyboard Mono	$400 used
Plus	68000-8 MHz 1Mb 4Mb	800K	Integrated Mono 9-inch 512×342	No slots 2 serial, SCSI, 2 ADB, floppy Mono	$600 used
SE	68000-8 MHz 1Mb 4Mb	800K 20Mb	Integrated Mono 9-inch 512×342	PDS 2 serial, SCSI, 2 ADB, floppy Mono	$1100 used (1/40)
Mac II	68020-16 MHz 1Mb 32Mb	800K 40Mb	Via Display Card Up to 24 bits/pixel 16.8 Million Colors	6 NuBus slots 2 serial, SCSI, 2 ADB, floppy Stereo	$2200 used (1/40)
Mac IIcx	68030-16 MHz 1Mb 32Mb	FDHD 40Mb	Via Display Card Up to 24 bits/pixel 16.8 Million Colors	3 NuBus slots 2 serial, SCSI, 2 ADB, floppy Stereo, 4 voice	$3000 used (1/40)
Mac IIx	68030-16 MHz 4Mb 32Mb	FDHD 80Mb	Via Display Card Up to 24 bits/pixel 16.8 Million Colors	6 NuBus slots 2 serial, SCSI, 2 ADB, floppy Stereo, 4 voice	$3600 used (4/80)

The Return of the Magnificent Seven

Now let's take a look at the seven "discontinued" Macs as of late 1990. These are summarized by Table 2-2. Stepping past the "clutter" of the table—you are comparing apples, oranges, peaches, bananas, etc., here (the many different models offering a wide range of capabilities)—to the Price column on the far right, notice the many bargains available. Here is where the Macintosh upgrade artist can come to full bloom. Do you want a new Mac IIsi, or a used Mac IIcx at the same price that is infinitely more expandable? Do you want a new Mac IIfx, or a used Mac II with an Apple IIfx upgrade at about half the price? The range of possibilities is enormous—and the reason for this book.

The 14 existing Macintosh models, the 7 "current" models and the 7 "discontinued" models offer you a tremendous spread of possibilities. However, you must sort through them first to find the best match to your needs. Here's where a little structure can help.

Macintosh models

Look at each of the Mac models in more detail. For each of the five categories of Macs, you'll look at the characteristics of its members and the pros and cons of using them: Clip-on Macs (Mac 128, 512, and Plus); one-slot Macs (Mac SE and SE 30); NuBus Macs (Mac IIcx and IIci—the three-slot members—and Mac II, IIx, and IIfx—the six-slot members); Apple's newest Macs (Classic, LC, and IIsi); and finally Apple's Mac Portable.

Hold up on that clip-on Mac purchase

The clip-on Macs all share a common heritage and a number of characteristics. Although Fig. 2-5 shows a Mac Plus, the unique and stylish design of its case and peripherals is shared by all clip-on Macs. Table 2-3 provides the comparison details and lets you see how you are really comparing apples to apples here—oops, sorry!

The 128, the 512, and the Plus all share the same clip-on Mac upgrade heritage of higher horsepower upgrades with memory, accelerator, and combination video cards all attached directly to the processor chip. This is done via a Killy clip, a 64-pin clip that snaps onto the top of the Motorola 68000 processor chip and makes contact with all pins and thereby has access to all its signals, power, ground, etc.

The Killy clip has its positive features and its drawbacks. On the plus side, it is quick and easy to connect or disconnect, positive contact is made, and no soldering is required. On the down side, clip-equipped Macs occasionally experience intermittent operation, with expansion/contraction of the logic board due to heating/cooling and oxidation/moisture being the most frequent reasons given for contact loss on pins.

Apple Computer, Inc.

2-5 The Mac Plus.

Table 2-3. Clip-on Macintosh comparison.

Model/features	128	512	Plus
CPU	68000	68000	68000
Clock speed	8 MHz	8 MHz	8 MHz
Memory management	No	No	No
Floating point	No	No	No
ROM	64K	64K	128K
Installed RAM	128K	512K	1Mb
Maximum RAM	4Mb	4Mb	4Mb
Slots	None	None	None
Internal floppy drive(s)	1-400K	1-400K	1-800K
External floppy drive	Yes	Yes	Yes
Internal hard disk	No	No	No
SCSI port	No	No	Yes
Internal video	Integrated Mono 9-inch	Integrated Mono 9-inch	Integrated Mono 9-inch
Color supported	No	No	No
External video port	No	No	No
Sound	Mono	Mono	Mono
Input/output ports	Keyboard and mouse	Keyboard and mouse	Keyboard and mouse
Serial ports	2	2	2
Cost or (used cost)	($200)	($400)	($600)

The Mac 128 was state-of-the-art when first introduced back in early 1984. Two quotes leap out at me from its first *Macworld* magazine hardware review:[11]

- "Until Burrell Smith[12] designed the Mac, no one believed it was possible to fit this much computer onto two small circuit boards stuck into a compact, lightweight case . . ."; and
- "The Mac (128) is the most sophisticated computer ever offered in its price range."

The Mac 512, or the "Fat Mac" as it was known, was a giant step forward when announced a few months later.[13] A glance at Table 2-3 shows why both of these models are not particularly well-suited for your needs today. They only have 64K of ROM, 400K floppy drives, and limited memory (by today's standards). They are "bargain"-priced, but you must upgrade them before you can use them with many of today's more powerful software programs.

The arrival of the Mac Plus was a quantum leap forward when announced in early 1986.[14] Table 2-3 shows why it opened up new horizons:

- 128K of ROM allowed more software routines in memory, with fewer disk accesses.
- 800K floppy drives gave more storage capacity and faster drives.
- The SCSI port provided a fast data path for high-speed disk drives and other peripherals.

Table 2-3 shows that the Mac 128 and 512 can be expanded to 4Mb of RAM. That's true, but not physically possible to do so on their logic boards without the help of a memory expander board. The Mac Plus makes that process a snap—just drop in four 1Mb SIMMs. This combination of features accounts for why the Mac Plus was one of the most popular Macs ever built (in terms of numbers shipped) and its unusually long—five years—production lifetime. Suitably equipped with the right peripherals, it can also do useful work for you today, and the price is right.

The clip-on Mac message in a nutshell is "upgrade them." Apple makes two upgrades that "convert" early clip-on Macs to Mac Plus versions. Third-party vendors make accelerators that can take the very earliest Macintosh to top-of-the-line 68030-based Mac performance and expansion, and video; other adapters are available. You need not feel limited by the fact that you own an early clip-on Mac.

In terms of buying a clip-on Mac at this point, I would counsel, "Don't do it." Third-party option vendors are developing their advanced products for other newer, more easily expandable Macs. If you buy a clip-on Mac today, you're limiting yourself economically and future flexibility-wise.

---

[11] Matthew Douglas, "Inside the Mac," *Macworld*, May/June 1984, p. 34. This was the Volume 1, Number 1 issue of *Macworld* featuring Steve Jobs standing over a row of Mac 128s on its cover.

[12] Burrell Smith or Larry Tesler or Steven Jobs depending on what version of history you read.

[13] Danny Goodman, "The Macintosh Deluxe," *Macworld*, November 1984, p. 56. The cover lead was the "512K Fat Mac Arrives!"

[14] Michael D. Wesley, "Macintosh Plus! Packed With Power," *MacUser*, March 1986, p. 38; David Ushijima, "A Change for the Plus," *Macworld*, April 1986, p. 86; and Steven Bobker, "The Macintosh Maze," *MacUser*, May 1986, p. 42.

SE or SE 30—go for it!

Now with the one-slot Macs, the SE and SE 30, you are buying into a target rich environment, as the military would say. Figure 2-6 shows an SE 30, but the case and peripheral design are shared by both members of this category. Table 2-4 provides the comparison details. There are a host, literally a wealth, of expansion option cards developed for both these models and will continue to be available for some time to come.

Apple Computer, Inc.

2-6 The Mac SE 30.

I've put the SE and SE 30 models into a category called the one-slot Macs although each of these two models comes with a different type of slot. The SE has a 96-pin PDS, and the SE 30 has a 120-pin 030 PDS that allowed direct access to their CPU chips. This allowed third-party vendors to standardize the design of add-on accelerator, video, and other option boards. Over time, powerful add-on boards have been developed to vastly improve the capabilities of the initial SE and SE 30. The Mac SE model, like its contemporary, the open-architecture NuBus equipped Mac II, was the first Macintosh model equipped with an Apple-sanctioned slot that provided for direct attachment to a processor chip. The SE 30 was the second.

The disadvantage of the one-slot Macs is—one slot! Once you make your choice as to what you're going to put into this slot, that's it. You don't have additional options. In other words, if you choose to use this slot for an add-on large

Table 2-4. One-slot Macintosh comparison.

Model features	Mac SE	Mac SE 30
CPU	68000	68030
Clock speed	8 MHz	16 MHz
Memory management	No	In CPU chip
Floating point	No	68882
ROM	256K	256K
Installed RAM	1Mb	2Mb
Maximum RAM	4Mb	32Mb
Slots	PDS	030 PDS
Internal floppy drive(s)	1-800K[1]	1-FDHD
External floppy drive	Yes	Yes
Internal hard disk	20 Mb	40 Mb
SCSI port	Yes	Yes
Internal video	Integrated Mono 9-inch	Integrated Mono 9-inch
Color supported	No	Yes
External video port	No	No
Sound	Mono	Stereo
Input/output ports	2 = ADB	2-ADB
Serial ports	2	2
Cost or (used cost)	($1100)	$3498

[1]A second 800K floppy drive was optional. FDHD upgrade was available.

screen video monitor, then you can't go back and also use this slot for an accelerator card. Of course, new designs put both these options on the same board to alleviate this problem, but still you don't have the flexibility of using anything more than a single board in this slot before you run out of expansion options. However, now Second Wave offers an expansion chassis that makes slot discussions a moot point. Its product, discussed in chapter 11, adds expansion slots to any Macintosh and makes it an "open" Mac. The down side is that you don't get something for nothing, and it costs you extra.

Introduced back in early 1987,[15] the Mac SE appeared at first glance to be nothing more than a repackaged Mac Plus. However, a look inside reveals the only parts shared in common are the CRT screen and the actual 800K floppy drive. Today, for only $500 more in cost (see Table 2-2; on the used market, the SE goes

---

[15] Lon Poole, "More than a Plus," *Macworld*, April 1987, p. 140; Jerry Borrell, "SE Close-up," *Macworld*, May 1987, p. 112.

for $1100, and the Plus for $600), you get an enormously more useful Mac, as Table 2-4 suggests:

- *256K ROM chips*   Gives you a 20% faster Mac than the Mac Plus with its 128K ROM chips.
- *Internal hard disk*   In addition to an external SCSI connector port like the Mac Plus, the SE has an SCSI connector on its logic board that allows it to accommodate an internal hard disk.
- *Two internal floppy disks*   The SE allows two internal floppy drives to be accommodated in addition to an internal hard disk—a tremendous flexibility.
- *Expansion slot*   Apple's SE 96-pin processor direct slot (PDS) was a first for any Mac model. It allowed vendors to custom-tailor a wide variety of accelerator, video, and upgrade option cards without the need for clipping onto the 68000 chip and really "opened-up" the Mac SE to the world.
- *ADB (Apple Desktop Bus) connectors*   Rather than just two dedicated connectors for keyboard and mouse, two ADB connectors permit easy attachment of these and 14 more peripheral devices if needed.
- *Lithium battery 7 year*   Already attached and mounted on the Mac SE logic board, it eliminated the need for a "battery door" on the case.

All these factors taken together probably account for the SE's popularity. Its four-year production run is second in longevity only to the Mac Plus. These factors are why you have so many upgrade options you can add to it today. While the Mac SE is discontinued, it is still an excellent choice to either buy or to add upgrade options to as a current owner.

A further study of Table 2-4 reveals why the Mac SE 30, first introduced in early 1989,[16] might even be a better choice for you:

- *68030 CPU chip running at 16 MHz*   Faster, later and greater in technology than the SE's 68000 chip, it will probably be around for a while because it handily runs Apple's new System 7.0 software. Plus no accelerators are needed unless you want a 25 MHz, 33 MHz, or 50 MHz 68030 screamer.
- *256K ROM SIMMs*   These SIMMs support color, gray-scale graphics, and video.
- *Eight RAM SIMM sockets like on the Mac II family boards*   These sockets support up to 32Mb of on-board RAM total when 4Mb SIMMs are used.
- *FDHD floppy*   Its benefits are many—speed, more storage (1.4Mb per diskette) convenience, and compatibility with DOS PC media.
- *40Mb internal hard disk*   The hard disk has twice the storage capacity and speed of the hard disk shipped with the Mac SE.
- *Expansion slot*   The SE 30's 120-pin 030 PDS is a superset of the Mac SE's and now an industry standard for option cards that fit other Mac models also, like the IIsi model.
- *Stereo sound*   The SE 30 brings it home to both your ears with fidelity!

---

16 Henry Bortman, "Much Ado About Something," *MacUser*, March 1989, p. 174; Bruce F. Webster, "The Mac SE Turns 030," *Macworld*, March 1989, p. 112.

The Mac SE 30 is one of Apple's current "Magnificent Seven" models and enjoyed a substantial price reduction in March 1991 to reposition it relative to newer models in the family. Many option boards are available for it today and, as long as it is manufactured, more will be developed in the future. The SE 30 is an excellent choice for you, although it presents an interesting study in contrasts at both ends of the price performance spectrum. You can buy one for about $1500 more than an SE costs, or you can upgrade into it from the SE you currently own for about the same figure. Either move gives you a 500% performance improvement over the Mac SE, plus a Mac that has full compatibility with the new Apple's System 7.0 software. At the other end of the power curve, you can add a blazing accelerator that cranks the SE 30 up to Mac IIfx performance levels, or buy two SE 30's each with a 33 MHz fast accelerator card for the price of one Mac IIfx!

Overall, the one-slot Macs are great to buy if you have a fixed target in mind for future expansion. In other words, if you foresee your operation never needing more than one expansion slot for the immediate and near-term future, then these Macs can do the job for you at the most economical price in addition to offering several other benefits.

Hitch a ride on the NuBus

What's a NuBus? Okay, a quick little primer on NuBus, the architecture designed by Texas Instruments and adapted by Apple. NuBus option cards are:

- Compatible across all Mac II models.
- True bus cards, so multiple cards can be used at the same time.
- Very intelligent cards; they automatically recognize what slot they are in and take care of their jumper settings, unlike DOS PC cards.

The NuBus family Macs, beginning with the Mac II, offer a broad breadth of expansion options that the one-slot Macs simply cannot match. With the NuBus expansion option, your flexibility goes up tremendously. Whether you choose a compact expandable Macintosh like the IIcx, or the top-of-the-line expansion afforded by the IIfx, you are betting on a sure future expansion winner when you choose a NuBus Mac.

I've put two subheadings in the NuBus category. The first includes the original Mac II, the Mac IIx, and the Mac IIfx. All three of these models share the same six-slot style NuBus case as the Mac IIfx shown in Fig. 2-7. The second includes the Mac IIcx and Mac IIci. These two models share the three-slot style NuBus case as the Mac IIcx shown in Fig. 2-8. Table 2-5 provides the comparison details.

The Mac II[17] was introduced along with the Mac SE in early 1987. Use Table 2-5 and look at its advantages over the Mac SE:

- *68020 CPU chip running at 16 MHz*   This chip gives four times the throughput of the 68000 chip used by the Plus and SE. The 68020 processor ran at

---

[17] David Ushijima, "Macintosh II: Opening to the Future," *Macworld*, April 1987, p. 126; Michael D. Wesley, "For the Best of Us," *MacUser*, April 1987, p. 74.

twice the clock speed of the 68000— 16 MHz versus 8 MHz moved twice as much data per cycle—32 bits versus 16 bits of data.

- *256K ROM*   The Mac II was the first Mac to support color monitors.
- *PMMU option*   The addition of this inexpensive memory management chip allows Mac II to run A/UX and Apple's System 7.0.
- *Internal hard drives*   Either 5¼-inch half-height or full-height or 3½-inch hard disks can be accommodated.
- *FPU option*   The addition of the 68881 chip allows even faster floating point calculation, far beyond that possible with the Mac SE.
- *Eight SIMM sockets*   Mac II supports up to 32Mb total of on-board RAM (with 4Mb SIMMs) versus the SE's four SIMM sockets.
- *Six NuBus expansion slots*   The Mac II was the first open architecture Mac. Its six NuBus slots were self-configuring, unlike a DOS PC, so you don't have to tell it what card was in what slot, set jumper switches, etc.
- *Stereo sound*   The Mac SE had monaural sound output.

The Mac II, far from being a dinosaur, is an outstanding price-performance proposition in a situation that can best be described as a "special buying opportunity." It offers speed, expansion, and color benefits compared to an SE. With the birth of the Mac IIfx, the Mac II becomes even more valuable because it shares the same chassis and power supply. If you already own one, you can use Apple's aggressively priced IIfx upgrade to expand its capabilities all the way to a top-of-the-line

Apple Computer, Inc.

2-7   The Mac IIfx.

Apple Computer, Inc.

2-8   The Mac IIcx.

Table 2-5. NuBus Macintosh comparison.

Model/features	Mac II	Mac IIx	Mac IIfx	Mac IIcx	Mac IIci
CPU	68020	68030	68030	68030	68030
Clock speed	16 MHz	16 MHz	40 MHz	16 MHz	25 MHz
Memory management	PMMU option	In CPU chip	In CPU chip	In CPU chip	In CPU chip
Floating point	68881	68882	68882	68882	68882
ROM	256K	256K	512K	256K	512K
Installed RAM	1Mb	4Mb	4Mb	1Mb	5Mb
Maximum RAM	32Mb	32Mb	32Mb	32Mb	32Mb
Slots	6 NuBus	6 NuBus	6 NuBus	3 NuBus	3 NuBus
Internal floppy drive(s)	1-800K[1]	1-FDHD	1-FDHD	1-FDHD	1-FDHD
External floppy drive	Yes	Yes	Yes	Yes	Yes
Internal hard disk	40Mb	80Mb	80Mb	40Mb	80Mb
SCSI port	Yes	Yes	Yes	Yes	Yes
Internal video	Display card to 24 bits/pixel	Display card to 24 bits/pixel	Display card to 24 bits/pixel	Display card to 24 bits/pixel	Display card[2] to 24 bits/pixel
Color supported	Yes	Yes	Yes	Yes	Yes
External video port	No	No	No	No	Yes
Sound	Stereo	Stereo	Stereo	Stereo	Stereo
Input/output ports	2-ADB	2-ADB	2-ADB	2-ADB	2-ADB
Serial ports	2	2	2	2	2
Cost or (used cost)	($2200)	($3600)	$8696	($3000)	$6397

[1]A second 800K floppy drive was optional. FDHD upgrade was available.

[2]The Mac IIci also supports 4 and 8-bit built-in video modes, no adapter card required.

IIfx. If you don't already own one, you can now buy one at a very attractive price and either use it as is, upgrade it, or use it as an intermediate step to obtain Apple's top of the line IIfx model at an attractive discount.

With the availability of the 68030 CPU chip, Apple evolved its product line in three directions at the same time. The SE 30 one-slot Mac is a contemporary of both the IIcx and the IIx. The SE 30 design in a six-slot Mac II chassis became the Mac IIx. The SE 30 design in a new, smaller footprint, three-slot NuBus chassis became the IIcx.

The Mac IIx, while sharing the identical chassis and six NuBus slots as the Mac II, extended its capabilities of the Mac II to the 68030 CPU chip and FDHD floppy drive, when quietly announced in late 1988.[18] Because you pay a premium of $600 over the IIcx model ($3600 for the IIx and $3000 for the IIcx on the used market) for the same capability, I would not recommend you buy the Mac IIx at this time unless you need the extra slots. Keep it if you own one, upgrade it if you like, but do not buy one.

If the Mac II family is a work of art, then the Mac IIfx is its highest form of art expression. You might choose to say that Apple just kept working at it until they got it right! Think about all the improvements you could make to a Mac IIx to move more data and move it faster:

- Fewer wait states so the CPU does not have to wait for faster memory.
- Cache memory so the CPU thinks it is looking at faster memory.
- Direct memory access (DMA) SCSI chip so the CPU gets hard disk data faster.
- Peripheral controllers so the CPU gets serial, floppy, and ADB port data faster.

What do you come up with? You get a Mac IIfx,[19] Apple's most powerful Macintosh. It comes in the same chassis as the Mac II and Mac IIx, offers the same six NuBus slots, but then you get a blazing fast 40 MHz 68030 CPU and 68882 coprocessor, a 32K static RAM cache, a PDS that is a superset of the processor direct slot on the SE 30, a SCSI DMA memory chip, custom I/O processors, and it supports Apple's new 24-bit video cards. The Mac IIfx with its six NuBus slots and PDS slot hedges your expansion bet in both directions! You are compatible with any NuBus card that ever lived, yet you retain the future capability to accommodate blazing fast IIfx-compatible PDS accelerator cards.

On the three-slot NuBus side, Apple's IIcx[20] immediately became its most

---

18 David Ushijima, "68030 at Last," *Macworld*, December 1988, p. 83; Gil Davis, "Meet the Mac IIx," November 1988, p. 34.

19 Jim Heid, "Power At A Price," *Macworld*, May 1990, p. 280; Russell Ito and John Rizzo, "The Mac IIfx: Fast Times at Apple Computer," *MacUser*, May 1990, p. 114; Nick Baran, "Apple's Special fx," *Byte*, April 1990, p. 111; and John Battelle, "IIfx puts Apple at head of performance pack," *MacWEEK*, 3/20/90, p. 1.

20 John J. Anderson, "Apple Mac IIcx: The Modular Macintosh," *MacUser*, June 1989, p. 120; Russell Ito, "Introducing the Mac IIcx," *MacUser*, May 1989, p. 30; and Lon Poole, "The Compact Mac," *Macworld*, April 1989, p. 130.

popular selling Macintosh model during the next year following its early 1989 introduction. It wasn't hard to see why. It delivered all the capabilities of the Mac IIx at a lower price. The Mac IIcx case had an innovative one-screw snap apart construction, could sit on either its bottom or its side (see Fig. 2-8) to minimize desk space, and weighed only 14 pounds without its monitor—actually lighter than Apple's Portable! Users found it could easily:

- Be upgraded to more powerful 25 MHz, 40 MHz, and 50 MHz 68030 versions.
- Accommodate internal 5^1/$_4$-inch hard drives if needed.
- Accept additional external FDHD floppy drives.
- Accommodate multiple monitor options in its three NuBus slots.
- Be transported as-is inside many standard padded bags.
- Take up less desk space due to its smaller footprint.

With the Mac IIci,[21] Apple added several additional capabilities to the already extremely capable IIcx. The result was all the benefits of the IIcx in exactly the same case plus:

- 25 MHz 68030 CPU chip (versus the IIcx 16 MHz).
- 120-pin cache controller so you can add cache cards to boost performance higher.
- 512K ROM adds 32-bit QuickDraw features.
- Uses main SIMMs for video RAM. The added on-board video circuitry allows you to drive an 8-bit color monitor without using a NuBus card slot using 80 ns RAM SIMMs as a video screen buffer.

In March 1991, Apple officially discontinued the Mac IIcx and lowered the price on its Mac IIci as the final coup de grace leaving users confronted with the difficult choice between the mouth-watering goodness of the IIci or the great price of the IIcx in the used market. My recommendation: Either. No, both. Wait, there's Uncle Fred . . . oh, heck, make that three of each.

Overall, the NuBus Macs are great and can't be beat in any category except price. Also, having the capabilities of Mac II and Mac IIcx models in the used market today at low price points is just a tremendous opportunity for the astute buyer.

New Macs and new opportunity

Saying that the new Macs announced by Apple on October 15, 1990 (the Mac Classic, Mac IIsi, and Mac LC shown from left to right in Fig. 2-9) represent a new opportunity has to be one of the all-time understatements. Take a look back at Fig. 2-2. The price performance curve for all these new Macs is shifted up and to the left away from all the Mac models introduced earlier. The translation is that you are getting a lot more performance for your investment dollar. Astute Macintosh buyers everywhere, seeing this basic shift in Apple's policy, snapped up these new

---

[21] Dan Littman and Tom Moran, "Apple Introduces a High Performance IIcx," *Macworld*, November 1989, p. 114; Russell Ito, "Macintosh IIci: New Speed Champ," *MacUser*, November 1989, p. 46.

Apple Computer, Inc.

2-9 The new Macs: Mac Classic, Mac LC, Mac IIsi.

models like hotcakes. Supply could not keep up with demand, Apple's stock went "through the roof," and Apple manufacturing managers reached for the aspirin bottle. Table 2-6 gives you the new Mac comparison details.[22]

Table 2-6. New Macintosh comparison.

Model/features	Classic	LC	Mac IIsi
CPU	68000	68020	68030
Clock speed	8 MHz	16 MHz	20 MHz
Memory management	No	PMMU option	In CPU chip
Floating point	No	68881	68882
ROM	256K	512K	512K
Installed RAM	2Mb	2Mb	2Mb
Maximum RAM	4Mb	10Mb	17Mb
Slots	Memory Card[1]	020 PDS	030 PDS or NuBus
Internal floppy drive(s)	1 or 2-FDHD	1-FDHD	1-FDHD
External floppy drive	Yes	No	Yes
Internal hard disk	40Mb	40Mb	40Mb
SCSI port	Yes	Yes	Yes
Internal video	Integrated Mono 9-inch	On Board 4 or 8 bit	On Board 4 or 8 bit
Color supported	No	Yes	Yes
External video port	No	Yes	Yes
Sound	Mono	Stereo I/O	Stereo I/O
Input/output ports	1-ADB	1-ADB	1-ADB
Serial ports	2	2	2
Cost	$1499	$2798	$4197

[1]Okay for memory and video options. Higher performance options clip-on to CPU chip.

---

[22] Rik Myslewski with Editors and Staff of *MacUser* and its Labs, "Three Cheers For Three New Macs," *MacUser*, December 1990, p. 90.

How did this come about? When Apple surveyed its user community it heard the message "low price" loud and clear. It also found out that the overwhelming primary usage for the first NuBus slot was for video, the second slot was split evenly between a second video card and communications—either Ethernet or Token Ring—and the third slot, a small percentage, was consumed by "other" uses like data acquisition and process control. Armed with this information, Apple developed a new generation of three different processors around three different "design points." Consider each of these new Macintosh models as a design point around which a whole family of future generations of Macs will spring. Apple can introduce successor models at both higher performance and lower price points.

At the low end, Apple developed a 68000-based Mac optimized for the lowest cost—the Mac Classic. At mid-range, Apple developed a 68020 Mac, optimized for both low cost and on-board color—the Mac LC. Above the middle, Apple developed a 68030, optimized for low cost and high functionality with one slot—the Mac IIsi. Each of these new Macs has only one expansion slot, and each Mac's expansion slot is slightly different in its capabilities. All of them differ from the one-slot expansion available to the SE and SE 30, which is why I put them in their own separate category.

The media has chipped about the power budget of these new Macs, and to a certain extent that complaint is valid.[23] You're not likely to buy a Classic or LC if your plan calls for extensive upgrading later on; that is not their design goal. And while the Mac IIsi, by virtue of the expansion chassis that has been discussed, is as upgradeable as any Mac ever built, that is not its design goal either. So by your initial choice of one of these Macs for exactly the right reasons today, you are in effect positioning yourself as unlikely to want to do a major upgrade to it in the future. This holds dire consequences for neither you nor Apple. When you're ready for more you can upgrade it, sell it, hand it down, or trade it for a more powerful model that Apple already has plans for on today's drawing boards.

A Classic occasion

Apple turned a new page in history in October 1990. You could buy a Mac with the capability of a Mac SE for the price of a Mac Plus. It's called the Mac Classic, and Apple forecasted more Mac Classics will be sold in their first year than any Mac ever built. Even 6 months after its introduction, most Apple dealers have two to three month order backlogs for the Mac Classic.

The Classic runs all the software in the Macintosh line, yet you can buy a floppy only model for $999, and a version with 2Mb of RAM and a 40Mb hard disk for $1499—an outstanding value by anybody's measurement.[24] Furthermore, you have a "memory expansion slot" to offer you additional memory and video capabilities plus accelerator capabilities via the clip-on attachment method. While they say that the expansion capability of the Classic is limited relative to other models because of its power budget, you can certainly add many option cards. Hard disks

---

[23] Andrew Gore, "Power trips up new Macs," *MacWEEK*, 11/6/90, p. 1.

[24] Lon Poole, "Mac Classic," *Macworld*, December 1990, p. 176.

that live within its power budget greatly increase its capabilities, and more cards are promised for the future. You're definitely still buying into an open Mac when you get a Mac Classic today, although it's not as open as some of the other Mac models. Overall, the guidance has to be the same as for the other one-slot Macs—you buy it only if you foresee a need for limited future expansion.

Let's C

As mentioned earlier, the Macintosh LC was optimized for low price and color. You get all the benefits of the original 68020-based Mac II—except NuBus slots—at a much, much lower price. The additional benefit of Mac LC is its Apple IIe emulator card that makes it instantly compatible with just about all the Apple II software ever written.[25]

To say this is a tremendous machine to own if you're in the education environment is another obvious understatement. Thank you, Apple. The Mac LC has outstanding on-board video support—not only in terms of Apple's products as shown in Table 2-1, but also in terms of third-party VGA monitors that just plug into the LC's video port—if you have the right cable. With suitable adapter cards, it also supports a flat-screen monitor, accelerator cards, internal modem, Ethernet card, on and on. Adding a third-party flat-panel screen to the LC gives you a portable unit that's almost as portable as the Mac Portable due to the LC's light weight and sleek, flat profile. Third-party vendors recognize a winner when they see one, and a substantial number of different option boards are already available for the LC.

If color on a Macintosh at a low price is your game, this is hands down the model for you. With so many vendors offering expansion options and more promised to come, you'd have to say that this is an absolutely expandable Mac. But overall, the guidance given for the LC has to be the same as given for the other one-slot Macs. You buy it with a fixed target in mind. You buy one because you're in the educational environment, want low cost color, and/or have only a limited future expansion goal in mind.

si Señor

Apple's new Mac IIsi is another nifty piece of well thought-out design. Current Mac users overwhelmingly occupied their first slot with a video card, so Apple designed on-board video into the IIsi. You could look at the Mac IIsi as a "headless" SE 30 although it has additional capabilities that the SE 30 doesn't have:[26]

- 68030 CPU chip at 20 MHz.
- 512K ROM, like the IIci's versus the 256K SE 30 ROM.
- On-board video monitor support, identical to that of the Mac IIci that uses any Apple monitor and doesn't waste a slot.
- Mac IIsi's unique PDS slot supports one SE 30 PDS or NuBus option card.
- Stereo sound, an 8-bit digital sound input/output.

---

[25] Cheryl Spencer, "Mac LC," *Macworld*, December 1990, p. 180.

[26] Jim Heid, "Mac IIsi," *Macworld*, December 1990, p. 188.

The Mac IIsi is price positioned very close to the Mac SE 30. Many of the reasons that would make you choose an SE 30 should make you take a close look at the Mac IIsi. Perhaps the Mac IIsi is a better choice for you over the longer term because of its greater flexibility in monitor and expansion options.

Of the Mac IIsi's two different adapter cards, one allows you to use NuBus expansion cards in it, and the other allows you to use SE 30 PDS expansion cards in it. Both adapter cards come with a 68882 FPU chip plus supporting chips on them and extend the base-level capability of the Mac IIsi. The theory here is that you would not add the FPU expansion capability until you need it.

If you own a Mac IIsi, you can be very comfortable in the fact that you can plug (power budgets notwithstanding) any SE 30 or NuBus card ever built into it. If you wanted to buy a Mac IIsi and didn't own one already, the primary reason you would buy it is because you wanted a mid-range machine with only the need for a single expansion slot in your future. This is not the machine to buy if you had an I/O intensive multimedia or process control application in mind that would later require several NuBus cards in your Mac.

Mac Portable

The last category is the Mac Portable shown in Fig. 2-10 with its characteristics summarized in Table 2-7.[27] The original Mac Portable was a thing of beauty, and the newest backlit LCD screen version is even better. Very few Portables are up for sale in the used equipment market, and you almost pay a premium to get them.

Apple Computer, Inc.

2-10   The Mac Portable.

---

[27] Bruce F. Webster, "The Macintosh Portable," *Macworld*, November 1989, p. 144; John J. Anderson and John Rizzo, "Mac To Go," *MacUser*, November 1990, p. 96.

Table 2-7. Portable Macintosh comparison.

Model/features	Mac Portable
CPU	68000
Clock speed	16 MHz
Memory management	No
Floating point	No
ROM	256K
Installed RAM	2Mb
Maximum RAM	9Mb
Slots	PDS, ROM, RAM, modem
Internal floppy drive(s)	1-FDHD
External floppy drive	Yes
Internal hard disk	40 Mb
SCSI port	Yes
Internal video	Integrated Mono 10-inch
Color supported	No
External video port	Yes
Sound	Mono
Input/output ports	1-ADB
Serial ports	2
Cost	$4199

Mac users love their Macs; Mac Portable users have that same feeling, but magnified. It is very hard for a Mac Portable owner to part with his or her machine. Is there a message in that?

The Mac Portable reflects Apple's initial attempt at portability not optimized for weight, size, or cost, but designed to be truly portable! Guess what? This baby is. You can take it to a mountaintop and have a Mac to do whatever you want with no power around. The Mac Portable's hardware and software has been optimized for low power consumption, and it does that extremely well. Take along an extra battery or two, and you could be there for a couple of days of uninterrupted computing. This is what Apple had in mind, a true portable that you can take anywhere—mountaintop, seashore, or woods—without power available, and carry on your Macintosh work. That's what I call portable.

Many of the original objections to the Mac Portable centered on price. Apple's recent bundling of features and backlit active matrix LCD display combined with price reductions do much to dispel the objections. Looking at Table 2-7 and reflecting on what you get, the Portable has to represent a true value. This is a Mac you can take anywhere. No playing around with transfer cables or anything else. When you get there you can plug it into your home station setup with a bigger monitor, etc. and enjoy it. It is 100 percent Macintosh.

The Mac Portable has a single PDS for expansion options plus a ROM slot, a RAM slot and a modem slot. Many upgrade options are available to expand it—mostly memory and modem options plus video and expansion options at your "home" site.

The Mac Portable you hold in your hands today—well, it ain't bad, but it's the tip of the iceberg with the best yet to come. Apple's future notebook class of portable models to be introduced later in 1991 will certainly close the gap between Apple and the DOS world, and you can rest assured that the future will provide even greater things to come from Apple.

Although it will decline in price, because of the uniqueness of your Mac Portable, there will definitely be a market for you to sell into when you get the new one. There will be willing and eager hands waiting for the model you have when you trade it for the next one to come that maybe you'll like even better.

So, the message in the Apple Portable area is if you currently own one you can certainly expand it and add other capabilities to it, and this will grow over time. If you're contemplating buying one, it's a better value than ever at the newer lower price with the backlit display screen, and you can feel comfortable that Apple will be adding at an ever increasing pace to its Portable Mac offerings.

In a nutshell

Here are the key points you have seen in this chapter:

- Apple has seven current Macintosh models to serve you, all set up with 2Mb of RAM, 40Mb hard disks, or more. At least four of them, the 68030 models, will run Apple's System 7.0 out of the carton.
- Apple also has seven discontinued Macintosh models to serve you. With the exception of the earliest clip-on Macs that can be upgraded at a cost, all of the discontinued models can also be set up to run Apple's System 7.0 out of the carton. Sometimes you obtain a substantial savings over new models by purchasing discontinued Macs at a bargain price in the used equipment market.
- Looking at the Mac model using the class framework to assist you makes life easier. The five categories of Macs are: Clip-on Macs (Mac 128, 512, and Plus); one-slot Macs (Mac SE and SE 30); NuBus Macs (Mac IIcx and IIci, the three-slot members, and Mac II, IIx, and IIfx, the six-slot members); Apple's newest Macs, the Classic, LC, and Mac IIsi; and finally Apple's Mac Portable.

Chapter 3
How used Macs can help you

Now that you've read about the advantages and benefits of the Apple Macintosh models, wouldn't it be great if you could get one for only a fraction of the Apple's list price? Well, let me introduce you to the used computer market. Whether you buy from a friend down the street, a stranger across the world, or a company in the business of buying and selling on a daily basis, you can really come out ahead if you use this source wisely.

Move over Superman

The heart of your Macintosh, or any Macintosh, is its logic board. This part simply does not wear out. You can break it by dropping it, by excessively heating or cooling it, or by zapping it with static electricity, but you cannot wear it out. Its solid-state integrated circuits are largely made of silicon, which is just a step removed from sand. The other parts on a logic board, the resistors, capacitors, and diodes, are equally reliable solid-state components.

The moving parts inside your Macintosh do wear out over time, but your logic board does not. Parts that wear out are your floppy and hard disks (along with your keyboard and mouse outside your Mac) and some of the non-moving parts that are subjected to high levels of electrical stress, such as your power supply and monitor.

New versus used car analogy

If you live anywhere in the Western world, you are quite familiar with the used car pricing phenomena (other parts of the world have their own variations of this game). You drive your brand new, shiny automobile off the show room floor, and it's immediately worth 40% less than you paid for it, despite the fact that you haven't driven it around the block yet. Over time, your new car will depreciate in value on a fairly predictable basis as the used car value tables show (Blue Book, Red Book, etc.). Eventually, after a certain number of years have passed, it will reach some stable base value. A ten-year-old car is not worth that much more than a fifteen-year-old car, but at some point in time, the price starts heading upward again as these cars become classics.

Used Macintoshes like used cars

There are parallels between the used car and the used computer market. From the minute you first buy your Macintosh computer (or mainframe, minicomputer, or DOS PC), the price drops. Now it's a used computer. Even though you got a good deal on it, it's not worth the same price as it was new. Over a period of time, the price of your Macintosh's value in the used computer marketplace will drop and eventually will reach a plateau value as it ages. It doesn't drop much below this base level. In this respect, it is very much similar to a used car. The only difference is the period of time—five years for your Macintosh versus ten years for an automo-

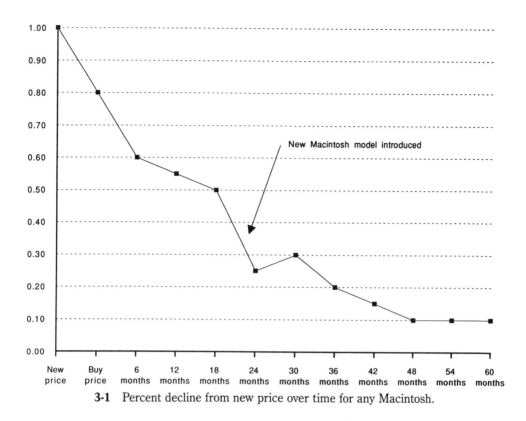

3-1 Percent decline from new price over time for any Macintosh.

bile to reach its base value. Figure 3-1 illustrates the general percent of new price decline versus time for any Macintosh computer.[1]

Used Macintoshes unlike used cars

The good news is the big difference between a car and your Macintosh. The difference is the heart of your Macintosh logic board will not wear out, whereas the heart of your car, the engine, will most certainly wear out. You can go out today and purchase an early generation Mac Plus that you can either upgrade or use as-is for a fraction of its original purchase price. With upgrades such as memory, accelerator, and hard disk added to it, and its other components replaced over time as they wear out, you have a perfectly good Macintosh that will run almost any Macintosh software available today.

---

[1] This chart, drawn from my own experience of the past several years, very closely resembles those in the book by Alexander Randall and Steven J. Bennett, *"Used Computer Handbook,"* Microsoft Press, 1990. Either all of us are wrong, or you are getting a good general idea.

Something for nothing?

Buying used Macs makes you a beneficiary of the interesting phenomena of early generation Macs being highly useable while greatly reduced from their original prices. Macintoshes are like cars in that they go out of favor, or out of style, and consequently decline in price with time even though they don't necessarily wear out. You might have to replace the power supply, monitor, hard disk, or floppy disk on your early generation used Macintosh 512 or Plus, but any one of these replacements will cost you less than having to go out and buy a brand new Macintosh of similar capability. As shown later in chapter 5, you can buy a used Mac 512, add all the things to it that make it have Mac SE 30 capability, and still pay less than you would for a Mac SE 30. Not a bad deal. Why? Because you're buying a used computer and the magic of used computers (and used Macintoshes in particular) is that they're just a great deal!

Tell me more

The reason you buy a used Macintosh is the same reason you buy a new Macintosh—because it does a particular job for you. If you are looking at a multi-slot Mac to fulfill a future need, fill that need at a better price by going into the used equipment market to buy your multi-slot Mac. You give up nothing and don't change what you want to buy. You just get it at a better price.

On the other end of the spectrum, if you have strictly a low-end word processing need, a Mac Plus will satisfy that extremely well today and in the future. You save money by buying it used versus buying a new Classic today, and it will give you many years of service to boot.

The rules of the game

There are three areas that distinguish buying a used Macintosh from a new Macintosh. These are the price, the model, and an area I'll just call business sense. Let's look at each one of these in turn.

The price

You will find that the best price you can get for a used Mac model of a particular kind typically occurs just before that model is about to be obsoleted. This is the well known phenomena identified by the premature "dip" in Fig. 3-1 shown at 24 months or so. Many people rushing to get rid of the old model to get the new one create an oversupply of that older model in the channel. Even though the model will drop lower in price later on, that decrease is usually more gradual. It might even recover in price to a higher level as shown at the 30-month point. But typically, right before a new Mac introduction, an older superseded Mac model drops to about 25% of its original list from the 50% level it was at about six months before. It might not drop to the 20% level for another six months or a year because it's basically overshooting its mark in anticipation of the new model. Keep in mind too, these are just approximate figures and will definitely vary with the individual Mac models both in the timing and pricing values.

When the overhang of supply runs out, just like in the commodities marketplace or the stock market, the demand for these unavailable models in the channel supports their price. So, in this regard, the sales price of Macs resembles the sales price of any other commodity. Buy your Mac at a time just before the new model is being announced to get the best price. What do you give up? You give up the latest and the greatest of the newest technology. This is why people's hearts pound faster and their salivary glands work harder when they go into a new car dealership. It's designed that way. The same thing happens to you when you watch an Apple commercial on TV, go into your friendly, local Apple dealer and see the new models on display, or read about them in your *Macworld, MacUser,* or *MacWEEK.* If you take advantage of the lessons that history has taught about the Macintosh used equipment channel, have patience, and can afford to delay your purchase, you can come out ahead dollar-wise by just "buying smart." Over time, this can amount to a considerable savings.

The model

Buy the same used model that you would buy new, but be wary of several hidden agenda items. Ideally, you want to buy the best equipment for the price. You do not want to buy models that lock you into a disadvantageous or limited upgrade option position in the future.

For example, the Mac Plus is an outstanding acquisition in terms of a low-end, single-purpose machine. If you bought it just to do word processing, it would be a tremendous benefit to you, and you might save a bundle. However, if you're planning on doing future upgrades to it and getting on to other things in your use of it then you really might be best served by buying a used Mac SE instead.

Perhaps this Mac SE also came with a hard disk and a video upgrade option card in it as part of the package. These are just a few examples of what buying a Mac SE, a more powerful model than a Mac Plus, might do for you. Same thing with buying a Mac II. Although you spend a little more money in the market for a Mac II than you would a Mac SE, you're going to be able to do a lot more with it in the future.

In terms of used Macintoshes, two rules and a few examples should summarize the point:

- Buy more used CPU than you need because it won't wear out.
- Buy as few used peripherals as you can because peripherals do wear out. Also, new ones are better.

For example, if you are offered a 2Mb RAM, 40Mb Mac SE and a 2Mb RAM, 40Mb Mac II at the same price (or about the same price), take the Mac II. On the other hand, suppose the deal is the same Mac SE as in the previous example versus a plain Mac II with no monitor or hard disk. Take the Mac II. Don't worry about the peripherals that come with it. You will be better off buying a brand-new monitor and hard disk to go with your used Macintosh base level system that has as its heart a logic board whose life runs well into the future. If you're buying an original Mac II with an early model hard disk and monitor, you should expect that they will at some point leave this world behind. Make your initial peripheral investment in new versus used products.

Business sense

Unlike buying a new Macintosh from your reliable, local Apple dealer, there's a good deal more risk involved when you buy used Macs because of who you are buying from. I'll identify five different sources here to give you the idea: a friend or business acquaintance, a local classified newspaper ad, a national classified newspaper ad, a mainstream mail order company in the business of buying and selling used and new computers, and a broker. Let's look at each of these in turn.

My good friend

If you buy from a friend or business acquaintance, there's a level of trust that is different than any of the other four categories. You still need to know what's on his or her agenda. Sometimes you can lose friends by loaning money to them. You can also lose friends by unwisely buying a Macintosh from them and not investigating before you invest. Be sure that what you are getting from your friend is a good deal. Check it out just like you would any other source.

Local classifieds

When you buy a used Mac through a local classified ad, you don't know who you're dealing with, how the equipment has been used, or where they got it. It's important that before you make an offer to go out and actually take a look at the equipment and ask the local party some questions. These should not be difficult questions, but they should be of the soul-searching variety. How long have you had it? What have you used it for? What sort of experience have you had with it? Are there any problems? Does it come with manuals? Will you give me a warranty?

Sometimes private parties will do that. At other times, when you buy it, you own it. When you walk out the door, it's your problem. Shop around for a good price, but make sure of what you're buying. First, see the unit in operation and get some sort of minimal warranty from the person so that when you take it home or to your place of business and the next day it dies you could say, "Gee, what have you sold me here?"

National classifieds

The next source of equipment is an ad placed in a national newspaper or publication by a private party or company selling a piece of capital equipment. Here's where you have to really be careful because you have no way of verifying the equipment ahead of time and you cannot see it. This situation is where some sort of iron-clad financial arrangement with the other party is the most important. Until you receive the equipment, have it up and operating, and see that it works to your satisfaction, the deal as far as the money is concerned is not closed.

The ideal situation is to have a third party hold your money in escrow until he or she receives a sign-off from you that the deal is satisfactory, i.e., that you received the equipment and it works. The party who is selling you the equipment would have an understanding with the third party that there is only a certain amount of time the money will be held. If the equipment is good, and you liked it and were not going to return it, then they are entitled to get their money. This is the ideal, but in practice you'll probably be working out some sort of similar arrangement.

Used equipment dealers

Perhaps the best way to buy a used Macintosh is through the used equipment channel as through any one of a number of dealers that advertise in the back pages of *Macworld, MacUser,* and *MacWEEK*.[2] Here you're dealing with a company that's known, does this for a living, and will with no questions asked, take the equipment back and give you a refund. You usually have to pay the freight.

Buying through a company whose business is reselling computers from its own stock is usually quite reliable because most of these sources usually take the time to recondition the equipment. They at least clean it and fix it up before they resell it to you. You might wind up paying a little more money for this service, but in the final analysis, it is usually worth a lot more, if not in out-of-pocket dollars then certainly in peace of mind. Buying from these companies is the best deal for you, and the best deal for them.

Brokers

Brokers are people who don't actually own the equipment but merely match buyers and sellers. Although you typically get a good deal, there is a risk in buying via brokers as well. Typically, your risk is higher than theirs. They sell equipment in volume from anybody. Sometimes, because of their volume of business, you don't get as good a piece of equipment in terms of the shape that it is in. In this case it is important to exercise your right to inspection and final acceptance before parting with your money.

For example, the Boston Computer Exchange, the oldest and the largest broker, does business the old-fashioned way: Their word is their bond. I have felt very comfortable dealing with them, but there are many other good brokers.

Another item is that not all used Macintoshes of the same model are created equal. Some of them might have been totally abused in their lifetime, whereas other models are in very good shape. Buying a computer sight unseen through a broker, you don't know in what condition the computer is that you are going to get. That's the big disadvantage to you. Before your one- or two-day inspection period is over, be sure to examine your used Macintosh very carefully and check it out from all aspects to make sure it is in good shape. Then you can send your money to the broker.

---

[2] Pre-Owned Electronics, Maya, and Shreve have all been quality used equipment dealers to work with if I could only pick three from my own experience. Obviously, there are many more.

Other important points to keep in mind

Apple products have a defined resale value. Third-party vendor products do not necessarily command the same respect. So when you buy your Mac, and the friendly salesman extols the virtues of your adding a Clatchett external hard drive with a Crontch large screen monitor and a Cruickshank non-Postscript laser printer, have him or her tell you what they'll be worth on resale. Third-party products tend to lose value more quickly than Apple products anyway, and non-mainstream third-party products drop in price like a rock. Buy with the idea of selling in mind. This is even a better idea when buying new equipment at the new equipment price. Need I say more?

As mentioned earlier, you should buy the most powerful, expandable, and flexible Mac model you can afford. Table 3-1, taken from *Boston Computer Exchange* March 1991 data,[3] shows why. Notice the SE and SE 30 prices. When new, the price difference was maybe $3000 plus, now it's only $1400. Is it worth the difference to you to go with the more powerful model? You bet! It's more than worth the difference because even an aggressively purchased upgrade would cost you more.

Look out for bottlenecks and obvious mismatches of capability. A fast 300Mb hard disk on a Mac Plus or a slow 20Mb hard disk on a Mac IIfx come quickly to mind as examples. Because they happen to be available for sale in that combination doesn't mean you should buy them. Buy one or the other. Or have a well-thought out plan to separate them after your purchase. Don't set yourself up to inherit someone else's problem.

Marquis of Queensbury rules (no rules) and *Caveat Emptor* (buyer beware) are the orders of the day when buying used equipment. You take a risk. If you do your homework, you minimize your risk. Are you looking at a particular Mac model?

Table 3-1. Used Apple Mac prices from the Boston Computer Exchange.

Item	BoCoEx sell price
Mac 128	$200
Mac 512KE	$400
Mac Plus	$600
Mac SE (20M)	$1100
Mac SE 30 (1/40)	$2500
Mac II (1/40)	$2200
Mac IIcx (1/40)	$3000
Mac IIx (4/80)	$3600
Mac IIci (4/80)	$4600
Mac IIfx (4/80)	$6400
Mac Portable (1/40)	$2900

---

[3] BoCoEx, as the Boston Computer Exchange calls itself, regularly publishes its pricing database on CompuServe. This database also appears in numerous magazines. Of course, numerous other sources such as "*The Computer Blue Book,*" National Association of Computer Dealers, Houston, TX (a quarterly), are available.

What does it normally sell for used? Ask around. Gather data. Talk to other sellers. Negotiate with your seller. What's the lowest offer he or she will take today? What happens if the machine goes belly-up tomorrow? Will he or she take responsibility? Hey, it's your money. After you buy your first mint-condition Mac IIfx for $3000 including hard disk, monitor, and keyboard, give me a call. My daytime telephone number is . . . .

What have you got?

Now that you know the pros and cons and a few other key items, what's the bottom line? What do you get buying used versus new?

Figure 3-2 answers that question and makes a few other points.[4] The horizon-

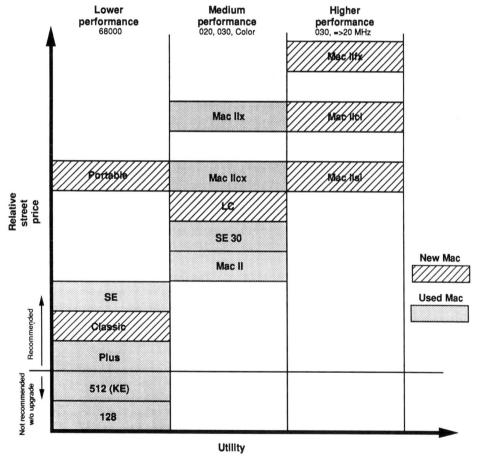

3-2   Macintosh used or street prices versus utility.

---

[4] The Mac SE 30, a "current" model on Apple's March 1991 price list, was priced as a used model to make Fig. 3-2 easier to read. The Mac IIx appears in the medium performance range for the same reason.

tal axis "utility" is divided into three categories: lower, medium, and higher perfor-mance. This is according to the power and speed of each Mac's CPU chip. The vertical axis "street price" shows used prices for both the seven "discontinued" Mac models and discounted new prices for the seven "current" Mac models in rel-ative position to one another.

Obviously, shopping the used market gives you more models from which to choose. More models give you more expanding or upgrading options and the abil-ity to exercise finer control over them.

Another picture also emerges. Would you rather have a new Classic or a more easily expandable used SE for a few dollars more? Want a new Mac IIsi or a used IIcx with more slots for the same price? Want a new LC or a used Mac II for a few dollars less? Oops, this is not a fair question because a used Mac II costs less than a new Mac LC, and you can upgrade the Mac II directly to a Mac IIfx! You get the idea.

Finally, returning to the point made at the beginning of this chapter, every new model becomes a used one the moment it is purchased. So you can get even the newest models and all their benefits at a better price by shopping for them in the used computer market.

In a nutshell

Here are the key points you have seen in this chapter:

- Used Macintoshes decline in price but contain a logic board that does not wear out. When appropriate upgrades are added, even the earliest models will satisfactorily run today's software products.
- Your Mac declines in value from the moment you buy it new. Like an auto-mobile, if you buy it used, someone else pays for the depreciation. You just get to pay the lower price.
- Buying your next new Mac computer "used" can save you a bundle if you are careful of what you buy, when you buy it, who you buy it from, and the price you pay for it.
- Always buy your Mac with the idea of reselling it someday in the back of your mind. This will help you to avoid mismatched or nonmainstream third-party components in your purchases—those items that drop greatly in value.
- Being able to buy any Mac model ever built, via the used computer market-place, greatly increases your flexibility to custom tailor your purchases to your needs.

Sources

Some used Apple Macintosh equipment sources are listed here:

Access II
26 Keewaydin Dr.
Salem, NH 03079
(800) 666-5612

Boston Computer Exchange
55 Temple Pl.
Boston, MA 02111
(800) 262-6399
(617) 542-4414

Campus Computers
Woburn, MA
(800) 447-1542

CRA Systems
700 S University Parks Dr., #650
Waco, TX 76706
(800) 950-8212
(817) 754-2120

MacHeaven
Chantilly, VA
(703) 263-2567

Maya Computer
P.O. Box 680
Waitsfield, VT 05673
(800) 541-2318

Micro Exchange
682 Passaic Ave.
Nutley, NJ 07110
(201) 284-1200

National Computer Exchange
118 E 25th St.
New York, NY 10010
(800) 659-2568
(212) 614-0700

Peripheral Outlet
314 South Broadway
Ada, OK 74280
(405) 332-6581

Pre-Owned Electronics
205 Burlington Road
Bedford, MA 01730
(800) 274-5343
(617) 275-4600

Rentex
Boston, MA
(800) 545-2313
(617) 423-5567

Shreve Systems
3804 Karen Lane
Bossier City, LA 71108
(800) 227-3971
(318) 635-1121

Sun Remarketing
P.O. Box 4059
Logan, UT 84321
(800) 821-3221

Chapter 4
Upgrade options overview

One of the famous commercials for a bank card begins, "Master the possibilities!" That same statement could be applied exactly to this particular chapter. There are so many options available to you in upgrading your Macintosh that it's almost difficult to see the forest for the trees.

This chapter has only two objectives. It introduces a classification structure for the upgrade options that I use throughout the rest of the book to make it easier for you to work with them. This chapter gives an overview of the Apple options that go across all option upgrade categories so you can compare them with third-party options.

Options, options, options—how to choose

The option chapters begin with chapter 6, and focus on the astounding if not bewildering array of options you can use to give your Macintosh more capabilities. This chapter will give you a road map to help you find your way through them.

The first Macintosh was designed as a "closed" box, and third-party vendors options could only offer attachments. Because of the difficulty of attaching to the early Macs, the number of upgrade options was small. Upgrade products of that time were either slow, expensive, or both compared to today's standards. Early serially attached hard disks were slow, early Mac accelerator boards were expensive because of the technical difficulties involved in attaching to the early Macs, or products were both expensive and slow, like the early internal hard drives.

The introduction of the SCSI port on the Mac Plus, Apple's standardizing on a PDS and NuBus slots on the Mac SE and Mac II, respectively, offered the flexibility to attach devices directly to the Mac's CPU or CPU bus from either inside or outside the Macintosh case. This changed the entire picture. These three new standards created an explosion in the number and variety of option devices introduced.

Today, you can attach very high speed accelerator, coprocessor, or bulk RAM options directly to the Macintosh CPU or NuBus. You can attach devices such as large, fast hard disks, both magnetic and optical, directly to the Macintosh SCSI port. Top-of-the-line Macs and 24-bit color displays open a whole new world of multimedia and desktop video. Simulation modeling, 3-D rendering, and computer-aided design and graphics were all areas denied to early Macs due to processing speed limitations. Your options will only get better.

There are so many options to choose from and so many types to go on so many Mac models. How do you choose? First, you need a plan.

Playing with blocks

Figure 4-1 shows the building blocks that go into any Macintosh. As you can see, the Mac is basically comprised of a few simple functions. At the heart or core of your Mac is its *logic board* containing the CPU, memory, and other chips that allow it to perform its functions. The functions the Mac performs are related to display,

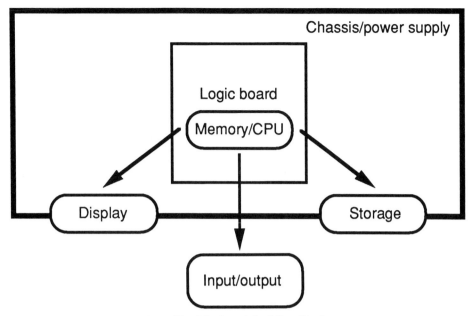

4-1 The Macintosh building blocks.

storage, and input or output of information that its memory and CPU are using. It performs these functions within a *chassis* or *case* that has a power supply in it.

Six blocks to remember

For convenience in looking at the upgrade process, the rest of the book will standardize on the hardware areas just introduced. These categories are memory/CPU (CPU chip, RAM, and ROM memory), storage (hard and floppy disks), display (monitors), input/output (keyboard, mouse, printer, and all the rest), and chassis. Chapters 6 through 11 will cover what's included in each area in more detail. Printers, a broad subject area in itself, earned its own chapter. Figure 4-2 gives you the outline of how the six chapters are organized.

In each of these major upgrade category chapters, I talk about the subject categories as follows. These areas are helpful in visualizing the upgrade process of your Macintosh. Each one of the areas affects you or your Mac to varying degrees:

- *Memory/CPU (memory, accelerator, and coprocessor upgrades)* Regardless of the Mac you have, this is the most likely first place you should look to get performance improvements.
- *Storage (short-term, working and long-term storage upgrades)* Your floppy and hard disk are the next most crucial areas that affect your Mac's performance.
- *Display (monochrome, color and video card upgrades)* Your monitor choice is something you have to look at every day. It affects both the Mac's performance and your own. Big screens bring productivity gains, and color helps even more. Both features also bring cost and performance tradeoffs.

- *Input/output (input data, audio and video, high speed, and communication and networking upgrades)*   Your keyboard and mouse are likewise important choices, but these choices affect you and your efficiency rather than your Mac's performance. Other more productive means to get data into and out of your Mac are available, such as scanners, sound, video, and high-speed digital.
- *Printer (dot matrix, laser, and other printer upgrades)*   Your printer choice is "how the world sees you." You and your organization's image is reflected in the quality of the product generated on your Mac as it appears on the printed page.
- *Chassis (expansion, repackaging, and clones)*   Apple's Mac chassis and case does it all, but other options are available to serve your special needs.

The primary focus of each chapter is to give you a product overview to show how each option can help you as an upgrade. For example, there are many different storage categories, but only those really relevant as a Macintosh upgrade option are examined. Rather than looking at every variation, I focus on giving you a direction. In some areas, I give you my specific recommendation—something I am comfortable with will also work for you. In other areas, I avoid any recommendations. All I am doing here is sorting out the options and bringing some areas into clearer focus. Ultimately, you must decide what upgrade is best for you.

What I cannot do here, of course, is tell you about every possible option that exists in every possible category. As mentioned in the Introduction, this task is already performed extremely well by the excellent weekly and monthly magazines

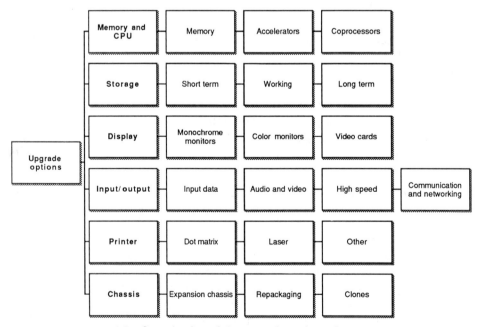

4-2   Organization of the upgrade options chapters.

and quarterly product guides that service the Macintosh community. See chapter 18 for the complete list.

Apple upgrades

The Apple upgrades are a special case, so I will treat them separately here. Apple is one of the few major manufacturers that provides upgrades to its products. You can go from a Mac 128 to a Mac Plus, a Mac SE to a Mac SE 30, a Mac II to a top-of-the-line Mac IIfx, and a Mac IIcx to a Mac IIci, which is just a step below the IIfx. No other major manufacturer can make this claim. Apple also provides upgrades across the broad spectrum of upgrade option categories just presented.

Because there is such a plethora of Apple upgrade options and products available, they need to be organized to give you an overview of availability plus one place to go to look at costs. Table 4-1 shows the results of my labors. It presents the cost of the various Apple options organized by the five Mac model classifications (across) and the five option category classifications (down). You might have to study Table 4-1 for a while because it has a lot of information to digest and it is rather busy.

Apple options come in many varieties and cover all categories. While you have to make the specific choice for yourself, I can give you some general guidelines at this point. You might not fully appreciate my comments here until you cover the upgrade chapters in detail—just remember to come back to this section when you need to look up the information. Here's the bottom line on Apple upgrades and options:

- Memory—Here's one area where it pays to pass on the Apple offerings. With the exception of the Classic memory card, Apple does not aggressively price its memory upgrade products.
- Logic board upgrades—Apple's logic board upgrades are always the best solution if your budget permits it.
- Floppy disk—Upgrade options come with ROMs and are your only choice. Second disk drives are a good choice, and you have the genuine Apple product.
- Hard disk—Like memory, this is another area where it pays to pass on the Apple offerings. Looking at the Apple prices versus third-party vendor prices shown in chapter 7 will quickly make this clear.
- Monitors—Apple makes the best! But you pay for what you get.
- Printers—Apple makes the best printer for your Macintosh. You pay for what you get, but there are no interface hassles to worry about and Apple printer designs are trouble free.
- Keyboard and mouse—Toss a coin! Apple makes good products, but this is purely your decision here.
- Coprocessor and networking—The Apple IIe emulator card is unique in the industry and aggressively priced. The Ethernet LC is also priced aggressively.

Table 4-1. Apple upgrade cost summary.[1]

Upgrade	Clip-on	One-slot	NuBus	New	Portable
Memory:					
Classic 1Mb Card	—	—	—	149	—
Portable 1Mb Card—	—	—	—	—	499
1Mb (4 256K SIMMs)	—	299	299	—	—
2Mb (2 1Mb SIMMs)	499		499	—	—
4Mb (4 1Mb SIMMs)	999	999	—	—	—
CPU:					
512 to Plus	799	—	—	—	—
512 to Plus	599	—	—	—	—
SE to SE 30	—	1699	—	—	—
PMMU chip	—	—	499	—	—
Mac II to Mac IIfx	—	—	2999	—	—
Mac IIcx to Mac IIci	—	—	2399	—	—
Mac IIci cache card	—	—	399	—	—
Mac IIsi NuBus adapter	—	—	—	249	—
Mac IIsi 030 PDS adapter	—	—	249	—	—
Co-processor cards:					
Apple IIe Card	—	—	—	199	—
Floppy disk:					
400K to 800K upgrade	299	—	—	—	—
Internal 800K	—	299	299	—	—
800K to FDHD upgrade	—	449	449	—	—
Internal FDHD	—	349	349	—	—
Internal hard disk:					
40Mb	—	1199	1199	—	1199
80Mb	—	1699	1699	—	—
160Mb	—	—	2599	—	—
Display:					
Backlit screen	—	—	—	—	1095
Display card 4/8	—	—	648	—	—
Display card 8/24	—	—	799	—	—
Mac LC VRAM SIMM	—	—	—	199	—
Macintosh 12-inch Mono	—	—	299	299	—
Macintosh 12-inch RGB	—	—	599	599	—
Apple Color Hi-Res RGB	—	999	999	—	—
Printer:					
ImageWriter	595	595	595	595	595
StyleWriter	599	599	599	599	599
Personal LaserWriter LS	1299	1299	1299	1299	1299
Personal LaserWriter NT	2599	2599	2599	2599	2599
LaserWriter II NT	3999	3999	3999	3999	3999
LaserWriter II NTX	4999	4999	4999	4999	4999
Keyboards:					
Standard ADB	—	129	129	129	—
Extended ADB	—	229	229	229	—
Option card:					
Ethernet LC card	—	—	—	199	—

[1]From Apple Computer's March 1991 Price List.

In a nutshell

Here are the key points you have seen in this chapter:

- Any Macintosh can be thought of in terms of its four key areas: memory/CPU, storage, display, and input/output.
- Looking at the upgrade options that are available for the Mac, it helps to organize them into six areas: memory/CPU, storage, display, input/output, printers, and chassis.
- Apple offers many Mac upgrades and options. Some are aggressively priced, and some are not. You need to choose wisely.

Chapter 5
How to make the best choice

Great, you say. Chapter 1 told me why I should do it, chapter 2 told me all about the different Mac models and upgrades, chapter 3 showed me what used Macs did for me, and chapter 4 told me about Apple and third-party upgrade options. But with so many choices and so little time, how do I make the best choice? How do I actually go about upgrading the Macintosh I have or buying a new one?

I'm glad you asked. Let's put what you just read in the preceding chapters to use and help you with your upgrade decisions.

On the theory that "a picture is worth a thousand words," Fig. 5-1 shows you the concerns you are likely to have starting with where you are now, either as a Macintosh "first time buyer" or "current owner." Notice that whether you are a first time buyer or a current owner, the questions foremost in your mind are almost identical. The answers to "what kind of Mac should you get?" and "how can you improve the Mac you have?" both boil down to what you want to do with it now, the money you have to spend, and future needs.

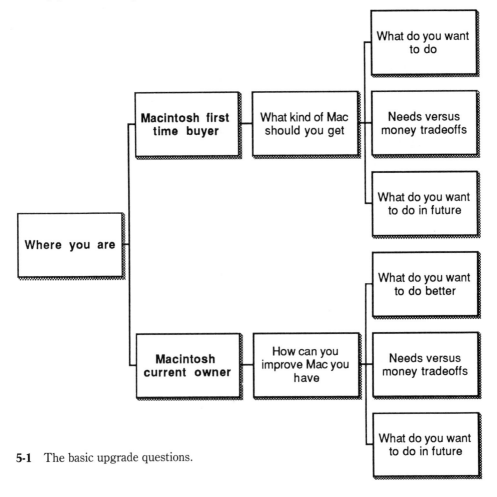

5-1   The basic upgrade questions.

The fundamental tradeoff

Millions of words have been written about the process of answering the basic questions just raised. I believe in the KISS principle, so I'll go right to the heart of the matter with the aid of a simple graphic analogy. When you were younger, you and your friend might have played on a teeter-totter similar to the one shown in Fig. 5-2. If you weighed 100 pounds, and he or she weighed 200 pounds, you moved farther away and got your companion to move closer in towards the fulcrum or balance point on the beam to balance the load.

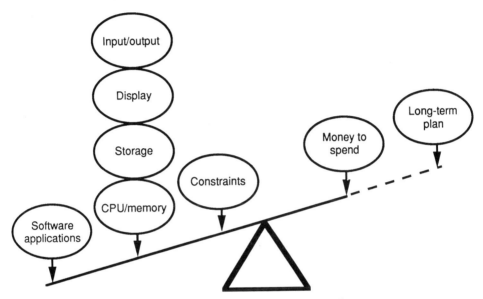

5-2   The fundamental upgrade tradeoffs.

The purchase or upgrade process works on a similar principle. You have certain needs, and you have only so much money to spend. These two must be in balance. Driving your needs on the one side are software applications, CPU/memory, storage, display, input/output needs, and some additional "constraints" needs. These are items that don't influence the outcome too much. On the other side, you have the money to spend plus your long-term plan. Long-term plans, depending on how you weight them in your decision process, can either be very important or unimportant. That is why the line is dotted.

Although Fig. 5-2 depicts the tradeoffs in an easy-to-visualize graphic, for some, the concept is better represented by an equation or formula, so here goes:

software + hardware + constraints = money + long-term plan

Graphic or formula, this is the message:

- What software applications you want to run are usually the most important factor in your decision. This consideration exercises the most leverage—has the greatest weight—that is why it is the element farthest away from the balance point.

- Hardware needs in CPU/memory, storage, display, and input/output are usually, but not always, driven by your software applications.
- Constraints include compatibility, networking, communications, equipment specifications, and aesthetic needs. Your data must also be compatible to be used on a DOS PC. Your machine must be connected to an Ethernet network for networking. Your machine must function as a dial up node for other remote locations calling in. Your machine must also have a tape backup unit in it like the others in your company do to match equipment specifications. What kind of keyboard or mouse would you like to match your own aesthetic needs. On and on. There might be few or many constraints, and they are usually subservient to your primary need, but not always.
- The money you have to spend is, of course, the most important consideration. It is the basic ingredient that makes all the other points either possible or moot. All things being equal, would you rather someone gave you a Lear jet or a new car? Same with computers. Of course you would rather have a top-of-the-line Macintosh IIfx rather than a Mac Classic. The issue always comes down to what can you afford.
- Your long-term plan is a vital ingredient to the equation that might be overlooked until it comes back to haunt you later. All it takes is up front asking the question, "What am I likely to need or be doing with my Macintosh during the next or future phase?" For example, don't buy a Mac now that makes it harder to add color if you know you are going to need color later on.

Whether you are buying your first Macintosh or upgrading the one you already own, each of these elements always enters into the picture. The relative weighting given the different factors is what makes each Macintosh purchase or upgrade decision unique. Only you can make the best decision for your set of circumstances.

Build on the foundation

Let's build on the foundation just established, the fundamental tradeoffs, by looking at how software affects the four hardware areas. The most important of all the elements in this equation is usually the systems software, followed by the application software you need to run. (This question is more subtle for Macs versus DOS PCs. Unlike the DOS PC world, Macintosh software runs on any model in the line. It just runs faster and better on the more powerful models.) Figure 5-3 graphically depicts the software tradeoffs versus computing power required. Visualize it as three concentric ovals each divided up into four quadrants.

The inner oval represents a lower demand placed on your computer chip. You can get by with the 68000 CPU chip found in low-end Macintoshes. The outer oval represents a higher demand. You need the power of the 68030 CPU chip found in high-end Macintoshes.

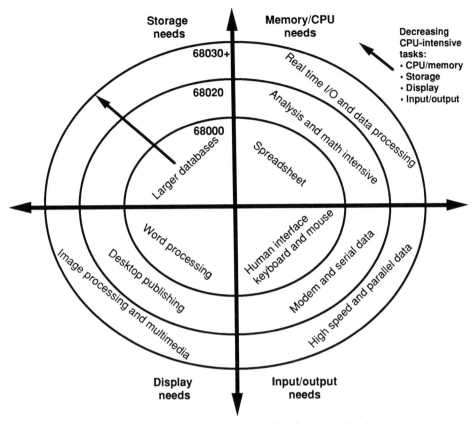

5-3 Macintosh software versus hardware tradeoffs.

The four quadrants represent your main computer hardware needs: CPU/memory, storage, display, and input/output. As you move from the inner oval to the outer in each quadrant, you increase the load placed on the computer by the needs of that quadrant. For example, word processing (inner quadrant) places little demand on a display device compared to image processing or multimedia (outer quadrant).

The highest need occurring in any quadrant determines your computer need. For instance, if you were doing only word processing (display quadrant—inner oval) but had an extremely large database (storage quadrant—outer oval), you would still be best served by a 68030 Macintosh.

In general, going around the quadrants counterclockwise from the Memory/CPU quadrant reflects decreasing loads placed on your Macintosh. In other words, memory or CPU-intensive tasks load up your Mac more than storage tasks or redrawing your Mac's screen and certainly more than you typing on the keyboard. System software affects hardware even more dramatically. For example, Apple's System 7.0 software won't run to its full extent unless you have a 68030 CPU (or the equivalent, a 68020 CPU plus a PMMU chip), and it won't run at all unless you have 2Mb of memory. How can this chart help you figure out, "What kind of Mac should you get?" Let's take a look:

- What kind of Mac you should get or upgrade to is determined uniquely for you by your own tradeoff equation:
  software + hardware + constraints = money + long-term plan
- Money available and software needs carry the most weight in determining your purchase or upgrade strategy (remember the teeter-totter graphic) and are related by the tradeoff equation to hardware, constraints, and long-term plan needs.
- Highest software need in any quadrant shown in Fig. 5-3 should be given heaviest "weighting" in your decision.
- Your software need determines what hardware you need and "usage" category you fit into, which one of the three ovals of Fig. 5-3: 68000 Lower, 68020 Medium, or 68030 Higher.
- Once you know the CPU you need, your money available determines the Macintosh model that you are able to buy within that category.

Now, let's put this information to practical use.

Where do I fit?

Let's take the fourteen Macintosh models introduced to you in chapter 2 and group them by "how you use" rather than by "how you expand" them categories. At the same time, let's carry forward the "usage" categories (entry-level, mid-range, and high-end) introduced to you in Fig. 3-2. (The usage categories of Fig. 3-2, Fig. 5-3, and Fig. 5-4 don't strictly agree—in each case I am emphasizing a different point. In Fig. 5-4, the point is simply you can do more with the high-end multi-slot 68030 Macs than the mid-range one-slot 68030 Macs.) The result is shown in Fig. 5-4:

- *Entry level*   Macs in this category are typically purchased for dedicated use. Yes, you can do virtually anything on your Mac Plus that you can with your Mac IIfx, but today you would normally find these handling dedicated word processing, spreadsheet, and light desktop publishing tasks or as light duty network nodes. (Remember the Mac Plus was the "top of the line" model when introduced back in 1986.)
- *Mid-range*   Macs in this category are more powerful, more expandable, and can handle color. Because of this, they can be applied to multiple uses on an ongoing basis.
- *High-end*   Macs in this category have powerful 68030 based CPUs and either three or six NuBus expansion slots. Even the least powerful Mac in this category can be expanded to top-of-the-line Mac IIfx capability.

Whatever Mac you now own will be found in one of the categories on this chart. As a general rule of thumb, you can expand or upgrade any Mac model into the next higher capability category without any problem. But if you are thinking of going from the lowest to the highest category, you are better off starting with another

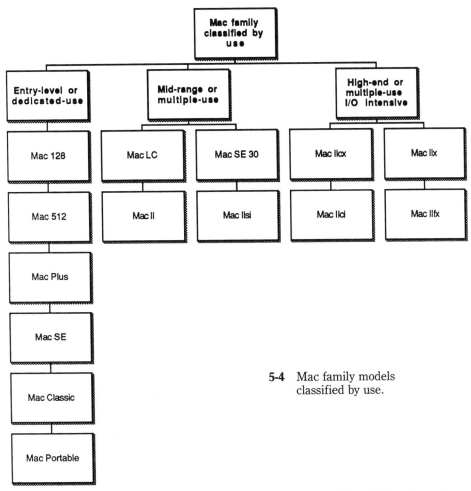

5-4 Mac family models classified by use.

Macintosh of higher capability. Yes, you can expand your Mac 128 to have almost the performance capability of a Mac IIfx, but after all is said and done, you would be better served by buying a Mac IIfx. Get a Mac IIfx used or at a good discount. Or sneak up on it by getting a Mac II, Mac IIcx, or Mac IIci and upgrading into it via Apple or third-party upgrades. Any of these alternatives can save you money and needless heartache in the long run.

Virtually any of the capabilities of the mid-range Macs are easily available to entry-level Mac owners, even color, by the addition of the appropriate accelerator board. Mac SE owners can get to color directly via the Apple SE 30 upgrade, and other Mac owners via third-party options. While Fig. 5-4 represents only a first cut grouping of the 14 Mac models on a usage basis, it can take you pretty quickly into the target area, the specific Mac model(s) you should look at more closely to do your particular application. The whole point is that one of the great benefits of the Macintosh is that virtually any software will run on a lower capability model, just not as fast. So you can buy as much as your pocketbook allows and upgrade later.

What's your goal?

Let's talk about minimums. As a general rule of thumb, in today's environment, you want to have at least 2Mb of memory across all classes of machines to at least be able to run MultiFinder. Entry-level Mac owners should at least have SCSI ports and 128K ROMs (i.e., be upgraded to the level of a Mac Plus). Mid-range Mac owners need to focus on upgrade strategies that allow them to run Apple's new System 7.0 software. This would imply a PMMU upgrade to 68020 Macs and at least 2Mb of memory. High-end Mac owners can kick back and sip a tall iced tea. The FDHD floppy offers numerous advantages. It should at least be on your wish list. Given their disproportionate low cost to high benefit ratio, you should certainly seek to own a high-speed 40Mb hard disk, either external or internal.

Now, let's talk about recommended Macintosh expansion targets. Figure 5-5 tells the story. You found the usage category for whatever Mac you own, entry level, mid-range, and high-end, in Fig. 5-4. Figure 5-5 has these same usage categories across the top, and nine of the most significant option or expansion choices down the side. Whatever you are doing with your Mac today, you should look at expanding it to these capabilities in the future. Why? Because these options match your Macintosh's capabilities. You would not place a four cylinder engine in your Lincoln Town Car. Why choke your Mac IIfx with a 40Mb hard disk? At the other end of the spectrum, why waste a two-page monitor on a Mac Plus? Sure, both of these will work. But they are not the highest and best use of your Mac system, your money, or your time. (Always there are exceptions. Forgive me if your needs specifically dictate the examples given.)

Some actual examples

Now that you have your trade-off foundation, understand your Mac's usage category, and looked at your hardware expansion goals, a few examples with real-world cost figures should make the upgrade benefits point clear.

Upgraded Mac 512 versus Classic

Refer to Table 5-1, that compares the cost of upgrading a Mac 512 to the capabilities of a standard Mac Classic with 2Mb of memory and a 40Mb hard disk. Although you could have paid $3195 for your Mac 512 back in 1985, upgrading it to the capabilities of the Classic only costs you $1100 today, $400 less than the cost of the Classic. (Before Apple's new low-cost Mac introductions in October 1990, "street price," what you could actually buy a new Mac for at an Apple dealer or through the mail, averaged about 20% to 30% off list. The margins on the new Mac models are lower, so their discounts range from 10% to 20% off list. Discounts to other special channels: education, government, developers are still higher. It's possible to do even better if you fall into one of these categories. You won't get a street price discount on a Classic. Apple is selling all the Classics it can make and still has two to three month backlogs.)

Some Mac users might object to the fact that you have an 800K floppy drive instead of 1.4Mb. The ROMs are different, as is the keyboard, mouse, and case.

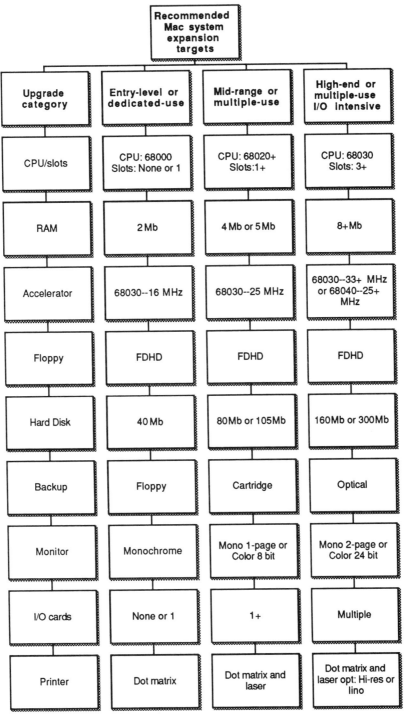

Recommended Mac system expansion targets			
Upgrade category	**Entry-level or dedicated-use**	**Mid-range or multiple-use**	**High-end or multiple-use I/O intensive**
CPU/slots	CPU: 68000 Slots: None or 1	CPU: 68020+ Slots:1+	CPU: 68030 Slots: 3+
RAM	2 Mb	4 Mb or 5 Mb	8+ Mb
Accelerator	68030--16 MHz	68030--25 MHz	68030--33+ MHz or 68040--25+ MHz
Floppy	FDHD	FDHD	FDHD
Hard Disk	40 Mb	80Mb or 105Mb	160Mb or 300Mb
Backup	Floppy	Cartridge	Optical
Monitor	Monochrome	Mono 1-page or Color 8 bit	Mono 2-page or Color 24 bit
I/O cards	None or 1	1+	Multiple
Printer	Dot matrix	Dot matrix and laser	Dot matrix and laser opt: Hi-res or lino

5-5 Mac system expansion targets.

Table 5-1. Apple Mac Classic cost versus Mac 512 upgrade cost.

Item	Mac Classic 2/40	List	Mac 512 to Classic upgrade	List
Logic board	Standard Classic	1499	Standard Mac 512	—
Accelerator	N/A	—	Newbridge NL1 + SCSI	300
Memory	2Mb SIMM	—	2Mb SIMM	100
Hard disk	40Mb 3-1/2-inch internal	—	Quantum 40Mb External	400
Floppy disk	Sony 1.4Mb	—	Apple 800K Upgrade + ROM	300
Keyboard	Apple Classic ADB	—	Standard Mac 512	—
Mouse	Apple Standard ADB	—	Standard Mac 512	—
Video display	9-inch mono	—	9-inch mono	—
Case and misc.	Standard Classic	—	Standard Mac 512	—
Total cost	—	$1499	—	$1100

Yes, you are correct, but 800K floppy media is still the overwhelming media of choice today. Why buy more than you need, if the 128K ROMs you get with the 800K upgrade work perfectly well? If you want a new keyboard and mouse, you can get either or both, and your upgrade price is still less. Yes, the 512 case is different from the Classic case, but it has the signatures of the original Mac development team in it. (By now a historical piece of Mac memorabilia, the signatures of the original Mac development team appear written into the plastic inside the back of the original Mac case. According to the original case maker, this outstanding touch of class was in the tradition of true artisans signing their work; this added considerable extra expense to the price of the original mold.)

Upgraded Mac 512 versus Mac SE 30

If you really want better performance, use an accelerator board in your Mac 512 instead of a memory upgrade board. Refer to Table 5-2. Now your savings are substantial, $1700 for the upgraded Mac 512 versus $3498 for the new Mac SE 30. In terms of performance, your Mac 512 accelerated to 25 MHz with a 68030 chip and a 68882 floating point chip handily beats the standard 16 MHz Apple SE 30. Do you still have floppy, keyboard, and mouse complaints? Get exactly what you want and still pocket substantial savings.

Table 5-2. Apple Mac SE 30 cost versus Mac 512 upgrade cost.

Item	Mac SE 30 2/40	List	Mac 512 to SE 30 Upgrade	List
Logic board	Standard SE 30	3369	Standard Mac 512	—
Accelerator	N/A	—	Novy 25 MHz + Killy + SCSI	900
Memory	2Mb SIMM	—	2Mb SIMM	100
Hard disk	Quantum 3-1/2-inch 40Mb	—	Quantum 40Mb external	400
Floppy disk	Sony 1.4Mb	—	Apple 800K Upgrade + ROM	300
Keyboard	Apple Standard ADB	129	Standard Mac 128	—
Mouse	Apple Standard ADB	—	Standard Mac 128	—
Video display	9-inch mono	—	9-inch mono	—
Case and misc.	Standard SE 30	—	Standard Mac 128	—
Total cost	—	$3498	—	$1700

Upgraded Mac SE versus Mac SE 30

What if you are a Mac SE owner? Look at Table 5-3. Upgrading a Mac SE with a third-party accelerator card produces even more spectacular cost savings than the Mac 512 upgrade because you have less to add. Your savings here are $1200 for the upgraded Mac SE versus $3498 for the new Mac SE 30. In terms of performance, your Mac SE accelerated to 25 MHz with a 68030 chip and a 68882 floating point chip also handily beats the standard 16 MHz Apple SE 30. Add the FDHD floppy if you prefer and still pocket big savings.

Table 5-3. Apple Mac SE 30 cost versus Mac SE upgrade cost.

Item	Mac SE 30 2/40	List	Mac SE to SE 30 upgrade	List
Logic board	Standard SE 30	3369	Standard Mac SE	—
Accelerator	N/A	—	Newbridge 25 MHz 68030	800
Memory	2Mb SIMM	—	2Mb SIMM	100
Hard disk	Quantum 3½-inch 40Mb	—	Quantum 40Mb internal	300
Floppy disk	Sony 1.4Mb	—	Apple 800K	—
Keyboard	Apple Standard ADB	129	Apple Standard ADB	—
Mouse	Apple Standard ADB	—	Apple Standard ADB	—
Video display	9-inch mono	—	9-inch mono	—
Case and misc.	Standard SE 30	—	Standard Mac SE	—
Total cost	—	$3498	—	$1200

Apple upgraded Mac SE versus Mac SE 30

Upgrading a Mac SE with an Apple SE 30 upgrade kit is the preferred choice of many because nobody can ever complain about the results. You now have the identical parts in your SE that come in a Mac SE 30, even down to the chassis and front panel bezel. While the cost savings are not as spectacular here, $2348 for the upgraded Mac SE versus $3498 for the new Mac SE 30, as shown in Table 5-4, you command a better price at resale time.

Table 5-4. Apple Mac SE 30 cost compared to Mac SE Apple Upgrade.

Item	Mac SE 30 2/40	List	Mac SE to SE 30 upgrade	List
Logic board	Standard SE 30	3369	Standard Mac SE	—
Accelerator	N/A	—	Apple SE 30 upgrade	1699
Memory	2Mb SIMM	—	2Mb SIMM	—
Hard disk	Quantum 3½-inch 40Mb	—	Quantum 40Mb internal	300
Floppy disk	Sony 1.4Mb	—	Apple 1.4Mb upgrade	349
Keyboard	Apple Standard ADB	129	Apple Standard ADB	—
Mouse	Apple Standard ADB	—	Apple Standard ADB	—
Video display	9-inch mono	—	9-inch mono	—
Case and misc.	Standard SE 30	—	Standard SE 30	—
Total cost	—	$3498	—	$2348

Apple upgraded Mac IIcx versus Mac IIci

Another Apple upgrade kit is the IIcx to IIci conversion. As Table 5-5 shows, your savings are substantial here, $2999 for the upgraded Mac IIcx versus $6397 for a new Mac IIci, and again the result is the genuine article.

Table 5-5. Apple Mac IIci cost compared to Mac IIcx Apple Upgrade.

Item	Mac IIci 4/80	List	Mac IIcx to IIci upgrade	List
Logic board	Standard Mac IIci	5969	Standard Mac IIcx	—
Accelerator	N/A	—	Apple IIcx to IIci upgrade	2399
Memory	4Mb SIMM	—	4Mb SIMM	200
Hard disk	Quantum 3½-inch 80Mb	—	Quantum 80Mb internal	400
Floppy disk	Sony 1.4Mb	—	Sony 1.4Mb	—
Keyboard	Apple Standard ADB	129	Apple Standard ADB	—
Mouse	Apple Standard ADB	—	Apple Standard ADB	—
Video monitor	Apple Hi-Res Mono	299	Apple Hi-Res Mono	—
Video card	Apple 8-bit	—	Apple 8-bit	—
Case and misc.	Standard Mac IIci	—	Standard Mac IIcx	—
Total cost	—	$6397	—	$2999

Apple upgraded Mac II versus Mac IIfx

Let's go to the other end of the Apple Mac model lineup. What if you are a Mac II owner and want to upgrade to a Mac IIfx? You could have paid $7145 for your Mac II back in early 1987, but you reap the benefits today. Refer to Table 5-6 that compares the cost of upgrading a Mac II to a Mac IIfx—$4048 versus $9145 using the Apple IIfx upgrade kit. You have the exact same Mac IIfx with shiny new upgrade parts. Even with a healthy Mac IIfx "street price" discount, you have still saved tremendously by upgrading your original Mac II.

Let's summarize. Figure 5-6 does just that. It compares the upgrade prices for the six variations just discussed. (If this figure looks familiar, it was the same one used back in chapter 1.) Notice that the upgrade cost, expressed as a percentage of

Table 5-6. Apple Mac IIfx cost compared to Mac II Apple Upgrade.

Item	Mac IIfx 4/80	List	Mac II to IIfx upgrade	List
Logic board	Standard Mac IIfx	8069	Standard Mac II	—
Accelerator	N/A	—	Apple IIfx upgrade	2999
Memory	4Mb IIfx SIMM	—	4Mb IIfx SIMM	300
Hard disk	Quantum 3½-inch 80Mb	—	Quantum 80Mb internal	400
Floppy disk	Sony 1.4Mb	—	Apple 1.4Mb	349
Keyboard	Apple Standard ADB	129	Apple Standard ADB	—
Mouse	Apple Standard ADB	—	Apple Standard ADB	—
Video monitor	Apple Hi-Res Mono	299	Apple Hi-Res Mono	—
Video card	Apple 8-bit	648	Apple 8-bit color	—
Case and misc.	Standard Mac IIx	—	Standard Mac II	—
Total cost	—	$9145	—	$4048

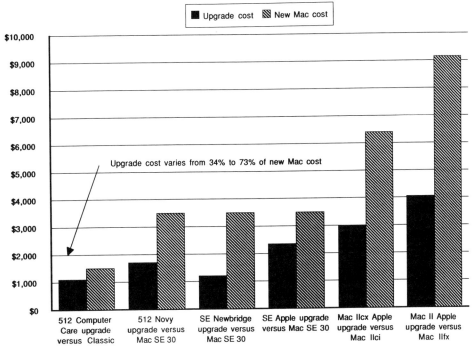

5-6 Summary of Mac upgrade versus new system costs.

the new Mac list price, varies from 34% to 73% of the new Mac cost. I doubt you'll be paying full list, but you will save a bundle by upgrading versus buying new. I'd like to draw your attention to several important items:

- *Mac 512 versus Mac SE upgrade to Mac SE 30* In general, it costs more to upgrade an older vintage model to the capabilities of a new one. The difference being the ROM, 800K floppy drive, SCSI port, and expansion connector are already available on the Mac SE. All this capability has to be added to the Mac 512.
- *Special situation, Mac SE 30* In the case of the SE 30, third-party vendors have priced their upgrades very aggressively, making it an extremely attractive alternative for Mac SE owners.
- *Apple versus third-party upgrades* In general, third-party upgrades are less expensive than standard Apple upgrades. Versus the standard Apple offerings for the Mac Plus, SE 30, Mac IIx, Mac IIfx, and Mac IIci upgrades, you will almost always do better by accomplishing your task via third-party upgrade/accelerator boards. This is an uneven playing field where the surface is constantly changed by Apple's new product announcements and third-party vendor product pricing adjustments. You must check out the prices at the time you are upgrading.
- *Special situation, Mac IIfx* In the case of the Mac IIfx, Apple has priced its upgrade very aggressively, making it an extremely attractive alternative for present Mac II owners.

Used Mac Plus upgrade costs less than new Mac revisited

If you recall back in chapter 1, I mentioned you could save money buying a used Mac and upgrading it versus buying a new Mac. Look at Table 5-7. Here you see some of the possible savings. Notice the savings range from 60% to 78% of list price and from $1198 to $2897 in dollar amount. Not too bad for just another alternative for you to keep handy in your upgrade bag of tricks.

Table 5-7. Used Mac plus upgrade versus new Mac cost.

Comparison	Used	Upgrade	Total	New	Money saved	Percent less
Used 512 versus SE 30	400	1700	2100	3498	1398	60
Used SE versus SE 30	1100	1200	2300	3498	1198	66
Used IIcx versus IIsi	3000	—	3000	4446	1446	67
Used IIcx versus IIci	3000	2000	5000	6397	1397	78
Used Mac II versus Mac IIfx	2200	4048	6248	9145	2897	68

A practical formula

I believe you have it. For whatever situation you face, if you can "pencil out" the numbers for the Macintosh upgrade option that does the job for you versus buying the new Mac model—just like what you've seen in Table 5-1 through Table 5-6—you can chart your own way. Or for the same Mac model new versus used. Use the techniques just discussed, but apply them to your unique situation. Figure 5-7 is a worksheet that you can consider using. Notice it looks similar to Fig. 5-5, the recommended Mac system expansion targets, except it has blank areas that you fill in yourself for either a new Mac system or an upgrade to your own Macintosh.

Beyond this form there are still other steps you can take.

Taking inventory

Your first step—really. It's important that you take stock of where you are. How much memory do you have? What kind of hard disk do you have—internal or external? How much capacity does it have? What's its speed? What kind of monitor are you using, the internal Mac or something else? What kind of keyboard and mouse do you have? Do they meet your needs? How about your backup techniques. Do you use an FDHD floppy or do you have an 800K or do you really need something larger? What kind of printer do have? Will it take care of your future needs? What kind of expansion chassis do you have, or do you think you might need down the road? All these and more are questions you should be asking yourself on a regular basis. You should be planning for the future.

Nothing says you have to buy everything you need at one time. If your Macintosh is serving the needs of your individual proprietorship business, maybe you can pick up the extra memory you need or a bigger hard disk as a result of a classified ad that appears in the local newspaper and get a great bargain in the process. If you're buying for a larger organization perhaps you could buy at greater quantity

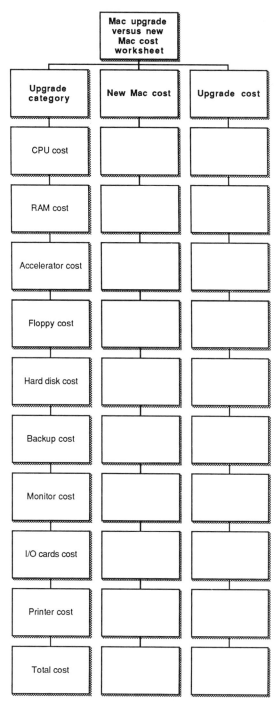

5-7 Mac upgrade versus new cost worksheet.

to take advantage of bulk purchasing discounts. There's no end, no limit to the amount of resourcefulness that you can exercise with a little planning in the area of your future Macintosh needs.

A plan for upgrading success

Going back to Yogi's comment at the beginning of the Introduction: "If you don't know where you are going, you will probably end up someplace else" is most appropriate here. First, you need a goal. Then you can figure out a plan to accomplish your upgrade strategy. Once you know what you want to do, then you can figure out the questions you need to ask. The more detailed your thinking, the better your results. If you don't work through a little Macintosh upgrade planning first, you could wind up spending more money than you have to on an upgrade that you don't need and/or doesn't do the job!

Here are some questions to help jog your thinking. It helps if you ask the right questions. You also might want to look at some articles that have appeared covering the broad subjects of buying a Mac and whether to upgrade or not.[1]

General

- What do you plan to do with your Macintosh in the future?
- Are your needs changing slowly or rapidly? How fast is your business growing? How many Macs per year do you need?
- What are the most significant constraints you face?
- Any special packaging, chassis, environmental, expansion, or reliability requirements?

Software

- What kind of system software—System 6.0x, MultiFinder, System 7.0, A/UX?
- What kind of application software? Word processing, spreadsheet, page layout, graphics, multimedia, etc.?
- Does your upgraded Macintosh support your software needs?

Money

- How much money do you have available for the complete system purchase?
- Is it a lump sum, or spread out over time?
- Will you lease or purchase? Capitalize or expense the purchase cost?
- Do you have a budget plan? Is it annual or multi-year?

---

[1] Jim Heid, "Getting Started with Buying a Mac," *Macworld*, January 1990, p. 253; Doug and Denise Green, "Round Up the Usual Suspects," *Infoworld*, 8/7/89, Target Edition No. 23.

CPU

- Does the CPU support your software needs?
- Does it support your storage, display, input/output, and printer needs?
- Does it support your constraints?

Storage

- What kind of short-term storage do you need? Are floppy disks sufficient?
- What kind of working storage do you need? Hard disks? Removables? What size, speed, type? What will you be saving, and for how long?
- What kind of long-term storage do you need? Optical? Tape?

Display

- Do you need a monochrome or color monitor?
- Do you need a VGA 14″, full page, or two page?
- Will it have high-resolution graphics, compression, or accelerators?

Input/output

- Do you like your keyboard and mouse?
- Do you have video/multimedia or sound requirements?
- Do you need any high speed or special input/output requirements?
- What do you require for communications and networking?

Printers

- What kind of printing will you need to do and how much?
- Is network or remote printing a requirement?
- Will you need dot matrix , laser, or other printer?

A worksheet for you

While Fig. 5-7 is excellent for individual use, buying or upgrading a Mac in a business environment requires a little more. You are looking at other costs besides just the hardware. There are software costs, networking, and communication costs, plus someone has to do the buying and that involves looking at multiple alternatives.

That is why the worksheet shown in Table 5-8 has been prepared. It includes all the items shown in Fig. 5-7 plus additional hardware, software, buying, and even an "other" contingency cost provision. As a business person, you can look at them as the "short form" and the "long form." I offer it as a starting guide to assist in your own upgrade tradeoffs. By going through a worksheet organized such as

Table 5-8. Total upgrade cost worksheet for a new Mac versus upgrade options.

Upgrade cost	New Mac	Mac upgrade A	Mac upgrade B
CPU	_____	_____	_____
RAM	_____	_____	_____
Accelerator	_____	_____	_____
Floppy	_____	_____	_____
Hard disk	_____	_____	_____
Backup	_____	_____	_____
Monitor	_____	_____	_____
I/O cards	_____	_____	_____
Printer	_____	_____	_____
Network cards	_____	_____	_____
Communications cards	_____	_____	_____
Subtotal hardware	_____	_____	_____
Software	_____	_____	_____
Buying	_____	_____	_____
Other	_____	_____	_____
Subtotal other	_____	_____	_____
Total cost	_____	_____	_____

that in Table 5-8, you can develop a quantitative way for your own organization to pin down precisely the figures involved with:

- Acquiring.
- Tradeoff new versus used.
- Tradeoff upgrade versus buy another piece of equipment.
- Trade-in, disposal, or salvage issues (not all the figures in the worksheet need to be positive numbers, you can subtract the cost of a trade-in).

You might wish to organize your chart differently, but the framework of the chart should give you the idea for the process, and you can adapt it for your own needs.

In a nutshell

This chapter has focused on the philosophy of how you make the best choice, given you a framework, worked through several examples, and provided you with two worksheets, a "short" and "long" form. Hopefully, you picked up some ideas and practical tools you could use.

Chapter 6
Memory and CPU upgrade options

More than in any other area, the improvements you make in the memory and CPU area will do the most to improve the performance of the Macintosh you own or the Macintosh you want to buy. This chapter covers the options available to you in this area for upgrading your Mac—the memory, accelerator, and coprocessor upgrade options. Beyond what appears here, some excellent articles have been written that can further extend your understanding.[1]

I'll begin by first expanding on the simplified Macintosh block diagram introduced in chapter 4, get a few definitions and some history out of the way, then cover this chapter's upgrade options, show you some products, make a few recommendations, and leave you with guidelines to make you own decisions.

The Macintosh in more detail

Figure 4-1 in chapter 4 introduced a rather simplified block diagram for establishing the framework of the option upgrade categories, or how you should look at them in terms of adding on to your Mac. Figure 6-1 shows that diagram in a little more detail generalized for all Macs with slots. Not every Mac has every feature. My intent is to show you what functions you are likely to find inside any Mac in general. Figure 6-1 shows the the CPU, memory, display, storage, and input/output functions you were introduced to earlier. In this chapter, you'll be looking at the functions above the "internal bus." The chapters following cover the remaining functions.

Notice the CPU block is connected to the bus as is the cache, RAM, and the ROM memory blocks on both sides of it. The RAM is also connected directly to the CPU via the cache. Notice also, that while the NuBus slots connect directly to the internal bus, the PDS slot and the cache slot come directly off the CPU and cache, respectively. Each one of these are discussed in turn.

The Motorola 68000 CPU chip family

If the logic board is the heart of your Macintosh, then the Motorola 68xxx central processing unit (CPU) chip is the soul of it. This microcomputer chip is the engine that makes your Macintosh go. Encased in a larger protective housing, the chip itself is no larger than your thumbnail, yet it offers more capability than the room full of electronics required by the IBM mainframes of the 1960s or the rack full of electronics required by the Digital minicomputers of the 1970s.

Thanks to the lessons learned from Digital and other minicomputer makers of the 1970s, Motorola has chosen a path that ensures your Macintosh software investment will not be obsoleted. Each newer chip is fully instruction set compatible with the previous one, while it contains significant performance improvements.

---

[1] Brita Meng, "Is Your Mac Obsolete," *Macworld*, February 1990, p. 124; John J. Anderson and Kristi Coale, "Making the Upgrade," *MacUser*, February 1989, p. 113. These articles should do for openers.

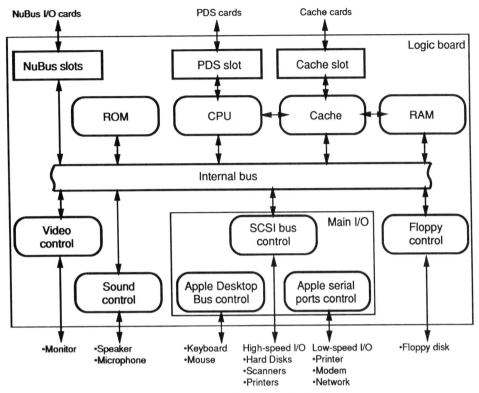

6-1 A generalized Macintosh block diagram.

Because of this strategy, you can replace an older chip with a newer one in your CPU line, and everything still runs—only faster. Of course, you do have hardware technical details to work out—how you talk to the chip, etc.—but your software code still works.

This is good news for every Macintosh owner. For example, using the Apple SE 30 upgrade, you can remove the SE logic board from your Mac SE chassis, pop in the SE 30 logic board, and everything works. It would also work for a 128 or 512 to a Plus, a II to a IIx, a IIcx to a IIci, and a II or IIx to a IIfx.

Figure 6-2 shows the trends in the Motorola 68xxx chip family on which the Macintosh is based. It took five years to go from 68,000 to 195,000 circuits on a chip in the early 1980s; it only took two years to go from the 68030 chip with its 300,000 circuits to the newly announced 68040 chip with its 1,200,000 circuits. No one knows exactly where CPU chip performance is going, but it is going there at an increasingly faster rate. Fortunately, it takes a while for the software to catch up with the hardware.

Enter the 68040

Some people say that the 68030 chip, used in all of Apple's newest Mac models, is already over the hill. Motorola officially unveiled its 25 MHz 68040 in January

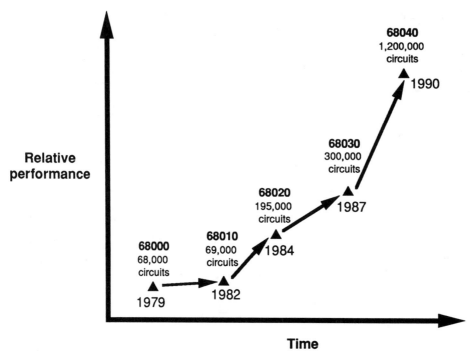

6-2 Motorola 68000 family growth trends.

1990; volume shipments began in January 1991. The 68050 is getting ready for a 1991–92 roll-out, and the 68060 is being considered for a few years beyond that. Apple should introduce a 68040-based Macintosh in 1991 if the chips are available in the quantities and price it requires. At the January 1991 Macworld convention, six smaller vendors announced 68040 accelerator card products. About that same time, articles on Apple's forthcoming 68040 tower machine appeared in the trade press. This is good news for Mac owners.

More good news for Mac fans, this time versus the DOS PC world. Motorola released performance results showing its 68040 chip delivered 20 Mips versus the Intel 80486 chip's 15 Mips. Each chip was running at 25 MHz during the measurement. The 68040 chip has a 33% performance advantage in throughput over the 80486 chip; Mac users can take heart that with the 68040, they are absolutely getting a hotter chip than their current generation DOS PC counterparts. Raw speed doesn't tell the whole story, however. As just mentioned, all chips are upward compatible in the Motorola 68000 family, whereas the applications written for the 80386 Intel chip have to be rewritten for the next generation Intel 80486 chip to take advantage of its power.

When talking about graphics, remember that Intel's entire line was never designed with graphics in mind. The 68040 will be a screamer for 3-D graphics and CAD at 350% faster than the 80486 in floating-point operations. In fact, 68040 performance is right up there with Motorola's 88000 RISC-base chip set.

A lot of optimized and parallel processing is going on in the new 68040 chip. As a result, the 68040 can execute the average instruction in only 1.3 clock cycles versus the 3.4 clock cycles required for the 68030 chip. Motorola says its 25 MHz 68040 offers three times the performance of a 25 MHz 68030; its integral on-chip floating point unit (no separate 68882 style chip needed) allows it to perform floating point operations ten times faster.

What this means to you is that if you drop the 68040 chip in place of the 68030 chip, your software will run faster. Before you get too ecstatic, however, not all applications will be able to fully exploit the 68040 when it first comes out because of the chip's architectural differences. The 68040 chip handles floating point operations and memory management in a way different from the 68030's. Like anything new, you can expect a period of adjustment while software patches are developed to catch up with the hardware capabilities. Another subtle corollary here is that you shouldn't pass up your currently-compatible 40 MHz and 50 MHz 68030 accelerator cards. They will still be faster than the 25 MHz version of the 68040.

The overall message to you is to be aware of this CPU chip trend and know that because of it, you are going to be presented with some increasingly attractive alternatives to the 10-year-old 68000 chip technology now used in the Mac Classic logic board. On the down side, just know that any Macintosh you have today will be surpassed in the future as Motorola introduces newer CPU chips in the family.

ROM, RAM, DRAM, SRAM, PRAM, cache, memory chips, SIMMs

No, you didn't just get a briefing from the military. However, before reading about memory, you should have a few definitions and a little history under your belt.

Binary numbers   Computers "think" in binary language composed of 1s or 0s—the circuit is either "on" or "off." In computer terms, each individual 1 or 0 is called a *bit*. In mathematical terms, the number 2 raised to a power is a binary number. If I had three bits in a row, such as 111, that represented binary numbers with values of 2^0, 2^1, and 2^2, their base ten values (the numbers we think in) would be 1, 2, and 4. The binary number 111 would represent the number 7. By changing the 1s and 0s pattern, the sum of their three digits could represent any number from 0 to 7, or eight different values. In this way, computer values are changed to those we understand, and vice versa.

Byte   The smallest computer *word*, or character, consists of 8 bits and is called a *byte*. With 8 binary bit positions, you can arrange them to define 256 different characters or symbols. This is how your computer keyboard works.

K or Mb   Although K or kilo usually means a thousand (and M means a million), a kilobyte isn't a thousand bytes. Because computers think in binary numbers, their counting system is based on the number two, not on the number ten. The number 2^{10} (or two multiplied by itself ten times) equals 1024. A kilobyte or 1K is really 1024 bytes. This shorthand notation has proliferated and become more in vogue in the computer industry. Today, depending on who you are talking to, either 1024 kilobytes or 1000 kilobytes equals 1 megabyte or 1Mb, and 1024 or 1000 megabytes equals 1 gigabyte.

Word length Earlier computers and chips "thought" in word lengths of 8, 12, 16, and 24 bits. They defined and moved data in chunks of that size. Two raised to that number defined the limit of memory they could directly address. Most of today's computers and chips use 32 bits and are able to directly address four billion address locations (2^{32} or four gigabytes).

Read only memory (ROM) ROM is a permanent storage medium that is uniquely "programmed" with data. Think of it as a chip with thousands and thousands of tiny fuses on it that are either blown or intact, in accordance with the instructions. You give any computer its unique personality by telling it how it will execute certain instructions. This is done by storing its programming instructions in ROM. The Motorola 68xxx processor chip at the heart of the Macintosh is also used in the Atari, Amiga, NeXT, and numerous other computers. The major difference between them (physical architecture aside) is the instructions stored in their ROM chips. When Apple first introduced the Mac 128, the 64K of instructions optimized and crammed into its ROM is what really made it a Macintosh. It represented countless thousands of man-hours, was the engineering marvel of its day (1982-83), and still is very impressive by today's standards. The 128K ROMs in the Mac Plus, 256K ROMs in the Mac SE and later models, and 512K ROMs in the Mac IIci and later models, each required successively more work. Yet put the tiny Apple Mac ROM chips into a clone computer and you have a Macintosh—not Apple's idea of a good time. Now you have at least a small idea of why Apple covets its ROM code so zealously.

Random access memory (RAM) Memory is also called *DRAM* or dynamic RAM (you have to refresh it constantly), *SRAM* or static RAM (SRAM does not need constant refreshing, and it has lower power consumption), *PRAM* or parameter RAM (a small amount of RAM powered by the Mac's internal battery is set aside to store a few user-definable settings so they are not lost each time the Mac is turned off). Today's semiconductor computer memory, like the processor chips, is very fast but volatile; when you turn the power off you erase memory. RAM memory only temporarily stores your data. (No power, no data.) In the mid-1970s, minicomputer memory used magnetic cores and was slower but nonvolatile. It permanently stored your data, but it was extremely expensive compared to today's semiconductor memory. It was also less dense. In those days, 32K of memory was a lot; top-of-the-line minicomputers had 256K. Computers used 4K memory chips, then 16K, then 64K, then 256K, then 1Mb, and now 4Mb. Soon they will use 16Mb chips, and 64Mb chips are in the labs now. More powerful and less expensive memory and CPU chips have fueled the personal computer explosion.[2]

Cache A cache is a small pocket or purse, like the change purse in a wom-

---

[2] Jim Heid, "Getting Started With Memory," *Macworld*, April 1990, p. 235. This article will definitely increase your ROM and RAM.

an's handbag. You look in it first to get your change. Mainframe and minicomputer manufacturers have for years used high-speed memory in front of regular processor memory to speed up their computers. Here's how it works: When your computer writes data in main memory, it leaves a copy of it in cache memory too. When your computer goes to read data, it looks first in cache memory. If it finds the data there, it doesn't bother with looking in main memory. If your cache and your program loops are of the right size, your computer hardly ever looks in main memory. The result is that everything runs a lot faster. Motorola, Apple, and a host of third-party vendors have integrated these concepts into their products. Motorola's 68020 has a 256-byte instruction cache, the 68030 has 256-byte instruction and data caches, and the 68040 has 4096-byte instruction and data caches. Apple has added RAM cache connector slots onto its newest logic boards, the IIci and IIfx. Third-party accelerator card vendors have designed a variety of products covering a wide price range using the cache concept.

Memory chips On the earliest Mac 128 logic boards, Apple soldered 64K RAM chips directly onto the board. In the 512 logic boards, Apple soldered on 256K RAM chips. Repairing or upgrading them was very difficult.

Single inline memory module (SIMM) A SIMM typically consists of two or eight individual RAM chips attached to a small printed circuit card. Some IIci and IIfx SIMMs use nine chips—the extra one is for parity, a quick way of checking your memory's health. Memory was revolutionized by use of SIMMs. First introduced with the Mac Plus in 1986, SIMMs made it possible to easily add additional memory to the Macintosh Plus logic board and to any Macintosh developed since then.

SIMM price trends

SIMM memory prices is an interesting subject. Good news for Mac users in general is that the price of SIMMs continues to slide downward. Look at Fig. 6-3 showing the price of 1Mb and 4Mb SIMMs between June 1989 and February 1991. I took this data straight out of the advertising pages of *MacWEEK*. The mail order price for 1Mb SIMMs has somewhat stabilized around the $40 point, while that of 4Mb SIMMs is at $180 and dropping. As the chart suggests, four of the 1Mb SIMMs are still less expensive than a single 4Mb SIMM, so the crossover point has not yet been reached. That point is rapidly approaching, and history has proven that 4Mb SIMM prices can be expected to drop significantly as volumes pick up. I believe 1Mb SIMMs will still be in the marketplace for quite a number of years, then the 16Mb versus 4Mb activity will come into play. Although the 16Mb area has begun to pick up as the leaders TI, Samsung, and Siemens AG have gotten beyond the pure prototyping stage, volume production here is probably not an issue until 1993. Beyond this, preliminary engineering papers have already been presented on 64Mb chips. All this activity prompted one semiconductor analyst to say that with the coming generations of chips, ''Memory will be almost free compared to the other things you can buy in a computer.''

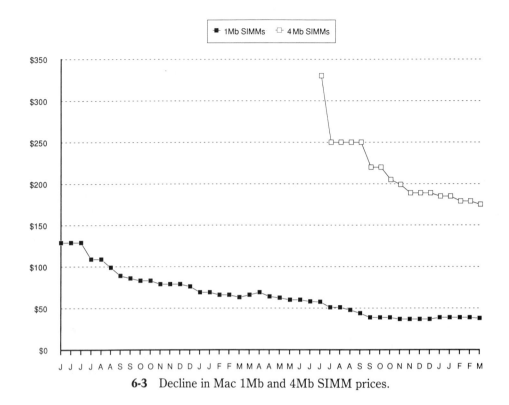

6-3 Decline in Mac 1Mb and 4Mb SIMM prices.

Playing the slots

Original clip-on Mac owners had no slots, and they griped. Today, 14 Mac models later, Mac owners have 11 different slot choices, and they still gripe. I say that strictly tongue in cheek. God bless slots. They are more reliable, easier to use, and although totally incompatible with one another save for the NuBus slot, their very existence and standardization ensures that a steady flow of products will continue to be made available to Mac upgrade buyers.[3] Let's look more closely.

NuBus, a trademark of Texas Instruments, was adapted from the TI design with changes by Apple.[4] In direct contrast to the hassle of putting option cards into a DOS PC, the NuBus option card system designed by Apple couldn't be simpler. There are no DIP switch settings to make, no slot locations to worry about, no batch files to install, nor is there any driver software or if there is, it's very simply done. It is the only expansion slot compatible across different Mac family models

---

[3] Clay Andres, "Expansion Choices: NuBus flexibility vs. PDS power," *MacWEEK*, 8/14/90, p. 33. While pre-dating the newest Mac introductions, this article is still a really excellent article on the subject and well worth a read.

[4] Bill Nowlin and John J. Anderson, "Hop on NuBus, Gus," *MacUser*, February 1989, p. 124. The article offers an excellent introduction to the subject and *Designing Cards and Drivers for the Macintosh Family, 2nd Edition* (Addison Wesley, 1990) covers the details.

and, by definition, only within the NuBus Macs unless expansion cards or chassis are added. Its greatest strengths are any NuBus card will work in any Mac IIxx family member, and with any Mac, it allows multiple devices concurrent access. Its greatest drawback is that while its 10 MHz transfer speed (NuBus has a fixed 100 ns system clock) was blazing speed when first introduced on the Mac II, it is a bottleneck on the IIci and up-class Macs today and to future high-end Macs. Apple has made the commitment to NuBus, and you can expect this standard to extend well into the future. You can also expect a "high-speed NuBus," whatever it is formally called, to be announced in the near future with Apple's new upper-end models. Figure 6-4 shows the six NuBus slots (to the left) on a Mac IIfx logic board.

6-4   Mac IIfx logic board showing NuBus slots and PDS.

The processor direct slot (PDS) has a different mission from the NuBus slot. Its only mission is to connect you with the Motorola 68xxx CPU chip in the most expeditious manner. Unlike the NuBus, it isn't even a bus—just wires and pins. Its greatest strength is any card plugged into a PDS has direct access to the CPU, making it higher in performance and less expensive than a NuBus card. Its greatest drawbacks are you can have only one PDS per Mac and, by definition, every new Mac PDS is totally unique to that Mac model and incompatible with every other. Today, there are PDS slots for the SE, SE 30, LC, IIsi, IIfx, and Portable. You can plug a 96-pin adapter into the SE, LC, and Portable, and you can plug a 120-pin adapter into the SE 30, IIsi, and IIfx. However, the pinouts and board size specs are all different, and the option boards won't work. The Mac IIfx PDS (directly in front of last NuBus slot on right in Fig. 6-4) is a superset of the SE 30's with additional capabilities. In Fig. 6-5, my finger points to the PDS connector on the SE 30 logic board. Tomorrow, you can expect processor direct slots to continue to proliferate as new models are introduced. Hey, why change a good thing?

6-5 Mac SE 30 logic board showing PDS connector.

6-6 Mac IIci logic board showing cache slot.

The cache slot is a single-purpose slot unique to the IIci. This slot gives direct access to the IIci cache memory area allowing its performance to be extended by the addition of an optional cache card with high speed memory on it. As the trend with each new Motorola CPU generation is to introduce even more cache functionality, this will probably not be the last cache slot you will see in the Mac family. Figure 6-6 shows Mac IIci cache slot directly in front of SIMM socket in center of Mac IIci logic board.

Modem and RAM slots are two single-purpose slots currently unique to Apple's only Portable Mac that permit internal modem and RAM cards to be added. You can believe that there will be more special purpose slots, both in future Mac Portable and Mac-mainstream family members. Figure 6-7 shows the Mac Portable with its back cover off. My fingers are resting on the RAM card on the left, and the modem card is on the right.

The memory card slot is a new slot unique to the Classic. This 44-pin slot is a receptacle for the Classic's memory card, and third-party vendors have also adapted it for video output. Figure 6-8 shows the Classic logic board in the center with its memory card slot visible at its lower edge with two memory cards beneath it—Apple's (left) and Computer Care's (right).

Now that you've covered a little background, let's get into the actual memory, accelerator, and coprocessor upgrade options. For each area, I'll cover the items, the pricing, offer comparisons or positioning information, and make recommendations or suggest a strategy for you.

6-7   Mac Portable showing RAM (on left) and modem card.

6-8 Mac Classic logic board with memory cards from Apple (left) and Computer Care (right).

Memory upgrades

If you've read straight through up to this point, you know memory is the best investment you can make in upgrading your Mac. It is also the easiest upgrade to do unless you have a Mac 128 or Mac 512 that has its memory soldered on.

Today, you should not have less than 2Mb of memory in your Macintosh. Why? Because 2Mb is the minimum amount of memory that will allow you to run Apple's System 6.0x MultiFinder or the new System 7.0 software. Both hold great productivity increases for you. With 1Mb SIMM prices at $50 or less, there is no excuse for you not to have at least 2Mb or more of memory in your Macintosh.[5] All the new Macs come with 2Mb already, except the Classic where 2Mb is Apple's first upgrade option. Perhaps Apple is telling us something.

Adding 4Mb or more is really necessary for any graphics or desktop publishing work. The best OCR scanner software requires 4Mb minimum for text. For

---

[5] Tom Thompson, "Mac at the Minimum," *Byte*, March 1990, p. 219 and Jim Heid, "More For Your Memory," *Macworld*, April 1990, p. 154. Lest everyone be carried away, Tom shows how much can be done in a 1Mb memory Mac and Jim shows how to best use your Mac memory, whatever its size.

graphics, 4Mb-and-up TIFF files are not uncommon for full-page scans. More memory is always better. Your memory upgrade strategy will vary, depending on the Mac you own. Early Macs with soldered-in RAM follow different rules, the Plus on up through the latest models all utilize SIMMs in varying amounts, and the Mac IIfx and Portable introduce a few new wrinkles. Let's look more closely.

Early Mac memory upgrades

As a general rule of thumb, owners of Mac 128 and Mac 512 models should seriously consider upgrading these machines to the level of a Mac Plus with 2Mb of SIMM memory. This means upgrading to an 800K floppy disk drive and the 128K ROMs it requires and adding a SCSI port, along with adding at least 2Mb more memory. While you can do this piecemeal, it is best done via either an Apple upgrade or a SIMM-based third-party daughterboard. Let me explain why.

You have four alternative memory upgrade strategies: fixed, Apple, daughterboard, and accelerator board. I no longer recommend fixed, strongly recommend accelerator, and recommend either daughterboard or Apple because you can take your SIMMs with you when you later get an accelerator.

As mentioned earlier, Apple soldered on 64K RAM chips to the Mac 128 logic boards and 256K RAM chips to the Mac 512 logic boards. Upgrading the Mac 128 logic board yourself, at this point, is not only difficult, but an unwise investment of your time and money. I don't recommend that you do it. Should you be so inclined, you can mail in your Mac 128 logic board and receive a Mac 512 logic board in return from several qualified sources.

Adding fixed memory upgrades to either the Mac 128 or 512 is not a good idea because they do not easily permit you to expand memory. On the other hand, they are inexpensive. The Dove MacSnap series 524S (1Mb) and 548S (2Mb) are probably the most popular user-installed fixed memory upgrade boards that come with the SCSI port adapter. With fixed 128 and 512 upgrades, what you have the first time you upgrade is what you get: 1Mb, 2Mb, or 4Mb. If expansion is important to you, you need to do something else. I don't recommend you do a fixed upgrade at this time.

The Apple upgrades are, by definition, expandable. Using them, you can take the Mac 128 to a 1Mb Mac Plus at $799 list or Mac 512 to a 1Mb Mac Plus at $599. As a prerequisite to either one of these, you need to add the Apple 800K floppy upgrade (it comes with the 128K ROMs) at $299 list. You can probably do better than list prices today. Whatever you pay, the result is an open-ended Mac Plus, and you wind up with the genuine Apple article that you can add SIMM memory upgrades to later on. Although pricey, if you want to keep the Mac you now own and maximize its resale value, I recommend you go the Apple upgrade route versus going out and buying a used Mac Plus—mostly because you know about what you now own, and the Apple upgrade parts you are buying new, so you are sure of what you are getting. When you buy a used Mac Plus, you are not totally sure of its history. Even if you wind up paying a few hundred bucks more, it should still be worth it to you in peace of mind. On the other hand, if you want a new platinum, color Mac Plus and/or its larger keyboard, by all means sell your Mac and get the used Mac Plus.

Daughterboards to the rescue

Computer Care and Newbridge have introduced a better way to expand a 128 or 512 logic board using a daughterboard that clips on to the 68000 chip on the Mac's logic board. Computer Care offers a board with 6 SIMM sockets for $250, and Newbridge offers a board with 8 SIMM sockets for $300. Each one includes a new 68000 chip, SCSI chip and cable, and Killy clip. You attach the clip to your existing logic board 68000 chip, plug in the daughterboard, add memory chips, set the jumper settings, and you are in business. You still need to add the Apple 800K floppy upgrade, but you get 20% greater than Apple Mac Plus performance and save a few dollars over the all-Apple upgrade cost. Plus either board lets you expand all the way to 4Mb of SIMM memory. This is probably your most cost-effective Mac 128/512 upgrade, and I recommend it, too. Figure 6-9 shows the Newbridge board (eight SIMM sockets; count 'em) being installed on a 512 logic board.

6-9 Newbridge memory upgrade board being installed on the Mac 512 logic board.

The best upgrades for 128 and 512 logic boards

Today, the best way to upgrade your Mac 128 or 512 is by adding a 68030 accelerator card, plus the 800K floppy and 128K ROMs. While this is the most costly option, it yields the greatest benefits. Accelerators let you add 4Mb or more of SIMMs plus a blazing 68030 chip under the hood that can bring you up to Mac IIci performance levels for a fraction of the cost. I highly recommend this approach if you have the budget.

SIMM memory upgrades for Mac Plus and up models

Owners of Mac Plus machines up through the latest Mac models introduced, with the exception of the Mac IIfx and Portable, have a much simpler memory upgrade task. If you own one of these models, you should definitely consider upgrading it to 2Mb with SIMM memory. Unlike the early Mac owners, you don't have to worry about upgrading your floppy disk drive ROMs along with memory. Everything you need is already there; just add the memory SIMMs. On the latest Mac models, you don't have to worry at all because most offer at least one variation that already has 2Mb installed. Let's get to the details.

You need to concern yourself with four areas when buying SIMMs:

- *SIMM types* SIMMs come in two flavors: dual inline package (DIP) and surface mount (SOJ). The RAM memory chip pins on DIP SIMMs are soldered on through holes, require a larger width SIMM circuit card, sit higher in their logic board socket, and cannot be used in height critical Plus or SE boards, but cost less. SOJ SIMMs are shorter in length than DIP SIMMs, and their pins are soldered onto the surface of the SIMM circuit card. They can be used in any SIMM socket and typically cost more.
- *SIMM sizes* Today's SIMMs come in three sizes: 256K, 1Mb, and 4Mb. (Let me not be hasty here. These are the standard sizes. Third-party vendors also provide SIMMs in 512K, 2Mb, and 16Mb flavors built up from the standard sizes to open up other memory upgrade possibilities for you. More on this later.) They can be mixed and matched, but you have to follow certain rules that are slightly different for each Mac model regarding size and speed. Figure 6-10 shows three different kinds of SOJ (surface mount) SIMMs. In the front is 1Mb SIMM with eight 80 ns RAM chips on it; in the middle a 256K SIMM with two 80 ns RAM chips on it; and at the rear a 256K SIMM with eight 120 ns RAM chips on it.
- *SIMM speeds* The suffix numbers on RAM chips mounted on the SIMM are important. They tell you the chip's speed. The " – 15" means you have a 150 nanosecond chip, " – 12" means you have a 120 nanosecond chip, " – 10" means you have a 100 nanosecond chip, " – 80" means you have a 80 nanosecond chip, " – 70" means you have a 70 nanosecond chip, etc. There is no advantage in using chips faster than your logic board needs; its clock speed and wait states are fixed and cannot take advantage of faster chips. Don't spend money on faster SIMMs than you need unless you plan on taking your SIMMs with you to a higher performance Mac model later. Any-

thing faster than 150 ns on your Mac Plus or SE and faster than 120 ns on your Mac II or SE 30 is wasted. On the other hand, the SE 30, Mac IIx, and Mac IIcx will take 100 ns, and your accelerator board might need 100 ns or better SIMMs to perform well. The IIci and IIsi use SIMMs for video RAM and require at least 80 ns chips. On the other hand, you cannot run slower SIMMs than your particular Mac requires, and you must exactly match the speed of all SIMMs used in any given Mac's memory bank if you wish to avoid erratic and intermittent operation of your Mac that results in data loss. Table 6-1 summarizes your memory speed options across all Mac models.

* *SIMM prices*   Use Fig. 6-3 as a guideline when you shop around.

My recommendation on your strategy here is very straightforward: Buy the most memory your pocketbook will allow. Numerous articles have been written that expand on this area more.[6]

6-10   Different Mac SIMM types: 1Mb (front) and 256K (middle and rear).

---

[6] If you only have time to read a few, choose: Owen W. Linzmayer, "SIMMple Pleasures," *MacUser*, April 1991, p. 194; Bob LeVitus, "Memory-Upgrade Options," *MacUser*, June 1990, p. 299; and Russell Ito, "The Persistence of Memory," *MacUser*, February 1989, p. 140. If you receive *Mac-WEEK*, David Ramsey's bi-weekly "Help Desk" articles are invaluable.

Table 6-1. SIMM speed options for various Mac models.

Model	150 ns	120 ns	100 ns	greater than 80 ns	Comments
Mac Plus	Yes	Yes	Yes	Yes	No 4Mb SIMMs
Mac SE	No	Yes	Yes	Yes	No 4Mb SIMMs
Mac Classic	No	Yes	Yes	Yes	No 4Mb SIMMs
Mac SE 30	No	Yes	Yes	Yes	
Mac II	No	Yes	Yes	Yes	
Mac IIx	No	Yes	Yes	Yes	
Mac IIcx	No	Yes	Yes	Yes	
Mac LC	No	No	Yes	Yes	
Mac IIsi	No	No	Yes	Yes	Apple ships 80 ns SIMMs!
Mac IIci	No	No	No	Yes	
Mac IIfx	No	No	No	Yes	64-pin SIMMs only
Portable	No	No	Yes	Yes	Low-power static RAM only

Mac Plus and SE SIMM rules

Both the Mac Plus and SE logic board have four SIMM sockets. As you look down on the Mac Plus board with the front edge toward you (as shown in Fig. 6-11), the SIMM sockets are numbered 1, 2, 3, 4 starting with the SIMM socket closest to the CPU chip. On the Mac SE board (with its front edge to the left in Fig. 6-12), there are two rows of SIMM sockets, with 1 (upper) and 2 (lower) in the row closest to the CPU, with 3 and 4 to the left of them, respectively. Although the four sock-

6-11 Mac Plus logic board SIMM layout.

6-12   Mac SE logic board SIMM layout.

ets are physically arranged differently in the Mac Plus and Mac SE, each have four identical allowable memory configurations using the 256K and 1Mb memory chips. Table 6-2 summarizes them.

**Table 6-2. SIMM configuration
options for the Mac Plus and Mac SE.**

Configuration	1Mb	2Mb	2.5Mb	4Mb
SIMM #1 (Old SE & Plus)	256K	1Mb	1Mb	1Mb
SIMM #2 (Old SE & Plus)	256K	1Mb	1Mb	1Mb
SIMM #3 (Old SE & Plus)	256K	—	256K	1Mb
SIMM #4 (Old SE & Plus)	256K	—	256K	1Mb
SIMM #1 (New SE board)	256K	—	1Mb	1Mb
SIMM #2 (New SE board)	256K	—	1Mb	1Mb
SIMM #3 (New SE board)	256K	1Mb	256K	1Mb
SIMM #4 (New SE board)	256K	1Mb	256K	1Mb

Apple has laid down some simple rules[7] that, if followed, make life much simpler. Here are the SIMM guidelines for either a Plus or an SE:

- Each SIMM must use 150 ns or faster RAM chips.

---

[7] Apple, *Guide to the Macintosh Family Hardware, 2nd Edition*, Addison Wesley, chapter 5.

- All RAM chips in a row must be the same speed and size.
- Each SIMM must be filled with eight RAM chips. The nine RAM SIMMs used in IBM PC chips will not work.
- All rows must either be empty or contain two SIMMs.
- The SIMMs with the larger RAM chips must always be installed in row 1.

There is also a corresponding need to be aware of what to do with the SIMMs resistors or jumpers on the Plus and SE logic boards. Table 6-3 summarizes it.

Table 6-3. Resistor/jumper options for the Mac Plus and Mac SE.

Configuration	2 SIMMs	4 SIMMs	All 256K	All 1Mb
On Plus; resistor R9 "one row"	installed	removed	—	—
On Plus; resistor R8 "256K bit"	—	—	installed	removed
On SE; resistor R36 "one row"	installed	removed	—	—
On SE; resistor R35 "256K bit"	—	—	installed	removed
On new SE; jumper on 1Mb	—	—	1Mb installed	—
On new SE; jumper on 2/4Mb	—	—	—	2Mb installed
On new SE; jumper off	—	2.5Mb installed	—	—
On new SE; jumper off	—	—	—	4Mb installed

Mac SE 30 and NuBus SIMM rules

On the SE 30, Mac II, Mac IIx, Mac IIcx, Mac IIci, and Mac IIfx logic boards, socketed SIMMs allow you to expand memory to 8Mb. There are eight SIMM sockets on all these logic boards. In Fig. 6-5, as you look down at the SE 30 logic boards with its front edge toward you and connectors away from you, the SIMM sockets are numbered from 1 to 8 starting with the SIMM socket closest to the CPU chip. On Mac II, Mac IIx, Mac IIcx, and Mac IIci boards with same orientation, SIMM number 1 is closest to the right edge. On the Mac IIfx board with same orientation, SIMM number 1 is closest to the rear. The five allowable memory configurations using the 256K and 1Mb memory chips are summarized in Table 6-4.

Apple's rules changed slightly for these logic boards, but there are no resistor changes to worry about. Here are the SIMMs guidelines for the SE 30, Mac II,

Table 6-4. SIMM options for the Mac SE 30 and NuBus Macs.

Configuration	1Mb	2Mb	4Mb	5Mb	8Mb	16Mb	17Mb	32Mb
SIMM #1 (bank A)	256K	256K	1Mb	1Mb	1Mb	4Mb	4Mb	4Mb
SIMM #2 (bank A)	256K	256K	1Mb	1Mb	1Mb	4Mb	4Mb	4Mb
SIMM #3 (bank A)	256K	256K	1Mb	1Mb	1Mb	4Mb	4Mb	4Mb
SIMM #4 (bank A)	256K	256K	1Mb	1Mb	1Mb	4Mb	4Mb	4Mb
SIMM #5 (bank B)	—	256K	—	256K	1Mb	—	1Mb	4Mb
SIMM #6 (bank B)	—	256K	—	256K	1Mb	—	1Mb	4Mb
SIMM #7 (bank B)	—	256K	—	256K	1Mb	—	1Mb	4Mb
SIMM #8 (bank B)	—	256K	—	256K	1Mb	—	1Mb	4Mb

Mac IIx, Mac IIcx, Mac IIci, and Mac IIfx logic boards:

- Each SIMM must use 120 ns or faster RAM chips (80 ns or faster for the IIci or IIfx, plus the fast page mode for the IIci).
- All RAM chips in a row must be the same speed and size.
- Each SIMM must be filled with eight RAM chips. Nine RAM chip SIMMs to enable parity checking may be used in IIci and IIfx models when equipped with custom parity checker and generator (PGC) IC on the IIci and custom RAM parity unit (RPU) IC on the IIfx model.
- All rows must either be empty or contain four SIMMs.
- The SIMMs with the larger RAM chips must always be installed in row 1.
- RAM SIMM pinouts are different for the IIfx and not interchangeable with other model SIMMs.

Mac Classic, LC, and IIsi SIMM rules

The rules change again for the Classic, LC, and IIsi models. The allowable memory configurations for them using the 256K, 1Mb, and 4Mb memory chips are summarized in Table 6-5. Each model is a little different.

On the Classic, 1Mb is already soldered to the logic board. You expand memory by adding the optional memory card. The Apple optional memory card comes with 1Mb already soldered to the card and two SIMM sockets. You get the various possible expanded memory combinations of 2Mb, 2.5Mb, or 4Mb of RAM by adding either none or two 256K SIMMs or two 1Mb SIMMs to the card. You cannot used 4Mb SIMMs.

On the LC, 2Mb is already soldered to the logic board, and you have two SIMM sockets on the logic board for add-in memory. You get the various possible combinations of 2Mb, 4Mb, or 10Mb of RAM by adding either none or two 1Mb SIMMs or two 4Mb SIMMs to the logic board.

On the IIsi, 1Mb is already soldered to the logic board and you have four SIMM sockets on the logic board for add-in memory. You get the various possible combinations of 1Mb, 2Mb, 5Mb, or 17Mb of RAM by adding either none or four 256K SIMMs or four 1Mb SIMMs or four 4Mb SIMMs to the logic board.

Table 6-5. SIMM options for Mac Classic, Mac LC, and Mac IIsi.

Configuration	2Mb	2.5Mb	4Mb	5Mb	8Mb	10Mb	17Mb
SIMM #1 (Classic)	Memory board	256K	1Mb	—	—	—	—
SIMM #2 (Classic)	Memory board	256K	1Mb	—	—	—	—
SIMM #1 (LC)	Standard	—	1Mb	—	—	4Mb	—
SIMM #2 (LC)	Standard	—	1Mb	—	—	4Mb	—
SIMM #1 (IIsi bank B)	256K	—	—	1Mb	—	—	4Mb
SIMM #2 (IIsi bank B)	256K	—	—	1Mb	—	—	4Mb
SIMM #3 (IIsi bank B)	256K	—	—	1Mb	—	—	4Mb
SIMM #4 (IIsi bank B)	256K	—	—	1Mb	—	—	4Mb

Mac IIfx SIMM rules

The rules don't change for the IIfx as much as the physical appearance of its SIMMs, memory slots, and memory slot orientation in the chassis. The big difference is shown in Fig. 6-13. Notice the IIfx 1Mb SIMM in the foreground is a 64-pin wide unit rather than a standard off-the-shelf 30-pin 1Mb SIMM for other Mac models shown in the rear. Apple improved the performance of its IIfx system by going to an overlapping read/write technique. Apple calls it *latched read/write*, where even though the IIfx's 68030 only supports 32-bit data paths, you grab data in the form of 64-bit words because your read and write accesses can overlap. The improved performance 64-pin SIMMs command a higher price than their standard cousins, but performance-conscious IIfx owners gladly pay the difference.

6-13　Mac IIfx 64-pin 1Mb SIMM (front) versus standard 1Mb SIMM (rear).

The metal clips on the IIfx SIMM sockets are a tremendous improvement over the standard plastic ones that are hard on your fingernails and are easy to break. Optimum board layout on the IIfx dictated that its SIMM memory slots be rotated 90 degrees from those in the Mac II and IIx. No big deal, it is just different.

My memory recommendations for the IIfx break the pattern from the other models in the Mac family. Hey, you've just bought a machine whose list price is over $10,000—and you probably have a hefty agenda of what you'd like to accomplish with it. Why short change yourself in the memory department? I would definitely load it up to 8Mb for openers, and more if you have the need.

Bulk memory

Piggyback four-for-one SIMM cards from Computer Care let you put four 256K SIMMs or four 1Mb SIMMs on a card that inserts into a SIMM socket in your Mac II or Mac IIcx. The card for a Mac IIcx is shown in Fig. 6-14. Mac II style

6-14 Computer Care four-for-one memory upgrade adapter card for Mac IIcx or Mac IIci.

cards are lower and wider in 2-by-2 side-by-side versus the 4-high arrangement for the Mac IIcx cards. This allows you to use up older 256K SIMMs and make 1Mb SIMMs out of them or, alternately, use less expensive 1Mb SIMMs to make 4Mb SIMMs—simple, inexpensive, and they work.

Remember an earlier mention that said you also have 512K, 2Mb, and 16Mb SIMM options? They are called composite SIMMs and are built up using different SIMM circuit boards and/or RAM chips variations. For example, Newer Technology has 70 ns 16Mb composite SIMMs. The 64-pin Mac IIfx version is shown in Fig. 6-15. Versions are also available in parity and nonparity styles for other Mac models using standard SIMMs.

If you're really in need of a lot of very fast memory, you need Newer Technology's SCSI Dart. Imagine a 512Mb 3½-inch hard disk with an access time of 0.2 millisecond! Newer's 3½-inch form factor package accommodates 256K, 1Mb, 4Mb, or 16Mb SIMMs in combinations up to 448Mb to give you the fastest hard disk you've ever seen. A built-in UPS battery back-up system gives you nonvolatile storage. Start with only the memory you need today, and expand to meet your needs. It makes a slick way for you to have bulk amounts of RAM memory at your disposal for very, very fast I/O tasks. Fig. 6-16 shows a picture of it.

Hey, who stole my memory?

Before I leave the subject of SIMMs, you've probably noticed that Table 6-5 has configurations using 4Mb SIMMs to give you 10Mb of RAM in an LC and 17Mb in

6-15 64-pin 16Mb composite SIMM.

6-16 SCSI Dart ultra-high speed memory.

a IIsi. Table 6-4 shows you can have 32Mb in any of your 68030-based Macs by substituting 4Mb SIMMs for 1Mb SIMMs—yes and no.

Under Apple's System 6.0x, in all its flavors, your Mac can "see" the memory attached to it but it can only "use" up to 8Mb of it. Because of limitations in System 6.0x, no matter how much memory you have attached, the System only allows you to use 8Mb. (Who would have thought 8Mb was a limitation a few years ago—that's a lot of 256K SIMMs!) This limitation makes for interesting phenomena. For example, in your 17Mb Mac IIsi running System 6.07 (the latest 6.0x variant, as of this writing), when you open your Apple menu and invoke the normally trustworthy "About The Finder..." command, the dialog box says you have 17Mb out there, and that the System is using 10Mb of it—oops!

Under Apple's System 7.0, you can see and use all that memory. You have options available to you besides Apple's System 7.0. Connectrix Corp. makes a product called Virtual 2.0x that lets you use up to 14Mb of system memory on any 68030 Mac (or PMMU-equipped Mac II) by using extra hard disk space the Mac system held in reserve for NuBus slots. Another Connectrix product called Maxima (distributed by Newer Technology) gives you the benefits of Virtual plus creates a high-speed nonvolatile RAM disk drive.

Still another Connectrix product called Optima (also distributed by Newer Technology) allows owners of "32-bit clean" Macs (the new Mac IIsi, IIci, and IIfx with 512K ROM—their ROMs support addressing four gigabytes of memory—if you had it!) to run 32-bit clean applications in System 6.0x Finder Mode (not Multi-Finder!) and bypass the 8Mb memory limitations. When used in conjunction with Maxima, you can give the System 14Mb and use all the remaining memory as a RAM disk. When used with 4Mb SIMMs, Optima allows you to access up to 32Mb of memory. When used with Newer Technology's 16Mb composite SIMMs, you can access up to 128Mb of memory! Optima certainly gives you a viable memory addressing alternative you can use in lieu of Apple's System 7.0.

On the other hand, if you fill up your Mac IIsi with four 2Mb SIMM chips, instead of 4Mb ones, you have 9Mb total in your IIsi, 8Mb of it is usable, and your SIMM investment is lower. I am going to leave you with the fact that today you have SIMM-ply an amazing amount of memory options for your Mac.

Mac Portable SRAM memory rules

With the Mac Portable memory, you have a whole new ball game. Here you are talking static RAM (SRAM) chips on a plug-in memory card instead of dynamic RAM chips on standard SIMMs. A wide selection of plug-in circuit boards from Apple and third-party vendors is available to fit the Portable's single memory upgrade slot.

The Mac Portable's memory addressing scheme supports up to 9Mb of memory. It comes with 1Mb of memory (32 100 ns 32K static RAM chips) soldered on its logic board. Static RAM chips consume much less power than dynamic RAM chips. For the Mac Portable, 32K RAMs are the optimum size to conserve the most power. This translates to less battery drain when the Portable is turned on and makes it much easier to preserve the contents of memory when the Portable is turned off.

Apple provides a 1Mb memory upgrade card providing 2Mb total memory, and third-party vendors provide upgrade cards with up to 8Mb on the card taking you up to the 9Mb limit. The 8Mb card is an innovation of newer packaging technology utilizing both sides of the memory card and high density pseudo-static RAM chips. Figure 6-17 shows Newer Technology's 2Mb (upgradable to 6Mb) Mac Portable memory card.

Newer Technology

6-17 Mac Portable memory card with 2Mb.

My recommendation here is to expand to 2Mb of memory minimum (to run all of today's software, etc.), but not add extra memory unless the Portable is your only machine or you definitely have a future need. An in-between step might be to purchase a third-party vendor memory card that allows you to start with 1Mb or 2Mb today and add more memory to it in the future. My criteria here is driven by dollar rather than lower power budget concerns. Lower power psuedo-static RAM chips are available to keep battery drain low today, and you know that lower memory prices are coming in the future. Don't buy more than you need today is the message.

In memory of

A brief review of memory and a few concluding thoughts—memory is either random access memory (RAM) or read only memory (ROM). RAM is temporary (volatile), and ROM is permanent. Macintosh memory upgrades come in several flavors:

- Option cards that you can add on to older machines to bring them up to the level where they can be upgraded with SIMMs.
- SIMMs, the most common form of upgrade memory universal across all Macintosh models except the Mac Portable that uses a single plug-in card with static RAM chips on it.
- Four-for-one cards let you piggy-back your older SIMMs into higher density memory configurations.

- Bulk memory chassis lets you utilize different capacity SIMMs to build large nonvolatile RAM memory configurations for use in high-speed, memory-intensive applications.

A few concluding thoughts on memory: RAM memory chips and SIMMs are a commodity. To get the best price on the SIMMs you need today, buy them direct or wholesale from reputable suppliers who guarantee their products. History has proven new memory replaces the old. Use up your 256K SIMMs on other projects or sell them. They can no longer compete on price or utility. Figure 6-3 showed you 1Mb SIMMs are now the most cost-effective with 4Mb SIMMs catching up rapidly.

Accelerator boards

Accelerator boards can be thought of as the surgeon's wonder bullet to the Macintosh owner. With them you can:

- Raise the dead—take an early vintage Macintosh you're considering getting rid of and make it useable again.
- Use like Geritol pills—add a lot more speed and efficiency to a Macintosh you're now using in a heavy production mode.
- Use like plastic surgery—combined with a video card option, it adds the ability to make over your Mac video area as well as providing increased performance.

Accelerator boards are the Mac owner's customizing tool. They come in all sizes, speeds, option configurations, and prices. They can be used to take your 128K Mac to a 4Mb 68030 screamer, your Mac II to a 68030 running at 50 MHz, or merely to double the speed on your 68000 SE chip from 8 to 16 MHz giving you a performance boost on the software programs you now run.

The Macintosh market has undergone a healthy growth and with it the market for accelerator boards and the number of board suppliers. When Apple makes a move, such as announcing its SE 30 logic board upgrade kit[8] or its aggressively priced Mac IIfx logic board upgrade kit,[9] third-party accelerator card suppliers move rapidly to adjust their prices and reposition their products.

Accelerators come in itty-bitty, middle-of-the-road, and heavy-duty flavors. Be sure you're getting the one you want when you sign on the dotted line. The newer accelerator boards are less expensive, easier to install, and provide a higher compatibility with existing software than their predecessors of just a few years ago. Performance levels have drifted higher as increasingly hotter chips become available and this trend will continue.

---

[8] Dale Coleman, "The Market For SE acceleration undergoes dramatic changes," *MacWEEK*, 4/4/89, p. 24.

[9] John Battelle, "IIfx puts Apple at head of performance pack," *MacWEEK*, 3/20/90, p. 1.

The menu please

The subject of accelerator boards is a broad one. My objective in this chapter is not to discuss the pros and cons of every one of them, but only to introduce you to the subject and discuss the five types of boards that can help you in upgrading your Macintosh:

- Full-function accelerator cards with memory and CPU chips provide significant increases in performance.
- CPU/clock cards merely speed up the CPU clock or bus.
- Memory cache cards speed up your cache memory.
- SCSI bus accelerator cards increase the speed with which your NuBus Mac can talk to SCSI peripherals.
- File Compression cards increase the speed of compressing and decompressing files.

First, I'll get a few definitions out of the way. As in the memory section, I'll cover items, pricing, offer comparisons or positioning information, provide my recommendations, and suggest a strategy for you.

Okay, accelerate me

Here are some definitions for terms you are likely to encounter in discussing accelerator boards.

CPU chip   Today, accelerators come in four chip flavors: 68000, 68020, 68030, and 68040. The 68000 chip has 68,000 transistors or switches on it with 32-bit internal architecture and 16-bit data input paths. The 68020 chip has 195,000 switches on it, full 32-bit architecture, and an on-board 256 byte instruction cache. The 68030 has 300,000 switches on it with an on-board PMMU and an additional 256-byte data cache. The 68040 has 1,200,000 switches on it and an on-board FPU, PMMU plus 4096-byte instruction and data cache. For additional speed, the 68040 chip adds parallel, independent instruction, and data buses that are accessed simultaneously.

Clock speed   68020 and 68030 chips in Mac II and Mac SE 30 logic boards, respectively, run at 16 MHz versus the 8 MHz clock speed of the 68000 chip used in the SE logic board. Two times the operating frequency means that twice as many operations are performed each second. Today, accelerator boards are available to run at up to 50 MHz.

Throughput   68020 and 68030 chips use 32-bit versus the 16-bit data paths in the 68000 chip. Two times the path width means that twice as much data is transferred each operation. Twice as much data moving at twice the previous speed means the 68020 and 68030 chips have four times the throughput of the 68000 chip.

Cache   As explained earlier, the cache is a small amount of faster memory in front of main memory. The CPU only has to look at it for the next instruction or piece of data. On-chip instruction cache in the 68020 with data cache added in the 68030 improves performance, especially of looping, iterating programs. Radius accelerator boards, for example, use the technique of very fast static RAM cache to achieve outstanding performance even with the slow RAM chips used for main memory.

FPU   The floating point unit (FPU) is an optional 68881 or 68882 chip (the 68882 is twice as fast as 68881) used in conjunction with the CPU chip to accelerate math intensive applications such as spreadsheets, graphics, and CAD programs.

PMMU   The paged memory management unit (PMMU) is the optional 68851 chip used in conjunction with the 68020, and already on the 68030 chip. This chip or function must be present to run the "virtual" software operating systems that use a part of your hard disk as memory. By definition it is not "real" memory, so it is called *virtual* memory. PMMU does nothing for your System 6.0x software, but A/UX (Apple's Unix Software), Connectrix's Virtual, and Apple's System 7.0 (Apple's first system software to have virtual capabilities) all use its features.

Memory options   Not all accelerator boards are created equal in this department. Some use their own RAM exclusively, some use your logic board's RAM, while some use both. Some specify that you must use faster SIMM chips than the 150 ns SIMMS that came with your Mac Plus or early Mac SE. Ask specific questions in this area because extra fast SIMMs increase your accelerator board cost.

Control software   Packaged with each third-party vendor's product, control software's most basic function is to allow you to disable the accelerator board or cache and keep using programs that work only in the 68000 native mode. All other control software features, such as copy ROM into high-speed RAM at startup, configure FPU options, set speeds, and size memory fall in the "nice to have" category.

Expansion options   Can you drive a video monitor or piggyback other option cards off your accelerator card? When Radius entered the market in 1987 with its complete expansion solution designed by Burrell Smith, the Mac's original hardware designer, it piggybacked video onto the accelerator card and set the standard for virtually all accelerator cards that followed. Today, all distinctions are blurred, and accelerator board manufacturers support their own video monitors, and vice versa. Radius, Mobius, Lapis, Newbridge, and Computer Care are typical examples.

Remember your mission

In your car, you can take out the four- or six-cylinder engine and replace it with a more powerful eight-cylinder one. The car body and everything else stays the same. The same principle applies in adding an accelerator board to your Mac. You take a new board with a more powerful CPU chip and either clip it on to your Mac's existing CPU chip or remove the old CPU chip entirely and plug the new board in its place. Everything else stays the same. Well, not exactly. You also need some additional software, and you might even want to reformat your hard disk for better performance. Most of your programs, or all of the major ones (word processors, spreadsheets, etc.), run exactly as before only faster.

Your goal is simple. Save money by upgrading with an accelerator board rather than buying another more powerful Macintosh model. Avoid spending more for your accelerator board and its options, however, than the more powerful Mac model would cost you. As chapter 3 pointed out, you are more likely to recover your investment in your Apple Mac than in its third-party upgrade options when it's time to sell.

As for the accelerator board subject area, a large amount of reference material is available to help you. Excellent comprehensive articles well worth a read on accelerator boards have appeared in the past few years.[10] Some articles on accelerator boards from 1988 are excellent, although now dated.[11]

Full-function accelerators

Full-function accelerators are your best investment overall if you choose wisely. Although more expensive than other accelerator solutions, you'll be happier with your immediate performance and position yourself better for future growth. Let me explain. Full-function accelerators use several design techniques in conjunction to achieve their performance gains:

- Use a "hotter" CPU chip running at a higher clock speed.
- Usually install a "hotter" FPU chip on-board.
- Put SIMM memory sockets right on the accelerator board so the accelerator board's CPU chip can access it faster.
- Add high-speed cache memory to increase its performance further.
- Provide faster SCSI "handshaking."

While none of these steps is earth-shattering in itself, using all of them in conjunction produces significant performance gains. People are usually quite satisfied with the results. I strongly recommend full-function accelerators because you will definitely see the difference and be happy if a board is giving you a 100% performance improvement. If you're only getting a 20% performance improvement, it's usually hard to see it and you're unhappy about how your money was spent.

Today, it's to your advantage to purchase only a 68030-based accelerator board. All new Macintosh software will be optimized for the 68030 products; the 68030 does everything the 68020 does and then some with speed. Accelerator boards with the same CPU chip running at the same speed with the same amount

---

[10] Robert Hollis, "The low (price) roads to high performance," *MacWEEK*, 9/25/90, p. 109; Winn L. Rosch and *MacUser* Labs staff, "Chasing the IIfx: Accelerators," *MacUser*, August 1990, p. 84; Cheryl England Spencer, "Full Speed Ahead," *Macworld*, August 1990, p. 134; John Rizzo, "Fast Cache IIci and Marathon Racer," *MacUser*, May 1990; Lawrence Stevens, "Add-on boards give stock Macs new life," *MacWEEK*, 4/17/90, p.39; Bruce F. Webster, "Pushing the Mac II Performance Envelope," *Macworld*, February, 1990, p. 135; Bruce F. Webster, "Processors: Is Faster Better?," *Macworld*, March 1989, p. 118; and Gil Davis, "Maximum G-Force," *MacUser*, February 1989, p. 169.

[11] Chip Carmen, Jim White, Steven Bobker, "Pedal to the Metal," *MacUser*, March 1988, p. 108; and Savant Labs, "Speed Thrills," MACazine, November 1988, p. 41.

of on-board memory from different vendors produce different results because of their design differences! Investigate thoroughly before you invest. I will just give you my best recommendation for each processor family.

Clip-on Mac accelerator strategies

My recommended accelerator upgrade for the 128, 512, or Plus clip-on Macs is from Total Systems. They have many years experience in this area and numerous product options that help you add up to 4Mb of RAM with a blazing 68030 chip under the hood of your clip-on Mac. Total Systems offers both *a la carte* and full meal choices.

Their recommended solution is the Gemini II accelerator board shown in Fig. 6-18. You get not only the accelerator board and Killy clip, but also an extra power supply with fan and mounting bracket, plus a heavy-duty power cable. Their years of experience have demonstrated that this combination provides the most reliable clip-on Mac installation. Owners of the earlier 68020-based Gemini board shown in Fig. 6-19 have an upgrade option. Notice the 68030 socket next to the 68020 chip on the board and also two of the four on-board SIMMs are visible. One of the Gemini accelerator board benefits is that any owner can upgrade merely by plugging in hotter chips.

Total Systems Mercury accelerator board shown in Fig. 6-20 is the *a la carte* choice. You can buy less to start with (for a lower cost) and expand it as your needs grow. The accelerator board is in the upper right of Fig. 6-20, the high-speed SCSI expansion card is upper left, and the 32-bit RAM expansion card is beneath them

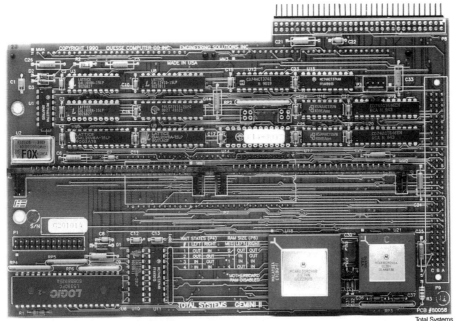

Total Systems

6-18 Gemini II accelerator board.

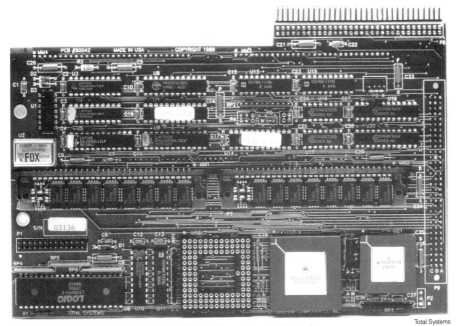

6-19 Gemini accelerator board.

Total Systems

6-20 Mercury accelerator board.

Total Systems

both. All this capability is already on the Gemini boards, giving you the *a la carte* option merely makes it easier on your budget.

Purchasing less than a 25 MHz accelerator is pointless at this time. Prices have come down, and 25 MHz gives you IIci performance in your clip-on Mac—that ought to keep you happy for a while!

One-slot Mac accelerator strategies

While many choices are available to you for the Mac SE, my recommended accelerator upgrade choices are either the Newbridge Microsystems Newlife 25 MHz or the Novy Quik 30 25 MHz shown in Fig. 6-21 on the left and right, respectively. (Newbridge licenses its design from Novy, so these are really the same products in different packaging.) The Newbridge version offers you an optional video interface that connects to a multisync monitor, but the Novy version has a better price. Installation couldn't be simpler; plug it into the 96-pin expansion slot on the Mac SE logic board, and that's it. Performance of the Novy or Newbridge (or the Gemini) 25 MHz accelerator boards is about the same—zoom! The SE board is less expensive than its Mac Plus accelerator board counterpart in every case because there is no need for the Killy clip or SCSI upgrade options. Any of these accelerator boards should make you happy because they all leave a stock Mac SE 30 in the dust and the upgrade cost is a lot less than buying a Mac SE 30.

If a high performance one-page or two-page video monitor is also what you need, you can simultaneously add it and a 25 MHz SE 30 accelerator to your SE to get the best of both worlds by getting the Mobius One Page or Two Page 030 Display SE. I'll talk more about this in chapter 8.

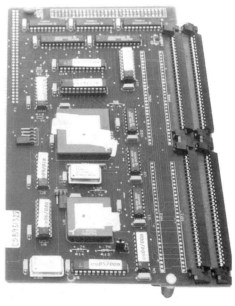

6-21 Newbridge Newlife 25 (left) and Novy Quik 30 accelerator boards.

By the way, there is absolutely nothing shabby about just going to the standard Apple Mac SE 30 Upgrade Kit either. You get a 16 MHz 68030 CPU with 68882 FPU chip that combine to give you 200% performance increase over your stock Mac SE. Also, you have the 8 SIMM slots on the board that you can load up, plus color and stereo sound capability—all for only $1699 list—a price you can probably do better on these days. While you will pay more for this than for any third-party solution, if your budget permits it, this gives you a total Apple solution with more functionality today and a higher resale value down the road. I definitely recommend it.

Speaking of the SE 30, the Total System Enterprise accelerator board shown in Fig. 6-22 is available in 25 MHz, 33 MHz, 40 MHz, or 50 MHz flavors and also works on the Mac LC and Mac IIsi. Installation is like the SE installation—plug it into the 120-pin expansion slot on the Mac SE 30 logic board, and that's all there is to it. In addition to delivering "Star Trek warp drive" performance to your Mac SE 30 (not that much of a slouch to begin with), the Enterprise accelerator board is field upgradable to different processor speeds, has optional 68882 FPU chips available, offers the expansion capability to run other third-party cards, and comes bundled with Connectrix's Virtual software.

Total Systems

6-22   Enterprise accelerator board.

NuBus accelerator strategies

Here your world of option opens up again. The most choices are available for the 68020-powered Mac II, whose performance is slower than its 68030-powered NuBus cousins. On the Mac IIcx, its 68030 chip being soldered to the board in later versions made upgrades more difficult; covet your Mac IIcx if it has a socketed 68030 on its logic board. On the Mac IIci, the 68030 CPU chip is also soldered on but Apple deliberately provided a cache slot for enhancement purposes. Mac IIci cache card recommendations are discussed in the section about cache card accelerators.

My Mac II, IIx, or IIcx accelerator board recommendation is simple here—the Powercard 030 from DayStar Digital. It comes in 25 MHz, 33 MHz, 40 MHz, or 50 MHz flavors to suit your dollar and power budgets, is also field upgradable to different processor speeds, has optional 68882 FPU chips available, leaves all your NuBus slots open, works with the SIMMs you already have, and runs all standard Mac software, even A/UX. Its installation takes a matter of a few minutes, and the entire process has been extremely well thought-out by DayStar. They provide outstanding documentation and even a chip puller tool that makes sure your expensive and delicate 68030 doesn't ricochet off the ceiling during the removal process! For the Mac II, IIx, or IIcx, the procedure is basically the same, unless you do not have a socketed Mac IIcx, in which event you ship your logic board to DayStar and they provide you with one at a nominal charge. Remove your present CPU chip (DayStar even provides an anti-static foam square you can store it in in case you want to later reverse the process), install the DayStar Power Card in the vacated socket, and attach the DayStar cache board to the power card via two 96-pin connectors. These two connectors, located at opposite ends of the board, "sandwich" the two boards together making a very positive connection assuring long-term contact and stability—unlike most other boards with only one connector on them whose other end is usually attached with tape to the nearest object handy.

By far the biggest bargain in today's upgrade world is the standard Apple Mac IIfx Upgrade Kit.[12] You can add a blazing performance Mac IIfx board to your stock Mac II for only $2999 list, a price I'm sure you can better. If you don't already own a Mac IIfx, you can go out and buy a Mac II and the upgrade kit and make one for about half the list price! Regardless of your tactics, moving to the Mac IIfx board gives you top-of-the-line Apple performance today and a high resale value in the future. I highly recommend it.

As far as the Mac IIfx is concerned, if you own one, enjoy it. Even the 50 MHz third-party accelerators don't keep up with it because of Apple's extremely well thought-out memory, SCSI bus, cache, and I/O designs. I have nothing to tell you here until a hotter 68040 accelerator board (greater than the initial 25 MHz offering) is announced or Apple itself provides an upgrade board.

The 68040 accelerator cards

Speaking of 68040 accelerator boards, at the Macworld convention in January 1991, no fewer than six vendors threw their hats into the ring for 68040-based products: Radius, Sigma, Venture Tech, Total Systems, Fusion, and ITR. Also, Apple's planned 68040 tower machine is getting more and more space in the trade press. Things are definitely happening here, but I haven't actually gotten to touch one because none are for sale—yet.

---

[12] The Apple IIfx upgrade board is so aggressively priced that after its announcement, third-party accelerator vendors were scrambling to lower their prices. See John Battelle, "Accelerator prices decelerate," *MacWEEK*, 3/27/90, p. 1.

Time for a brief reality check here. Today, the first 68040 chips are only available in the 25 MHz flavor. Even though it is a 68040 chip and its internal logic executes at approximately three times the cycle speed of the 68030, a 25 MHz 68040 is not going to do that much more for you, if anything at all, than a third-party 40 MHz or 50 MHz 68030 board. No boards, not even 50 MHz 68030 accelerators, are faster than the Macintosh IIfx.[13] The simple reason is that they do not have the same amount of parallelism and optimization going into them as on the Apple-designed Mac IIfx board. At this point, the 68040 upgrade is a worthwhile upgrade for a low to mid-range Macintosh owner. For hotter performance, you are still better off going to a 40 MHz or 50 MHz 68030 accelerator card or the Mac IIfx.

New Mac accelerator strategies

In terms of full-capability accelerator board options for the new Macs (the Classic, LC, and IIsi), Total Systems again has the answers. Its Gemini Classic in 20 MHz, 25 MHz, 33 MHz, 40 MHz, or 50 MHz flavors gives you all the Classic upgrade choices you could possibly want. It attaches to the Classic's CPU chip via a Killy clip in identical fashion to the clip-on Macs, is field upgradable in speed, uses standard SIMMs, supports an optional 68882 FPU chip, and comes bundled with Connectrix's Virtual software.

The Total Systems Enterprise accelerator board would be my recommendation for the Mac LC and IIsi. At this time, the Enterprise only supports up to the 40 MHz option on the LC (only!). Its speed capabilities, along with all its other benefits for both the Mac LC and the Mac IIsi, are identical to those mentioned earlier for the SE 30. On the LC, it plugs into the 96-pin PDS 020 slot. On the IIsi, plug it into the 120-pin, PDS 030 slot. That's all there is to it.

CPU/clock accelerators

At the other end of the spectrum from the full-function accelerators boards are the CPU/clock speed-up cards. These boards have no memory on them, only a faster CPU and, optionally, a faster FPU chip. All you are doing is working with one of the performance elements—a higher CPU/clock rate—and optionally a higher performance FPU. The good news is these little goodies are easy on your pocketbook and sometimes provide just the speedup you need to make the difference between happiness and drudgery in running programs on your Mac.

The performance of the 8 MHz 68000-based Mac SE can be enhanced approximately 50% by the addition of a CPU/clock board with 16 MHz 68000 CPU and 16 MHz 68881 FPU chips on it—little else. These are available at prices around $300 to $500 from AOX (Double Time), Newer Technology (MacSElerator), and Siclone (Turbo SE).

The Dove Marathon 030/SE 30 uses a board with a 32 MHz 68030 CPU on it to improve the performance of the 16 MHz 68030-based SE 30 approximately 40%. On the down side, this particular board doesn't let you format FDHD flop-

---

[13] See previously cited Spencer, *Macworld*, August 1990, article p. 137.

pies at speed; you have to turn off the acceleration function. However, it is an inexpensive way to pump up your SE 30 at the $699 list price. Dove also has a Marathon 030 for the 8 MHz 68000-based Mac Classic at $799 list that uses a 68030 CPU running at 16 MHz.

Brainstorm recently introduced its Mac Plus Brainstorm Accelerator that adds a 16 MHz 68000 CPU chip and has designed special circuits in its on-board application specific integrated circuit (ASIC) to reconfigure the Mac's bus also allowing memory and I/O chips to run at 16 MHz. The two-chip card is said to run 28% faster than a Mac II and has a list price of only $249. Mac SE and Mac Classic versions are also planned.

Memory/cache accelerators

Apple created an entire new market almost overnight with the cache slot in its Mac IIci model. The premise is simple. If a little amount of faster static RAM in front of your main RAM gives increased performance, then a lot more still faster SRAM should do even better. Apple validated the market even further by introducing its own 32K Mac IIci Cache Card at $399, an aggressive price at announcement time. Third-party vendors responded by offering more memory at Apple's list price and dropping their list prices. The cache card user is the real beneficiary of these marketing moves. Adding a cache card gives you a nice boost to your IIci's performance for little more than the cost of a 4Mb memory upgrade. Total Systems (Quick Cache IIci) and Micron (Xceed IIci-128) offer cache cards with 128K of 25 ns SRAM. DayStar Digital (Fast Cache IIci), Siclone (ciCACHE), Technology Works (64K Cache Card), and UR Micro offer cache cards with 64K of 25 ns SRAM.

My recommendation, from another universe of performance entirely, is DayStar Digital's Power Cache IIci shown in Fig. 6-23. It contains 32K of 25 ns SRAM

DayStar Digital

6-23 SCSI Power card

and a 40 MHz or 50 MHz 68030 chip. Rather than offering the approximately 30% performance gains of the unaccelerated cache cards, DayStar's Power Cache IIci card brings your Mac IIci right up to near Mac IIfx performance levels. If your budget permits it, the 40 MHz version at $1299 list price ($1599 list with FPU) or 50 MHz version at $2299 list price ($2699 list with FPU) is the best investment you can make as a Mac IIci owner today. DayStar Fast Cache owners even get a rebate credit toward purchase. It is also field upgradable to different processor speeds, has optional 40 MHz or 50 MHz 68882 FPU chips available, leaves all your NuBus slots open, and runs all standard Mac software and A/UX. Its installation takes a matter of a few seconds.

SCSI bus accelerators

Although the Mac IIfx SCSI/DMA controller chip enhances the SCSI bus by providing devices on the bus with direct access to memory, the Mac SCSI bus is still a bottleneck, particularly to the faster peripherals. An "intelligent" NuBus boards from DayStar Digital, the SCSI Power Card shown in Fig. 6-24 changes this picture.[14] DayStar uses an on-board 16 MHz 68000 as an independent background I/O processor that relieves the Macintosh CPU from dealing with SCSI transactions. It makes extensive use of up to 16Mb of on-board SIMM memory to support buffering writes and caching reads to accomplish a 5 megabytes per second SCSI transfer rate. Of course, to obtain its full benefits, you have to use it with high-capacity, high-transfer-rate disk drives such as the 400Mb, 600Mb, or 1200Mb drives with 2Mb to 3Mb per second transfer rates from the Seagate/Imprimis Wren family. If your applications need this capability, it costs about $1000 to $2000 depending on memory options—plus the cost of your high-capacity, high-transfer-rate disk drive that you put into your NuBus Mac.

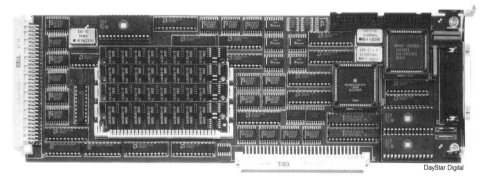

DayStar Digital

6-24   Power cache card IIci.

---

[14] Beware of some older technology products from other companies that have the same product name "SCSI Accelerators" but don't do the same job. Read Tim Standing, Paul Yi, and *MacUser* Labs staff, "SCSI Accelerators," *MacUser*, March 1990, p. 175 for details.

File compression accelerators

Sigma Designs Double Up NuBus Card shown in Fig. 6-25 uses its Stac 9703 40 MHz data compression coprocessor to boost data compression speeds to 1Mb per second and data decompression speeds to 5Mb per second. It comes bundled with Disk Doubler software that gives you compression capabilities of 2:1 on average, with up to 15:1 possible. It provides no-loss, real-time file compression that means data, images, and applications can be compressed and decompressed at speeds that are virtually unnoticeable, and no data is ever lost or altered. This is a painless way to optimize your NuBus Mac, particularly if you handle a lot of graphics and database files.

Sigma Designs

6-25   DoubleUp card.

The envelope please

That about covers it. Table 6-6 summarizes my accelerator recommendations for you. What board should you choose and why? The answer depends on your budget and how much performance you want. Buy the one that gives you the best price performance. Buying an entry-level 68030 full-function accelerator board mail order costs under $1000; a 68000 CPU/clock card will set you back about $300. Cache cards run about $250. If you own a Mac II, Apple's Mac IIfx upgrade is still the best game in town today. The Apple SE 30 upgrade is not a bad choice for SE owners either. If you own a Mac IIcx or Mac IIci, DayStar has a solution for you with either its Power Card or Power Cache Card, respectively. If you already own a Mac IIfx, just relax, kick back and sip a tall iced tea—and see if it can calculate the value of pi to 10^{20} decimal places before the ice melts in your glass.

Table 6-6. Mac full-function 68030 accelerator board recommendations.

Manufacturer/accelerator	Logic board	CPU speed	Street price
Total Systems Mercury 030	128, 512, Plus	25 MHz	500
Total Systems Gemini II 030	128, 512, Plus	25 MHz	1000
Novy Quik 30	SE	25 MHz	700
Newbridge Newlife 25	SE	25 MHz	800
Apple SE 30 Upgrade	SE	16 MHz	1500
Total Systems Gemini Classic	Classic	25 MHz	1000
Total Systems Enterprise	LC	33 MHz	1500
Total Systems Enterprise	SE 30	33 MHz	1500
Total Systems Enterprise	Mac IIsi	40 MHz	2000
DayStar Powercard	Mac II, IIx, IIcx	40 MHz	2000
DayStar Power Cache	Mac IIci	40 MHz	1400
Apple Mac IIfx Upgrade	Mac II, IIx	40 MHz	2700

Here are some pitfalls you want to watch out for when you buy accelerator boards:

- Do not purchase a 68020 accelerator board at this time; go directly into a 68030 model. All new Macintosh software will be optimized for the 68030 products, and the 68030 does everything the 68020 can and more with speed.
- Make sure the board works with the applications software you're using now and want to use in the future.
- Make sure the board works with future system software. Have the accelerator card vendor give you assurances (written) that it has System 7.0 compatibility.
- Make sure it doesn't bomb or otherwise wipe out the use of a system function that you're presently enjoying or utilizing quite heavily. An example of this would be the ability to read and write FDHD floppies. If this ability is important to you and the accelerator card you're considering requires that you turn off the accelerator mode every time you use this feature, maybe you should look at another card.
- Because the accelerator card and your Macintosh are almost inseparable, it behooves you to go with a quality product from one of the brand-name vendors. You have a lot of things to look at. The best guidance I can give is especially true of the accelerator area: Investigate before you invest.

Coprocessors

Coprocessors come in several different flavors, and they basically allow your Mac's CPU chip to do more useful work in the same time either by offloading it, accomplishing some of its tasks in parallel, or doing something entirely different. You've already come across several in this chapter; the PMMU and FPU chips serve the offload function, and the SCSI Bus and File Compression Cards accomplish tasks in parallel. Now it's time for you to discover something entirely different. How about a new computer in your Macintosh?

DOS coprocessors

Need to run DOS PC programs in your NuBus Mac? Orange Micro's Mac 286 (shown in Fig. 6-26) and Orange386 DOS emulator boards are NuBus cards that you merely drop into any NuBus Mac. (Orange Micro's Mac86 is available for the Mac SE. Univation, Inc., also makes a DOS coprocessor for the Mac II family.) You can instantly run DOS programs on your Macintosh concurrently with your Macintosh programs. The 286 version occupies one-slot, and the 386 version occupies two NuBus slots. Compatibility is a non-issue because it is a DOS PC that you have under the hood of your Macintosh—it is just squeezed down in size to fit on one or two cards. Otherwise it uses your Mac monitor, hard disk, and floppy disk—

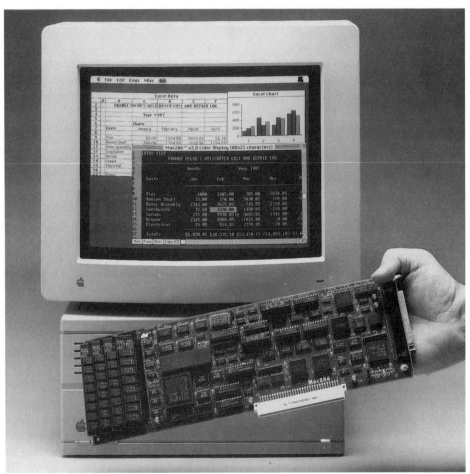

Orange Micro

6-26   Mac 286 coprocessor card.

although you can add a 1.2Mb PC floppy, a PC IDE hard disk, and PC serial and parallel ports to it. Talk about contrasts—it is one thing to talk about Mac versus DOS PC in abstract terms, it is another thing entirely to have them both present on your desktop at the same time. Once you get over the strangeness of the view, however, it's a handy tool to be able to cut and paste Lotus data from DOS or Windows 3.0 into the Excel spreadsheet on your Mac—if you really need this capability. It is a lot less crowded to have only one CPU, monitor, and keyboard (and mouse!) on your desk all for about the same price you'd pay for a good DOS PC clone.[15]

Do you have a 4Mb Mac IIci, a casual need to run DOS PC programs, but a low budget? For a street price of around $500, Insignia Solutions offers a program called SoftPC with an EGA/AT module that does it all in software. Although it runs about the same speed as an original IBM PC XT, it is also a good solution if you want to have a high degree of DOS compatibility between the two environments and only have one Mac on your desktop.[16]

Apple II coprocessor

If you have school-age children or work in or around the education field, the one ability you have always wanted for a Mac is the ability to run your Apple II programs on it. The Apple Mac LC makes that possible. At announcement, Apple introduced an add-in option board (it attaches to the LC's 020 PDS connector) that makes it possible to run Apple II and IIe programs including those with copy protection (a nontrivial technical feat here!) on your Mac LC. It does not run IIGS software, but I suspect that is a marketing rather than a technical issue. What it amounts to is the technical wizards at Apple shrunk the whole Apple II to fit on a small card (M0444LL/A) at $199 list. The cleverly designed board contains a 65C02 processor (just like you'd find in an Apple IIc) and 256K of RAM, and uses all the Mac LC's peripherals as if they were its own.

With the board installed, the Mac LC's FDHD floppy drive can read and write both Mac and Apple II 3½-inch floppy diskettes. It can read Apple 5¼-inch diskettes when an external Apple 5¼-inch floppy drive is connected to the Apple II board. This is slick because today, there is no handy way to read Apple 5¼-inch diskettes in a Mac. You need to find an Apple II and convert them to 3½-inch disks first, from then on it is easy with Apple File Exchange, etc. The low Apple price for the board has to be one of the great bargains of all time. The Mac LC with color monitor and Apple II board is an incredible package. I'm sure the "Early Adapters" in school systems everywhere will jump on it.[17]

---

[15] Read Tom Moran, "Orange Micro Puts a PC in Your Mac," *Macworld*, November 1990, p. 139; Henry Norr, "DOS coprocessor card shrinks to one slot," *MacWEEK*, 6/12/90, p. 16; and Henry Norr, "Orange386 will bring OS/2, Windows to Mac screens," *MacWEEK*, 7/31/90, p. 3.

[16] Dale Coleman, "Added power, slower disk access," *MacWEEK*, 5/22/90, p. 59 has more details.

[17] For more, read the sidebar in Cheryl Spencer, "Mac LC," *Macworld*, December 1990, p. 180.

RISC coprocessor

In the super exotic class are the NuBus reduced instruction set computing (RISC) coprocessor cards. These custom-programmable cards, available from several different third-party vendors, are designed for offloading very high-speed graphics, high-speed peripheral I/O, and compute-intensive programs from the Mac's CPU. Newbridge's Newlife Image Accelerator Card is designed around a 33 MHz Am29000 RISC chip (the same chip adopted by Apple for its 8×24 GC Quick Draw accelerator), YARC's MacRageous around a 67 MHz version of the same chip, and Levco Sales 860i around a 40 MHz version of the Intel i860 chip. At prices starting in the $2000 range, these boards typically come with software tools to help you in doing your own customizing.

In a nutshell

The key points in this chapter are:

- Memory is the first upgrade area where you should look. For only a small investment, adding memory to your Mac will disproportionately increase the performance you get. You've now seen the wide variety of memory options available to you and can make the best choice for your Mac.
- Numerous add-on cards are available to you to improve the performance of the Mac CPU you have or add a newer, hotter CPU. Although you've also seen a wide variety of accelerator options, you now know why I generally recommend the full-function ones as the best choice for your Mac.
- You can add another coprocessor CPU that gives you the capability to run DOS programs or Apple II programs on your Macintosh. You've also seen that programmable RISC coprocessor boards are available to customize your Mac for high-speed processing applications.

Sources

Some memory upgrade sources are:

Computer Care
420 North Fifth St., #1180
Minneapolis, MN 55401
(800) 950-2273
(612) 371-0061

Dove Computer Corp.
1200 N. 23rd St.
Wilmington, NC 28405
(800) 622-7627

Newbridge Microsystems
20 Edgewater St.
Kanata, Ontario CANADA
(800) 267-7231

Some SIMM memory sources are:

Add On America
433 N. Mathilda Ave.
Sunnyvale, CA 94088
(800) 292-7771
(408) 746-1590

Aurora Industries
60 Skiff St., #1011
Hamden, CT 06517
(800) 426-1591
(203) 624-9018

Chip Merchant
9541 Ridgehaven Ct., #A
San Diego, CA 92123
(800) 426-6375
(619) 268-4774.

Computer Care
420 North Fifth St., #1180
Minneapolis, MN 55401
(800) 950-2273
(612) 371-0061

Delta Research Laboratories
26072 Merit Circle, #119
Laguna Hills, CA 92653
(800) 999-1593
(714) 367-0344

Dynamic Electronics
8 Argonaut, #100
Aliso Viego, CA 92656
(800) 845-8228
(714) 855-0411

ELKCO Corp.
41A North Main St.
N. Grafton, MA 01536
(800) 243-5526
(508) 839-2111

LLB Company
4296 E. Mercer Way
Mercer Island, WA 98040
(800) 848-8967
(206) 236-2009

Memory Plus
43 Hopkinton Rd.
Westboro, MA 01581
(800) 388-7587
(508) 366-2240

Micron Technology
2805 Columbia Rd.
Boise, ID 83706
(800) 642-7661
(208) 368-3800

Peripheral Outlet
314 S. Broadway
Ada, OK 74820
(800) 332-6581
(405) 332-6581

Shecom Computers
22755 Savi Ranch Pkwy.
Yorba Linda, CA 92687
(800) 366-4433
(714) 637-4800

Technology Works
4030 Braker Lane West
Austin, TX 78759
(800) 688-7466
(512) 794-8533

Tercom
6920 Roosevelt Way NE, #193
Seattle, WA 98115
(800) 827-1257
(206) 575-8361

Some bulk memory sources are:

Newer Technology
1117 S. Rock Rd., #4
Wichita, KS 67207
(800) 678-3726

Atto Technology
1576 Sweet Home Rd.
Amherst, NY 14228
(716) 688-4259

Connectrix Corp.
125 Constitution Dr.
Menlo Park, CA 94025
(415) 324-0727

Some accelerator sources are:

Aox Inc.
486 Totten Pond Rd.
Waltham, MA 02154
(800) 232-1269
(617) 890-4402

Atto Technology
1576 Sweet Home Rd.
Amherst, NY 14228
(716) 688-4259

Brainstorm Products
1145 Terra Bella Ave.
Mountain View, CA 94043
(415) 964-2131

DayStar Digital
5556 Atlanta Hwy.
Flowery Branch, GA 30542
(800) 962-2077
(404) 967-2077

Dove Computer Corp.
1200 N. 23rd St.
Wilmington, NC 28405
(800) 622-7627
(919) 763-7918

GCC Technologies
580 Winter St.
Waltham, MA 02154
(800) 422-7777

Insignia Solutions
526 Clyde Ave.
Mountain View, CA 94043
(800) 848-7677
(415) 694-7600

Irwin Magnetics
2101 Commonwealth Blvd.
Ann Arbor, MI 48105
(313) 930-9000

Levco
6181 Cornerstone Ct. E., #101
San Diego, CA 92121
(619) 457-2011

Microtech International
29 Business Park Dr.
Branford, CT 06405
(800) 325-1895

Newbridge Microsystems
603 March Rd.
Kanata, ON K2K 2M5 Canada
(800) 267-7231
(613) 592-5080

Newer Technology
7803 E. Osie St., #105
Wichita, KS 67207
(800) 678-3726
(316) 685-4904

Novy Systems
1862 Fern Palm Dr.
Edgewater, FL 32141
(904) 428-0411

Orange Micro
1400 N. Lakeview Ave.
Anaheim, CA 92807
(714) 779-2772

Orchid Technology
45365 Northport Loop W.
Fremont, CA 94538
(415) 683-0300

Peripheral Land Inc.
47421 Bayside Parkway
Fremont, CA 94538
(800) 288-8754
(415) 657-2211

Radius
404 E. Plumeria Dr.
San Jose, CA 95131
(800) 227-2795
(408) 434-1010

Second Wave Inc.
9430 Research Blvd.
Echelon II, Suite 260
Austin, TX 78759
(512) 343-9661

Siclone Sales and Engineering
107 Bonaventura Dr.
San Jose, CA 95134
(800) 767-8207
(408) 456-5060

Sigma Designs
46501 Landing Pkwy.
Fremont, CA 94538
(800) 933-9945
(415) 770-0110

SuperMac Technology
295 N. Bernardo Ave.
Mountain View, CA 94043
(415) 964-8884.

Technology Works
4030 Braker Lane West
Austin, TX 78759
(800) 688-7466
(512) 794-8533

Total Systems
99 W. 10th Ave., #333
Eugene, OR 97401
(800) 874-2288
(503) 345-7395

Fusion Data Systems
8716 Mopac North, #200
Austin, TX 78759
(512) 338-5326

UR Micro
1659 N. Forest Rd.
Williamsville, NY 14221
(800) 876-4276
(716) 689-1600

Venture Technologies
111 Yachting Circle
Lexington, SC 29072
(803) 951-3600

Chapter 7
Storage options

After the CPU and memory, the next most significant step you can take to upgrade your Macintosh is to improve the speed and capacity of whatever storage devices you have attached. Storage affects your Mac in three forms: short term, working, and long term. The respective products that address these requirements today are floppy disk drives, hard disk drives, and backup devices: floppy, hard, removable, optical, and tape drives.

This chapter will cover the options available to you in this area for upgrading your Mac. I begin by first getting some history and a few definitions out of the way, then cover this chapter's upgrade options, show you some products, make a few recommendations, and leave you with guidelines to make you own decisions.

A brief overview and history lesson on storage

Parkinson's law applied to computer data storage would be, "Data expands to fill the space available for it." You know—just like the closets in your apartment or house. Fortunately, the history of data storage is one of capacities growing and prices declining every year.[1] Unfortunately, your graphically based Macintosh has a voracious appetite for storage. Using the newest software applications, and particularly the high-performance graphics or database types, will just exacerbate the problem. It helps if you view the Macintosh storage area from its functional standpoint.

Short-term storage

For short-term storage, all you really need is a device for getting data in and out of your Mac. Floppy disk drives do this job nicely and are commonly used today. Their performance has steadily improved over time. Early Macs used only two 400K floppy disks. One had the system software on it, and the other had applications and data. Today's standard is the 800K floppy, with the 1.4Mb FDHD floppy coming on strong. Future larger capacities are now on the horizon. Given the cost versus performance benefits of hard disks today, a floppy disk drive should never be the only storage device on your Mac.

Working storage

For your working storage, you want the device for storing and using your Mac's data on a day-to-day basis to have speed and capacity. Hard disk drives fit these criteria perfectly and offer the additional benefit of low price. During the Mac's brief lifetime, they have overwhelmingly improved in performance and dropped in price. The earliest 20Mb Mac hard disks were slow, attached to the Mac's serial

---

[1] A brief but excellent article that talks about all kinds of storage devices, their past and future, is James Anderson, "Memory will drive the future," *Computer Reseller News*, 1/8/90, p. 74. Two other excellent overview articles are: "The state of Mac storage," *MacWEEK*, 10/23/90, p. 46; and Amy Bermar, "More, more, more: The storage story," *MacWEEK*, 4/10/90, p. 73.

port, and cost you at least $2000.[2] Today's 20Mb hard disks are faster, attach to the Mac's faster SCSI port, and versions that come complete with enclosure and power supply cost you under $300. Or you can get a much faster, internally-mounted 40Mb hard disk in the same price range.

Today's new Apple Mac models are all equipped with 40Mb or more hard disks. You should follow the same guidance. Versus the standard 800K floppy disk drive, even the slowest of today's hard disks provide you a 20-fold increase in capacity and a 10-fold improvement in speed. Treat yourself to a hard disk as a present if you don't already have one. You will never go back. If you already own a hard disk, think in terms of quadrupling rather than doubling your storage—20Mb hard disk owners should consider 80Mb to 105Mb drives, 40Mb to 60Mb owners should consider 150Mb to 300Mb drives, and 300Mb owners now have options in the 1 to 2 gigabyte range. Prices have dropped so dramatically that you will probably pay less than your original investment for the upgrade.[3]

Long-term storage

For your long-term storage, you want a device to back up your data for safety and/or to preserve your data for archiving. In this area, the smallest Macintosh owners—those with dedicated Macs—are today thoroughly taken care of and will be taken care of into the foreseeable future using floppy disks. As you go up in size, both in your system and the amount of data you want to store, removable cartridge or read/write optical disks come into play with tape as a lower-cost alternative.

In the backup area, when floppy disks no longer do the job for you, my experience suggests that you next consider a removable cartridge disk or read/write optical disk. Both are quicker than a tape unit in storage/retrieval. With a disk, you go directly to the data you need versus having to look through an entire tape serially. While disk storage is far more efficient and practical, you get a lot more tape drive and media for your money than with their disk counterparts. The gap is closing on this, and if your budget allows it, I would certainly recommend disk over tape for backup.

For archived storage, optical wins over magnetic media. No matter what you do—dehumidifiers, air conditioning, etc.—your valuable data will gradually fade from its magnetic media. Yes, I hear you. Just ask the music recording industry how they feel about it! Also, be sure you select a machine and a drive mechanism that will be around as long as the media so you can read your data![4]

---

[2] Hey, I'm not kidding. Look at Gary Phillips and Donald J. Scellato, *Macintosh Expansion Guide*, TAB Books, 1985. Chapter 12, "Disk Drives" was "state-of-the-art" when published, it was hard to find even 10Mb Mac hard disks for less than $2000. Remember the popular GCC Hyperdrive 10Mb that fit inside your Mac 512? Its list price was $2795. My, how time flies.

[3] Paul Bendix, "Hard disks: Save now or pay later?," *MacWEEK*, 10/23/90, p. 54.

[4] Paul Hyman, "Poof! Into Thin Air," *Electronic Buyers' News*," 3/11/91, p. 31. Paul observes that the government recently noticed it might be losing its 1960-1980 Census Data and its NASA Space Programs Data from 1958 onward, all carefully stored on reels of low-density magnetic tape, for this very reason. But look at the bright side, the IRS is gradually losing all your earlier tax return data for the same reason!

Store me

First, a brief detour for a few definitions.

Platters   Platters are also called the "media." This is the flexible disk medium in a floppy diskette, typically of thin plastic with an even thinner magnetic coating on both sides of it. Or it is a rigid disk medium in a hard disk of a metallic alloy or glass, again magnetically coated.

Cylinders, tracks, sectors   Like a phonograph record, floppy and hard disk platters have information stored on each side. Unlike a phonograph record's spiral, a computer disk's platter is recorded in concentric areas. Each side of a platter is called a *cylinder*. *Tracks* are the pattern of concentric circles or rings on the disk's surfaces established by the formatting software onto which the data is written. Frequently, cylinders and tracks are interchanged in usage. A used equipment listing had a Rodime 105Mb hard disk with 868 cylinders for sale. *Sectors* are the subdivided portions of the tracks. They are also called *blocks* and refer to a specific location on a given track onto which data is written. A Mac disk might be formatted with 512 bytes of data in a sector or block. The interface reads or writes one sector at a time regardless of the amount of data actually being read from or written into the sector.

Heads   Sometimes heads are called "read/write heads." Like the tone arm to the phonograph record except ... not quite. It would have to be a tone arm with no weight at its needle end, and one that could go to any spot on the record instantly and transfer information at an almost unbelievable rate once it got there. On a floppy drive, heads on opposite sides of the media press it between them, and the tiny electromagnets at the tip of the heads either read or write data. A hard disk functions the same way except the heads float on a cushion of air and never touch the platter's incredibly flat surface. A particle of dust is a giant boulder to a hard disk's heads, so all hard disks are sealed to prevent contamination.

Formatting   When you first obtain a floppy or hard disk, although it has been tested at the factory, it is a clean slate to you as far as your purpose is concerned. Much like you would take a blank wall inside a post office and build sorting bins into it, the formatting step puts these specific track and sector "pockets" into your hard disk. It builds exact locations where you can later find data. To move data on and off the disk quickly, formatting identifies certain tracks as directory tracks. These tracks contain information tags, or flags or pointers, that point to or identify the location of data on the disk. When you delete data on a PC DOS machine or throw an icon into the trash on a Mac, all you are doing is deleting its entry from the directory. The data is still there—until you write over it.

Capacity   *Capacity* refers to the amount of binary data in 8-bit bytes that can be stored on the disk platter's surface. Raw capacity is greater than when formatted. Sections set aside for directory and housekeeping usage are not available for data. Formatted disk capacities depend on the computer, disk controller, and formatting software used.

Average access time   The average access time refers to the amount of time it takes, on average, to position the read-write heads over the track that holds the data. Again be aware—not all disk average access times are stated equally. Technically, it is defined as seek time (time to find the track) plus settling time (time to stabilize over the track) plus latency time (time to bring the sector data on the track under the head). Some manufacturers ignore both the average consideration and the latency factor to publish better times.

Interleave Depending on the speed of the computer attached to the hard disk, it might not be fast enough to read all the data from one sector transferred by the disk interface, or to write it in one rotation of the disk. To avoid this problem, disks initially being formatted to work with slower Macintoshes have their sectors interleaved. A slow Mac Plus requires a 3:1 interleave. That means the next logical sector that the controller reads or writes data on actually skips two sectors over from the last "physical" sector located on the disk. A faster Mac SE requires a 2:1 interleave. The next logical sector read or written actually skips one sector over from the last physical sector located on the disk. The Mac II, Mac SE 30, and up use a 1:1 interleave. The next logical sector read or written by the controller is identical with the physical sector located on the disk.[5]

Fragmentation On a new disk, files are written onto continuous and connected (called *contiguous* in computer parlance) sectors and tracks. As you use the disk—erasing files, writing new ones, etc.—all the contiguous space eventually gets used up, and new files are then written in pieces or *fragments* all over the disk. This is called *fragmentation* and greatly reduces disk performance.

SCSI interface Small computer system interface refers to a high-speed bus that transfers data at 1.5Mb per second and allows you to daisychain up to seven devices (disk drives, CD-ROM drives, tape drives, scanners, printers, etc.). Each device is generating its own input and output traffic on the bus. SCSI hard disks contain an embedded controller, meaning an intelligent controller board is part of the disk drive package.[6]

Size and height *Size* refers to the diameter (its width) of the disk inside the enclosure. The sizes are 5¹/₄ inch and, increasingly today, 3¹/₂ inch. *Height* is a carry-over from early IBM DOS PC days. *Full height* refers to a disk that takes up the entire height of the original PC front bezel opening designed to fit 5¹/₄-inch wide disk cases. *Half height* means half that dimension. You can stack two drives in that space. For today's new Mac's one-third height (approximately one inch high), 3¹/₂-inch disk drives are the norm.

MTBF The letters stand for *mean time between failures*. An MTBF rating of 50,000 hours does not mean each hard disk will last that long before needing repair. It means that in a population of 50,000 hard disks, one will fail every hour, 24 hours per day, or about 18% of the drives will have to be repaired before year's end. Over a three-year period, over one-half (54%) of the original 50,000 hard disks

[5] Brett Glass, "Interleaving: The Right Place at the Right Time," *Infoworld*, 12/10/90, p. 69. Has a great explanation with a visual graphic.

[6] Several articles provide an excellent introduction to SCSI: Thom Hogan, "A Beginner's Guide to Daisy Chains," *MacUser*, August 1990, p. 243; Jim Heid, "Getting Started With Troubleshooting," *Macworld*, August 1989, p. 233, has an excellent sidebar: "A SCSI Primer;" and Ted Drude, "Macintosh SCSI Drive Secrets Revealed," *Computer Shopper*, September 1988, p. 28.

will require some amount of service. The bottom line is buy the hard disk with the higher MTBF, but disregard the actual number because every manufacturer uses a scheme that puts its products in the best light.[7]

Short-term storage—floppy disks

For short-term storage today, floppy disk drives do the best job of getting data into and out of your Mac. Their performance has steadily improved over time. Today, Macintosh 3¹/₂-inch floppy disk drives come in three storage capacities: 400K or single-sided, 800K or double-sided, and 1.4Mb or high-density. In the near future, Mac owners will also have 4Mb and 20Mb 3¹/₂-inch floppy disk drive options. I discuss several types and my recommendation.

Mac 400K floppy

Today the 400K floppy disk drive is a dinosaur—unfortunately, not yet extinct. Yes, it is inexpensive, you can probably pick one up for $25 to $50, and it makes an excellent companion to your Mac 128 system. However, it is the slowest of all floppy drives, offers the least storage capacity, and at this point is a solution only if you are contemplating a hobbyist or low-utilization word processing use. If it breaks on you, you could have difficulty finding parts to fix it. If you are using one today, I would implore you in the strongest terms to upgrade to an 800K floppy drive.

Mac 800K floppy

Today the 800K floppy drive and 800K floppy diskette media are the standard. It's number one as the mainstream floppy of choice for the majority of Mac users. Why? It's compact and cheap. An 800K floppy diskette with 100 to 200 typewritten pages on it fits into your shirt pocket and costs under 50 cents! You can select from two 800K drives for your Macintosh. The Sony drive is the one that Apple uses and sells. The Fujitsu drive is repackaged and sold by everyone else. The Apple external 800K floppy drive (A9M0106) lists for $399. The Apple internal floppy drive for the Mac II (M0136) or internal upgrade for the 128/512 (M2516) lists for $299. All have a one-year warranty. The Fujitsu drive is repackaged by Cutting Edge and other third-party vendors and is available from various mail order sources at $149. It comes with a one- or two-year warranty.

Macintoshes (both 800K and 1.4Mb models) that support the external floppy drive connector all support an 800K external floppy drive. However, the newer 1.4Mb FDHD floppy drive equipped Macs will not support the older 400K external floppy.[8]

---

[7] Steven L. Kaczeus, "MTBF for hard disks: An unreliable indicator," *Computer Reseller News*, 6/18/90, p. 12. Extrapolating from his article, 50,000 hours translates to a continuous 24 years of 8 hours per day use!

[8] Pin 10 on the floppy connector is permanently wired to +5V (not connected on the Mac Portable) on the newer FDHD Macs. The older 400K used this for its motor speed control signal.

Mac 1.4Mb floppy

Here's where the action is. Because Apple now offers a 1.4Mb FDHD floppy disk drive on every new Mac sold from the Classic on up through the Mac IIfx and including the Mac Portable, it is only a question of time before the 1.4Mb floppy drive overtakes its 800K cousin.

This "question of time" is especially true in the media area. High-density 1.4Mb floppy diskettes are already at the crossover point. A 1.4Mb floppy diskette costs just under $1, twice the cost of an 800K floppy diskette. The rate of price decline on 800K diskettes has slowed, and the 1.4Mb diskette's price decline is accelerating.[9]

Mac bytes DOS PC

The 1.4Mb floppy disk drives do everything the 800K floppy drives do, and then some. They can also read and write DOS PC 3½-inch floppy diskettes.

First, a little background. Macintosh 400K and 800K floppy disk drives both used the *group-coded recording* (GCR) technique and rotated at different speeds when writing to different areas of the diskette. Both 400K and 800K diskettes contain 80 tracks. Both diskette specifications are identical, with the difference being the 800K diskettes are written on both sides. They step down in density (1 sector at a time in groups of 16 tracks) from having 12 sectors each on the outermost 16 tracks, to 8 sectors each on the innermost 16 tracks. The rotational speed when accessing the outermost and innermost tracks is 394 and 590 rpm (revolutions per minute), respectively.[10] The famous IWM (Integrated Wozniak Machine) chip adjusts the drive rotation speed as the read/write head moves across the diskette.

However, DOS PC 720K and 1.4Mb floppy disk drives use the MFM (modified-frequency modulation) technique that rotates their diskettes at a constant speed. Who are you gonna call? Apple's simple and elegant solution: couple a 2Mb Sony drive mechanism to a SWIM (Super Wozniak Integrated Machine) disk-controller chip. The result is Apple's Floppy Drive High-Density (FDHD) SuperDrive. And it is a super drive. The FDHD SuperDrive can read, write, and format 400K, 800K, and 1.4Mb Mac 3½-inch diskettes. Using the Apple File Exchange utility software, the SuperDrive also reads and writes DOS PC 3½-inch disks formatted at 720K and 1.4Mb. Neat, eh? You bet. Now you know why Apple offers a 1.4Mb floppy disk drive on every new Mac sold, and why it is offered as a retrofit kit to earlier Mac II or Mac SE models.

The Apple FDHD SuperDrive (M0112) lists at $399 for the external version, which is the same as its 800K model. Are you getting the message yet? Either external package appears like the unit sitting next to the Mac Plus in Fig. 2-5 of chapter 2. The Apple FDHD internal floppy drive upgrade kit including the ROM/SWIM upgrade for the Mac SE (M0652/A) or Mac II (M0651/B) lists for $449.

---

9 "High-density floppies lead drop in disk prices," *MacWEEK*, 1/9/90, p. 75, had a chart showing the trends clearly, although the information is now dated.

10 If you must know exact tracks, sectors, and speed it is: 00-15/12/394, 16-31/11/429, 32-47/10/472, 48-63/9/525, and 64-79/8/590. Satisfied?

The Apple FDHD add-on internal floppy drive (M0247) for the Mac SE, II, IIx, or IIfx, that presumes you already have an existing FDHD drive installed, lists for $349. All have the standard Apple one-year warranty. You will compare both Apple internal 800K and FDHD drives in chapter 14.

Third-party high-density floppy drives

High-density floppy disks are also offered by third-party vendors. A *MacUser* February 1990 article summed up the subject nicely.[11] However, the list has expanded, and vendor offerings have changed since the article was written. You can now choose from at least five 1.4Mb drive vendors in addition to Apple: Applied Engineering, Dayna, Kennect, PLI, and Quadmation. All of the drives can read and write Mac and PC high-density disks, but they are not equal in all other respects.

Kennect's Drive 2.4 and its Rapport drive controller are shown in the center of Fig. 7-1, flanked by Kennect's 360K and 1.2Mb 5¼-inch floppy drive offerings on either side. Drive 2.4 and the Rapport drive controller that plugs into the Mac's disk drive port are an alternative to the Apple FDHD and available through mail order for $329 and $199. It can do everything the Apple FDHD can, plus it has proprietary software that can squeeze up to 1.2Mb and 2.4Mb onto Macintosh 800K and 1.4Mb diskettes, hence its name. It can also attach to Macs that do not have the SWIM kit installed—a Mac Plus for instance—and comes bundled with Fastback II, a backup utility that offers data compression, thus further increasing the Kennect 2.4's capacity. On the down side, the separate drive and controller pricing probably makes it more expensive than the Apple offering on the newer Mac models. It has a one-year warranty.

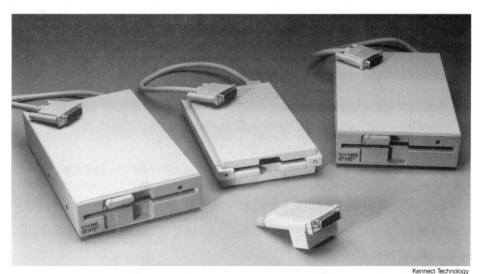

Kennect Technology

7-1 Drive 360, Drive 2.4, Drive 1200 behind the Rapport drive controller.

---

[11] Owen W. Linzmayer, "High-Density Floppy Drives," *MacUser*, February 1990, p. 221.

The DaynaFILE II is one of the best suited for dedicated use in a PC-intense environment. It comes in three flavors: two 5¼-inch drives that read and write DOS PC 360K diskettes, one 1.2Mb that reads either format, and one 3½-inch drive that reads and writes DOS PC 720K or 1.4Mb diskettes. The 3½-inch drive also reads and writes Macintosh 1.4Mb floppy diskettes, but not the older Mac 400K and 800K diskettes—DaynaFILE cannot switch to GCR mode. A Dayna-FILE II external 5¼-inch unit is shown in Fig. 7-2. All DaynaFILE II models come with software that mounts these drives directly from the Finder just as if you were working with a Mac disk. They have a $599 list price and come with a one-year warranty.

PLI's Superfloppy 1.4 drive is available through mail order for $359. It can also do everything the Apple FDHD can, plus it connects to any Mac via its SCSI port. It therefore supports daisychaining and higher transfer rates. It comes with a one-year warranty.

Applied Engineering and Quadmation's offerings repackage the Sony high-density floppy disk drive at a better price than Apple's, which is typically around $249 through mail order. They both come with a one-year warranty.

Dayna Communications

7-2   DaynaFILE II 5¼-inch external floppy for the Mac.

Do not coerce your floppy diskettes

The subject is floppy diskettes and getting something from nothing. That is, making 1.4Mb floppy diskettes for your Macintosh from 800K ones by just punching another hole in the corner and making your 800K diskette *look* just like a 1.4Mb diskette. My advice is don't do it. I know you've read it. I know there are even tools available to help you, and I know that a lot of you have already done it, just like myself. The bottom line is it will work perfectly for you for a long time, and then the other shoe will drop. Chances are Murphy's law will come into play, and this will be exactly at the time when you don't want it to happen to you. By then, it's too late.

The short form reason for this? The word is called *coercive force*. The dictionary says that this is the amount of force required to overcome residual magnetism. The difference between your 1.4Mb high density floppy diskette and your standard 800K double-sided double-density floppy diskette is more than just an extra hole in its rectangular outside case jacket. Inside, its magnetic media is different in terms of its coercivity. and retentivity. Because the magnetic bits in an 800K diskette are packed a lot closer together than they were intended to be when you punch your hole and reformat it into a 1.4Mb diskette, eventually these bits can demagnetize and you lose data. Conversely, once you reformat your 1.4Mb diskette as an 800K diskette, you lose the ability to ever again reformat it as a 1.4Mb diskette. The 1.4Mb diskette's smaller magnetic footprint gets lost inside the 800K diskette's larger and deeper magnetic footprint. You cannot coerce your 800K diskette into being a 1.4Mb diskette—or you should not. Sooner or later, somewhere down the line, you will have to pay the piper.

What should you do? I've been able to use Stuffit, Disk Doubler, and the new Fastback with compression. All these features allow me to put more data onto my 800K diskettes without my actually having to trick them or mess around with cutting extra holes in them. I do it with less risk by just selecting a piece of software to do the data compression rather than trying to get more disk space out of the disk by formatting it at a higher density than it is supposed to be formatted at. The final choice is yours, but I believe you'll sleep better at night if you follow this guidance.

Future Mac magnetic floppy disks

A lot of Japanese floppy disk drive manufacturers are cranking up 4Mb models. For a while, it was difficult to pick up any computer or electronics magazine and not notice Toshiba's advertising spread touting its new 4Mb (2.8Mb formatted) $3^1/_2$-inch extra-high-density floppy diskette and its new perpendicular recording technology advantage. New IBM and NeXT computers already incorporate it. Can Apple be far behind?

While reading about the nifty features of barium ferrite in the Toshiba ads, I noticed they also slipped in the fact that they and others are utilizing this magnetic technology to produce floppy diskettes above 20Mb in storage capacity. This area in particular, shows great promise because floppies could then rival tape as a backup media. Apparently, the biggest stumbling block at this point is getting all the various manufacturers to agree on a format standard, like Beta versus VHS. Stay tuned.

20Mb in your shirt pocket!

Imagine taking a high-density $3^1/_2$-inch floppy diskette, stamping an indelible servo track optical pattern into its media surface, and being able to store 20.8Mb rather than just 1.4Mb on it. All this for only 4 or 5 times what you pay for the standard floppy diskette! It's called a *floptical disk*, and I was impressed during a hands-on demonstration at the Insite Peripherals booth at fall 1990 COMDEX.[12] Bernoulli and Commodore Technology have licensed Insite's technology for future products, Microcomputer Manager's Association has selected it as a standard,[13] and Brier Technology has jumped in to compete with its Flextra disk drive with a 20Mb read/write floppy/optical with a SCSI interface. Insight has recently redesigned its current product to fit a one-inch case height and run off a single 5 volt power supply for broadest market appeal. It has even attracted competitors. Recently, DJK Development Corporation announced plans to ship a Mac floptical drive by mid-1991, although pricing for the external drive unit has not yet been set.

Toshiba has licensed its 4Mb technology to 12 drive and 18 diskette makers. Its 4Mb product is downwardly compatible with earlier 2Mb offerings, and its 4Mb drives don't need to resort to expensive servo-based head positioning technology that the 20Mb floptical drives require. While IBM, the ultimate standards maker, has not yet spoken, I believe you will see the 4Mb floppies go to large-volume production soon. On the other hand, the 20Mb floppy is technologically neat. Floptical drives might cost more, but their diskettes will be close in cost to today's high-density units. Ultimately, the market forces will decide.

The envelope please

Just as less expensive 256K DRAM chips drove out 64K ones, and 800K floppies replaced 400K ones, the relentless push of technology will cause the 800K floppies to be displaced by 1.4Mb ones. They, in turn, will be replaced. You say, "Gee, just when I was getting used to them and had finally switched over all my data from 400K floppies." I wrote in earlier books that you should not pay extra for what you don't use, but lately I've rescued several clients by using 1.4Mb floppies and Apple File Exchange to import DOS PC documents into their Macs. Several of my clients are also using them more for storage of large system and TIFF file backup material plus backups of other larger programs that are just more convenient to carry around unstuffed. My message is that I am beginning to see the handwriting on the wall. You should look at it, too. Meanwhile, watch the developments in the 4Mb and 20Mb floptical areas, and don't get too comfortable with your 1.4Mb floppy drives.

Working storage hard disks

For your working storage, you want the device for storing and using your Mac's data on a day-to-day basis to have speed and capacity. Hard disks fit the bill nicely. But hard disks come in fixed and removable flavors, and with magnetic, optical, and combination media. Which type should you use? Although there are excep-

---

[12] Chuck Moran, "Spreading wings to 25M-byte superfloppy," *Computer Reseller News*, 8/13/90, p. 12.

[13] Jill Miller, "Japanese Disk Drive Firms Eye U.S. Move," *Electronic Buyers' News*, 11/12/90, p. 6.

tions, your working storage needs are today best met by fixed magnetic media hard disks. Because hard disks fit the speed and capacity criteria perfectly, and offer the additional benefit of low price, I will deal first with them. The following section on long-term storage needs covers removable and optical drives.

Magnetic media hard disks have changed drastically since their first introduction in the 1950s. This technology trend continues today. Next to memory and CPU chips, they are probably the number one reason for the increase in the number of personal computers installed. Today, 2 gigabyte 5^1/$_4$-inch hard disks and 600Mb 3^1/$_2$-inch disks are a fact of life.

Quantum's Prodrive LPS 52S/105S 3^1/$_2$-inch one-third height disk drive, intended for use in all Apple's new Mac models, typifies the mainstream of today's offerings. It is shown in Fig. 7-3. The 2^1/$_2$-inch form factor hard disk market is heating up.[14] Connor's Pancho Series 2^1/$_2$-inch 30Mb unit shown in Fig. 7-4 typifies the offerings in this new market segment. There is no end in sight. Over the next 10 years, the ability to store information on a given form factor is expected to increase tenfold.[15] Their increased storage capacity, smaller size, reduced access time, and much lower cost has brought their benefits within reach of every personal computer user.

Quantum Corp.

7-3   Prodrive LPS 52S/105S SCSI hard drive for the Macintosh.

---

[14] Greg Garry, "2.5-in. Disk Drive Marketplace Becomes Crowded Playing Field," *Electronic Buyers' News*, 12/3/90, p. 17.

[15] Mark Brownstein, "Hard Drive Capacities, Performance Improve," *Infoworld*, 11/19/90, p. 23; Greg Garry, "Drive Makers Boost 3.5-in Lines," *Electronic Buyers' News*, 10/8/90, p. 26; and Mark Brownstein, "Hard Disk Drives Getting Bigger, Better," *Infoworld*, 9/10/90, p. 29.

Connor Peripherals

7-4   Pancho Series 2¹/₂-inch 30Mb hard disk drive.

Remember the old time music jukebox in the corner restaurant? It had its 78 or 45 rpm record platters in a stack or bin. When you made your selection, the record with your music on it would be moved into place, and the pickup arm with the needle in it would be moved over the starting groove on the record. Although Connor's Summit Series 3¹/₂-inch 510Mb hard disk as shown in Fig. 7-5 is a universe away technology-wise, it works in a remarkably similar fashion. The platter is a highly polished metal or glass disk rather than a vinyl plastic one. It is perfectly flat, with a thin magnetic oxide layer deposited on it to a high tolerance of purity and uniformity. Rather than grooves, the read/write head is a tiny electromagnet at the end of an arm that has been optimized for minimum mass, rather than a pickup arm with a phonograph needle in it. The read/write head goes directly to the part on the disk it wants, just like today's CD players go right to the music track you selected. These heads are positioned by slower, less expensive, stepper motors (heads move in fixed increments or steps across the disk) or faster, more expensive

Connor Peripherals

7-5   Summit Series 3¹/₂-inch 510Mb hard disk drive.

voice coil and servo track mechanisms (the heads move in precise increments using servo feedback technology). The electronic data going to and from the heads is formatted and controlled by circuitry adhering to well-defined interface specifications, such as the modified SCSI standard used by the Macintosh.

In the hard disk area, you are inundated with data. You have so many choices and so many advice-givers that it almost becomes overwhelming. My objective here is to KISS it. I'll cut through the chaff and clutter, answer the basic questions, give you the framework to make your own hard disk choices, and give you my recommendations. In addition, I'll give you some excellent articles that have been written on hard disks during the last year and earlier.[16]

Why buy a hard disk

Far more Mac users buy hard disks for their Macs than do PC users for their machines because of the graphics intensive nature of the Mac. Anyone buying a Macintosh today and wanting to do any kind of serious work on it should add a hard disk. Why? The main three reasons are speed, cost, and convenience. Even the smallest of the hard drives sold today, the 20Mb, gives you ten times faster access time versus a floppy disk. Prices have come down to where you can buy a mail order 40Mb hard disk for the same list price of an Apple 3½-inch External FDHD Floppy Disk Drive. (Table 7-1 shows APS offered the External 40Mb Quantum for $349 in March 1991, same as Apple's external FDHD floppy.) Plus, all your applications are always instantly available on the desktop—provided you have purchased a large enough disk drive.

What size hard disk

Today, the 40Mb drive is the most popular choice,[17] but it really depends on your individual needs as they are now and projected into the future. With Word, Excel, PageMaker, and a couple of other graphics and business programs loaded, 20Mb of your disk is already filled. How much more space you need for data is up to you. Let history and your own memory help you. If you have been a computer user for several years, think about the number one complaint you have had (after speed)— not enough disk space. When the first DOS PCs came out with their 10Mb hard disks, they were considered huge. Once you used your DOS PC for any length of time, you found out quickly that 10Mb of hard disk storage wasn't that much. As a rule of thumb, think about Parkinson's Law about data expanding to fill the space available on your hard disk, and buy more than you need. Today, 40Mb would be an

---

[16] Cheryl England Spencer, "Midrange Hard Drives," *Macworld*, March 1991, p. 137; Owen W. Linzmayer and MacUser Labs staff, "Moving Up To A Big, Fast, Hard Drive," *MacUser*, December 1990, p. 114; Lon Poole, "Huge Hard Disks," *Macworld*, November 1990, p. 174; Cheryl England Spencer, "Best Buys in Low-Capacity Drives," *Macworld*, September 1990, p. 189; Tom Badgett and Corey Sandler, "Buyer's Guide: Hard Disk Drives," *Computer Shopper*, March 1990, p. 101; Winn L. Rosch, "101 Hard Drives," *MacUser*, February 1990, p. 153; and Cheryl England Spencer, "Turning 40," *Macworld*, September 1989, p. 172.

[17] Martin Marshall, "40Mb 3½-Inch Drives Are Dominating Market." *Infoworld*, 5/7/90, p. 43.

absolute minimum, 80Mb to 105Mb probably about right. What is Apple doing? Figure 7-6 compares the original Quantum 40Mb offered in a Mac II with the new Quantum 160Mb that comes with a Mac IIfx. Apple fits the profile.

A byproduct of buying a larger disk is that speed usually increases (or access times go down) as disk capacity rises. Your larger disk will also be faster than your smaller hard disk. Don't let anyone tell you different—faster is always better.

7-6   The Apple 160Mb Mac IIfx drive (left) and Apple 40Mb Mac II drive.

Who to buy it from

Hard disks involve three levels of vendor functions: manufacture, repackaging, and distribution. The hard disk manufacturers list has undergone some consolidation recently, but the main players would include Seagate, Quantum, Connor, Maxtor, Rodime, Fujitsu, and Sony, to name a few. All the other vendors repackage these manufacturers' disk drives. The distinction between vendors who package versus those who distribute hard drives has become increasingly blurred because the market has become lowest-cost driven as more purchases are made through the less-expensive mail order channel. In a sense, these vendors are also victims to today's better quality products. The quality of the raw disk drives along with that of external disk enclosures, power supplies, internal mounting brackets, SCSI/power cables, and formatting software has somewhat eliminated the need for a middleman.

So my "who you buy from" advice has to be somewhat generalized. Buy a quality product. Buy a mainstream hard disk drive with a good reputation and specifications from a high-profile quality vendor, someone you asked about and they have checked out as good. Then be sure you are getting at least a one-year warranty (some vendors offer more) and an unconditional full return privilege if the product doesn't meet your specifications. None of the quality distributors would hesitate to honor these terms. By taking these steps, even if this is your first attempt, you can sleep nights.

Now owned by Quantum Corporation, LaCie (whose Tsunami and other hard disk offerings are shown in Fig. 7-7) typifies the quality third-party vendors who package hard disk products today. Alliance Peripheral Systems who repackages Quantum and Seagate hard disk offerings into their cases typifies the quality third-party vendors who distribute hard disk products today. Figure 7-8 shows a Quantum drive on top of an APS case. JMR Electronics typifies the quality third-party vendors who manufacture hard disk enclosure products today. Their MacZero half-height hard disk and removable media enclosures are shown in Fig. 7-9. Because there are hundreds of hard disk manufacturers, distributors, and resellers not mentioned here, some excellent sources to begin your vendor search are the *Macworld* and *MacUser* hard disk articles referenced earlier and also the *Macintosh Product Registry*.[18]

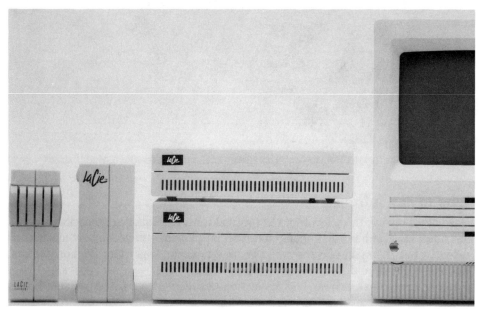

LaCie Ltd.

7-7   LaCie Tsunami and other Mac hard drive products.

How much to spend

How much should you pay? Get the best drive from a reliable vendor, but don't spend more than you have to. Disk drive pricing has dropped drastically since the

---

[18] *Macintosh Product Registry*, Redgate Communications Corp., Vero Beach, FL, 1990.

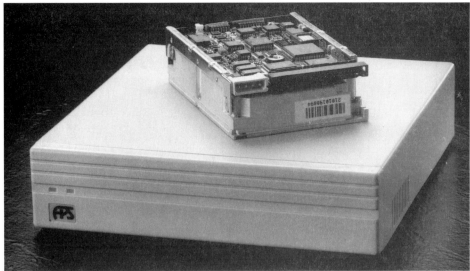

Alliance Peripheral Systems

7-8   Quantum drive with APS external Mac case.

JMR Electronics, Inc.

7-9   Mac Zero half-height enclosures for hard disk and removable media.

early days of the Macintosh. The last few years have provided an acceleration of this trend as $3^1/_2$-inch drives take over the spotlight from the $5^1/_4$-inch models and manufacturing overproduction floods the retail channels.

Figure 7-10 shows you the decline in Quantum hard disk prices since January 1990. The prices shown, taken from one mail order vendor's published prices in *MacWEEK*, are for internal drives with mounting brackets. Notice the price for the 105Mb drive has almost dropped in half in the past year, from $700 versus $379, while the 40Mb drive somewhat stabilized around $300, and recently dropped to $259. It makes you definitely want to get the larger drive!

The other part of the story, pricing from Apple and others for different disk models as summarized in Table 7-1, can be considered a snapshot in time. Note that you are looking at Apple's list prices (from Apple's own March 1991 price list) and third-party vendors' street prices (from advertisements in *MacWEEK, Macworld,* and *MacUser*). Please consider this information subject to change early

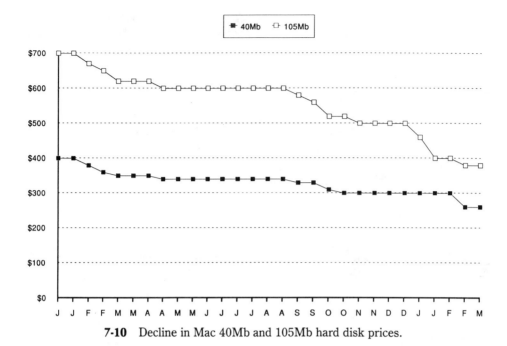

7-10 Decline in Mac 40Mb and 105Mb hard disk prices.

and often, and refer to your actual hard disk supplier for current updates. From Table 7-1, you might assume I prefer Seagate and Quantum hard disks, and your assumption would be correct. There are numerous other manufacturers of hard disks, and I am sure they provide the same quality. It is just that, over the years, I have obtained consistently good results from these two, with only occasional lapses. I am familiar with their performance, idiosyncrasies, pricing, and also where to send them for repairs when they break.

What else can you glean from Table 7-1 and Fig. 7-10?

- Even with generous discounts, you are probably paying more when buying a disk drive from Apple. Unless you are on Apple's discount schedule, or you must have the Apple logo on your desk (a decal is cheaper), the equivalent drive purchased from a third-party vendor is probably a more cost-effective choice. (In all fairness to Apple, who has not changed its disk prices in over a year, it's pricing structure shown in Table 7-1 is a product of its situation of being "locked-in" to steep discount schedule contracts. I would suggest that very few individuals or companies pay full list for Apple hard drives in the current market.)
- It pays to shop around. Notice the same drive varies widely in price among the different suppliers. This is reflecting their own supply/demand and competitive situation at any given point in time.
- More costs less. Looking at the 40Mb versus 105Mb situation, you get 2.5 times the capacity for only $100 more, $300 versus $400. Buy the bigger drive if your budget allows it.

Table 7-1. Mac SCSI hard disk price comparison (March 1991 prices).

Manufacturer/model	Capacity (Mb)	Internal	External
Apple			
HD 20SC	20	699	799
HD 40SC	40	1199	1299
HD 80SC	80	1699	1799
HD 160SC	160	2599	2699
Alliance Peripheral Systems			
Quantum 40	40	259	349
Quantum 105	105	379	469
Quantum 170	170	729	829
Wren 173	173	999	1099
Quantum 210	210	799	899
Wren 300	300	1249	1449
Wren 600	600	1699	1899
Hard Drives International			
Seagate 20	20	249	295
Quantum 40	40	259	319
Quantum 80	80	379	439
Quantum 105	105	349	399
Quantum 210	210	769	819
Mac Land			
Quantum 40	40	299	399
Quantum 105	105	399	459
Quantum 120	120	589	689
Quantum 170	170	679	779
Quantum 210	210	849	959
Wren 300	300	1349	1449
Wren 600	600	1799	1899

One other little tidbit. If you are offered a "great deal" on a used, closeout, or refurbished disk drive, take a long, hard look at it before you sign on the dotted line. Consider what you are paying versus getting the same disk capacity with full return and warranty privileges for the latest brand new disk drive. Hard disk drives are electromechanical. They do wear out. Do you want to place your important data on an older, obsolete, or nonmainstream vendor disk drive that might fail and leave you in a situation where not only the repair parts are difficult to find but virtually no one knows how to fix? Your good data is still on the surface of the drive but no one can get to it for you!

The industry's largest supplier, Seagate, is being attacked by Quantum and Connor on two fronts. Not only are Quantum's faster 3^1/$_2$-inch drives with two-year warranty available from mail order sources at prices approaching Seagate pricing for slower drives, but Quantum and Connor with their fast, reliable, and inexpensive one-third height (one inch) drives have opened up a new front. Quantum and Connor are also used by Apple in its Portable, LC, and IIsi models.

At the high end, the 300Mb to 2000Mb hard disks, Seagate's Wren drives are still unmatched for reliability and price performance. When combined with

MicroNet's SCSI NuPORT card, either in single-drive or drive arrays as shown in Fig. 7-11, you get the best of all worlds. You get up to 3.7Mb per second synchronous transfers and 5.4 millisecond average access times!

New generation hard disks constantly offer still better price performance. Quantum has staked out its turf in the higher-capacity end of the 3½-inch drive market with its ProDrive 330 and 425Mb models list priced at $1350 and $1595, respectively. Seagate has countered with its ST 1400 (331Mb) and ST 1480 (426Mb) models. Stay tuned.

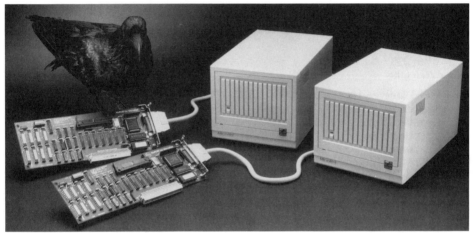

Micronet Technology, Inc.

7-11 Mac disk array system with Raven disk drive and SCSI NuPORT cards.

The envelope please

Regardless of what size hard disk you buy, what kind it is, who you buy it from, and how much you pay, you are far better off than the Mac owner with no hard disk at all.

All of you who already own a hard disk know what I mean. If you own a slower, first generation hard disk consider this. On a disk-intensive database job, an older 20Mb 65 millisecond access time hard disk might take five minutes to do a sort or prepare a report that a newer 40Mb 15 millisecond disk could complete in one minute. How important is that to you? Is it worth a $300 or $400 upgrade investment? (This is precisely the point I made in the chapter 1's "quick payback" example.) I would not advise anyone to buy less than a 40Mb hard disk today unless you had a strictly low-end word processing Mac use or price was a critical issue. Today you can buy a Quantum 105Mb with a two-year warranty shipped to you the next day via mail order, already preformatted, with system and public domain software already loaded on it, ready to run for under $500! Apple's external HD 80 is $1799 list price! I believe you got my message. Price, speed, what disk model, and which vendor you buy it from are pretty much up to you. Numerous choices await you in the pages of the Macintosh magazines. As mentioned, get the best deal you can from a high-profile vendor that gives you a good warranty and a liberal return privilege. No matter what investment you have made in your hard disk, the relentless march of technology will obsolete you. Just think about how you are going to back up your 6-gigabyte 3¹/₂-inch hard disk in the year 2000. Time marches on.

Removable long-term storage

For your long-term storage you want a device to back up your data for safety and/or preserve your data for archiving. Floppy disks take care of you if you have a dedicated Mac situation. Other Macintosh owners should look at more powerful solutions. Beyond floppy disks, I recommend you consider a removable cartridge disk or read/write optical disk for backup use. I would recommend tape as a lower cost alternative. Let's get into the details.

You want to remove my hard disk?

The easiest way to make a "removable" hard disk for your Mac is to buy an external half-height DOS PC drive case that has a 5¹/₄-inch drive bay accessible from the front, mount a removable hard disk bracket (made by Wetex and others) in it, and mount your 3¹/₂-inch drive in the carrying frame that slides into this bracket. The result is a 3¹/₂-inch hard disk drive that can be removed at will just by unlocking and sliding it out of its holder. You then put the carrying frame into the carrying case that comes with it for portability and protection, and you can transport to another location for safer storage or use.

Say you have a 40Mb drive in the Mac SE 30 you're using regularly for your work. Your "removable" backup Mac disk drive sits in a "zero-footprint" type case under your Mac SE. At the end of the day, you just power down, slide your removable 40Mb backup disk into its zero-footprint case bracket, power on, reboot your Mac, back off whatever you want onto it, then shut down and remove it. A quality hard disk utilized just a few minutes a day as a backup device should practically last indefinitely. Several 3¹/₂-inch hard disks kept circulating this way make a very reliable and/or secure backup system.

Believe it or not, this is nothing new. Tandon pioneered it with its removable Digital Data Pak for DOS PC machines in 1987.[19] On the Mac side, Advanced Gravis Computer Technology (HardPac), Golden Triangle Computers (Gemini), Mega Drive Systems (Disk Pack), Mirror Technologies (RD Series), and Tradewinds Peripherals (TravelDisk) all offer similar ready-made products today. It is a viable alternative. Remember, you always need the drive mechanism as well as the media to get at your information. With this alternative, it is always available together in the same spot. The down side, of course, is that it costs much more to use the entire mechanism as a storage device rather than just using the media itself. Ultimately, this is probably why it has not become more popular, although it has definitely found support in niche markets.

---

[19] Mark Brownstein, "Removable Disk Drives Slim Down," *Infoworld*, 6/18/90, p. 23.

45Mb in your coat pocket

Building on the removable thought, if removing the whole disk is great, then removing just the media and leaving the heavy and more delicate electromechanical components behind should be even better. You bet. The result is the broader and more common category of removable hard disks as defined today by SyQuest, Iomega (Bernoulli), and newcomer Ricoh.[20]

Make a stack of 1.2Mb 5¼-inch DOS PC diskettes about five diskettes high in a uniform pile. That's about all the space you need to fit a 45Mb SyQuest, Bernoulli, or Ricoh removable disk cartridge. You get 9 times as much data in the same amount of space, plus a bonus. You can get at it 10 times as fast, at 25 millisecond hard disk access rates rather than at floppy disk speeds.

The 45Mb removable cartridge, in its three distinct and noncompatible flavors, has become the *de facto* media of choice for backup, archiving, securing storage, and transporting large files.[21] While not perfect for any one of these missions, it does a highly satisfactory job that undoubtedly accounts for its widespread use. Stated in another way, it gives you data security and the portability and flexibility of a floppy disk combined with the performance of a relatively fast hard disk. While this offers the same performance as some hard disks—some users do employ these as their only disk drive—it would not be my recommendation as they are not intended for continuous heavy-duty usage. This is the exclusive and unrivaled domain of the fixed hard disk.

Alliance Peripheral Systems and MicroNet Technology offer attractively packaged ready-to-go SyQuest solutions. They are shown in Fig. 7-12 and Fig. 7-13,

Alliance Peripheral Systems

7-12 Mac SyQuest cartridge system.

---

[20] Steve Costa and MacUser Labs staff, "Portable, Secure, Unlimited-Storage, Cartridge Drives," *MacUser*, February 1991, p. 206. A great article covering 30 products using all three technologies.

[21] Or as MicroNet Technology says in its SyQuest ads, "Boot, Backup, Restore, Archive, Add, Secure, Ship, Share, and Store..."

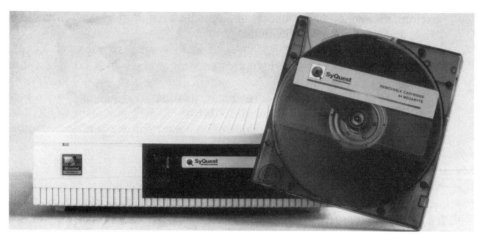

Micronet Technology, Inc.

7-13 Micro/removable SyQuest cartridge system.

respectively. I highly recommend either of these quality vendor's SyQuest products for their high performance and low price.

I do recommend you consider this technology as your next step-up solution when you begin to outgrow your floppy disks. My experience has shown that personal preference, more than anything else, dictates a user's choice of drive technology and cartridge. My counsel would be to study the offerings, ask lots of questions, and take your best shot. My experience has also shown that the low priced SyQuest drives in the hands of experienced users are often exceptional values. If you don't accidentally put your thumbprint on the media, insert the cartridge backwards, or remove the cartridge from a still spinning drive, they tend to work quite well. I have seen one accidentally erased, but I have never seen one lose data.

The subject of removable drives encompasses optical drives as well, but I will include it in a category all of its own.[22]

Optical long-term storage

You will never have to wonder about what my first choice for a backup device is: Optical ... all the way. (The answer should really be spoken in the tone used by Richard Gere in the movie *An Officer and A Gentleman*, when asked what he wanted to fly: "Jets ... all the way, Sir.") Optical drives are the jet planes of the storage business. In their three forms, each holds the most promise for future dominance in its market niche:

- *Magneto optical or erasable optical* With these, you can read and write. It is a backup device with 600Mb per cartridge and is in widespread use for

---

[22] Mark Brownstein, Linda Slovick, and Zoreh Banapour, "You Can Take It With You," *Infoworld*, 4/2/90, p. 51. This interesting article compares seven products in all three categories: optical drives, cartridges, and removable hard drive units.

backup, archiving, and transport of larger files required by scientific, database, and CAD/CAM applications.

- *Write-once read-many (WORM)* A WORM is an archival device with 600Mb to 800Mb per cartridge that is widely used as a computer-age replacement of microfiche.
- *CD-ROM* CD-ROM storage is read only, just like those in your stereo system. It is an archival device with 400Mb to 500Mb per disk. CD-ROMs enjoy widespread use for distribution of computer software and information because of the convenience of the media.

My jet plane analogy is founded on reason. Jets make most efficient use of the airflow. No propeller cuts the air in front of or behind the plane. Optical drives in similar fashion are technologically elegant. No electromechanical device interacts with the media, so there is nothing to wear out and no risk of head crashes ever. Everything is done with a beam of light. If the drive mechanism is elegant, the media itself is the *creme de la creme*. It has the longest shelf life of any media, it has removability, portability, and large capacity. Enough pontificating—here's what they can do for you.

Erasable optical drives

For your backup needs, optical disks have definite advantages over magnetic disks. They are not subject to head crash and media wear. They are also highly resistant to strong magnetic fields, radiation, and deterioration of magnetic oxide coating with age which are all problems associated with conventional magnetic media. Removable optical cartridges also offer additional advantages over magnetic tape as a backup device: high capacity, random access, and removability. Like magnetic removables, storage capacity is unlimited because optical drives also use cartridges. At $200 for a 600Mb cartridge (300Mb per side), that works out to 33 cents per megabyte. This is about the cost of an 800K floppy, and about one-twentieth the cost of a hard disk. Optical cartridges will outlive either floppy diskettes or hard disk media, and nobody would contest the convenience of a 5$1/4$-inch optical cartridge, which is about the same size as a SyQuest removable cartridge, versus handling 600 floppy diskettes!

Optical drives are as easy to use as floppy diskettes. You can boot up your Mac from them like a floppy diskette, they can be partitioned into smaller volumes like hard disks, and they are less prone to the debilitating failure modes that affect removable magnetic drive mechanisms. Because of these reasons, the optical drive has really begun to catch on. As its market widens, prices should drop further, making them more widely accessible.[23]

---

[23] Read a great article on the subject: John Rizzo and MacUser Labs staff, "Maximum Movable Megabytes: Erasable Optical Drives," *MacUser*, November 1990, p. 102; and its predecessor John Rizzo, "Letting in the Light," *MacUser*, November 1989, p. 132. Other interesting articles are: Chris Clark, "Wave of the Future," *Computer Reseller News*, 7/16/90, p. 75; Barbara Kent, "Promise of Rewritable Disk," *Computer Reseller News*, 1/1/90, p. 43.

How do they work? The short form answer is to imagine a clear plastic sandwich with some magneto-optical material in between. Now imagine in the tracks of this optical sandwich there are little tiny magnets pointing up and down. To write to the disk, a stronger laser beam heats the tiny magnet while a nearby magnet "magnetizes" it with one polarity or the opposite. To read from the disk, a weaker laser beam looks at the end of the tiny magnet and "sees"[24] what polarity it is. You don't want to see the long form answer. Because magneto-optical material can only change polarity when heated, it is impervious to magnetic fields, unlike floppy or hard disks.

There are many erasable optical drives (the excellent *MacUser* article cited reviewed 20 of them), but I believe seeing is believing with optical drives, too. That is you have to see them, use them, and try them out to really see if you like them. After going through this exercise, I have but one recommendation. As always, decide for yourself.

The SuperMac LaserFrame shown in Fig. 7-14 is hands-down the best erasable optical drive you can buy for your Mac at any price. Using a specially enhanced version of the Sony 650Mb (288Mb per cartridge side formatted) mechanism that boosts performance, it is among the fastest of the erasable optical drives on the market today, and its drivers have been especially optimized for storing and retrieving image files.[25] It is well engineered, handsomely designed, and comes

SuperMac Technology

7-14   LaserFrame 650Mb removable optical storage for the Mac.

---

[24] Actually, the laser beam's rotation, due to Kerr effect, allows optic reader to determine magnetic direction of bit. Brian Gillooly, "Magneto-optical technology slated to impact mass-storage market in next five years," *Computer Reseller News*, 5/7/90, p. 146. One of the best and shortest explanations I've read, complete with a diagram.

[25] Eric Adams, "Magneto-optical drives getting faster, less costly," *MacWEEK*, 10/23/90, p. 41; Ric Ford, "Erasable-optical refinements," *MacWEEK*, 10/23/90, p. 67; both articles echoed the LaserFrame accolades as did the earlier referenced *MacUser* article.

with a preformatted cartridge and outstanding instructions so that you can probably have it up and running within 15 minutes after opening the box. After using the LaserFrame, it is difficult to go back to anything else. Its street price is around $4500. If not on today's list, put it at the top of your future upgrade list.

WORM optical drives

For your archival needs, write-once read-many or read-only optical disks have the same advantages over magnetic disks and tapes as do erasable optical drives. They are not subject to head crash and media wear, and they are highly resistant to strong magnetic fields, radiation, and deterioration of magnetic oxide coating with age, while they offer high capacity, random access, and removability. Like erasable optical drives, storage capacity is unlimited because WORM drives also use cartridges.

While the WORM media itself is closely related to its erasable optical kin, in write-once technology the laser permanently alters the disk in one of three ways: ablative (burns a hole in the disk), phase-change (heats a spot in the disk and changes its crystalline structure), and dye (heats a spot in the disk and changes its color). Because these multiple techniques are available, WORM standardization has not yet achieved the levels of erasable opticals. Sony media predominates, and is freely interchangeable between different vendor products. Notwithstanding, the WORM market in units shipped is approximately four times as large as the erasable optical market today. The growth in either exceeds 100% annually, and the erasable market growth rates are accelerating faster than the WORM's. This is perhaps due to standardization.[26]

A typical 800Mb cartridge (400Mb per side) from Maxtor costs $200. That works out to 25 cents per megabyte, which is slightly under the erasable optical media cost. WORM optical cartridges are superb and unsurpassed choices for legal, accounting, programming, audit trail, and other archival needs requiring long-term, permanent storage. You will find them especially useful in automating any area using microfiche today.[27] Expect to spend about what you would for an erasable optical drive (that would be in the neighborhood of $3000 to $5000). I have no recommendation to offer you here, but go with a drive vendor in the mainstream. You want your drive to at least last as long as your data!

CD-ROM optical drives

The exact same technology that has replaced the phonograph record and raised home music quality to near perfection is revolutionizing the way software and information is distributed today. Service technicians that once had to sort through

---

[26] Greg Garry, "Optical Disk Drive Business: Clearly, A Brighter Outlook," *Electronic Buyers' News*, 9/10/90, p.26.

[27] T.C.Doyle, "Banks 'tidy up' offices," *Computer Reseller News*, 7/16/90, p. 101. This article makes the point that financial institutions nationwide are dumping records by the tons thanks to new court rulings identifying WORM records as permanent storage media allowing users to exclusively rely on optical media.

reams of microfiche in their briefcase now make quick work of it with a portable CD-ROM reader attached to their laptop computer. Resellers can have an entire store full of software in a desk drawer by copying the software and documentation to the user's diskette at the time of the sale. Anyone can have a library at his or her fingertips with a collection of CD-ROMs that occupy less than one shelf in a small bookcase.[28] Talk about a revolution!

Closer to home, what this means to you is that upgrades can open up new vistas and horizons for you at 650Mb of CD-ROM diskette at a time. Examples of this are the Apple CD-ROM drive (M2700/B) at $899 list or Toshiba XM-3200 or NEC CDR-72 CD-ROM drives at about $600 mail order.[29] Check them out.

Tape long-term storage

While removable magnetic and optical cartridges give you faster access to your backed-up data, if you don't need this capability, you get a lot more for your money with magnetic tape drives and media versus their disk counterparts.

While very slow, and not random access compared to disks, nor usable as a startup device, nor as invulnerable to magnetic fields as is optical media, with the additional burden of existing in several incompatible formats, tape still finds widespread use as a routine backup device for Macintosh networks. Just start your tape backup and walk away and let it do its thing overnight. Alternately, one tape drive and multiple controller cards (one in each Macintosh) is another popular and economical way to do your backups. Just plug in, backup, and move to the next Mac.[30]

The most popular quarter-inch tape format for the Mac, DC2000, stores 40Mb on it, lets you pack 50 floppies worth of information onto a cartridge the size of a credit card, and was first popularized by Apple's tape backup 40SC (M2640/B) at $1499 list. Today, DC 2000 formats provide up to 120Mb of storage on extended-length cartridges. The next most popular quarter-inch tape format for the Mac, DC600, closely resembles your video cassette in size. Its larger format cassettes typically hold 150Mb, 250Mb, 320Mb, or even 525Mb. You're talking some serious backup here of the kind that you would typically want for backup of larger network file servers or large audio or graphics files. TEAC data cassettes, which look like standard audio cassettes, are also a popular choice. Its cartridges, originally available in 60Mb flavors, now have given way to the 150Mb varieties. Of course reel-to-reel tapes of the variety that still proliferate in the mainframe and minicomputer data centers (and old science fiction movies!) are also available for the Macintosh (Qualstar, Blackhole Technology). Typically, if you have specialized conversion needs. At 40Mb to 250Mb per reel you are talking $10 to $20 each.

---

[28] Steven B. Adler, "CD-ROMs Are Coming," *VARBusiness*, April 1990, p. 76.

[29] John Rizzo and MacUser Labs staff, "Most Valuable Players," *MacUser*, March 1990, p. 150. A very informative article covering six different drive models, but some of the products are dated today.

[30] Tom Negrino, "Tape Backups," *Macworld*, November 1990, p. 167. The article tested 43 drives. Maybe you can find one you like.

If you want to play in the big leagues of tape backup, DAT (Digital Audio Tape) or 8 mm tape is the way to go. The largest capacity DAT tape systems, based on 4 mm tape, hold 1.2 gigabytes. The largest capacity 8 mm, based on videotape, hold 2.2 gigabytes.[31] The future holds promise of greater densities to come.

Your DC2000, TEAC, and DC600 tape backup solutions are all in the same cost ballpark as the removable magnetic cartridges, from $500 to $1000. Media cost is lower because tape cassettes cost less than removable cartridges. Your reel-to-reel, DAT, and 8 mm tape solutions are in the same cost ballpark with erasable optical and WORM drives ($3000 to $5000), and again the media cost is less.

Other than Apple's tape backup unit, I can offer you no specific tape backup recommendation. (Hey, I know it's slow, but it works!) Check out the product, the warranty, the company support, and return policies, and go with a tape drive vendor in the mainstream.

In a nutshell

Here are the key points you have seen in this chapter:

- After your CPU and memory, the next most significant improvement you can make to your Mac is to upgrade your storage area. Regardless of what application you are using your Mac for today, you should at least have a hard disk and 800K floppy drive on it. In storage devices, faster speed and higher capacity is almost always better.
- For short-term storage, you should be using at least an 800K floppy drive to help you here and a 1.4Mb FDHD version if interacting with DOS PCs.
- For working storage, a 40Mb hard disk should be your minimum size. Buy with your growth needs in mind. Hard disk pricing is extremely competitive today, so always go for the highest capacity and fastest speed your budget will allow.
- For long-term storage, you must back up your work. Backups are ridiculously cheap in terms of your initial equipment investment and your ongoing time investment as compared to the alternative of losing it all and redoing the work. If you are using your Mac in a small business at home, your floppy disk drive is probably adequate. Everyone else should at least consider a dedicated backup device. This could take the form of a portable hard drive, removable cartridge, read-write optical drive cartridge, or some form of tape.

Now that you know my true preference, if you happen to have a SuperMac LaserFrame for sale at a good price, call me; my daytime number is....

---

[31] Brian Gillooly, "Technological leaps for data's life jacket," *Computer Reseller News*, 8/20/90, p. 71.

Sources

Here are some hard disk sources:

Advanced Gravis Computer Technology
7033 Antrim Ave.
Burnaby, BC V5J 4M5 Canada
(604) 434-7274.

Alliance Peripheral Systems
2900 S. 291 Hwy., Lower H
Independence, MO 64057
(800) 233-7550
(816) 478-8300

Areal Technology, Inc.
2890 N. First St.
San Jose, CA 95134
(408) 954-0360

Club Mac
7 Musick
Irvine, CA 92718
(800) 258-2622
(714) 768-8130

CMS Enhancements
1372 Valencia Ave.
Tustin, CA 92680
(714) 259-9555

Connor Peripherals
3081 Zanker Rd.
San Jose, CA 95134-2128
(408) 456-4500

Cutting Edge Inc.
97 S. Red Willow Rd.
Evanston, WY 82930
(307) 789-0582

Deltaic Systems
1701 Junction Ct., #302
San Jose, CA 95112
(800) 574-1240
(408) 441-1240

DJK Development Corp.
8325 Riverland Dr., Ste. 4
Sterling Heights, MI 48314
(313) 254-2632

Ehman Engineering Inc.
P.O. Box 2126
Evanston, WY 82931
(800) 257-1666

FWB Inc.
2040 Polk St., #215
San Francisco, CA 94109
(415) 474-8055

GCC Technologies
580 Winter St.
Waltham, MA 02154
(800) 422-7777
(617) 890-0880

Hard Drives International
1912 W. 4th St.
Tempe, AZ 85281
(800) 234-3475
(602) 967-5128

IDS Systems, Inc.
2107 N. First St., Ste. 280
San Jose, CA 95131

JMR Electronics
19320 Londelius St.
Northridge, CA 91324
(818) 993-4801

LaCie
19552 SW 90th Ct.
Tualatin, OR 97062
(800) 999-0143
(503) 691-0771

Liberty Systems
120 Saratoga Ave., #82
Santa Clara, CA 95051
(408) 983-1127

MacLand
5006 S. Ash Ave., #101
Tempe, AZ 85282
(800) 333-3353

MacProducts USA
8303 Mopac Expwy., #218
Austin, TX 78759
(800) 622-3475

MacTel Technology
3007 North Lamar
Austin, TX 78705
(800) 950-8411
(512) 451-2600

Microtech International
158 Commerce St.
East Haven, CT 06512
(800) 626-4276
(203) 468-6223

Mirror Technologies
2644 Patton Rd.
Roseville, MN 55113
(800) 654-5294

Maxtor Corp.
2111 River Oaks Pkwy.
San Jose, CA 95134
(800) 356-5333
(408) 432-1700

MicroNet Technology
20 Mason
Irvine, CA 92718
(714) 837-6033

Micropolis Corp.
21211 Nordhoff St.
Chatsworth, CA 91311
(818) 709-3300

NexSys
296 Elizabeth St.
New York, NY 10012
(212) 995-2224

Pinnacle Micro
15265 Alton Pkwy.
Irvine, CA 92718
(800) 553-7070
(714) 727-3300

Peripheral Land Inc.
47421 Bayside Pkwy.
Fremont, CA 94538
(800) 288-8754
(415) 657-2211

Procomm Technology
200 McCormick Ave.
Costa Mesa, CA 92626
(714) 549-9449

Quantum Corp.
1804 McCarthy Blvd.
Milpitas, CA 95035
(408) 432-1100

Relax Technology
3101 Whipple Rd., #22
Union City, CA 94587
(800) 848-1313
(415) 471-6112

Rodime
901 Broken Sound Pkwy. NW
Boca Raton, FL 33487
(800) 688-9390
(407) 994-5585

Ruby Systems
188 S. Whisman Rd.
Mountain View, CA 94041
(800) 888-1668
(408) 735-8668

Seagate Technology Inc.
920 Disc Dr.
Scotts Valley, CA 95066-4544
(800) 468-3472

Sony Microsystems Company
651 River Oaks Pkwy.
San Jose, CA
(408) 434-6644

Storage Dimensions
2145 Hamilton Ave.
San Jose, CA 95125
(408) 879-0300

SuperMac Technology
485 Potrero Ave.
Sunnyvale, CA 94086
(408) 245-2202

Third Wave Computing
1826B Kramer Ln.
Austin, TX 78758
(800) 284-0486
(512) 832-8282

Toshiba America Information Systems
9740 Irvine Blvd.
Irvine, CA 92718
(800) 456-3475
(714) 583-3000

Total Peripherals
(508) 480-9042

Tulin Corp.
2156H O'Toole Ave.
San Jose, CA 95131
(408) 432-9025

Wetex International Corp.
1122 W. Washington Blvd., #D
Montebello, CA 90640
(800) 798-7041

Some floppy disk sources follow:

Applied Engineering
3210 Beltline
Dallas, TX 75234
(214) 241-6060

Cutting Edge Inc.
97 S. Red Willow Rd.
Evanston, WY 82930
(307) 789-0582

Dayna Communications
50 S. Main St., 5th Floor
Salt Lake City, UT 84144
(801) 531-0203

DJK Development Corp.
8325 Riverland Dr., Ste. 4
Sterling Heights, MI 48314
(313) 254-2632

Fujitsu America
3055 Orchard Dr.
San Jose, CA 95134
(800) 626-4686
(408) 432-1300

Insite Peripherals
4433 Fortran Dr.
San Jose, CA 95134
(408) 946-8080

Kennect Technology
120-A Albright Way
Los Gatos, CA 95030
(800) 552-1232

Microtech International
158 Commerce St.
East Haven, CT 06512
(800) 325-1895

Mirror Technologies
2644 Patton Rd.
Roseville, MN 55113
(800) 654-5294

Peripheral Land Inc.
47421 Bayside Pkwy.
Fremont, CA 94538
(800) 288-8754
(415) 657-2211

Quadmation
1120 Stewart Ct., #L
Sunnyvale, CA 94086
(408) 733-5557

Chapter 8
Display options

Monitors are the most visible choice of your Macintosh upgrade options. I don't mean this as an oxymoron. The fact is that you have to live with your selection everyday. If you made a good one, you'll love yourself, forget about it, and go on more efficiently than ever. If you made a bad choice, you're going to be kicking yourself about it and hoping the product you got came with a 30-day return privilege. More than in any other area, except the keyboard and mouse, your decision here is important and not just aesthetic.

This chapter covers the options available to you in this area for upgrading your Mac: monochrome and color monitors and video cards. I begin by first getting some history and a few definitions out of the way, then I cover the options, give my recommendations, and leave you with guidelines to make your own decisions.

The Macintosh monitor story

Originally, there was no decision to make. You got the monitor that came with your Macintosh—the 9-inch screen. Before there were larger monitors (yes, there was such a time—how quickly we forget), nobody complained about the size of the screen they had on their Macintosh. It was the only screen you got, it was the only screen you could get.

However, a trickle of complaints started and eventually became an avalanche. Customers would come into a computer store and complain about the Macintosh screen. Sophisticated corporate users complained about their loss of productivity, unsophisticated users just complained about its small physical size. In 1988, this shortcoming was addressed by Radius, E-Machines, and then a multitude of other companies with full-page and two-page monochrome monitor offerings in the 15 to 19 inches and up range. SuperMac and others added color a short while later. Grayscale monitor capability became available about that same time. In 1989, Apple legitimized the market by introducing its own big screen monitors.

The original Macs had their video contained onboard; there was nothing else to add. With the advent of the Mac II family in 1987, a video interface card was introduced that had the ability to be either 4-bit video to drive Apple's monochrome monitor or 8-bit video to drive Apple's 13-inch RGB hi-res color monitor—depending upon the number of video RAM chips you put in it. Today you have 24-bit color, 32-bit color, and very sophisticated multimedia video cards, with new ones being introduced in ever increasing numbers.

After addressing the high end of the market and monitor products that delivered full-page, two-page, grayscale, and color monitors, vendors turned their attention to the low end. Today, you can put a relatively inexpensive monitor, identical to those used on DOS PCs on your Mac and enjoy all the benefits of a larger screen. Merely plug a video card into your SE logic board adapter, plug the monitor into this video card, and you've done it. Monitor software lets you use either one or both Mac screens. The trend is, increasingly, to put accelerator and video functionality on the same add-in board, because they usually have mutually dependent needs. Today finds this problem solved in numerous clever ways.

Apple's open Mac II family architecture gave Macintosh monitor and video interface vendors the same opportunity to provide the wide variety of choices the DOS PC world had with two important differences—simplicity and graphics.

Just pick the monitor you like and plug its video interface card into a Mac II NuBus slot. NuBus slots let you have as many monitors attached to your Mac as you want—limited only by your imagination and your slots. I dare you to even put a second monitor on your DOS PC machine, plug a card into a slot, click a screen with a mouse, and have your monitor set up running within five minutes! Yet on a Mac II, it's just that simple to do.

Graphics on the Macintosh, a machine designed from the chips up to be a graphics machine, has always been better than that on the DOS PC machines, first with monochrome video and later with color. The newest offerings make it even better. Today's Mac color offerings are just outstanding—they have to be seen to be believed. The original Mac color capability at 8 bits per pixel was pretty impressive. The newer color monitor and video card offerings that display 24 and 32 bits of color information are nothing short of phenomenal. Looking at a 19-inch 32-bit color Mac screen is like looking at a photographic slide. I know slides have 5000 and up lines per inch resolution and the Mac doesn't even come close to this, but your naked eye is a believer!

Monitor me

First, a brief detour for a few definitions to get our basic vocabulary straight.

Video monitor Somewhat redundant in usage, the term *video monitor* refers to the monitor reproducing a visual image on a television or computer screen. This is as opposed to an audio monitor that would monitor sound frequencies.

Pixel *Pixel* is short for "picture element." It's the smallest dot that a monitor can display.

Pixel density *Pixel density* is the number of dots per inch (dpi) on the screen.

WYSIWYG What You See Is What You Get. One of the benefits of the Mac interface is what you see on the screen is reproduced faithfully by the printed output. To accomplish it, Apple specified that Mac compatible displays have a one-to-one ratio between the 72 dots per inch on the display and the 72 dots per inch at which the Apple ImageWriter prints. Some third-party monitor vendors bent this rule to suit their needs. The tradeoff is a higher than 72 dpi fits more information on the screen, but shrinks it—it's harder to read; lower than 72 dpi fits less information on the screen, but enlarges it—it's easier to read.

Size Monitor sizes, sometimes called viewing area, are measured diagonally from corner to corner. The 9-inch Mac screen is actually $7^1/_2$ inches wide by $5^1/_2$ inches high.

Resolution The number of pixels across and down—sometimes called pixel dimensions—is the amount of information displayed. The 9-inch Mac screen paints a picture that has a resolution of 512 pixels across by 342 pixels down for a total of 175,104 pixels.

Size versus resolution The size of the monitor does not determine its resolution. By just hooking up a larger 14-inch monitor to your Mac and not changing the amount of information fed to it, you make the viewing area larger, but you don't increase the amount of information displayed. To state it in another way, you are making your 512 × 342 image viewing area larger, but not increasing your productivity, because it takes the same scrolling time to view information on the screen. On the other hand, you can hook up the same monitor through a video card to get resolutions of 720 × 350 pixels (252,000 total, an increase of 144%) or 640 × 480 pixels (307,200 total, an increase of 175%). At the high end, an E-Machines Big Picture 17-inch 1024 × 808 monitor increases the pixels by 473%, or adding a full two-page 21-inch 1280 × 960 monitor increases the pixels by 702%. You get the picture?

Full-page or portrait monitor A full-page or portrait monitor reproduces the vertical format 8½-by-11-inch (or A4 European) page you are used to working with on the screen. This is good for heavy word processing work where it is helpful to see the entire page at a glance.

Two-page or landscape monitor A two-page or landscape monitor gives you two full side-by-side pages and is useful for doing page layout work. It is also useful for working with spreadsheets—it can either show many cells of a spreadsheet at one time or enlarge a few cells at a time for better viewing in group presentations.

Transistor to transistor logic (TTL) Although, strictly speaking, this definition applies to a type of electronic interface, this label has also come to apply to the whole universe of the simplest and least expensive (under $100 monitors) you can buy because they use that interface.

Multisync The ability of a multisync (more expensive than TTL) monitor is that it adjusts itself to a wide range of video input signal frequencies and thus is usable for a large variety of applications implemented over numerous computer platforms.

Grayscale Each pixel can display up to 256 shades of gray as opposed to just black or white available in a standard monitor. Many monitors can be converted into grayscale just by changing the interface card driving them. You can see much more of the tonal range if you are working with scanned photographs.

All monitors are not created equal

One of the principal benefits of upgrading your Mac is the wide range of options from which you can choose. Nowhere is this more true than in the monitor area—but it is a highly subjective decision. There are monitors, and there are monitors. You can compare all you want with pencil and paper, but buying a monitor is one area where seeing is believing. Fortunately, numerous articles have been written about video monitors and their features to help you. Excellent articles appeared in the past few years.[1] Other excellent articles on monitors, although now dated, also appeared previously.[2] If possible, I would encourage you to always look at the results on the screen of the monitor you are thinking of buying before you make your final decision.

What to look for

Certain selection criteria that can help you regardless of whether you are looking at the lowest priced TTL solution, a large screen color monitor at the other end of the price scale, or something in between.

Let me give you a few items to consider when shopping for a monitor. Some may be more important to you then others—it's your choice—but you should at least be aware of all of them. I divided my list into five areas: the physical viewing screen, the tube itself, the interface, the packaging, and the price-performance.

Physical viewing screen

This section covers the overall characteristics of your monitor:

- *Resolution*   One of the most important decisions. Yes, a 640 by 480 monitor is a nice size, but if you are working mostly with full-page text, 640 × 860 (one full page) would be a better choice.
- *Pixel density (dpi)*   Are you getting 72 dots per inch? If not, do you know why you are getting more or less? Do you agree that it's the best choice?
- *Refresh rate and flicker*   Excessive flicker is a strain on the eyes; no flicker is best. A high refresh rate reduces flicker. At 60 Hz (the screen image is redrawn 60 times per second), most people notice it. At 65 Hz, a few people notice. Above 70 Hz, you get a rock solid display.
- *Brightness*   Does your monitor image appear bright or is it washed out? Can you adjust the brightness? Monitors decrease in brightness with age, and being able to adjust can help compensate for the dimming.
- *Contrast*   Do you have a good range between the light and dark areas? With good contrast, you have dark blacks and bright whites. Is contrast adjust-

---

[1] Among the best are: Kelli Wiseth and MacUser Labs staff, "Picture Perfect Portraits: Full-Page Displays," *MacUser*, February 1991, p. 176; Kelli Wiseth, Paul Yi, and MacUser Labs staff, "Do-It-Yourself Screen Tests," *MacUser*, February 1991, p. 198; Robert C. Eckhardt, "Color Monitor Put To The Test," *Macworld*, July 1990, p. 146; Amy Bermar, "Many users stand firm for monochrome," *MacWEEK*, 5/15/90, p. 33; Winn L. Rosch and MacUser Labs staff, "In Living Color," *MacUser*, May 1990, p. BG32; Eric R. Azinger, Jeff Eckert and Serge Timacheff, "Monochrome VGA Monitors," *Infoworld*, 4/30/90, p. 53; Robert C. Eckhardt, "Monochrome Monitor Mania," *Macworld*, April 1990, p.123; Rik Myslewski and MacUser Labs staff, "A Study in Black and White," *MacUser*, April 1990, p. 182; Ken Milburn, "Evaluating display systems: There's more than meets the eye," *MacWEEK*, 7/25/89, p.36; Alexander Rosenberg, "In Focus: Apple, Radius monitors," *MacWEEK*, 4/4/89, p.34. The last article features a sidebar "What makes a good monitor?"

[2] Try Philip Robinson, "Black & White & Read All Over," *MacUser*, August 1988, p.102; and Savant Labs, "Introduction to Monitors," *MACazine*, August 1988, p.41.

able? This control along with brightness can also compensate for other ills such as the monitor's physical placement in room and ambient lighting.

- *Color* Do you like the tint or color of the screen? Is it blue-white (preferred Mac standard), gray, or yellow-white? Are your colors rich and on track and uniform in tint over the entire screen?

Tube

The overall characteristics of the picture tube that goes into your monitor can be very important:

- *Focus* How clear is the information appearing on your screen? Do you get crisp, readable text? Is the focus uniform over the entire screen area?
- *Color alignment* Is the color pattern uniform in all areas of the screen or do you have patches where it appears wavy or splotched?
- *Pin cushioning* Are the screen edges wavy or distorted? Are the corners cramped or misshapen?
- *Phosphor persistence* Is there ghosting—do movements of you white cursor across a dark screen leave a noticeable afterglow?
- *Flatness* Is the tube face flat or curved? Some older tubes made you feel you were looking into a fish bowl. Flatter is better.
- *Scanning* How straight are the edges of the electronically scanned area in the display? Are they in physical alignment with the tube, or rotated, twisted, or horizontally or vertically skewed?
- *Glare coating* Does the tube have one? Does it interfere with the image? Either too much or too little is bad. Too much makes the screen appear unfocused; too little reflects too much ambient light off the screen face.

Interface

This section raises the questions about the hardware and software interface of your monitor:

- *Compatibility* Can the monitor be used across all Macs? Does it have optional interface adapters—i.e., SE, SE 30, NuBus—so you can take your favorite monitor with you should you change Mac models down the road?
- *Software* Does it have the software features you want—e.g., tear-off menus, tool-palettes, or multi-screen features if you are working with an SE or SE 30?

Packaging

Packaging describes the physical aspects of your monitor:

- *Overall* Is it the right size and weight for your needs? A 50-pound color monitor is not portable! Does the case color match your room drapes?
- *Ergonomics* Does it come with a tilt-swivel stand and/or other extras?

Price-performance

Price-performance has to do with the value aspects of your monitor. Bigger monitor screens definitely enhance productivity—numerous studies have proven it. Even a 14-inch monitor will give you significant benefits over a standard Mac 9-inch screen because it cuts down the scrolling time to view information on a page; obviously the 15-inch full-page displays and 19-inch two-page displays even more so if you can afford it.

Match your machine to the monitor you need at the outset. Yes, you can now add color capability to the traditional Macs, but it really is better to start off with a Mac II and up to begin with if you need color.

Note that most corporate users prefer color despite cost. Basically this is aesthetics, but many corporate users cite further productivity gains with color.

Grayscale is a worthwhile investment if your business justifies it, such as corporate publishing departments that work with halftones.

- *Avoid obsolescence* Look for features that let you expand later and don't lock you in. What is the next step you are likely to take with your display?
- *Quality/vendor* It is worth it to pay more for quality. Buy the best quality you can get from a vendor you can trust.
- *Price* I put price last because it should be last in your mind when monitor shopping. Only after getting all the features you want should you consider the price and where to get it from. If someone has helped you look at 50 different monitors in the store, it is a nice touch if you buy one from them.

Monochrome monitors

First, let me talk about my favorite choices in several different monochrome monitor categories. I arrived at these after going through the preceding tradeoff list. Will these monitors please everyone? No way. I qualified monitor decisions at the beginning of this chapter as being a highly subjective area! But it is a starting place for you to look at when you begin your own monitor quest.

Low-end monochrome monitors

Today, just one step up from the Macintosh 9-inch screen, you're able to put a very fine monochrome PC monitor on your Macintosh. It could be a multi-scanning monitor, it could be as simple as just a plain TTL monitor, or most likely it would be a VGA monitor (video graphics array—an analog DOS PC display standard introduced with IBM's PS/2 computers). VGA has become such a popular standard on the PC side that in recognition of this, Apple's newest model, the Macintosh LC, even comes straight out of the box with a standard VGA adapter. You can plug a VGA monitor right into the back of your Mac LC. All you need is the right cable. Here are three low-end monochrome monitors that I can recommend to you:

- *Apple 12-inch Monochrome Display* Originally announced as the Hi-Res Mono Monitor (M0400) at $399. Today's version (M0298LL/A) offers substantially the same performance at a $299 list price. Either way you get 640 × 480 resolution, 72 dpi, and external brightness and contrast controls in a "bulletproof" monitor design that will give you years of trouble-free service. Fig. 8-1 shows it sitting on the new Mac LC.

- *Princeton Graphics Max-15* A multisync 14-inch monitor with a street price around $250 that offers more capabilities than the Apple monitor at the same price. Figure 8-2 shows it. In addition to the same 640 × 480 resolution on a larger 14-inch screen, the Princeton has seven (!) more external screen adjustment controls, can be driven in additional modes by the Lapis video cards and offers an extra adjustment control to fine tune your viewing area further to suit your taste. It has more of a gray phosphor screen than the blue-white of the Apple monitor. I have used one and loved it for years. On the other side of the coin, last year Princeton moved its production facility and you couldn't get a Max-15 anywhere.
- *NEC GS2A* A 14-inch VGA monitor with a street price around $250 that offers the same Apple 640 × 480 resolution on a larger 14-inch screen at the same price. It is shown in Fig. 8-3. When driven by the Lapis video cards, it offers an outstanding rock-solid screen view in the same blue-white range as the Apple monitor but covering a larger viewing area. It's very nice. I have used one and loved it for days.

Apple Computer, Inc.

8-1 Macintosh 12-inch Monochrome Display on Mac LC.

Notice I did not mention DOS PC TTL monitors here. Yes, you can use them on your Mac—they work great with the Lapis video cards—but the 512 × 348 Mac screen displayed on a 12-inch or 14-inch monitor in its original 9-inch screen size really doesn't do too much for me. For example, no matter how I tweaked the

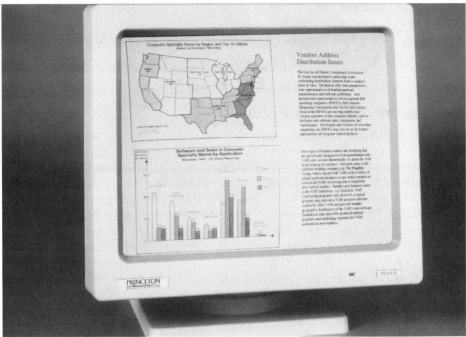

8-2 MAX-15 High-Resolution Multisync Monitor.

8-3 Multisync GS2A 14-inch Grayscale Monitor.

intensity and adjusted the contrast of my amber TTL Samsung monitor, I found it harder on my eyes compared to the paper-white Mac screens I have viewed for years. It worked great, though. I know this is heresy to some Mac users, but the original green IBM mono monitor also worked as good with the Lapis card as the Samsung did. The green monitor screen was also harder on my eyes, and I never could get used to seeing the logo on the case—IBM.

One-page monochrome monitors

Nowhere else can the adage "you get what you pay for" be demonstrated as graphically as in this monitor category. In my opinion, the very best displays available on the Macintosh today are available in this category. (Most Mac monitor vendors perceive a mainstream Macintosh use to be putting words on the screen and printing them to an $8^1/_2 \times 11$ sheet of paper, hence the popularity of the one-page monitor.)

While I will not name names, the very worst displays for the Mac are also to be found here. Some low-priced one-page and two-page monitors are not even in the same league (perhaps "universe" should be substituted) with those recommended here. And why should they be? You are paying a lot less. Notice I said "some"—others are outstanding values, but you must shop carefully. As for me, it's my eyeballs, and I'll take the best I can afford. Here goes:

- *Apple Macintosh Portrait Display*   Apple wasn't quick to enter this market niche. It watched carefully as third-party vendors defined and refined their offerings. Apple's market and product study efforts were not wasted. When it finally did announce a product, it had clearly distilled the essence of the Mac market's needs into one of the best offerings—and set the standard for everyone else to match. The result is Apple's 640 × 870 resolution, 80 dpi Mac Portrait Monitor (M0404) at $1099 list. Its Toshiba CRT, refreshed at 75 Hz, produces one of the brightest, crispest displays combined with good glare protection. It is easy to see why it won the five mice (highest) award from *MacUser* magazine and placed at or near the top of every one-page monitor evaluation conducted. You can see it in Fig. 2-4 (the Apple family portrait) sitting on the Mac IIci. Or, better still, see it at your Apple dealer.

- *Radius Pivot One-Page Display*   Hands down, this is the best monitor of any type you can buy for your Mac at any price.[3] It wasn't easy for anyone to top the Apple one-page monitor, but Radius, the original founder of the Macintosh one-page market with its FPD (full-page display), pulled it off. Pivot's 640 × 864 resolution, 78 dpi, and 69 Hz refresh, priced at $995 for the monitor and $695 for the card, offers a bright, crisp, rock-solid screen, outstanding software, excellent documentation, and an attractive, ruggedly designed case—everything you'd buy a monitor for. Plus, it is technologically slick—you can shift effortlessly from portrait to landscape viewing mode with just a slight pressure from your hands—software and electronics make it all

---

[3] Don't just take my word for it. Read John Battelle, "Radius sets monitor market on its ear," *MacWEEK*, 3/6/90, p. 6; Kirk van Druten, "Pivot turns screen viewing on its side," *MacWEEK*, 4/10/90, p. 114; Neil McManus, "Radius Pivot turns to IIsi, IIci video," *MacWEEK*, 1/8/91, p. 4; and Kristi Coale and Patricia J. Pane, "Radius Colorizes Pivot Monitors for Mac," *Infoworld*, 3/11/91, p. 8.

transparent to you! Originally offered with controller, a later version for the Mac IIsi was controlled only through software and plugged directly into it. Its latest announcement is a color Pivot monitor in both controller board and software-only versions. Try a Radius Pivot, and you too will find it is very difficult to go back to anything else. Figure 8-4 shows it tilted—any way you like.

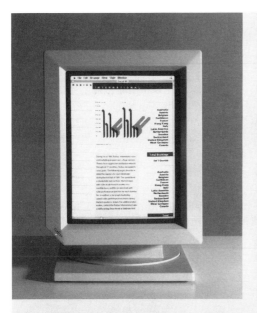

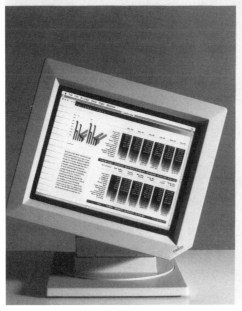

Radius.

8-4 Radius Pivot One-Page Display.

• *Mobius One-Page Display* Apple and Radius are heavyweights, but Mobius had a better idea. Take an outstanding CRT from Zenith, add a video interface and software, then add a full-function 68030-based accelerator, and offer the whole product as a package directly to the end user. The result is the Mobius One-Page Display 030 featuring 640 × 870 resolution, 78 dpi, 75 Hz refresh, and a price of $1395.[4] Even without the add-ons, the Mobius Display offers the flattest, glare-free view, in addition to delivering brightness, crispness, great contrast over the entire viewing area, and the preferred blue-white tint all on a rock-solid screen, with innovative and useful software. Mobius, no newcomer to the field, has been providing video interfaces to mid-range Macs for the last several years; Mobius has certainly got the formula right on this one. Try it; it won't disappoint you. Figure 8-5 shows—but doesn't do justice to—the Mobius One-Page Display on the left. Figure 8-6 shows the full function Mobius accelerator card; notice it has an FPU chip and on-board SIMM memory in addition to the 68030 CPU chip.

Two-page monochrome monitors

Beyond one page lies the realm of two-page monitors. With more screen area to cover, there is nowhere to run or hide to cover up imperfections in a two-page monitor. The extra-large screen makes it especially important to go for the gold in this

Mobius

8-5 Mobius One-Page Display (left) and Two-Page Display.

---

[4] See Neil McManus, "Mobius accelerator and display card for SE uses new '030 chip," *MacWEEK*, 1/8/91, p. 14.

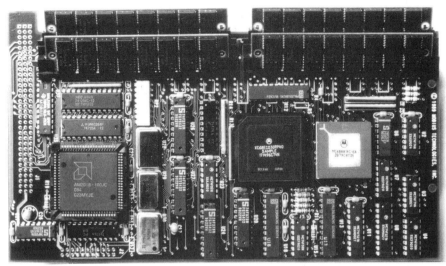

8-6 Mobius Full-Function 68030 Accelerator and Video Card.   Mobius

high end of the monitor market. Also, driving a two-page monitor with anything less than a Mac SE 30 or NuBus Mac is like filling up a large swimming pool using a garden hose—you can get there, but it takes a long time. You should have a NuBus Mac, plan on getting a NuBus Mac, or should plan on accelerating the Mac you have to 68030 levels and checking out accelerator versus monitor compatibility before making your monitor choice.

Unlike the one-page game, the two page market has no clear-cut winners. The top six contenders are only a hairsbreadth apart, making it the most subjective of all categories to call. My three recommendations for 19-inch two-page monitors follow, but your three could be different. While a 19-inch monitor might or might not allow you to get exactly all of two full pages on the screen depending on its dpi, I'm not sure you need a 21-inch two-page monitor. A quality 21-inch monitor just takes more real estate on your desk, costs more, yet doesn't do that much more for you versus a 19-inch unit. I believe you actually start losing productivity because of the extra time you spend moving your mouse on the screen to drag files to the trash, etc. As before, you decide:

- *Radius Two-Page Display* Radius wins this contest, but only by a narrow margin this time. It has 1152×882 resolution, 82 dpi, and 71 Hz refresh. TPD, priced at $1990 for the monitor and card, offers the best balance of brightness and other important screen characteristics especially contrast and sharpness. In color hue or tint, it appears closer to the original blue-white Mac screen standard than any other unit.
- *Sigma Designs L-View Multi Mode* Sigma Designs is another winner. It offers you a choice of six resolutions under software control from 36 dpi 512 $\times$ 384 to 120 dpi 1664×1200 resolution (WYSIWYG 72 dpi is one of them) and up to 92 Hz refresh. It also offers Sigma's trademarked Low-Emission design. Priced at $1999 for monitor and card, Sigma offers a bright, sharp,

well-focused product with perhaps the best software features, including pop-up menus, dual-screen capability, cursor size, screen saver, large menu fonts, screen capture, and the widest variety of screen modes. It's easy to see why it won MacUser's 1990 Eddy Award. Figure 8-7 shows it.

Sigma Designs

8-7 L-View 19-inch Multi-Mode Display System.

- *RasterOps ClearVue/II* RasterOps also has a winner. It has 1024 × 768 resolution, WYSIWYG 72 dpi, and 72 Hz refresh. ClearVue/II priced at $1995 for monitor and card, also offers a bright, sharp, well-focused product with a good balance of other important screen characteristics. It has excellent software featuring pop-up menus and its 200% and 400% zoom modes should be especially useful to graphic artists working with individual pixels. In color hue or tint, it appears blue-yellow compared to the Radius two-page monitor but was otherwise not at all objectionable. It is shown in Fig. 8-8.

Grayscale monochrome monitors

Beyond two-page monitors are the two-page grayscale monitors that give you an almost photographic quality output on your Macintosh screen.[5] Picture a grayscale

---

[5] For more information read: Owen W. Linzmayer and MacUser Labs staff, "The Golden Age of Gray Scale," *MacUser*, October 1990, p. 150; Diana Bury, "Monitor Choices: Shades of gray," *MacWEEK*, 5/15/90, p. 33; and Owen W. Linzmayer and MacUser Labs staff, "Grading the Grays," *MacUser*, October 1989, p. 182.

RasterOps

8-8 ClearView/II 19-inch High-Resolution Display System.

monitor as a color monitor without the color feature—the pixels are different shades of gray rather than being different colors. Because they still require the color QuickDraw feature in your Mac, they only work on the SE 30 and NuBus Macs. That is absolutely not a problem because as mentioned earlier, you don't want to use anything slower than these in terms of CPU horsepower. I'll recommend two 19-inch two-page grayscale monitors, but you have to decide for yourself:

- *SuperMac 19-inch Platinum Display* SuperMac, a major player in the color monitor market, wins this contest hands down. Its Platinum Display has 1024 × 768 resolution, WYSIWYG 72 dpi, 75 Hz refresh, and a price of $2399 for the monitor and card. Its Philips CRT offers the brightest, sharpest, highest contrast, best focus, and screen factors. It also comes with a color-capable card, hardware pan and zoom, virtual desktop, glare protection, and tilt and swivel stand. What more can I say?
- *RasterOps ClearVue/GS* RasterOps also has a winner with its grayscale offering. ClearVue/GS has 1024 × 768 resolution, WYSIWYG 72 dpi, 75 Hz refresh, and a price of $2195 for monitor and card (it has an SE 30 card option). Its Ikegami CRT also offers the brightest, sharpest, highest contrast, best focus, and screen factors—just a shade below those of the Super-Mac offering overall. Like its standard two-page cousin, it again has excellent software featuring pop-up menus.

Color monitors

Bruce Webster said it in one of the first Mac color monitor reviews, "Color in computers is what everyone wants but nobody is really sure how to use."[6] His point is just as well taken today. For three-quarters of the Mac community that use their machines for word processing, spreadsheets, simple desktop publishing, and then output to a standard printer, his meaning is that color is complete overkill. While I know that statement will draw someone's wrath, its logic is irrefutable. Let's look at the other quarter of the community. If you're in magazine publishing prepress, outputting to a color printer, color video production, multimedia in any form, you just need color—no questions asked. If you are doing production database work, working with large quantities of I/O data to be tabulated, doing CAD or any of it variants, preparing presentation slides, doing complicated desktop publishing (even if your output is only in black-and-white printed form), you should take a look at how color can help you. If you know how to use it correctly, it can really enhance your productivity. The reason why color is really important is that it holds out the possibility of doing this for anyone.

As with monochrome monitors (again using the tradeoff criteria outlined earlier), here are my favorite choices in several different color monitor categories. Will *this set* of monitors please everyone? No, I have told you from the beginning of this chapter that this is a highly subjective area. My choices are only intended to be a starting place for you on your monitor quest.

Low-end color monitors

Two Apple models set the standard for the low-end color monitors:

- *Apple 14-inch Color High Resolution RGB Display*   The one and only original Apple color monitor (M0401) lists for $999. First introduced with the Mac II in 1987, it set the standard for all other monitors to live up to; even today, most others do not. Its monitor, built by Sony, used Trinitron technology that later became the *de facto* standard for superior Mac color performance in all monitor sizes from all vendors. Personally, I have never seen another monitor of its size and class measure up to it. Even Sony's own CPD series is not on the same par. When used with Apple's Mac II video card, you get 640 × 480 resolution, 70 dpi, 67 Hz refresh, and a 0.25 mm dot pitch. It gives an extremely, bright, clear, sharp display with true blacks and very reliable color representation.
- *Apple Macintosh 12-inch RGB Display*   Introduced with the Macintosh LC in late 1990, this color monitor (M0297LL/A) at $599 is the first new Apple color monitor offering in years. It's well done, but targeted at a completely different market from the original. This monitor features a 512 × 384 resolution at 64 dpi and is perfectly matched to the Mac LC in case size. Upon first review, industry pundits panned its resolution as being little more than

---

[6] Bruce F. Webster, "Looking through the Mac II kaleidoscope," *Macworld*, December 1987, p. 90.

the original Mac's 512 × 342 resolution, 9-inch screen, but Apple studies have shown that users prefer the lower-resolution color monitor. Text can be read more easily when its enlarged from the 72 dpi WYSIWYG standard, and the Mac LC along with this monitor is specifically targeted at the Apple II market to whose users it will be love at first sight. I was impressed with its bright, clear, sharp high-contrast display with true colors; I would say Apple had come very close to the original with this economy model.

High-end color monitors

Many offerings are available at this end of the spectrum, but two manufacturers really stand apart from the rest in the quality of their offerings. Both SuperMac and E-Machines have focused on the quality end of this market, and it is well reflected in their products. SuperMac defined the high-end color niche as its market from the very start; E-Machines grew into it from its position as one of the original Mac large-screen vendors.

- *SuperMac 19-inch Trinitron Color Display* The original Sony Trinitron technology 19-inch color monitor (shown in Fig. 8-9) with Spectrum 8 NuBus card (shown in Fig. 8-10) is priced at $5799. SuperMac obviously went to the same school as Apple. This 19-inch monitor is superior to virtually any other color monitor except Apple's, which is only offered in the smaller size. When used with the Spectrum 8 video card, you get 1024 × 768 resolution, 72 dpi, 75 Hz refresh, and a 0.31 mm dot pitch. It had far and away the best display: bright, clear, sharp with black blacks and brilliant colors. Plus, you get a hardware pan, a zoom virtual desktop, and a host of other neat software. A little pricey, this package will never disappoint you, nor will you be criticized by others for choosing it.
- *E-Machines ColorPage T16* E-Machines simply had a better idea: Take proven Sony Trinitron technology, put it in a 16-inch color monitor, match it with your best video card, and offer it at $3595, mid-range between Apple and SuperMac. E-Machines' razor-sharp 16-inch monitor has won all the awards in its class and gives you 832 × 624 resolution, 72 dpi, 67 Hz refresh, and a 0.26 mm dot pitch. It has the best display in its class. Being closer to the Apple in dot pitch size, it actually has a slightly sharper display than the larger SuperMac. The ColorPage T16 is bright and clear, with good contrast and true colors. Include E-Machines' excellent software, and you have a product that you very rarely find in the used equipment market— users love their T16s.

Flat panel displays

A little side trip before you leave the subject of displays: Flat panel displays have been around for years in portables, but look for them to assume more of a role on your desktop in the years to come. They take up less desk space and consume less power, VDT radiation injuries are eliminated, and there are never any tube-related issues such as focus, alignment, distortion, and degradation with age.

SuperMac Technology

8-9 SuperMac 19-inch Trinitron Color Display.

SuperMac Technology

8-10 SuperMac Spectrum/8 NuBus video card.

E-Machines

8-11   E-Machines 16-inch ColorPage T16 color display.

Flat panel displays come in liquid crystal displays (LCD), electro luminescent (EL), and plasma (works like a fluorescent lamp).

In the LCD area, both Dynamac Computer Products and Nutmeg Systems offer 9½-inch 640 × 480 resolution (plus 16 shades of gray) backlit paper-white LCD monochrome displays especially targeted for the Mac LC in the $1000 price range. The combination of the LC's light weight and flat form factor are complemented by those of the flat panel displays. The result is a 14-pound combination you can take with you—no lugging required. In Focus Systems has announced a 10-inch color LCD add-on display to any Macintosh SE or Mac II in the $2500 price range and choice of either 64 or 4913 colors.[7] It should be shipping to OEMs later on in 1991.

In the EL area, Planar Systems, one of the world's largest EL display manufacturers, announced one of the world's largest EL displays in mid 1990—an 18-inch model called its MAX Terminal[8] shown in Fig. 8-12. Featuring NuBus compatibility and 1024 × 864 resolution with black on amber pixels, it measures only 4 inches deep and takes less than 50 square inches of desk space. While still fairly

---

[7] See Gregory Quick, "In Focus adds display," *Computer Reseller News*, 11/19/90, p. 65.

[8] See John Webster, "Planar ships big flat-panel display," *MacWEEK*, 6/19/90, p. 15.

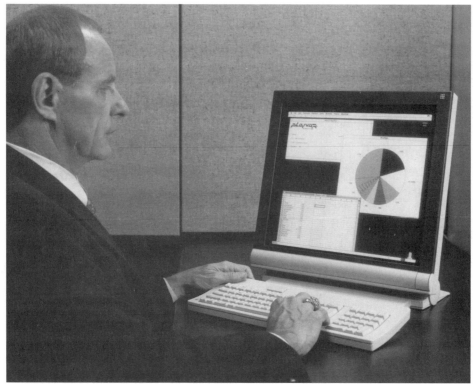

Planar Systems

8-12 MAX Terminal 18-inch EL Display.

pricey (you'd have to trade in your Mac IIci to buy one), it has already found several niche market applications. It will definitely come down in price as volume picks up, and it is absolutely the wave of the future.

Video cards

Video cards are the go-betweens that allow you to connect the monitor you like to the Mac that you like. Unfortunately, its not always that simple. In the beginning, God created heaven and earth, and Apple only one Mac model. You didn't have to worry about any video cards because it was already inside the box and done for you. Since that time, it has been all downhill.

　　While you could hang a large screen on a Mac Plus, and early products introduced when the Mac Plus was the zenith of Apple's Mac offerings gave you just that capability, the results were disappointing. The bottom line was that while you can probably hang any monochrome monitor on any Mac and any color or grayscale monitor on any NuBus or SE 30 Mac, you don't want to go about it in that way. Here's why.

　　You want to match the Mac to the monitor and vice versa. At the low-end and high-end, that's no problem. In the middle is where it gets a little dicey. Because there are so many options, users invariably try to shoehorn the monitor they want into the Mac they have rather than stepping back, looking at the overall picture, and getting the monitor and Mac to drive it as one package. My advice is to keep it simple. If you feel you have to add an accelerator to the Mac you have just to drive the monitor you want, seriously consider getting a more powerful Mac instead.

In this section, you'll see the offerings available for each Mac family to help you with your upgrade decisions.

Clip-on Macs

Computer Care and Newbridge, using video extensions to the boards I introduced to you in chapter 6, offer the best way to add video to either your clip-on Mac 128 or 512. Just get their option with video expander. Either will handle a wide variety of monochrome TTL, Multisync, or VGA monitors.

With the Mac Plus, you have to go with monitors that already have their interface card bundled with them. You have a wide variety of choices. Check out E-Machines, MegaGraphics, Nutmeg Systems, and Radius for openers.

One-slot Macs

If you are a Mac SE owner, totally new horizons are opened to you. Lapis has boards that allow you to attach virtually any Mac or DOS PC monitor to your Mac SE. Figure 8-13 shows the Lapis DisplayServer SE Video Card. If you find the choices too overwhelming, Mobius gives you an outstanding one-page or two-page monitor and card solution, as mentioned earlier. Mobius also offers a 25 MHz 68030 accelerated version prematched to the capabilities of the monitor and its video card. The accelerated choice has expansion options with room for FPU and memory chips to be added as your needs grow. The monitor manufacturers supporting the Mac Plus: E-Machines, MegaGraphics, Nutmeg Systems, Radius, plus Sigma Designs; a host of others all offer bundled monitor video card solutions.

8-13 Lapis DisplayServer SE video card.

An SE 30 owner's video options are almost identical to the Mac SE owner's. Here you can again use the Lapis solution—the Lapis DisplayServer SE 30 Video Card with IIsi adapter shown in Fig. 8-14—or solutions from Mobius, plus E-Machines, MegaGraphics, Nutmeg Systems, Radius, Sigma Designs, and a host of others. SE 30 owners have the color or grayscale option as well. Here you can make your own choice using the SE 30 Lapis color card or ready-made solutions from RasterOps, E-Machines, and a number of others.

8-14   Lapis DisplayServer SE 30 video card with IIsi adapter.

NuBus Macs

The original Apple Mac 4 or 8-bit video card (depending on onboard video RAM) has stood the test of time. In its 8-bit flavor (M0121PA/A) at $648, this card did an excellent job of driving the Apple 13-inch RGB hi-res monitor and was the standard for quite some time. Since that time, Apple has announced its 8/24 (M0507PA/A) at $799 (upgradable to 24 bit via 8 to 24 VRAM kit at $249), 8/24GC accelerator (M0122) at $1999, and there have been 24-bit and 32-bit video cards along with QuickDraw accelerators introduced in ever increasing numbers.[9]

New Macs

After only a few months since the announcement of the new Macs, an avalanche of products have been introduced for these Macs. Here is the picture.[10]

Classic   No fewer than eight manufacturers have announced interfaces or adapted their products for the Classic. Computer Care features a video interface on its Mac Stretch Classic memory board. Most other manufacturers have redesigned

---

[9]   See Cheryl England Spencer, "The 16 Million Color Question," *Macworld*, January 1991, p. 153 on which 24-bit display is best and Cheryl's "Fast Color," article on p. 136 of the same issue comparing 24-bit QuickDraw accelerator cards.

[10]   See Clay Andres, "Display systems for low-cost Macs," *MacWEEK*, 2/5/91, p. 51.

clips to fit the surface-mounted Mac Classic 68000 CPU chip. Continuing its product leadership edge in designing video cards to adapt the widest number of available DOS PC and third-party monitors to the Mac, Lapis provides a Display Server Classic board. Ehman, Generation Systems, Mirror, RasterOps, and Sigma have all announced complete solutions, featuring monitors and video cards.

Mac LC Lapis provides a Display Server LC-FPD board that drives five displays and is bundled separately with Ehman's LC monitor offering. RasterOps offers full-page and color/grayscale boards for third-party Apple compatible 13-inch and 19-inch monitors as well as bundled with its own line. Sigma Designs also introduced an L-View Multi-Mode Video card for the Mac LC's 020 PDS slot that brings the capabilities of the Sigma's 19-inch monitors with software variable dpi to the Mac LC. Nutmeg and Dynamac make backlit LCD displays as mentioned earlier in the chapter. Also mentioned earlier in the chapter, Apple's Mac LC has VGA capability; you can plug a VGA monitor right into the back of your Mac LC, and all you need is the right cable. Table 8-1, courtesy of *Infoworld*,[11] shows you how to do it. Be sure to connect pins 7 and 10 together on the Mac LC side as noted in the table—otherwise things won't work! The LC's built-in video also lets you drive an Apple mono, Apple's Hi-Res RGB Color, Apple's 12-inch RGB Color, or other compatible monitors directly at 640 × 480 resolution.

Table 8-1. Pinouts for connecting a Mac LC to a VGA monitor.

Signal	Mac LC pin #	VGA Monitor pin #	Comments
Red ground	1	6	
Red signal	2	1	
Green signal	5	2	
Green ground	6	7	
(Wired together on Mac LC connector)	7 and 10	—	(To turn-on VGA oscillator on LC logic board)
Blue signal	9	3	
Composite/vertical sync ground	11	4	
Vertical sync	12	14	
Blue ground	13	8	
Horizontal sync ground	14	10	
Horizontal sync	15	13	
Not connected	3, 4, 8	5, 9, 11, 12, 15	

Mac IIsi The special adapter cards for the IIsi allow either NuBus or SE 30 PDS cards to be adapted. Of course, the best solution is no card at all. Radius provides this with its Pivot monitor that plugs directly into the Mac IIsi's video slot and runs under software control. For the Mac IIsi, Lapis provides a Display Server IIsi-FPD board that drives the world of DOS PC and FPD monitor offerings. Vendors with existing NuBus video cards—Micron Technology, Radius, RasterOps,

11 Martin Marshall and Anne Kaliczak, "Connecting a Mac LC to a VGA Monitor," *Infoworld*, 3/11/91, p. 38.

and SuperMac—all tested their products to work with the Mac IIsi as did the vendors of existing SE 30 PDS products—Ehman, E-Machines, Nutmeg, and Radius. Power budgets were found to be extremely tight. Do yourself a favor and check for the latest on this before you buy would be my counsel.

Other video solutions

I told you all along that you need an SE 30 or NuBus Mac to run color. Well, not exactly. Aura Systems Scuzzy Graph shown in Fig. 8-15 lets you add color to your Mac Plus, SE, Classic, even your Mac Portable! At only $695, it is an economical option that works with most industry standard monitors including Apple's 13-inch RGB Color, Portrait, and VGA monitors plus Aura's own 19-inch color and monochrome monitors. It attaches to your Mac SCSI port and handily sits under your Macintosh just like a zero footprint hard disk case would, or it sits under your monitor or next to your Mac Portable. The SCSI interface allows it to be used on older, clip-on Macs as well as shared or moved as you upgrade to newer Macs. It is quite a nifty, handy device, and you don't lose anything in the bargain—well worth a look in my book.

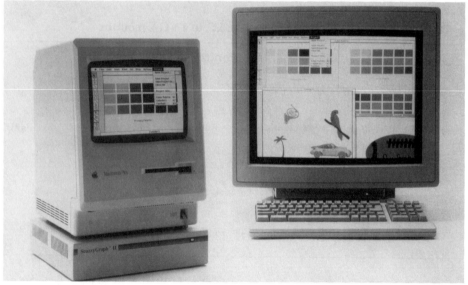

Aura Systems

8-15 ScuzzyGraph Color Display interface.

In a nutshell

Here are the key points from this chapter:

- After your hard disk, the next most rewarding improvement you can make is to your video monitor and interface adapter. Regardless of what type you choose, chances are it will be larger than Apple's traditional 9-inch offering.

There is nothing wrong with the Apple offering—the test of time has proven it—but in video monitors, bigger is almost always better.

- Shop around, ask questions, look at as many different monitors as possible, and then make your decision. Skimp in other areas, but get the best monitor your budget will allow. Only one set of eyeballs per person per lifetime, so you decide.
- A 14-inch monitor or a one-page or full-page monitor is better than the Mac's own 9-inch screen. But two-page monitors are better only if you need its extra capability. The same is true with color. Don't get color unless you need it, then get the best you can afford.
- Make sure your accelerator board is compatible with your video card. Better still, get them at the same time along with the monitor so you know the entire package works the way you want it to.
- And now you know too, that if you offered me a Radius Pivot monitor for sale at a good price, I would probably follow you anywhere.

Sources

Some video adapter sources are:

Aura Systems
P.O. Box 4576
Carlsbad, CA 92008
(619) 440-2304

Data Translation
100 Locke Dr.
Marlboro, MA 01752
(508) 485-3322

Lapis Technologies
1210 Marina Village Pkwy., #100
Alameda, CA 94501
(415) 748-1600

Mass Microsystems
810 W. Maude Ave.
Sunnyvale, CA 94086
(800) 522-7979
(408) 522-1200

Mobius Technologies
5835 Doyle St.
Emeryville, CA 94608
(800) 669-0556
(415) 654-0556

Power R
1606 Dexter Ave. North
Seattle, WA 98109
(206) 547-8000

Some video monitor sources are:

Cutting Edge Inc.
97 S. Red Willow Rd.
Evanston, WY 82930
(307) 789-0582

Ehman Engineering Inc.
P.O. Box 2126
Evanston, WY 82931
(800) 257-1666

E-Machines
9305 SW Gemini Dr.
Beaverton, OR 97005
(503) 646-6699

In Focus Systems
7770 SW Mohawk St.
Tualatin, OR 97062
(503) 692-4968

MegaGraphics
439 Calle San Pablo
Camarillo, CA 93010
(805) 484-3799

NEC Technologies
1255 Michael Dr.
Wood Dale, IL 60191
(800) 826-2255
(708) 860-9500

Optimal Technology
650 Main St.
Amhearst, MA 01002
(800) 637-0088

Planar Systems
1400 NW Compton Dr.
Beaverton, OR 97006
(503) 690-1100

Princeton Graphic Systems
601 Ewing St., #A
Princeton, NJ 08540
(609) 683-1660

Radius
1710 Fortune Dr.
San Jose, CA 95131
(408) 434-1010

RasterOps
2500 Walsh Ave.
Santa Clara, CA 95051
(800) 468-7600

Sigma Designs
46501 Landing Pkwy.
Fremont, CA 94538
(800) 933-9945
(415) 770-0110

SuperMac Technology
485 Potrero Ave.
Sunnyvale, CA 94086
(408) 245-2202

Chapter 9
Input/output options

The preceding chapters covered CPU and memory, storage, and display options, which are the most crucial areas in terms of improving the performance of your Macintosh. Input and output options are different. Most input/output options do not affect the performance of your Mac directly; they improve it as part of a total picture, custom-tailor it for specific applications, or connect it to the outside world. Some options do directly affect performance, like high-speed I/O options or multimedia. Other options are more aesthetic. Hey, do you want a chartreuse keyboard to match your paisley drapes? By all means, go ahead. The options for aesthetically enhancing your Mac are unlimited.

Chapter 5 introduced the fact that outside conditions could impose constraints on your Mac upgrade decisions. The communications and networking areas covered in this chapter are prime examples. Whether you must interface into an AppleTalk or Ethernet network, maintain a direct link into the corporate mainframe, dial information services, or send faxes, at some point there will be constraints imposed on you by your environment. If you've equipped your whole company with one kind of option card and standardized on it because of the network you own, it is very difficult to suggest upgrading to another type of Macintosh for which that option card doesn't exist. This is a constraint with a capital "C."

Input/output affects your Mac in four areas. I'll cover each of these areas from the upgrade option point of view and provide my recommendations. In this chapter, because of the sheer numbers of options available, all I can do is sketch briefly some of what's available and leave you to do further research as to what best suits your needs. The final decision is always up to you, but you have an enormous amount of help here because there are many outstanding publications (*MacWEEK*, *MacUser*, *Macworld*, etc.) to help keep you posted on the latest changes. Also the sources cited at the end of the chapter are an excellent place to gather information. Here are the four areas this chapter focuses on:

- *Input data* How you get most of the data into your Mac. A keyboard and pointing device is used on all Macs; a scanner is used for graphics or text input if you have a lot of information or must do it quickly.
- *Audio and video* Voice input is standard on Apple's newest mid-range Macs but available on almost all using optional accessories; MIDI and multimedia are upward extensions of this capability also requiring specialized hardware and software.
- *High speed* Processing and control requires using its own special hardware and software on your Mac.
- *Communication and networking* How your Mac communicates and connects to other computers and peripherals across the room or around the world, whether it be AppleTalk connectors, Ethernet cards, adapter boards, modems, or whatever.

Input data

When Apple first introduced the Macintosh your choices were simple. There was one type of keyboard and one type of mouse. Not so today. Apple offers three types of keyboards and two types of mice, plus a keyboard and trackball for the Mac Portable. Third-party keyboard and pointing device makers offer numerous alternatives to Macintosh owners. All this, of course, is a benefit. The chances are that you can find a keyboard and mouse whose performance really pleases you and meets your specific needs. For the data input area, it all boils down to personal preference and matching the tools you need to the job you have to do. First, a brief detour on how they are connected to your Macintosh.

ADB versus non-ADB

There are only two games in town on both the keyboard and the mouse. They are *Apple Desktop Bus* (ADB) and *non-ADB*. On the Mac 128, 512, and Plus, you need a non-ADB keyboard and mouse. For use with every other Mac, you need an ADB keyboard and mouse.

The Mac 128, 512, and Plus models (the clip-on Macs) communicate with the keyboard and mouse over separate interfaces. The keyboard has its own cord, very similar to a coiled telephone handset cord with RJ11 plugs on each end, that plugs into the front of the Mac. The mouse has a DB9 connector on the end that plugs into the back of the Mac.

The Apple Desktop Bus is now the Apple standard serial communication bus that allows you to connect up to 15 ADB input devices such as keyboard, mouse, joystick, puck, other pointing/motion devices, and graphics tablets to your SE and newer Macintosh. It allows the devices to be connected in daisychain fashion. Your mouse can be connected to the side of the keyboard (left or right) easiest for you to work. Devices are connected using mini 8-pin connectors, ADB keyboards typically have two, Mac SE and up models have two (only one on the newest Macs), and mouse-type pointing devices come with their own single plug. The bottom line to you is increased flexibility at minimal increase in cost.

Keyboards, keyboards, keyboards

For most of us, the keyboard is the main method of getting information into our Mac, in addition to controlling what it does. You have to live with your choice of keyboard daily, therefore the keyboard selection process is quite personalized and "aesthetic" variables usually enter into the decision process in addition to the normal "functional" choices.[1]

Non-ADB keyboards are available from mail order, used equipment resellers, and Apple dealers as a spare or replacement part because Apple no longer sells the clip-on Mac models. Apple Mac Plus keyboards with the numeric keypad are typically priced at $99. The increased capability, PC look and feel, extended keyboard from Datadesk goes for $119 and up. Used keyboards can be had for $50 or so.

Apple offers its standard ADB Keyboard (M0116) and ADB Extended Keyboard II (M0312), priced at $129 and $229, respectively, as add-ons for its Macintosh SE and up models. (Apple upgraded its Extended Keyboard at no price

---

[1] Mark Brownstein, "Keyboards Evolve at a Slow Pace," *Infoworld*, 1/8/90, p. 19.

increase to meet current international ergonomic standards. The new model features continuous slope adjustment, from 6 to 14 degrees at the user's preference.)
Figure 9-1 compares Apple's standard ADB Keyboard (front) with its non-ADB
Mac Plus keyboard. Figure 9-2 compares all of Apple's current ADB keyboards:
the new keyboard shipped with the Mac Classic (front), standard keyboard (middle) and extended keyboard (rear).

9-1   The Apple standard ADB keyboard (front) versus the Mac Plus keyboard.

The main third-party ADB keyboards providers are: Cutting Edge/Ehman,[2]
Datadesk, and Key Tronics at around $99 to $159 mail order. Datadesk's Switchboard has to be the most innovative of the current Mac keyboards.[3] This product
offers you the modules, keyboard, keypad, function keys, etc., and lets you "create" your own. Creation has its price, however. My recommendations are:

- MacPro   Key Tronics manufactures my current keyboard of choice shown
  in Fig. 9-3. My wife, who is a power typist, found it very comfortable with
  an amazingly quick key rollover that's like having another gear available in
  your transmission! As for myself, a two-finger typing specialist, I never

---

[2] Cutting Edge and Ehman are two sides to the same company. Cutting Edge sells to dealers and distributors who resell their products. Ehman sells direct via mail order. Sometimes Cutting Edge's
price offered through dealers is lower!

[3] Ric Ford and Rick LePage, "Datadesk takes new approach to keyboard design," *MacWEEK*, 9/11/
90, p. 47; Patrick Lyons, "Datadesk's Switchboard Ushers in the Age of Modular Keyboards," *Infoworld*, 8/20/90, p. 75; and Dale Coleman, "Datadesk's modular keyboard with slots lets Mac, PC
users do it their way," *MacWEEK*, 4/24/90, p. 14.

9-2 Apple ADB keyboards: Classic (front), Standard (middle), Extended (rear).

9-3 Professional Series MacPro Plus keyboard.

KeyTronic

found that gear, but this keyboard has a nice touch and feel to it plus my big fingers found the oversized Return key handy. The extra function keys allowed me to easily move around in Word.[4]

- Power Key   From Sophisticated Circuits, it is shown in Fig. 9-4. Hey, this is not a keyboard at all. Right, it's a handy little device, pre-Mac II family, ADB keyboard owners can use to get the same benefits of easy power turn-on of your Mac from your keyboard. That's what the button at the top center of all Apple's standard ADB keyboards and top right of every vendor's extended ADB keyboard is for. Plus you get extra switched outlets, surge protection, and software that lets you start up your Mac at specific times or on a regular schedule—neat.[5]

Sophisticated Circuits

9-4   Power Key automatic Mac power turn-on device.

What keyboard should you choose? You can read about every keyboard made, but there is no substitute for hands-on experience. I would never buy a keyboard without first trying it. If you live near a city populated with computer stores, your task

---

[4] Dale Coleman, "Keytronic keyboard welcome alternative to Apple board," *MacWEEK*, 9/26/89, p. 69. At least one other person agrees with me.

[5] Henry Norr, "Third parties bring keyboard startup to SE," *MacWEEK*, 5/15/90, p. 14.

is somewhat easier. Go into a store and try them. Return policies being offered by most mail order suppliers also make the try-before-buy option easy, although if you return every keyboard you order, they will probably ask you to shop somewhere else.

Pointing the way

Unlike the keyboard, few of us, if anyone, were familiar with pointing technology— or a mouse—until Apple popularized it first with the Lisa computer, and then with the Macintosh in the early 1980s. The *mouse* is an object about the size of a small bar of soap with one or more *buttons* on it that you typically hold in your hand and use to control the movement of a *cursor* arrow on the computer screen. When combined with software featuring pull-down menus and icons, it is the key element that makes the Macintosh easy to learn and easy to use. All you have to do is point and click.

Let's talk about conventional mice first. Apple and Mouse Systems are the main providers for both ADB and non-ADB mouse devices. This would include Apple's mechanical mouse, a product of the early 1980s that, with minor improvements, still sells today, and Mouse Systems' optical mouse (more than one million optical mice sold) whose earliest predecessor was first introduced in 1982. Look at Fig. 9-5 to get an idea of the relative differences between them. The standard Apple ADB mouse is on the right, the new ADB Little Mouse from Mouse Systems is on the left.

A rubber coated steel ball in the mechanical mouse turns between two rollers as the mouse is moved and sends x and y electrical direction signals back to a chip

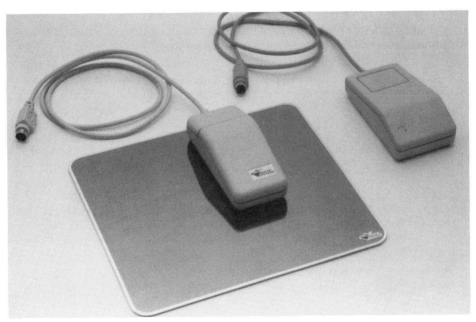

9-5 Mouse Systems Optical Mouse (left) and Apple Standard Mouse.

on the logic board. It's a relative motion device that communicates the direction and distance it has moved—not its location. Typically, it is used on a *mouse pad*, purchased separately by the user, that cushions and protects it, gives it a stable surface to roll on.

As seen in Fig. 9-5, an optical mouse comes with its own special mouse pad. The special mouse pad has a nonreflective x-y grid laid over a highly reflective mirrored surface both sandwiched together under a layer of optically transparent plastic and bonded to a rubberized backing layer. Inside the mouse, a photodetector senses changes in the light reflected back off the mirror pad from its LED source, and sends relative motion x and y electrical direction signals back to a chip on the logic board. Because there are no moving parts and nothing to wear out or clean, Mouse Systems claims a 30-year MTBF and offers a lifetime warranty.

The Apple ADB mouse, part number 661-0338, is available from Apple dealers as a spare part for around $90. The ADB Little Mouse from Mouse Systems typically goes for about $75. I recommend Little Mouse from Mouse Systems. Being a long-time Apple mechanical mouse user, both ADB and pre-ADB, I found the optical mouse extremely gratifying to use, once I got the hang of it. It took a couple of days of getting used to, but after that, the effortless ease of use, the better pointing accuracy, and the thought of no moving parts wearing out and not having to take it apart and clean it periodically, made me a convert.

On the other hand, Apple's new ADB mouse sports a new teflon pad and improved internal design to reduce wear in a new shape that provides a real solid feel. What mouse should you buy? Again, I would advise a try-before-buy approach.

Eek, a mouse invasion

Or, more correctly, an unconventional pointing device explosion. There has been a dramatic increase in the numbers and types of pointing devices available to attach to your Macintosh. Entire articles have been devoted to them.[6] You can now choose from all sorts of mice,[7] trackballs,[8] and graphics tablets.[9] More devices appear on publishers' press release stacks weekly. Here are a few of them that I would recommend:

- Felix from Altra   This is a low-profile 5-inch-square device with a knob-like device in the middle of it, like the lid you would have on a kitchen pot if it were square. Upon closer inspection, the knob-like device is actually a fin-

---

[6] Stuart Silverstein, "Mouse, input options multiply," *MacWEEK*, 6/5/90, p. 51; Chris Ferino, "Four Alternative Input Devices," *Macworld*, May 1990, p. 394; Ben Templin, "Four Alternatives to a Mouse," *Computer Shopper*, February 1990, p. 614; and Jane Berliss and Peter Borden, "Building a Better Mouse," *MacUser*, October 1989, p 124.

[7] Brian Gillooly, "New faces for the mouse," *Computer Reseller News*, 12/11/89, p. 71.

[8] Tracey Capen, "Shopping for a Mouse? Trackballs are a Viable Alternative," *Infoworld*, 2/26/90, p. 72.

[9] Timothy E. Johnson, "Closer to that pen-and-paper feel," *MacWEEK*, 4/24/90, p. 45.

gertip control enabling you to direct extremely smooth and precise movements of the cursor on your Mac screen while your fingertips never leave a 1-inch square "action" area. No matter how unique it looks, it works great—so good that the astronauts took it aboard a shuttle mission.[10]

- Unmouse from Microtouch   This is a simple device. Only your finger on a horizontal 3- × -4½-inch tablet that has a 1000- × -1000 point resolution. It is capacitance driven, just like the flat electronics control panel on your kitchen microwave. Unlike your microwave's panel, when you touch the pad a cursor appears on the screen and moves in precisely the way you guide it. It works great, plus has many unique features like its ability to let you program areas on it to act as keys or the entire tablet to emulate a 16-key keypad.[11] Figure 9-6 shows it with its keypad templates.

- Expert Mouse from Kensington   This is not a mouse—it's a trackball. I'm not particularly a trackball fan, but the oversize ball, smooth motion, and easy left or right-handed control at least made me a believer. Kensington, a household word in the accessories field, has sold this unit to the DOS PC world for some time and has done its homework well. It is shown next to a standard Apple keyboard in Fig. 9-7.

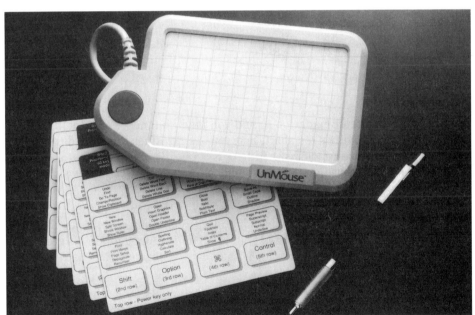

MicroTouch

9-6   UnMouse Mac pointing device.

---

10 Henry Norr, "Mac Portable, Felix aboard *Discovery* for cursor testing," *MacWEEK*, 10/16/90, p. 6; Yvonne Lee, "Altra Ships Point Device Alternative," *Infoworld*, 3/12/90, p. 24; Henry Norr, "Felix now chasing SE and II mouse users," *MacWEEK*, 9/26/89, p. 18.

11 Mark Brownstein, "Unmouse Keypad, Works With Stylus, Fingertip Input," *Infoworld*, 9/17/90, p. 24.

Kensington

9-7 Expert mouse trackball.

What keyboard or pointing device should you buy? You must make the final decision. Just remember, life's too short, and you are not stuck with the devices that came with your Apple Macintosh. Although I might quickly add that the Apple Mac keyboard and mouse products are among the best offered.

Scanning the future

The earliest scanners were crude, clumsy, inefficient, and error-prone. Today, all that has changed. Whether you have text, a drawing, a photograph, or even color materials to input, you can do it much faster with a scanner and the results are simply breathtaking!

A scanner is nothing more than a copying machine whose results go to an electronic digitized storage media rather than the printed page. Copier companies have offered models with both of these capabilities for some time. At its simplest, you scan a line of your input document and transmit the light or dark information you receive to another device for storage and later interpretation. The early Mac ThunderScan scanners displayed this principle quite openly and even required your Apple ImageWriter printer as part of its mechanism.

Your scanner should at least handle 256 shades of gray today, and color is a nice touch. If you have to input a lot of text or if you have to massage line art or photographs on your Macintosh for a living, upgrading your Mac with a good scanner and software is a sound investment that will pay for itself in a short time. I'll leave you to read about and investigate the options in hand scanners[12] at the low end and slide and color scanners[13] at the high end and focus on the mainstream,[14] mid-range scanners that can do it all at a nominal price. As always you must make the final decision. I have two recommendations:

- Apple Scanner (A9M0337) at $1799 list. It certainly is not the prettiest, the fastest, the newest, or the most expensive, but it works reliably and is foolproof and bulletproof. I have used one for years. It's a flatbed-type scanner, and I appreciate its ability to accommodate legal size 8½ × 14 inch documents in one pass. It comes with great software for scanning graphics. Because most of my work is text and line art, I couldn't care less about it only being a 4-bit scanner.[15] Actually, what made it fantastic for me was the OmniPage OCR (Optical Character Recognition) software from Caere.[16] I had searched for years (at one point almost buying a $10,000 Kurzweil DOS PC scanner) until finding this painless software product that I have used since its version 1.0 release (now 2.1). Earlier software either didn't work(!) or required you to "train" it to read—a painstaking process at best. This does it all at the touch of a button. At $795 list, it pays for itself in a short time.
- Hewlett-Packard ScanJet Plus at $2190 list with Mac interface is also a flatbed scanner. Versus the Apple model, this unit has 8-bit capability, gives you 256 shades of gray, has 8½ × 11 inch letter capability rather than legal, and offers an outstanding document feeder option in place of its standard top cover lid. On the down side, I thought the Mac interface was poorly designed—you wind up with three different boxes: scanner, Mac interface, and interface power supply. You also have to pull the plug to turn off power to the Mac interface! On the upside, the software is really good, even better than Apple's, and 8 bits does make a difference if you mainly work with graphics rather than text. Figure 9-8 shows it.

You have to choose a scanner to suit your needs. Here again it really helps if you can try a few before you decide. If there is a copy shop or graphics shop near you with a scanner you can try out and ask questions about, by all means, grab the opportunity.

---

[12] Eric J. Adams, "Hand-held scanners still novelties," *MacWEEK*, 1/22/91, p. 22; Pamela Pfiffner, "Caere takes OCR in hand," *MacWEEK*, 8/7/90, p. 1; and Pamela Pfiffner, "Getting a grip on new hand-held scanners," *MacWEEK*, 5/8/90, p. 11.

[13] John Ronga and Luther Sperberg, "Color Scanners, Pick from a Growing Field," *Macworld*, August 1990, p. 152.

[14] Owen W. Linzmayer, "An inside look at Scanners," *MacUser*, September 1990, p. 132;

[15] Actually Abaton offers an 8-bit upgrade for the Apple unit bundled with photo software at $595. Read David L. Foster, "Apple Scanner Upgrade Kit," *Macworld*, May 1990, p. 369.

[16] Philip Robinson and MacUser Labs staff, "Character Witnesses," *MacUser*, July 1990, p. 120. This article contrasts Caere's automatic OCR approach versus the trainable OCR programs.

Hewlett-Packard Company

9-8 ScanJet Plus scanner.

Audio and video

To write all there is to say about Macintosh audio and video would take another book in itself. Hmm.... In the audio/video I/O niche, a phenomenal number of tools exist to customize your Mac beyond your wildest dreams.

Mr. Bell, is that you?

Regardless of what was said when Alexander Graham Bell first tinkered with his telephone device, being able to transmit voice was a tremendous breakthrough. The new Mac LC and Mac IIsi bring Apple's latest innovation of built-in recording circuitry, and each includes a microphone. Previously, you bought Farallon's MacRecorder if you wanted to add this capability to your Mac. Scotty would not have to talk into his Mac mouse as he did in the scene from the *Star Trek IV* movie featuring the save the whales plot; he could use the real Mac LC microphone I am holding in my hand in Fig. 9-9.

Being able to understand spoken voice input commands, store voice with your text, play it back with a mouse click, or transmit it on a floppy diskette or over a network is also a tremendous breakthrough. These voice hardware/software products are here now. Voice Navigator II from Articulate Systems[17] and Voice Express from MacSema,[18] with their ability to recognize (after a brief training period) a rea-

---

[17] Henry Norr, "Articulate making itself heard with Voice Link, new Navigator," *MacWEEK*, 8/7/90, p. 16.

[18] Raines Cohen and Henry Norr, "MacSema's $499 Voice Express puts speech recognition on NuBus," *MacWEEK*, 5/15/90, p.14.

9-9 The Apple microphone for the Mac LC

sonable spoken (by you) vocabulary should prove quite useful in many applications areas. Voice Link from Articulate Systems enables you to integrate voice messaging, voice annotation, and sound into your mainstream Mac applications at the click of a button.

Make your own kind of music

If you've been in a music store recently you know you can't walk very far without bumping into a MIDI (Musical Instrument Device Interface) on a musical instrument. Although today's musical instruments resemble stereo devices (and are heading toward Sony Walkmans in size) rather than keyboards, the store manager will be happy to tell you that Macintoshes are an industry standard (he'll also mention Atari).[19] If you keep the conversation going, you'll also learn that many instruments can be connected to your Mac that let you enjoy the luxury of recording the notes you play on your instrument, then playing them through your Mac—with the results displayed on your Mac's screen in music notation. This ability is the product of Apple's Mac hardware design and its MIDI Manager System level software.

---

[19] An early 1990 *Keyboard* magazine survey showed 25% of readers owned Macs, 21% Atari, 19% Commodore, and 26% DOS PCs. When questioned about new 1990 purchases, 50% said they would buy Macs, 19% Atari, 2% Commodore, and 23% DOS PC. Something is definitely happening in Mac-musicland!

The process is straightforward. You take your music keyboard (with sampled sound module, etc.) and/or other instrument with MIDI interface, connect it to Apple's MIDI interface (A9M0103) at $99 list or a third-party MIDI box (DigiDesign, Opcode Systems, and Mark of the Unicorn provide special multi-input adapters), and then connect the MIDI interface box to your Mac. On your Mac, you need to add sequencing software such as that provided by Opcode Systems (EZ Vision, Vision, StudioVision) or Mark of the Unicorn (Performer) or Steinberg/Jones (Cubase). If you add a Digidesign Audiomedia NuBus card and its optional Deck[20] software package, you have a complete four-track digital recorder/mixer for preserving your masterpieces to audio tape.[21]

Launch the software, dial in the right musical instrument(s) and recording track(s), click record, and start playing. After you are done, click stop and immediately click save. That's all there is to it. Now you can edit what you've played note by note, change instruments or tempo, or transpose your composition into a different key. Even more software is available to help you edit your electronic compositions as you would edit and format word processing documents and drawings into a finished publication. The possibilities are endless. If you have some talent and aptitude, this is a wide open field you can try. Some Mac musicians in my local area subsidize their music habit by renting time in their Macintosh digital recording and editing studio to others. Regardless of your ultimate use, this is an upgrade you can certainly enjoy.

Light and sound

Light added to sound introduces yet another dimension. To manipulate digitized sound (20 kHz signals) requires CPU horsepower and plenty of storage space. To manipulate moving digital images in color (5 MHz and up signals), you're talking about some serious CPU horsepower and large storage space. That's why you start hearing about dedicated signal processors and image compression algorithms. As you have seen in the CPU area, hardware is one thing—software takes a while to catch up. The gains introduced by the Motorola 68000 in 1979 are still being digested by the software in 1991. The same applies here. Text processing is well in hand today, sound is almost getting there, but the best video processing software taking advantage of all the Mac's features is still to come.

Apple is staking the company on it. And I believe rightly so. Why shouldn't it be as easy to cut and paste a full-motion color video image clip together on your Mac and send it to another computer halfway around the world as it is with a paragraph of text? The challenge is to combine text, still and animated video and sound

---

[20] *MacUser* in its 6th Annual Editors' Choice awards, March 1991, p. 104, rated Deck from DigiDesign the best music product and gave honorable mentions to MacProteus from DigiDesign and Encore from Passport Designs.

[21] Here are some great articles for your further study: Bruce F. Webster, "Making Music," *Macworld*, March 1991, p. 85; Christopher Yavelow, "Digital Audio at Last," *Macworld*, February 1991, p. 161; and Ken Gruberman and Lon McQuillan, "Multimedia and Audio," *MacUser*, February 1991, p. BG38.

and voice (prerecorded and synthesized) in efficient and profitable new ways. Apple covers it all under the umbrella of *multimedia*. However, even that term fails to totally encompass the broad nature of this market—and your upgrade possibilities.

At the one end you can take snapshots with your electronic camera and import the results directly into your Mac for electronic editing. You can watch TV in a section of your larger Mac screen while you go about your other Macintosh duties. You can capture images from TV or video tape and edit them. You can use your Mac to edit raw videotapes into finished videotapes at either the home-video or the industrial-quality level. You can display brilliant images in 24-bit color after scanning them in from a color scanner and output the results to a color printer. You can create, animate, and colorize your productions and caption them with sound. You can store your finished product featuring images of faraway places and accompanying dialog on laser disks for use by travel agencies as a sales promotion device. You can produce detailed HyperCard stacks on CD-ROM for training manuals complete with sound annotation. There is no end in sight as far as you can look, and the horizons are receding ever more rapidly!

Looking at the shopping list of the preceding paragraph makes you start thinking, doesn't it? Surely you could find a use for a technology that lets you combine film, animation, speech, music, graphics, and pictures in digital form that can then be edited into full-motion video within your business, department, or company. Yup, you could, and that's the problem. Where do you start?

A few categories are in order. Let's do the familiar ones: input, processing, display, storage, and output. Your input is coming from live TV, video camera (still or moving), VCR, laser disk, CD-ROM, or scanner plus sound. To process it, you have option cards that capture the image, compress/decompress it, accelerate the speed of the color display to view it, convert it from/to a standard video format, and display live TV along with your video image, and coprocessor cards that accelerate the entire process or any part. To display it, you have your standard Mac digital display plus an NTSC compatible monitor—or maybe they are one and the same. To store it you have large, fast hard disks for your working storage. Output is to erasable optical disks for transmission or backup, or to a video tape or color printer. Your mission is to select the options you need from each of these categories. I won't do injustice to the area by attempting to tell you all you need to know in a paragraph or two. Besides, then you would miss all the fun of looking. Here are a few of the best articles to get you started.[22]

High speed

While multimedia takes center stage, the Macintosh processing and control field is totally unknown to most Mac users. Yet a highly visible (and vocal—just ask

---

[22] Peter S. Marx and Franklin N. Tessler, "Mac Video, Take II," *Macworld*, February, 1991, p. 178; Peter S. Marx and Franklin N. Tessler, "Prime Time Video," *Macworld*, September 1990, p. 206; and Lon McQuillan, "Multimedia and Video," *MacUser*, February 1991, p. BG4. Honorable Mention Radius TV, MU, 3/91, 102.

Apple!)[23] community of educators, researchers, scientists, and engineers consider the Mac as only another processing and control platform.

In this field, one that requires its own dedicated upgrade options because of its special needs, the action (from DC to hundreds of MHz) can take place rapidly and you need to be there to observe, record, and/or control it. Unlike the other "sanitary" Mac application areas, where if you need a piece of hardware or software you go to a store or mail order catalog and buy it, the leading edge innovators in this market segment must break out their soldering irons out of necessity to "build" from scratch or roll up their shirt-sleeves to program their own software control code. It is a different world.

Monitor and control

In this field, you are measuring "something," displaying or printing it, then storing the results and analyzing what you have. If it's a process control application, you're doing all the above in real-time plus providing a feedback control signal to keep the process on track. One way to categorize this area is by speed. You have the slower IEEE-488 or GPIB cards and the devices that attach to the Mac via the serial port; then the mainstream cards that attach directly to the SE, SE30, or NuBus slots; then the high-speed I/O cards. Then you need the software to run it. Hardware cards have the capability for:

- Connecting directly to a lab instrument—IEEE-488 or GPIB cards.
- Analog input or output, high level (volts) or low level (millivolts).
- Digital input or output.

The lab instrument standard

Of the thousands of laboratory instruments, most adhere to the IEEE-488 or GPIB (General Purpose Interface Bus) standard.[24] By plugging in a card to your SE or Mac II that has this interface capability, the Mac instantly becomes a controller for laboratory testing, production testing, and process monitoring and control equipment that utilize this interface. IEEE-488 cards are available from:

- GW Instruments (MacAdios 488NuBus, MacAdios 488SCSI).
- IOtech (Mac488Serial, Mac488SCSI, Mac488NuBus).
- National Instruments (GPIB-SE, GPIB-SE 30, GPIB-NuBus).

In addition, many companies make complete systems or packages that attach through the Mac's serial ports. These systems or packages would be suitable for use on older 512 and Plus Macs:

- Biopac Systems (MacPacQ Model MP10).

---

[23] Apple wisely established the Consortium for Laboratory & Industrial Applications of the Macintosh and takes input from this user group very seriously. It numbers many Fortune 500 members in its ranks.

[24] A new standard has recently been introduced, VXI, that promises faster, more flexible, and eventually less expensive ways to connect instruments and controllers.

- GW Instruments (MacAdios Model 411).
- IDAC (IDAC/1000).
- Remote Measurement Systems (ADC-1 Data Acquisition & Control System).
- World Precision Instruments (MacLab).

SE, SE 30, or NuBus I/O

These cards let you design your own customized I/O system. Manufacturers include:

- GW Instruments.
- IOtech.
- Keithley/Metrabyte.
- National Instruments.
- Strawberry Tree.

The following cards let you do a high-speed I/O system or process data faster once you have it. Manufacturers include:

- Data Translation (Topflight)—data acquisition at 750 kHz.
- Dolphin Scientific (Desktop Signal Processor)—25 to 450 Mflops.
- National Instruments (NB-DSP-2300)—33 Mflops.
- Spectral Innovations (MacDSP)—25 Mflops.

Mac I/O control software

These companies provide I/O control software for the Macintosh:

- GW Instruments (MacAdios Manager II, MacInstruments, Superscope).
- IDAC (Macontrol).
- National Instruments (LabVIEW 2).[25]
- Strawberry Tree (Workbench Mac 3.0).

There you have it—a brief snapshot and overview of the Macintosh processing and control field. In this area, I have no doubts that you'll be doing more homework.

Communications and networking

Networking and communications are where the Macintosh really shines. When Macintosh was first introduced to corporations, the concept that sold it was the Mac Plus, the LaserWriter, and AppleTalk. The idea that a work group could share or network an expensive (at that time) LaserWriter peripheral among a number of individual Macintoshes was the seed idea that sold Macintosh into corporations—at first through the back door and then through the main gates. Today, any

---

[25] Roger Wilson, "Mac IIfx, LabVIEW helps trace shuttle leak," *MacWEEK*, 6/19/90, p. 9; The most visible, probably the *de facto* standard in Mac Laboratory software. *MacUser* in its 6th Annual Editors Choice awards, March 1991, p. 103, rated it best data acquisition analysis product.

Macintosh you buy already has AppleTalk on it. There is nothing more to add except a simple external connector—the little one shown on the cover of this book. All your networking is done for you. All you have to do is hook up a few cables, add some software, and you're done. That's the beauty of the Mac.

Apple's adoption of Ethernet, the industry standard for higher-speed networking, is merely an extension of Apple's networking commitment. It offers more speed and greater performance while remaining equally transparent to the user as AppleTalk is today. In the future, any Mac you buy will have Ethernet already built-in.[26]

As the new kid on the block in the established corporations of America, the Macintosh was barred from entry unless it could connect with and talk to the existing machines already there. The Mac had to be better than anything else—just to get in the door! Recognizing this need, Macintosh developers focused first on DOS PC connectivity, then connectivity to mainframes and minicomputers. The result is that Macintosh connectivity and products are today superior to those for any other computer.

AppleTalk

You will probably be using and deriving the benefits from AppleTalk long before you know about it—especially if you hook an Apple PostScript LaserWriter up to your Mac. (Technically, LocalTalk, the hardware provided by Apple, is what lets you connect a group of Macs to a LaserWriter. Apple's AppleTalk network-protocol system is built into every Mac. But I will blur the distinction and go with the more common usage here.) You probably will not think about AppleTalk or connectivity until you add a second Mac and begin to think about networking the two Macs together.

AppleTalk was perhaps one of the best kept secrets at Apple. Nobody touted it until one day (probably around the time the AppleTalk PC card was announced as a product) somebody noticed that you got AppleTalk as a by-product of buying any Macintosh, whereas it was a separate card that had to be added to a DOS PC.

Because of this phenomenon, you will be pleasantly surprised when you find out all you need to get your network up and running is another connector and two TOPS software packages (they are serialized), one for each Mac. Making the connection and copying the software onto the two Macs should take you about 15 to 30 minutes—tops! And you are in the networking business—bona fide, big time. Copy files, share data, knock yourself out.

One computer retailer had a sales training exercise where the one sales team set up an entire five-station AppleTalk network and had it running before the other team was even able to get a single DOS networking card installed in the first DOS PC. Then they changed sides with the same results. So hands down, one would have to conclude that AppleTalk is a better idea. It certainly is simpler to use and definitely easier to install and get running. In all fairness to the DOS PC product

---

[26] John Rizzo and Jon Zilber, "How I learned to stop worrying and love connectivity: Networking the '90s," *MacUser*, January 1991, p. 93. An outstanding overview article.

area, at the high-end Apple networking software definitely lacks the bells and whistles of a Novell NetWare or Banyan Vines product. However, Apple Macintosh owners will soon have numerous options available to them from all the high-end DOS PC network vendors: Banyan, 3Com Corp, Microsoft, and Novell.[27]

Head for port

What do you need to upgrade your Mac to network it using AppleTalk? The answer is a Farallon PhoneNET[28] connector (or its equivalent from a number of third-party vendors) and a length of standard telephone cable. Figure 9-10 shows the whole story. Even your serial ImageWriter dot matrix printer can have an AppleTalk interface added to it to be used on a network as shown in Fig. 9-11.

9-10 Sitka (formerly TOPS) AppleTalk products for Macintosh.

9-11 AppleTalk interface for ImageWriter dot matrix printer.

---

[27] Margie Wylie, "Network Giants lumber Mac-ward," *MacWEEK*, 9/18/90, p. 1.

[28] PhoneNET has basically supplanted Apple's LocalTalk hardware standard because of its many advantages: less expensive, supports higher speeds, longer cable runs, uses standard telephone cables and modular jacks, and interfaces with phone system wiring already in most buildings.

There are two kinds of PhoneNET connectors, depending on the connectors used by your Mac's serial ports. Older Macs, original LaserWriters, and DOS PC cards use the 9-pin type. Today's Macs and printers all use the circular-8 connector. The cable is standard 4-wire telephone cable with RJ11 modular plugs on each end. PhoneNET lets you run up to 3000 total feet of cable in your network before you need a repeater. If you have DOS PCs on your network, the Sitka TOPS FlashCard (or equivalent) needs to be installed in the DOS PCs; the PhoneNET connector then hooks up to it. Add a copy of Sitka TOPS software for each computer on the network, and you are in business.[29]

Ethernet

Ethernet is not new to Macintosh. Dove, Kinetics (now Shiva), and others have made Mac connectivity products for it for years. Only Apple's formal endorsement and definition of it for the Macintosh world by the introduction of its own products is new. When you look at the overall picture, Apple's adoption of it is not that surprising.[30]

AppleTalk (LocalTalk) supports transmission at 230 kilobits per second while Ethernet supports transmission at 10 megabits per second. Ethernet is a super-highway compared to Apple's LocalTalk two-lane highway in terms of its data-moving ability. Ethernet is also the industry standard and is widely used by all computer manufacturers. Apple's LocalTalk and its offshoots are the standard within the Macintosh community. Today's more powerful Macintoshes, faster hard disks, more powerful video and graphics software applications demand the ability to transfer larger amounts of data at a faster rate. AppleTalk is not able to satisfy this need, but Ethernet can.[31]

Let's talk about Ethernet cabling for a moment. Ethernet traditionally supported "thick" and "thin" coaxial cabling. Thick cabling, 10Base5 (RG 8—50 ohm coax) supported runs up to 3280 feet. Thin cabling, 10Base2 (RG 58—50 ohm coax) supported runs up to 1000 feet. With the approval of IEEE standard 802.3,[32] a new Ethernet wiring standard has emerged; it is called *unshielded twisted pair* (UTP) cabling, or *10BaseT*. The event is roughly the equivalent of what happened to AppleTalk with PhoneNET. Ethernet users can now use existing installed phone cable, and only one type of cable has to be installed for phone and computer equipment.

True to its superior networking form, Apple has not deferred to the status quo in Ethernet either. Apple's Ethernet implementation is as elegant as its AppleTalk

---

[29] Brita Meng, "Networking for the novice," *Macworld*, December 1990, p. 202. This article has it all. Dave Kosiur, "Managing Networks," *Macworld*, February 1991, p. 152. For the larger network user.

[30] Margie Wylie, "Apple brings new simplicity to high-speed networking," *MacWEEK*, 1/8/91, p. 1; and Andrew Gore and Margie Wylie, "Ethernet moving into Macs," *MacWEEK*, 12/4/90, p. 1.

[31] Henry Bortman, "Apple Gives Nod to Ethernet," *MacUser*, March 1991, p. 197; and Brita Meng, "Apple Announces Plug-and-Play Ethernet," *Macworld*, March 1991, p. 105.

[32] David Coursey and Jodi Mardesich, "10BaseT Formalized as Official IEEE Standard," *Infoworld*, 10/8/90, p. 5.

implementation. Rather than leaving the transceivers for the different cabling schemes on the Ethernet hardware card, Apple standardized the cards and offered the cable transceivers—thick, thin, and 10BaseT—as plug-in transceiver connectors like its LocalTalk implementation. A further nicety is Apple has a 68000 chip with 512K of upgradable RAM on its NuBus Ethernet card; this allows Apple or third parties to download TCP/IP, DECNet, or other protocols to be processed directly on the card, relieving the main CPU of that task. Finally, Apple introduced self-terminating connectors that eliminate the problem of an entire Ethernet network going down when a single cable is pulled loose. As with AppleTalk, Ethernet is essentially transparent to you—you select it from the Chooser and go.

This time, Apple's Ethernet is not a secret at Apple or anywhere else. Apple has announced its commitment to it with its own offerings. Future Macintosh computers will have both AppleTalk and Ethernet interfaces built-in. High-speed peripherals such as laser writers will also. Look for it.

Any port in a storm

The combination of Macintosh requiring a heavier duty networking interface and the introduction of new easier and less expensive twisted pair wiring standard has resulted in a Macintosh Ethernet explosion with many vendors offering products. This can only be good news in both the short term and the long term for Macintosh users.

What do you need to upgrade your Mac to network it using Ethernet? You have many options and choices. Whether you choose Apple or third-party products, your procedure is the same. You need to find the Ethernet card that fits your Mac, and you need to use the transceiver, adapter, or card to match your wiring. If you're going the Apple route, Apple's Ethernet NB Card and its three transceivers are shown in Fig. 9-12, your Ethernet card choices are:

- Apple Ethernet NB Card for $424 (the new card, not the older EtherTalk card).
- Apple Ethernet LC Card for $200.

Then you need to add the transceiver to match your wiring scheme:

- Apple Ethernet AUI Adapter at $175 (thick).
- Apple Ethernet Thin Coax Transceiver at $175 (thin).
- Apple Ethernet Twisted Pair Transceiver at $175 (10BaseT).

If you're going the third-party route, your Ethernet card choices are somewhat(!) more extensive. Vendors have Mac Plus, SE, SE 30, NuBus, and SCSI offerings, so be sure to check around. Here's a partial list:[33]

- Asante Technologies   Multiport Adapter (thick, thin and 10BaseT in one), Mac LC, Mac IIsi. Asante's Mac LC MacCon+ Ethernet Card, featuring

---

[33] Dimitri Zarboulas, Philip Zarboulas, and *MacUser* Networkshop staff, "Are You Ready For Ethernet?," *MacUser*, June 1990, p. BG20. If you only have time to read one Ethernet article, this is the article to read.

10BaseT and Thin interfaces plus Floating Point Coprocessor Option on the card, is shown in Fig. 9-13.

- Dayna Communications   Mac LC, Mac IIsi (requires Apple PDS Adapter), EtherPrint Adapter for LocalTalk printer on Ethernet network.
- Dove   FastNet Mac Plus, SE, SE 30, SCSI.
- Farallon Computing   PhoneNET to Ethernet adapter, star controller.
- National Semiconductor   SE 30, NuBus.
- Network Resources   NuBus, Mac IIsi (requires Apple NuBus Adapter).
- Shiva (now owns Kinetics)   EtherGate for linking remote LANs, device sharing, dial-in.
- Tri-Data   SE 30, NuBus.

Beyond this list are additional ones offering you options to upgrade your network via bridges, gateways, repeaters, concentrators, hubs, and accelerators. Enjoy yourself.[34]

9-12   Apple Ethernet NB card and 10BaseT (top), thin coax (middle), AUI thick (bottom) transceivers.

---

[34] Clay Andres, "Ethernet products: you can get there from here," *MacWEEK*, 9/11/90, p. 47; and Meng, "Networking for the novice." This previously referenced article gets you started here, too.

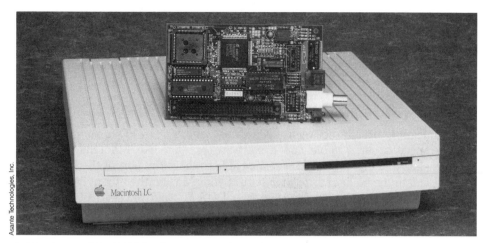

Asante Technologies, Inc.

9-13 Asante Mac LC MacCon+ card with 10BaseT and thin coax interface with a FPU option.

Mac to the rest of them

Macintosh "connects" to the world. You already know that. The fact that Mac communicates with DEC, HP, Data General, Wang, Burroughs, and NCR computers is nice, but academic. The world is IBM. When doing a networking or communication upgrade to your Mac, you will most likely to be "constrained" by encountering IBM in one of three forms. Let's discuss the three areas and how easily the Mac accomplishes them today. The three areas are:

- Communication with DOS PCs.
- Communication with mainframes, IBM 3270 style.
- Communication with minicomputers, IBM AS 400 style.

Mac to DOS PC communications

When communicating with DOS PC machines, there are several straightforward methods available to Macintosh owners today.[35] They are:

- *Sneaker Net*   Read a DOS PC floppy in your Mac.
- *Direct connect a Mac and DOS PC*   Use serial cable.
- *Network connect a Mac and DOS PC*   Put an AppleTalk card in DOS PC, then standard AppleTalk hookup, and TOPS software on both machines.

Sneaker Net

Sneaker Net is the easiest of the three methods. Take your DOS PC diskette and read it on your Macintosh. As mentioned earlier, Apple's FDHD diskettes and

---

[35] Don Crabb, "Mac-to-Pc Connectivity," *Infoworld*, 8/6/90, p. 55. This excellent article tells you all you need to know.

Apple File Exchange software makes this painless if you have a 3½-inch diskette coming from the DOS PC side. If it's a 5¼-inch diskette, use an Apple 5¼-inch drive (360K diskette) or a Dayna 5¼-inch drive (360K or 1.2Mb diskettes) on your Macintosh to read it. Today, reading DOS PC diskettes on your Macintosh is a piece of cake.

Direct Mac-DOS PC connection

Communicating directly between a Macintosh and a DOS PC is almost as easy. You just need a serial cable and a software product like MacLink Plus from DataViz shown in Fig. 9-14. Connect the cable to the serial port of the DOS PC on one end and to the modem or printer port of your Mac on the other. Two pieces of software come in the kit. One loads on your DOS PC, and you set it up so that it's acting as the remote slave. The other loads onto your Macintosh, and you set it up to use as the master. From your Mac, you establish communication with the DOS PC, then look through its files for those you want to pull over, mark them, then go. It's a piece of cake after you've done it once.

DataViz

9-14 Mac Link PC Plus software.

Network Mac-DOS PC connection

Network communication between a Macintosh and a DOS PC is only slightly more difficult. You communicate over an AppleTalk network. Remember, you already have that network capability inside your Mac. You need to put an AppleTalk card into your DOS PC. Then you connect an AppleTalk or Phone Net connector to your Macintosh, and another one to the AppleTalk card on your DOS PC, and connect the two together with the appropriate cable you have selected. From that point on, you load TOPS software on your DOS PC and a matching TOPS software module on your Macintosh. Set it up on your DOS PC so that files you want are in the public area, then go over to your Mac and pull them over in much the same way you did when the two machines were connected directly together.

That was easy. Regardless of what method you use, translators are available today from a number of sources that make it easy and painless to move text or spreadsheet data. Of course, you will have the best results and can even move graphics data across intact from DOS PCs to Macs when you choose software that exists for both platforms such as Microsoft Word, Excel, Works, Aldus PageMaker, WordPerfect, and Adobe Illustrator.

Mac-to-mainframe communications

For MIS Managers bold enough to try this experiment, replacing a 3278/9 terminal on a user's desk with a Mac capable of 3270 emulation gives that user a real computer in place of a 3270 compatible terminal. In the short term, you might take some heat, but over the long term (say, one week later!) that user will love you. The biggest problem facing the MIS manager today is finding the right Macintosh 3270 product:[36]

- *Avatar (MacMainFrame)* SE, SE 30, NuBus card. Avatar's MacMainFrame Coax Gateway hardware and software is shown in Fig. 9-15. Its Mainframe Coax Workstation Product for the Mac LC is shown in Fig. 9-16.
- *DCA (MacIRMA)* SE, SE 30, NuBus card.
- *Tri-Data (Netway 1000)* External chassis. It supports additional Macs via LocalTalk.

The simplest and least expensive 3270 approach is the direct connect. Put a card into your Macintosh, hook the coax cable up to the card, and run it over to the 3270 cluster controller, exactly as if it were hooked up to a 3278/9 terminal. From that point on, you can use your Macintosh for whatever 3270 terminal tasks you were doing before. The hooked up Mac supports multiple sessions and color (if your Mac has it) with the additional benefit of the Macintosh. Cut and paste information from 3270 sessions over to your Macintosh for later text or spreadsheet analysis, or store it on the Mac's hard disk to work on later. Talk about power—an MIS manager who has just replaced his or her users' 3270 terminals with 3270-like Macs has real clout. These users will wage a holy war at the highest company management levels for the MIS manager who dares.

---

[36] Dave Kosiur, "Connecting With IBM Mainframes," *Macworld*, September 1990, p. 214; Don Crabb, "Face to face with a 3270 mainframe," *MacWEEK*, 5/8/90, p. 49; and Ernest H. Mariette, "Mac-to-Mainframe Mating," *MacUser*, January 1990, p. 260.

Avatar

9-15 MacMainframe Coax Gateway hardware and software.

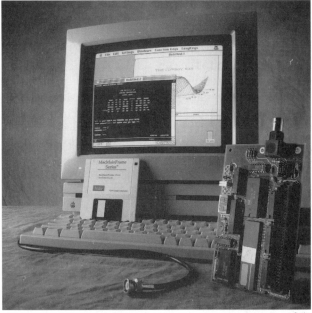

Avatar

9-16 MacMainframe Coax Workstation hardware and software for Mac LC.

Mac to minicomputer communications

Ditto the previous section minus much of the politics. Connectivity to IBM mid-range AS/400 computers is just as easy. Here the players are:[37]

- *Andrew/Emerald (MacTwin)*   SE, SE 30, NuBus card.
- *Andrew/KMW (TwinAxcess)*   SE, SE 30, NuBus card.
- *IDEAssociates (Ideacomm Mac)*   SE, SE 30, NuBus card.

Again the simplest and least expensive AS/400 approach is the direct connect. Put a card into your Macintosh, hook the twinax cable up to the card and run it over to the AS/400 (or System 34/36/38 or 5294 Remote Controller) exactly as if it was hooked up to a 5251/5291 terminal. From that point on, you can use your Macintosh for whatever AS/400 terminal tasks you were doing before (it supports multiple sessions) with the additional benefit of the Macintosh. Cut and paste information from 5251/5291 sessions over to your Macintosh for later text or spreadsheet analysis or store it on the Mac's hard disk to work on later. If you need more Macs attached, different multi-drop products are available from these vendors. These vendors also make DOS PC products, so editing AS/400 information from your Mac for a DOS PC user to pick up off the AS/400 later is a piece of cake.

Modems

"You've come a long way baby" would be the most appropriate statement to make in this area. I recently offered my Apple 1200 baud modem that sat under my phone and served me well for a number of years for sale for $25. It doesn't seem like that long ago that I bought it along with software for several times that amount.

Today, you should be looking for least a 2400 baud modem[38] for your mainstream data needs. If you're heavily communicating with another site, the two of you should at least equip yourself with 9600 baud modems.[39] Other than that, I have no specific recommendations for your modem upgrades. The Apple Modem 2400 (C0002LL/A) at $349 and offerings from Anchor Automation, Hayes, Prometheus, and Zoom Telephonics are all good choices at 2400 bps. Farallon, Hayes, and U.S. Robotics offerings at 9600 will all get you there, too. If you want to install a modem in your Mac rather than connect one up to it, Applied Engineering's Data Link Mac NuBus card modem, shown in Fig. 9-17, offers you a solution. Apple's MacTerminal 3.0[40] (M0708) at $125, Micro Phone II 3.0,[41] VersaTerm Pro 3.11,

---

[37] Paul Bendix, "IBM connectivity: New options for mid-range," *MacWEEK*, 4/17/90, p. 30.

[38] Steven Satchell and MacUser Labs staff, "Thoroughly Modern Modems," *MacUser*, January 1991, p. 100; and Steven Schwartz, "Choosing a 2400-bps Modem," *Macworld*, May 1990, p. 330.

[39] Dave Kosiur, "High-Speed Modems," *Macworld*, November 1990, p. 190; and Gordon McComb, Rik Myslewski, and MacUser Labs staff, "Modems: 9,600 bps and Counting," *MacUser*, January 1990, p. 180.

[40] Henry Norr, "MacTerminal gets big rewrite," *MacWEEK*, 8/14/90, p. 3.

[41] Doug and Denise Green, "Linking Up on Your Mac," *Infoworld*, 3/5/90, p. S1.

9-17 Data Link Mac modem on a NuBus card.

and White Knight (successor to Red Ryder) are all outstanding communications software packages you should consider for use. I believe that about covers this area.[42]

Fax

Fax modems are relatively recent newcomers to the Macintosh ranks, but they are making up for lost time with a vengeance; the last time I counted there were over 30 from which to choose.[43] If you don't have one or aren't using one, you're really missing out—particularly if you do a lot of faxing. Do look into the area because it is easy to write your fax on your Mac, press a button, and have it transmitted to a stored name on your fax address book list and receive your answer back in background mode while you are doing something else. If you want hard copy, generate it now or at a later time.

Before you buy though, you really need to look at your setup and how you want to be organized. Not all fax/modems will have what you need and, on the other hand, why spend money for features you will never use. Also, it gets a little tricky when you are sharing your one phone line between a telephone, fax, computer, and telephone answering device (TAD). If at all possible, get your vendor to agree to a try-before-buy policy to see if it works in your setup first.[44]

If you have a fax machine already and just want to send occasional faxes, the Prometheus ProModem 2400MFax works great, and the price is right. Orchid Technology's OrchidFax and Abaton's Interfax 24/96 are two outstanding full function fax modems you might consider.[45]

---

[42] Robert Hollis, "Sorting through the modem maze," *MacWEEK*, 4/3/90, p. 43.

[43] Steven Schwartz, "Fax-Modem Influx," *Macworld*, August 1990, p. 168; and Carolyn Said, "Tide of fax/data modems for the Mac still surging," *MacWEEK*, 7/31/90, p. 28.

[44] Joel West, "Ins and outs of buying a Mac fax modem," *MacWEEK*, 3/20/90, p. 34.

[45] Steven T, Satchell and Heather Barbara Clifford, "High speed, unified fax/data modems make debut," *MacWEEK*, 4/3/90, p. 43.

I personally use a Dove Fax that is about the size of a pocket transcriber. It is easy to use and set up, and it accommodates all my needs perfectly. I understand, in its newest incarnation, the Dove Fax Plus does everything except cook your breakfast. Seriously, it has voice mail, answering machine capability, and a slew of other features. Check out the Dove Fax Plus, if this kind of upgrade is useful to you.

In a nutshell

Here are the key points you have seen in this chapter:

- Like your wardrobe, keyboards and mouse/pointing device decisions are among the most personal you can make. Like monitors, it pays to try before you buy because you have to live with the results of your decision daily.
- If you are heavily involved in word processing or graphics, a good scanner can make you more productive.
- Processing and control is a highly specialized field, but the Mac, with its graphical interface, high-resolution color capabilities, and upper end CPU horsepower has much to offer.
- MIDI helps you make music with your Mac. Multimedia helps you make video productions. Voice input is the wave of the future, but can help you now. Any of these upgrades can help you earn more money from your Mac.
- You'll encounter AppleTalk right away—Ethernet if you have heavier duty needs. In addition to being an outstanding graphical machine, the Mac is an excellent communications machine. Today you can enjoy "connectivity" to the world by adding the appropriate interface.

Sources

Some sources for keyboards are:

Cutting Edge Inc.
97 S. Red Willow Rd.
Evanston, WY 82930
(307) 789-0582

DataDesk International
7651 Haskell Ave.
Van Nuys, CA 91406
(800) 826-5398

Ehman Engineering Inc.
P.O. Box 2126
Evanston, WY 82931
(800) 257-1666

Keytronic
P.O. Box 14687
Spokane, WA 99214
(509) 927-5515

Some sources for the keyboard power turn-on feature are:

Practical Solutions
1135 N. Jones Blvd.
Tucson, AZ 85716
(602) 322-6100

Sophisticated Circuits Inc.
19017 120th Ave. NE , #106
Bothell, WA 98011
(206) 485-7979

Here are some places to start looking at pointing devices:

Abaton Technology
48431 Milmont Dr.
Fremont, CA 94538
(415) 683-2226

Altra Technology Inc.
1200 Skyline Dr.
Laramie, WY 82070
(800) 726-6153
(307) 745-7538

Asher Engineering Corp.
15115 Ramona Blvd.
Baldwin Park, CA 91706
(818) 962-4063

CH Products
1225 Stone Dr.
San Marcos, CA 92069
(619) 744-8546

Curtis Manufacturing Co.
30 Fitzgerald Dr.
Jaffrey, NH 03452
(603) 532-4123

Forte Communications Inc.
1050 E. Duane Ave. # J
Sunnyvale, CA 94086
(408) 733-5100

Information Strategies Inc.
888 S. Greenville Ave., # 121
Richardson, TX 75081

Kensington Microware Corp.
2855 Campus Dr.
San Mateo, CA 94403
(415) 572-2700

Kurta Corp.
3007 E. Chambers St.
Phoenix, AZ 85040
(602) 276-5533

Micro Touch Systems Inc.
55 Jonspin Rd.
Wilmington, MA 01887
(800) 866-6873

Microspeed, Inc.
44000 Old Warm Springs Blvd.
Fremont, CA 94538
(415) 490-1403

Mirror Technologies
2644 Patton Rd.
Roseville, MN 55113
(612) 633-4450

Mobius Technologies
5835 Doyle St.
Emeryville, CA 94608
(800) 669-0556
(415) 654-0556

Mouse Systems Corp.
47505 Seabridge Dr.
Fremont, CA 94538
(415) 656-1117

Practical Solutions
1135 N. Jones Blvd.
Tucson, AZ 85716
(602) 322-6100

Scanner sources are listed here:

Hewlett-Packard
19310 Pruneridge Ave.
Cupertino, CA 95014
(800) 752-0900
(408) 323-4122

Caere Corp.
100 Cooper Ct.
Los Gatos, CA 95030
(800) 535-7226

Some audio and video sources are:

Farallon Computing Inc.
2000 Powell St., #600
Emeryville, CA 94068
(415) 596-9100

MacSema
29383 Lamb Dr.
Albany, OR 97321
(503) 757-1520

Articulate Systems
99 Erie St.
Cambridge, MA 02139
(617) 876-5236

Start your search for high-speed processing and control tools with these
companies:

Data Translation
100 Locke Dr.
Marlboro, MA 01752
(508) 485-3322

GW Instruments
35 Medford St.
Sommerville, MA 02143
(617) 625-4096

IDAC
P.O. Box 397
Amherst, NH 03031
(603) 673-0765

IO Tech
25971 Cannon Rd.
Cleveland, OH 44146
(216) 439-4091

Keithley Metrabyte
440 Myles Standish Blvd.
Taunton, MA 02780-9962
(508) 880-3000

National Instruments Corp.
6504 Bridge Point Pkwy.
Austin, TX 78730
(800) 433-3488
(512) 794-0100

Spectral Innovations
4633 Old Ironsides Dr., #450
Santa Clara, CA 95054
(408) 727-1314

Strawberry Tree
160 S. Wolfe Rd.
Sunnyvale, CA 94086
(408) 736-8800

Networking and communication sources:

Anchor Automation
20675 Bahama St.
Chatsworth, CA 91311
(818) 998-6100

Andrew/Emerald
18912 N. Creek Pkwy., #102
Bothell, WA 98011
(206) 485-8200

Andrew/KMW
100 Shepherd Mountain Plaza
Austin, TX 78730
(800) 531-5167
(512) 338-3000

Asante Technologies
404 Tasman Dr.
Sunnyvale, CA 94089
(800) 662-9686

Avatar
65 South St.
Hopkinton, MA 01748
(800) 282-3270
(508) 435-3000

Cayman Systems
26 Landsdowne St.
Cambridge, MA 02139
(617) 494-1999

DataViz
35 Corporate Dr.
Trumbull, CT 06611
(203) 268-0030

Digital Communications Associates (DCA)
1000 Alderman Dr.
Alpharetta, GA 30201
(404) 442-4000

Dove Computer Corp.
1200 N. 23rd St.
Wilmington, NC 28405
(800) 622-7627
(919) 763-7918

Farallon Computing Inc.
2000 Powell St., #600
Emeryville, CA 94068
(415) 596-9100

Hayes Microcomputer Products
P.O. Box 105203
Atlanta, GA 30348
(404) 441-1617

IDEA Associates
29 Dunham Rd.
Billirca, MA 01821
(800) 257-5027
(508) 663-6878

Network Resources Corp.
2450 Autumnvale Dr.
San Jose, CA 95131
(408) 263-8100

Novell
122 East 1700 South
Provo, UT 84606
(801) 379-5900

Nuvotech
2015 Bridgeway, #204
Sausalito, CA 94965
(800) 232-9922
(415) 331-7815

Orchid Technology
45365 Northport Loop W.
Fremont, CA 94538
(415) 683-0300

Practical Peripherals
31245 La Baya Dr.
Westlake Village, CA 91362
(800) 442-4774
(818) 706-0333

PSI
2005 Hamilton St., #220
San Jose, CA 95125
(408) 559-8544

Shiva Corp.
1 Cambridge Center
Cambridge, MA 02142
(617) 252-6300

Sitka/TOPS
950 Marina Village Pkwy.
Alameda, CA 94501
(800) 445-TOPS
(415) 769-2449

Tri-Data Systems
3270 Scott Blvd.
Santa Clara, CA 94054
(408) 727-3270

Ungermann-Bass
3900 Freedom Circle
Santa Clara, CA 95054
(800) 873-6381
(408) 496-0111

U.S. Robotics
8100 N. McCormick Blvd.
Skokie, IL 60076
(708) 982-5010

Ven-Tel
2121 Zanker Rd.
San Jose, CA 95131
(408) 436-7400

Chapter 10
Printer upgrade options

${\rm M}$acintosh printer upgrade choices are made for how you want the world to perceive you. Printers are the part of your Macintosh system the outside world "sees" and the other half of the Mac's WYSIWYG advantage. The wisdom of your Macintosh printer choice is visible every day in black-and-white hard copy for all the world to see. It can either greatly enhance or completely wipe out this advantage. Everyone will rave over the output from your PostScript LaserWriter printer. No one has to know it was generated on a Mac Plus. No one will rave over the output from a low-end, DOS PC, 9-pin dot matrix printer hung onto your Mac IIfx as an afterthought. No one would believe it was generated on a Macintosh.

This chapter covers the Macintosh printer options available to you: dot matrix, laser, and other printers. I leap right into my recommendations after getting a few general points out of the way.

The Macintosh printer story

The most significant upgrade you can make to your Macintosh other than buying a faster logic board or hard disk is going from a dot matrix to a laser printer. Not only does it result in an increase in speed, in pages per minute as opposed to lines per minute, but it puts you in a totally different class in terms of professionalism, and in terms of the quality of your output. For that reason alone, it's worth the difference in cost.

Of all my clients, most started small and grew with their businesses. None started small and went smaller. The point is that if you buy a little more printer than you need to begin with, and then step up to a laser printer, it can only serve you better as your business grows. In addition, I recommend you buy a PostScript capability laser printer to begin with. Why? My client experiences have proved it. PostScript gives you all the capability you need right out of the starting gate plus. Combined with AppleTalk networking, it gives you the ability to expand later to the system you need when your business is larger.

Even if you only keep it in your office at home for personal use, you get a higher quality, much more pleasing result. Also, you enjoy a greater degree of compatibility with existing software and fewer glitches. Your initial cost is not that much greater.

If you strictly do it by the numbers, the laser printer wins the battle of the cost tradeoffs, too. If you look at laser printers versus alternative choices in the categories of paper cost, supplies cost (ink, ribbon, toner cartridges), and the amortized cost of the printer itself, then the numbers are close. When you throw in time as a factor (cost of salaries, utilities, etc.), laser printers win hands down because of their greater speed and efficiency.

Having said that, what kind of laser printer should you get? When are other kinds of printers suitable? Let's get to the specific categories.

Dot matrix printers

The established workhorses of the printer world are the dot matrix printers. They print continuous form mailing labels, plus other labels with adhesive backing a LaserWriter can't handle such as multi-part forms and badges. Individual owners and corporate departments use them for first drafts, memos, and correspondence when they can't get to or don't have a laser printer.

The paper movement in a dot-matrix printer works just like a typewriter. It has a print head, ribbon, paper, platen, but the print head is different. The paper can be advanced by friction feed, just like a typewriter, or by tractor feed. Specially designed computer paper has holes along its outside edges that are easily removed from the body of the paper because of its perforated edges.

Today's dot-matrix printers usually have 9- or 24-pin print heads that form characters by printing a series of dots resembling each character in the ASCII alphabet in a tiny cell. With a 9-pin printer, you can still see the dots. An improved near letter quality (NLQ) mode is available that makes two passes with the second slightly shifted from the first and the holes between the dots are filled in by the dots from the second pass.

With a 24-pin printer, you can hardly tell the difference from a typewritten page, and you get the results much faster. These printers are so superior in type appearance and speed that they have driven the older daisywheel and thimble printers (those that printed fully formed characters like a typewriter) from the market.[1]

Here I have two printers I can recommend to you:

- Apple ImageWriter II (C0090LL/A) at $595   Apple in its wisdom has only one low-end dot matrix printer, the ImageWriter II shown in Fig. 10-1. For

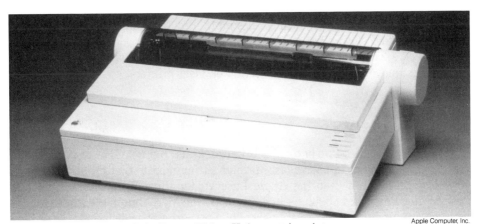

Apple Computer, Inc.

10-1   Image Writer II dot matrix printer.

---

[1] Charles Seiter, "Printing Without PostScript," *Macworld*, June 1990, p. 172.

many of my clients, it's the best solution I could have possibly recommended for them at any price, even if I spent a lot more time searching. It's extremely reliable and has a nice tractor feed that does an excellent job on mailing labels. It also lets you feed single sheet stationary and #10 size business envelopes through it. Plus you can add a sheet feeder option. It prints in color if you add a color ribbon and works on an AppleTalk network if you add a network board. Equipped with the Beverly Hills and Palatino fonts, it does a credible job on business correspondence although it is obviously not letter quality output. Yes, there are many other low-end dot matrix printers, but by the time you get the cables, the software, and find out about all their little quirks in working with each individual Macintosh software program, you are better off with the Apple ImageWriter II. It is a rugged, bulletproof workhorse. Just feed it a new ribbon and vacuum it out now and then. It works for me, as the man says.

- Toshiba P321SL at $699   The results look better on a 24-pin dot matrix printer versus a 9-pin. Also, you get 360 dpi (but only 68,000 versus the 90,000 dots per square inch of a 300 dpi laser printer) versus the 72 dpi of the ImageWriter II. You get a lot more speed: 216 cps draft and 72 cps in LQ mode. Paper-handling capabilities are on par with the ImageWriter's with sheet feeder and tractor options. A color model is available (P321SLC at $899), as is a wider carriage 132 column version (P341SL at $949). Beyond that, things get a little more complicated. You need to add MacMatrix software (Toshiba, $49), PrintLink 4.0 software (GDT Softworks, $99), or a Grappler LX parallel printer hardware interface as shown in Fig. 10-2 (Orange Micro, $199) to get the Toshiba printer to perform like an Image-Writer does on the Mac. But if you need more speed and higher quality dot matrix output on your Mac than an ImageWriter provides, this is the way.

My philosophy on dot matrix printers is simple. Buy the Apple ImageWriter II. It may be older and slower, but it is rugged and flexible and won't let you down. If you do need a 24-pin dot matrix printer, take a look at Toshiba. If you want more capabilities, move along to the next section on laser printers.

Laser printers

Laser printers are the stars of today's printer market, but not all laser printers are created equal. The inexpensive laser printer sitting next to that DOS PC clone is nowhere the equal of even the Apple LaserWriter Plus. Why? PostScript. The LaserWriter Plus has a 68000-based CPU as do the Mac's but in the same cabinet with the printer engine. It is very smart. The PostScript page description language tells the printer about each line, curve, halftone, and character that makes up the image, where to put it, how large to make it, how to fill it, what shade to use, what angle to set it at, and on and on. The bottom line is that everything is WYSIWYG. The screen, its text, graphics, everything is reproduced perfectly on the page with

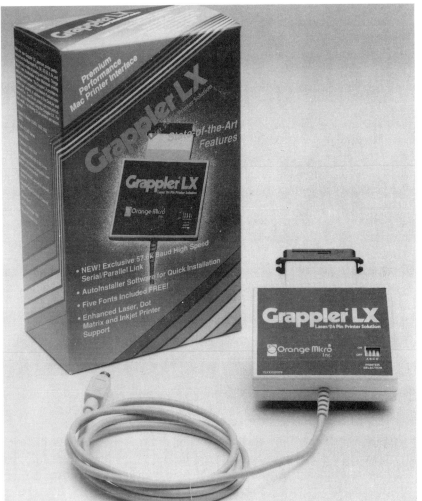

Orange Micro

10-2   Grappler LX printer interface.

no dot matrix style printer "jaggies." You don't get that out of an inexpensive laser printer.[2]

It don't mean a thing if it ain't got that PostScript swing

My philosophy on laser printers is also simple. It comes in three parts:

- Why buy a non-Apple laser printer when there are so many good Apple choices today?

---

[2] A particularly good, but now dated, article on PostScript laser printers was: Henry Bortman, Aileen Abernathy, and MacUser Labs staff, "Fit To Print," *MacUser*, September 1989, p. 179.

- Why buy a non-PostScript laser printer that limits you in terms of desktop publishing and graphics? Buy a PostScript model and get top-drawer performance.
- If you must buy a non-Apple PostScript printer, go for quality all the way. You might spend more when you buy it, but you'll more than make up the difference at resale time. I believe Hewlett-Packard fills the bill nicely here. And NEC, the other vendor I recommend, has a dandy product.

My experience has been that the average user tends to outgrow non-PostScript printers very quickly, and the difference between what you pay for the printer without the PostScript capability versus what you pay for the one with it is simply not worth the small, initial difference in investment. Plus, whatever non-PostScript printer you have, something funny is always happening with some of your standard software. I wish I had a nickel for every time I had to answer a customer question about a particular quirk. It was always something that wouldn't have happened with a standard PostScript laser printer.

I would recommend five PostScript laser printers to you and mention one non-PostScript laser printer. My experience has shown that you will be very satisfied with any of the following and one should fall in your budget range. The six are:

- Apple LaserWriter Plus.
- Apple LaserWriter II NT.
- Apple Personal LaserWriter NT.
- Hewlett-Packard LaserJet III (with Apple PostScript and AppleTalk).
- NEC SilentWriter 2 Model 90.
- Apple Personal LaserWriter LS (non-PostScript).

The one, the only, the original LaserWriter

The Apple LaserWriter Plus, the later version of the Apple LaserWriter that originally created the desktop publishing revolution when it was first introduced in 1987, is the one single product more responsible for putting the Apple Macintosh on the map in the corporate business world—with good reason. It's a bulletproof workhorse, and its cost and the cost of its consumables are very low.

- *Bulletproof* Very rarely will you ever find a piece of software the LaserWriter doesn't work with. It's not quirky. Its 1Mb of ROM, 1.5Mb of RAM, 35 resident typefaces, and version 38 PostScript make for a very stable, workable platform.
- *Workhorse* I have seen Apple LaserWriters (Cannon CX engine-based) with hundreds of thousands of copies on them working as if they were brand new out of the box. They have very high reliability and high serviceability.
- *Low cost of consumables* Service companies have sprung up all over the country whose sole purpose in life is to refill Apple LaserWriter toner cartridges at an attractive price. You can get three refills out of the original toner cartridge and, taking care to recycle your own toner cartridge, each refill is going to cost you in the area of $30 to $40 versus its $90 to $100 ini-

tial cost. You can get four uses out of your toner cartridge at 3000 copies each (12,000 copies) for about $180.

- *Low cost* The best part. Apple no longer makes the Apple LaserWriter Plus. The only way you can buy it is on the used equipment market, and the market in LaserWriter Pluses flourishes. These units sell today for $1500. You can buy one for the same price as a non-PostScript laser printer and the difference is strictly no contest.

Every Apple dealer on the planet knows how to fix and service them. In the unlikely event anything should occur, you have an instant ready source of someone with expertise to fix it. What else can you ask for?

Although the LaserWriter has declined in price, it hasn't become any less desirable, as its flourishing activity on the used equipment market attests. A dot matrix or non-PostScript printer will also give you hard copy from your Macintosh, but the LaserWriter can put you on the map as far as the quality of the printed output is concerned. Your correspondence and other printed output earn you respect both from your Aunt Martha and other businesses in your business dealings. No one can tell whether you generated your letter on an older, original LaserWriter or the newest top of the line LaserWriter II NTX. It's laser output—period.

The new champion

The Apple LaserWriter II NT continues the tradition of the Apple LaserWriter Plus with some outstanding enhancements. Figure 10-3 shows today's Apple LaserWriter lineup from left to right: Personal LaserWriter LS (the only non-PostScript one), Personal LaserWriter NT, LaserWriter II NT, and LaserWriter II NTX.

- *Reliable* Not quite as rugged at its predecessor, but even more reliable. As the standard in Mac LaserWriters today, all software products work with it because all software is tested on it.
- *Expandable, upgradable* A simple controller board swap takes you from the lowest non-PostScript (II SC, recently discontinued) model to the highest 68020-based (II NTX) model.
- *Faster, improved* Using a Canon SX 8 page per minute printer engine gives you blacker blacks, additional memory (2Mb RAM) and a new version of

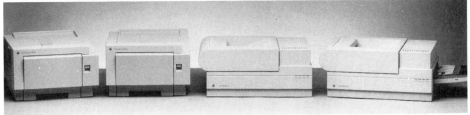

Apple Computer, Inc.

10-3 Today's Apple LaserWriter printer family.

PostScript (version 47) lets you download more fonts and print them faster, and a flatter printer path extends your printing options to heavier stock.

- *Low cost of consumables* LaserWriter and LaserWriter II toner cartridges cost about $100, and produce 3000 and 5000 copies, respectively. LaserWriter II's, made with more sensitive drum materials, are more difficult to refill, so you'll only get three uses out of them at 5000 copies each (15,000 copies) for about $200.
- *Reduced in cost* Apple LaserWriter II NT (M6210) was reduced to $3999 in March 1991. That puts its new street price in the $2800 to $3200 ballpark. This printer is also available in the used equipment market, usually locally only, for around $2000 to $2400.

I'll say bottom-line on this printer, it's everything that you got in the LaserWriter Plus and then some. It's an outstanding choice.

The new kid on the block

The Apple Personal LaserWriter NT continues the innovative example and heritage of the Apple LaserWriter family with some new wrinkles.[3] Figure 10-4 shows a better picture of it. Figure 10-5 shows the controller board that makes it into an NT model. This board, the rival of any of Apple's 68000 Macintosh logic board, comes standard with 2Mb of memory and is expandable to 8Mb.

- *Reliable engine* The NT shares the same 4-page-per-minute Cannon P-110 print engine used in the HP LaserJet IIP, but improves on it with a standard 250-page paper cassette. The blacks are even superior to the SX engine blacks.
- *Expandable, upgradable* Like its bigger, older brother, a simple controller board swap takes you from the non-PostScript Personal LaserWriter SC to the Personal LaserWriter NT model.
- *Faster, improved* Using a peripheral interface controller (PIC) chip that offloads AppleTalk traffic from the main processor and a new version of PostScript (version 51.8) with the same amount of memory (2Mb), the Personal NT is even faster than the II NT on printer jobs requiring many fonts and heavy downloading.
- *Low cost of consumables* Personal LaserWriter NT toner cartridges cost less than the II NT's and are rated at 3500 versus the 5000 copies of the II NT cartridges. The jury is still out on refills.
- *Lower cost* Apple Personal LaserWriter NT (B0325LL/A) was reduced to $2599 in March 1991. That puts its new street price in the $1800 to $2000 ballpark.

Even though the NT is called a personal printer, it's very definitely AppleTalk-compatible just like its predecessors. You have a lot of Apple LaserWriter options in the $2000 to $3000 range for some pretty outstanding printers.

---

[3] Henry Bortman, "Laser Lite: Apple's New Personal LaserWriters," *MacUser*, September 1990, p. 213; Jim Heid, "LaserWriters for Less," *Macworld*, August 1990, p. 129; and Bruce Foster, "Personal LaserWriter NT small, solid," *MacWEEK*, 8/7/90, p. 118.

Apple Computer, Inc.

10-4 Apple personal LaserWriter NT printer.

Apple Computer, Inc.

10-5 Apple personal LaserWriter NT controller board.

Hewlett-Packard LaserJet III alternative

In my mind, up to this point there was really no viable alternative to the Apple LaserWriter offerings. However, within the last year, Hewlett-Packard, the world-wide leader in the laser printer market, has taken dead aim at Apple's laser printer market with its LaserJet III product and Apple-specific options.[4] The Hewlett-Packard LaserJet III is shown in Fig. 10-6.

Hewlett-Packard's LaserJet III basic unit with its new resolution enhancement print technology lists for $2395. Then you add the Hewlett-Packard Post-Script cartridge at $695, AppleTalk interface kit at $275, and 2Mb of memory at $560 list. Pacific Data Products offers the equivalent package at $699 (AppleTalk interface is included), and 2Mb of memory is $299. If you go Hewlett-Packard all the way, your total list is $3929 that translates to a street price of roughly the same as Apple's LaserWriter II NT. Using the third-party AppleTalk and PostScript upgrade alternative brings it down to $3397 list.

What have you done? Versus the Apple LaserWriter II NT, the Hewlett-Packard LaserJet III gives you a less expensive solution with superior variable dot print technology that improves print quality. It also has more memory capability (up to

Hewlett-Packard Company

10-6   Hewlett-Packard LaserJet III printer.

---

[4] Arlan Levitan, "The Michael Jordan of Laser Printers?," *Computer Shopper*, September 1990, p. 198; and Serge Timacheff and Jeff Eckert, "HP's New LaserJet II Raises Laser Printing to a New Level," *Infoworld*, 3/19/90, p. 76

4Mb of Hewlett-Packard or 8Mb of third-party memory can be added as needed as opposed to the 2Mb fixed Apple total) the same number of genuine Adobe typefaces (35), and the identical 8 page per minute printer engine using the identical toner cartridge.

NEC SilentWriter 2 model 90 alternative

From no viable alternative to the Apple LaserWriter offerings to two—NEC, one of the world's electronics giants, has also taken dead aim at Apple's laser printer market with its SilentWriter 2 Model 90 product[5] shown in Fig. 10-7.

With a 6-page-per-minute Minolta engine, 35 resident Adobe fonts, and making the most efficient use of it with PostScript version 52.2 using a 16.67 MHz 68000 CPU chip and 2Mb of RAM, this baby is for real. The best news is its price at $2495. That translates to a street price of about $1800. NEC is extremely well-connected, too, and sports AppleTalk, serial, and parallel interfaces. NEC also provides a support kit of screen fonts and the printer's resident Adobe and HP fonts.

The bottom-line result of all this is that you're getting both PostScript and AppleTalk and a great new printer, smack in the middle of the range between a used II NT, new Personal NT, and used LaserWriter Plus. So, it's something you should definitely investigate.

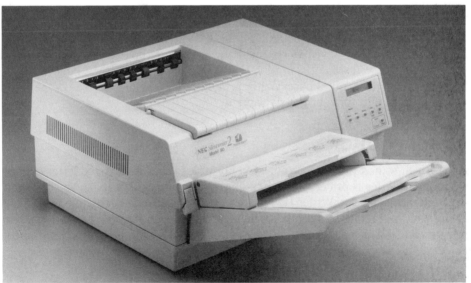

10-7   NEC SilentWriter 2 Model 90 option printer.

---

5 Bruce Fraser and MacUser Labs staff, "Personal PostScript Laser Printers," *MacUser*, March 1991, p. 116; Bruce Fraser, "Personal PS printers go head to head," *MacWEEK*, 11/6/90, p. 47; and Pamela Pfiffer, "NEC PostScript laser boasts 6-ppm engine at $2,495," *MacWEEK*, 8/14/90, p. 14.

Apple's non-PostScript printer has panache and low price

Apple's Personal LaserWriter LS (B054LL/A) at $1299 list was announced in March 1991, replacing the $1999 Personal LaserWriter SC.[6] It uses the same Cannon LX engine the SC did, offers 300 dpi, but premiers True Type, Apple's System 7 typeface technology. A True Type startup INIT offers 13 True Type fonts and does not conflict with Adobe Type Manager (ATM) Type 1 PostScript fonts, so users can also print these. By using data-compression technology, its internal 512K of RAM works like it was 2.5Mb, and much of the page processing is offloaded to the Mac it is connected to via a SCSI cable. It almost looks identical to Apple's Personal LaserWriter NT.

A couple of things are happening here. After Apple's System 7.0 ships, True Type will be included as standard with every Mac sold. True Type automatically creates smooth screen fonts of any size and automatically prints smooth fonts on any QuickDraw printer. ATM does the same. By offering both ATM and True Type capabilities on the same printer, Apple offers you the best of both worlds. By aggressively pricing its newest laser printer offering, Apple substantially lowers the "umbrella," under which third-party vendors must price their products, and moves Macintosh-compatible laser printing into the price realm formerly occupied only by ink-jet and high-end dot matrix printers.

I've extolled the virtues of PostScript throughout, so why do I even mention this printer? Because this newest, least expensive member of the Apple LaserWriter family should have a street price around $900 and offers you several interesting alternatives. If you you just bought a Mac Classic and are using your Mac for medium to heavy text-based work, this baby is going to do a great job for you. If you connect it to your Mac IIsi or Mac IIci, it would do even better. I believe Apple has again, as with its initial LaserWriter printer, struck the mother lode of the right printer, at the right time, at the right price.

Other printers

What if you want a printer for your Mac Portable? What if you need letter quality at an ImageWriter II price? What about high-end printing? What can you do if you need more than a LaserWriter II NTX? I'm glad you asked. For solutions in these areas, you are talking about other printer technologies: thermal printers, ink-jet printers, and enhanced, accelerated, or typesetting printer alternatives. Lets take a look.

A thermal printer for your Mac Portable is cool

Kodak's Diconix M150 + printer is just the ticket to accompany Apple's Portable Mac on off-road trips. The M150 + runs on AC or five rechargeable nickel cad-

---

[6] Neil McManus, "Apple preparing to spring True Type printers," *MacWEEK*, 12/4/90, p. 1; Kelli Wiseth and MacUser Labs staff, "Affordable Laser-Quality Quick Draw Printers," *MacUser*, November 1990, p. 134.

mium C-sized batteries that fit within the platen. While battery life is about an hour (nowhere near the Mac Portable's 6 to 12 hours), you aren't likely to be printing solid for that length of time either. The four-pound printer at $699 list uses thermal paper and is very quiet, so you won't disturb the other creatures when you're alone in the wilderness with your Mac.

Apple's ink-jet bubbles to the top

Apple also announced its StyleWriter Printer (B0438LL/A) in March 1991 at $599 list. It is shown in Fig. 10-8. The Apple StyleWriter, a 7.5-pound, ink-jet printer based on the Cannon BJ-10e Bubble Jet engine, also comes with True Type fonts.[7] Offering printing speeds of 2 minutes a page at 360 dpi and 1 minute per page at 180 dpi, the StyleWriter is roughly comparable in speed to the ImageWriter II, whose $595 price is almost identical. The StyleWriter is much quieter. Like the ImageWriter II, it attaches to your Mac via the serial port. Now you can have letter quality at an ImageWriter II price. Or use them both as an unbeatable combination for generating address labels and correspondence at a low, low price.

Apple Computer, Inc.

10-8   Apple StyleWriter printer.

---

[7] Neil McManus, "New inkjet: High style, low price," *MacWEEK*, 3/12/91, p. 1.

The high-end is hot stuff

If you are enjoying your present Apple LaserWriter very much and just want to add more speed to it, Xante has a solution for you with its Accel-a-Writer accelerator board. Priced starting at $1695 with a hot AMD 29000 RISC processor on board, it can kick up the resolution to 1200 by 300 dpi and increase performance by up to 20 times.

If you prefer to build from the ground up, Laser Max might have the solution you seek. Its LaserMAX 1000 delivers 1000-×-1000 dpi and puts you into the typesetting business, using plain paper, at a very affordable $7995. Or use its LaserMAX MX6 controller to boost resolution to 400-×-400 dpi or 800-×-800 dpi with prices starting at $2795.

The real thing, 1270 and 2540 dpi typesetters, for the Mac with raster interface processor (RIP) has been offered by Linotronic for some time. Products are steadily improving and prices are coming down as more competitors such as AGFA CompuGraphic, Varityper, Autologic, and Monotype enter the market. You are talking some serious dollars here. Prices start at $20,000 for 1270 dpi units, and 2540 dpi is in the $50,000 and up range.

What lies beyond the void

Apple has seen the future, and it is 68030-based laser printers at the high end and not too far away.[8] Apple plans to bracket the current three-year old 68020-based LaserWriter II NTX model with the lower cost and higher performance 68030-based LaserWriter models based on the Cannon SX engine by mid-1991. Can 68040 LaserWriters be far behind?

In a nutshell

Here are the key points you have seen in this chapter:

- The best dot matrix printer investment you can make for your Macintosh is the Apple ImageWriter II. It is a reliable workhorse, perfectly matched to your Mac, and will give you years of service for a very nominal outlay.
- A LaserWriter printer is the best investment you can make, other than your original Macintosh investment. A PostScript LaserWriter is an even better choice.
- Other types of printers may be the best choice at the low- or high-end of the market or to fit specialized needs such as a companion to the Mac portable.

---

[8] Connie Gugliemo, "New '030-based printers to redraw LaserWriter line," *MacWEEK*, 2/5/91, p. 1.

Sources

Eastman Kodak Co.
901 Elmgrove Rd.
Rochester, NY 14653
(800) 344-0006
(716) 724-5393

Epson America
20779 Madrona Ave.
Torrance, CA 90509
(800) 289-3776

Hewlett-Packard
19310 Pruneridge Ave.
Cupertino, CA 95014
(800) 752-0900
(408) 323-4122

Lasermax Systems
7150 Shady Oak Rd.
Eden Prairie, MN 55344
(612) 944-9696

NEC Technologies
1414 Massachusetts Ave.
Boxborough, MA 01719
(508) 264-8000.

Newgen Systems
17580 Newhope St.
Fountain Valley, CA 92708
(714) 641-8600

Pacific Data Products
9125 Rehco Rd.
San Diego, CA 92121
(619) 597-4659

Toshiba America Information Systems
9740 Irvine Blvd.
Irvine, CA 92718
(800) 456-3475
(714) 583-3000

Chapter 11
Chassis options

This chapter talks about two viable alternatives for upgrading your Macintosh, and a third not so viable one. You can add an expansion chassis to almost any Mac to give it expansion slots, or you can repackage the Macintosh logic board you have into another chassis to make it more functional. The third alternative, the Mac clones, is potentially hazardous to your health.

This chapter will cover the Macintosh chassis options available to you: expansion chassis, repackaging, and clones. I'll jump right into the subject matter and give you my recommendations.

Expansion chassis

Let's start off with the good stuff—a Mac expansion chassis. Second Wave, out of Austin, Texas, offers a series of products that can help any Mac owner, from a Mac Plus on up through a NuBus model. Using the Second Wave chassis, you can increase your Mac's capability and protect your investment. What better way can you enjoy your Macintosh? Second Wave expansion chassis options can add two slots to your Mac Portable, four slots to your Mac Plus through Mac IIci, or eight more slots to a six slot NuBus Mac making 14 slots total! Plus, there are a number of other options in between. Let's take a look.

The open Macintosh

In talking about the Apple Macintosh family in chapter 2, I mentioned that the earliest Macs were closed Macs. You couldn't get inside the box. The later ones became open Macs, and every model since then has been an open Mac. The Second Wave expansion chassis options enable your closed Mac Plus to join the open Mac world, provide tremendous expansion flexibility for your Mac SE or SE 30, and add an entirely new and greater expansion dimension to your NuBus Mac. The bottom line is that the Second Wave expansion chassis completely changes your Mac upgrade expansion opportunities for the better. Here are a few examples.

On your Mac Plus, SE, or Portable you'd want to add the following cards:

- Accelerator boards.
- Larger monitors.
- Communications and networking.

On your Mac SE 30, you'd want to add:

- Memory boards.
- Accelerator boards.
- Color monitors.
- Communications and networking.

On your NuBus Mac your card list and application areas could grow to:

- Memory boards.
- Accelerator boards.

- Color monitors.
- Communications and networking.
- Co-processors: artificial intelligence, MS-DOS, RISC, transputers.
- Processing and control: data acquisition, digital signal processing, industrial process control.
- Manufacturing burn-in and testing.
- Multimedia and image processing.
- Engineering NuBus and SCSI device development.

All these possibilities are now available to you. Let's see how.

A home for your Mac Portable

For your Mac Portable your needs are simple. You'd like to connect a larger screen monitor to it and hook into the network or into a larger mainframe computer system when in the office. The ExpanSE Home BaSE expansion chassis at $995 list price, shown in Fig. 11-1, makes that and other possibilities easy.

The ExpanSE Home BaSE expansion chassis is the smallest in Second Wave's line, but it serves your needs just great if you are a Mac Portable owner. It acts as a base station for your Mac Portable and plugs into the Portable's PDS slot—for which there are not many options—and gives you two standard Macintosh SE 68000 PDS card slots—for which there are many expansion options. Home BaSE is a wedge-shaped unit, similar in shape and dimensions to the Mac Portable. Your Mac Portable sits neatly on top of Home BaSE if you like. It contains a 25 watt power supply and cooling fan, in addition to the two SE PDS slots. Only a single cable has to be disconnected from the Home BaSE chassis and you are again . . . portable!

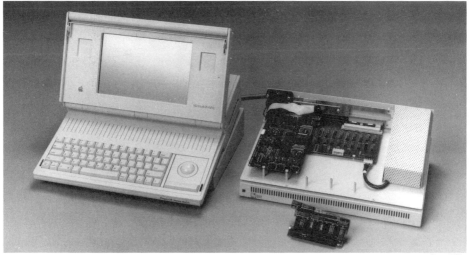

Second Wave

11-1 ExpanSE Home BaSE expansion chassis.

A growth path for your Mac Plus or Mac SE

For your Mac Plus or SE, your needs are also simple. Perhaps you'd like to upgrade either one of them to have multiple slot expansion capabilities. Enter the ExpanSE Plus at $795 list or ExpanSE expansion chassis at $995 list to make that a reality for you. Figure 11-2 shows the ExpanSE expansion chassis that fits either Mac.

The Macintosh Plus has no internal card slots. ExpanSE Plus opens up the closed architecture of the Mac Plus to accommodate four SE PDS cards! The standard 68000-based Macintosh SE has one PDS slot. ExpanSE increases the single SE PDS option card capability to four SE PDS cards. Creating a 68000 SE slot environment greatly increases your expansion option choices on your Mac Plus. With four slots at your disposal, there are quite a number of SE monitor and accelerator options you can now add to pump up your Mac Plus to the horsepower and flexibility of the latest Mac models. The same, of course, applies to the Mac SE.

ExpanSE Plus and ExpanSE use the same four-slot chassis, but each has a different interface card to connect to the appropriate Macintosh. The interface card for the Plus attaches to the Plus motherboard using a Killy clip to the CPU. The interface board for the SE occupies the single slot in the SE. ExpanSE Plus and ExpanSE come complete with the interface card, internal and external cables, and the expansion chassis. The expansion chassis contains a 50 watt power supply, cooling fan, and four SE 68000 PDS card slots. The external cable assembly disconnects from the back of the Macintosh to maintain its transportability.

Second Wave

11-2 ExpanSE Expansion Chassis for the Mac Plus or the SE.

An outstanding growth option for your Mac SE 30

For your Mac Plus or SE 30, your needs are also simple. You want to extend the high-performance capability of this compact, transportable Macintosh to be able to add multiple NuBus slots so you can use color monitors and a wide assortment of other options with it. ExpanSE/30 offers four slots at $1295 or Expanse II/SE30 offers eight slots at $2295 to make your dreams come true.

If you have an SE 30 to start with, these expansion chassis open up new vistas for you. Add multiple NuBus cards to your SE 30, while taking advantage of its ability to do color, and you can operate it in a "docking adapter mode." The chassis with a larger color monitor stays at your stationary site while you continue to enjoy the portability of your SE 30 and take it with you on the road—a nice setup.

These chassis systems convert the single Macintosh SE 30 PDS slot into multiple Mac II family NuBus slots. ExpanSE/30 fits neatly underneath the Macintosh SE 30 or sits next to it and gives you a 50 watt power supply, cooling fan, four NuBus card slots, plus the electrical and mechanical hardware to install one $3^1/2$-inch SCSI hard disk drive.

If you need more room, the Expanse II/SE30 sits next to your SE 30, contains a 130 watt power supply, cooling fan, eight NuBus card slots, and room for three $3^1/2$-inch SCSI hard disk drives! Either chassis connects to the Macintosh SE 30, a SE 30 PDS card and a single cable. You can have the best of both worlds with the powerful, transportable Macintosh SE 30 and NuBus expansion capability!

How easy is it to add the ExpanSE/30 to your Mac SE 30? Let's just see. First you open up the case as shown in Fig. 11-3. Then you remove the blank panel covering the opening for the NuBus card connector on the back panel as in Fig. 11-4. My finger points to DIP switch settings you have to change only when moving the chassis to another style Mac. Then you add your NuBus card as shown in Fig. 11-5. Optionally, you can add an additional hard disk inside the expansion chassis as shown in Fig. 11-6. My other finger points to the NuBus card already installed. Figure 11-7 shows the final setup, cabled to your Mac SE 30, ready to go. The whole process took less than 30 minutes.

Making a big league NuBus Mac

For your NuBus Mac, your needs are not so simple. You want to do everything with it. The NuBus Mac open architecture and processing power has moved the Mac into sophisticated application environments: advanced workstation environments, image processing, data acquisition, measurement and control, engineering design and simulation, digital signal processing, etc. Now you want the slots to take care of these applications. Second Wave's Expanse NB4 at $1295 gives you 4 more NuBus expansion slots that extends the slot capacity of your Mac IIcx/IIci to 7 slots total. Second Wave's Expanse II at $2295, shown in Fig. 11-8, gives you 8 more expansion slots and extends the slot capacity of your Mac II/IIx/IIfx to 14 slots total. This is the maximum number of NuBus slots you can have on a Mac. Now you can accommodate any option card's intensive applications!

11-3 Opening the ExpanSE/30 case.

11-4 Removing the NuBus connector slot cover.

11-5 Adding Your NuBus card.

11-6 Adding an optional hard disk.

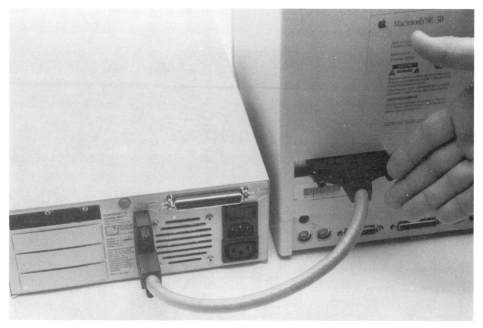

11-7 The ExpanSE/30 case cabled to your Mac SE 30.

Second Wave

11-8 The Expanse II Expansion Chassis for the Mac II family.

Expanse NB4 and Expanse II are the same four-slot and eight-slot NuBus expansion chassis as ExpanSE/30 and Expanse II/SE30 with a NuBus interface card instead of a PDS interface card. Either one of these options lets you tap more of the potential of your NuBus Mac, and also gives you more slots to handle NuBus card intensive applications at significantly less cost than dedicated solutions. Check them out.

Expanding the new Macs

At this time, Second Wave has no plans to offer a chassis expansion upgrade for the Classic, and is actively working on a Mac LC expansion solution. The Mac IIsi is expandable via the Expanse NB4 and Expanse II, as are the other NuBus Macs.

Repackaging your Mac

My earlier book, *Build Your Own Macintosh and Save a Bundle*,[1] was devoted entirely to the concept of repackaging your Mac. You take an Apple Mac logic board, put in a chassis of your choice, and surround it with third-party vendor components. Put a board in a box and save a bundle. Time has proven that it's a market whose time has come.

At other times the need occurs out of necessity. Industrial applications require a special rack or enclosure, Embedded Control Applications must meet stringent temperature or environmental specs, DOD requires Tempest specs be met for sensitive military applications, or your Macintosh just might be handier if it were packaged in an equipment rack along with your other multimedia, MIDI, or laboratory equipment. Users will always be finding new and creative uses for their Macs. There are specialized industrial control and military repackaging companies that offer you "ruggedized" Macs in their enclosure for a mere $30,000 a copy. And darn well worth it, I might add.

Beyond needs are the convenience aspects. You enjoy your Mac SE, but would like to have only one big-screen monitor on your desk, not a monitor and your Mac. You would really like to take your Mac with you but you don't enjoy lugging around your Mac SE or SE 30, and the current Apple Mac Portable is too much of an additional investment. You only need one Mac. On and on. You get the idea.

Here's where you can help yourself. Enter MicroMac Technology and its SE and SE 30 Upgrade Systems. MicroMac's pre-made kits save you time, make it easy, and are relatively inexpensive. Atlanta Technical Specialists also offers you solutions.

The MicroMac solution

Let's review why you might want to do this. You love your Mac SE or SE 30, but not its smaller screen. Also, it's not as portable as you would like it to be. The MicroMac SE upgrade system, shown in Fig. 11-9, allows you to address both

---

[1] Bob Brant, *Build Your Own Macintosh and Save a Bundle*, Windcrest, 1990.

MicroMac Technology

11-9 MicroMac SE Upgrade System.

these needs. Rather than having two monitors on your desk taking up space, you get exactly the monitor you want the first time, and you have a small footprint package sitting under it with lots of room to do other things on your desk. By repackaging your Macintosh SE or SE 30 logic board and floppy drive into a small but sturdy enclosure, it allows you to really make it truly portable so you can take it with you wherever you go. All you need is a small flat carrying case. Wherever you go, the chances are there will be a VGA monitor available from a DOS PC. Take your MicroMac SE or SE 30 out of its case, plug in your keyboard and mouse, plug in the standard VGA monitor, configure the system with the installation diskette for the connected monitor, and you're home free.

The MicroMac SE with 15-inch full-page monochrome monitor is $995 list, the SE 30 with 15-inch full page monochrome monitor is $1075 list. Either model gives you all you need. Just take the logic board, floppy, keyboard, and mouse from your Mac SE or SE 30. Putting together your MicroMac couldn't be simpler. It is an extremely rugged, well engineered, quality product where much attention has been paid to the little details. It should give you years of trouble-free service. It comes with a full set of detailed instructions, everything fits together perfectly, and assembling it is straightforward.

How easy is it to repackage your Mac SE into the MicroMac case? After you take apart you Mac SE, one phillips-head screwdriver and about 30 minutes should do it. MicroMac ships a completely sealed chassis, a rugged plastic outer enclosure that covers a metal chassis that completely encloses and protects your Mac SE's delicate parts. After you take the MicroMac chassis apart, you get to the foundation shown in Fig. 11-10. Your next step is to put your SE logic board into it and fasten it down onto the standoffs with the screws already provided, as I'm doing in Fig. 11-11. Next, add your Mac SE floppy drive as shown in Fig. 11-12. Next, add your one-third-height hard drive to the MicroMac hard drive bracket as shown in Fig. 11-13. Figure 11-14 shows the next step, connecting your hard drive cables and putting it into the chassis. Next, you put the video card in and button up the chassis as shown in Fig. 11-15. Figure 11-16 shows you can take it with you. Here, I'm putting it into an old ImageWriter printer carrying case, and it worked great. MicroMac provides you a much nicer one as an option.

Having written the build-your-own-Mac book, I have seen a lot of products. I would be truly proud to put my "signature" on this one. Look MicroMac up; you'll be happy you did.

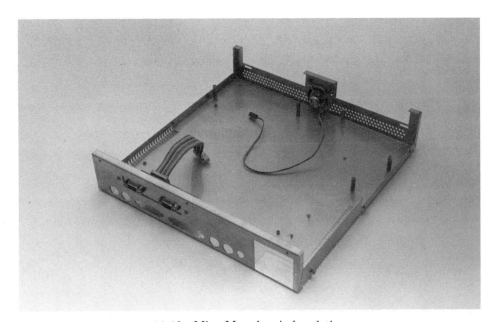

11-10   MicroMac chassis foundation.

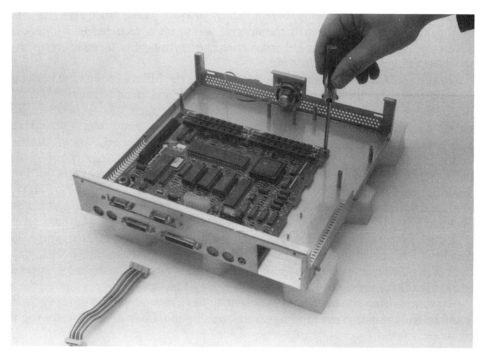

11-11 Adding your SE logic board to the MicroMac chassis.

11-12 Adding your SE Floppy drive to the MicroMac chassis.

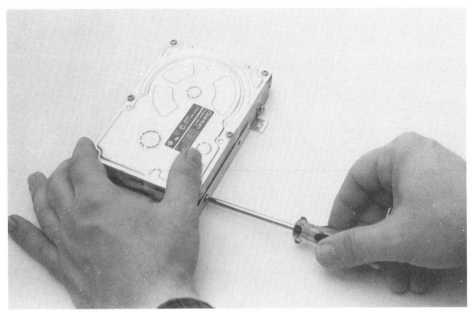

11-13   Attach your hard drive to the MicroMac bracket.

11-14   Adding your hard drive to the MicroMac chassis.

11-15   Putting the cover on the MicroMac chassis.

11-16   Putting the MicroMac chassis into an ImageWriter printer carrying case.

The Atlanta Technical Specialists solution

Atlanta Technical Specialists (ATS) has a long heritage as DOS PC specialists and integrators that it brought to the Macintosh and applied to a number of successful products including its Convertible SE and Convertible SE 30 Kits. These offer you repackaging opportunities within conventional style DOS PC cases as shown in Figure 11-17. ATS comes at it from the other end and offers you piece-by-piece solutions starting at $400 for the basic SE case kit and $475 for the basic SE 30 case kit. These include a low-profile PS/2 style DOS PC case, power supply, 800K floppy, video adapter card and SCSI, floppy, and power cables. All you need to add is a logic board, hard disk, monitor, keyboard, and mouse. ATS also handles "unconventional" repackaging requests. Like MicroMac, ATS is also a quality company. Check them out.

Atlanta Technical Specialists

11-17 The ATS Convertible SE kit.

Mac clones

My position on clones was clearly stated in *Build Your Own Macintosh and Save a Bundle*. They are a high-risk proposition because of Apple's legal posture against them. I made the point that while Apple is strongly supportive of the used equipment market because it helps sell more new equipment, Apple is not giggly about clones and illegal use of its ROM chips because it amounted to an infringement upon Apple's substantial and ongoing investment in its Macintosh ROM code that makes the 68000 CPU inside your Mac a Macintosh. It is one thing to repackage your Mac, to take its logic board, freely available in the used equipment market or out of another Macintosh, and put it inside another housing. No rules broken, no harm done. It is another matter entirely to clone it.

I'm sure you understand that you can't go around ripping labels off other people's software diskettes, putting on your own, and reselling them. Yet that is precisely what a number of Macintosh clone makers have tried to do to Apple. Macintosh clone makers do away with the Apple logic board entirely. They use their own logic board, electronics, and box but still use Apple's set of Macintosh ROM chips! This applies to either real or illegally copied chips. Either way, it's still a rip-off. Apple's not particularly interested in giving all its technology away for free. You wouldn't be either.

So I believe a clone manufacturer—any clone manufacturer—is strongly at risk, and Apple has a substantial legal process in place to defend its rights and has shown a history of not hesitating to do so when provoked. One of the clone manufacturers I mentioned in *Build Your Own Macintosh and Save a Bundle* is no longer in business. A sting requested by Apple revealed several of its employees were illegally copying Apple ROMs which, of course, was the kiss of death. I rest my case.

Clones have not yet been successful in the Macintosh world. But why would anyone be interested in a Mac clone anyway? Lower price? How is a clone maker, given Apple's state-of-the-art worldwide manufacturing capabilities and new-found commitment to low-priced Macintosh models, going to keep up with Apple? Recall the third-party resale value discussion from chapter 3, the low-or-no resale value. So you must weigh the advantages from your own perspective. Is saving a few dollars worth all the risk, given the many alternate sources and good pricing you can buy the genuine Apple article at today? It's doubtful that it is. Why should you risk buying a product that has virtually no resale value from a company that might not be around tomorrow, or whose price advantage may be swept away by Apple's next announcement?

However, the interest in Apple Macintosh clones has remained quite high and, recently, the media has been ablaze with just such a company.[2] Like the efforts of Chips and Technologies and Phoenix Technology who created the IBM-compatible chip sets and BIOS, Nutek Computers supposedly engineered from scratch a very close approximation of the Apple ROMs. When used with OSF's Motif interface, it supposedly will look like Apple System 6 software with Finder and Apple System-like files that contain a Nutek version of MultiFinder. You can bet your socks and shorts on Apple's legal department taking a long and hard look at them. Time will tell.

---

[2] Kristi Coale, "'Clean' Mac Compatible To Run Apple's Gauntlet," *Infoworld*, 1/28/91, p. 1; and Allison Calderbank, "Nutek to test Macintosh clone market," Computer Reseller News, 1/28/91, p. 3.

In a nutshell

Here are the key points of this chapter:

- An expansion chassis is the ultimate upgrade-your-Mac customizing tool. You can use it to expand virtually any Mac. It makes logical and economic sense to take a look at it before you sell or throw away what you have and invest in an all new Macintosh setup.
- Repackaging your Mac might be a necessity, or it might be a convenience, but it is today a reality. Pre-made kits save you time, make it easy, and are relatively inexpensive.
- Clones have not yet been successful in the Macintosh world. Given Apple's state-of-the-art, worldwide manufacturing capabilities, and new-found commitment to low-priced Macintosh models, it is doubtful whether they ever will be. Why should you risk buying a product that has virtually no resale value from a company that might not be around tomorrow or whose price advantage might be swept away by Apple's next announcement?

Sources

Atlanta Technical Specialists
3550 Clarkston Ind. Blvd., #B
Clarkston, GA 30021
(404) 292-6655

MicroMac Technology
9 Sorbonne, Suite B
Laguna Niguel, CA 92677
(714) 363-9915

Second Wave
9430 Research Blvd.
Echelon II, #260
Austin, TX 78759
(512) 343-9661

Sixty Eight Thousand Inc.
10 Victor Square
Scotts Valley, CA
(408) 438-1777

Chapter 12
Upgrade process overview

${O}$kay, you're in the homestretch, the last leg of your journey. The rest of the book is devoted to how you actually upgrade the particular Macintosh you have. This chapter introduces you to the subject. The following five chapters cover the specific upgrading steps and provide illustrated examples of what you need to do to replace the memory, change a floppy, add a hard disk, or put in an option board. Find your Mac in its chapter category: clip-on, one-slot, NuBus, new, and Mac Portable.

Once you've installed one NuBus card or SE hard disk, other installations are going to be very, very similar. Once you've read all the chapters, there will be very little you won't be able to handle. My objective is to give you the tools and examples to get you started rather than show you every possible thing you can do. After you get through and put down this book, the notion that upgrading a Macintosh is difficult will be forever dispelled from your mind.

This chapter focuses on the tools you need, some dos and don'ts, and some troubleshooting steps during and after the upgrading process. It also gives you a few checklists.

My basic assumption

My assumption is that you are taking a perfectly good Macintosh that you already own and upgrading it to make it even better. If you have a defective Mac, your best bet is to take it or the defective part to your local Apple dealer or third-party repair specialist. (Obviously this comment and those that follow on repairing your own Mac do not apply if you are a trained Macintosh repair person and just happen to be reading this book!)

You wouldn't undertake to repair or diagnose your late-model car casually. Why spend valuable time in repairing or diagnosing your Mac? Your late-model car has electronics interfaces; trained technicians plug into your car's diagnostic module, quickly find out what's wrong, then fix it. Trained Macintosh technicians at Apple dealers and third-party repair specialists work the same way. They have the tools and experience that enables them to quickly isolate and troubleshoot the problem with your Mac.

The upgrade process is simple. You take apart your Mac, you take out the old product, and you put in the new. Anyone can do it given a little guidance, and the likelihood of success is extremely high. However, when you undertake to repair your Macintosh, your level of expertise is necessarily higher. You're spending more time learning what to do than fixing the problem.

Can you fix your Mac? Yes, absolutely! Should you fix it? Probably not. My purpose is not to dissuade you from fixing or repairing your own Macintosh; it's merely to suggest that your valuable time is better used doing something else—using your Macintosh.

Myths and disclaimers

With a Macintosh or upgrade option kit, you receive three different warnings:

- If you open your Mac, you void the warranty.
- Danger, high voltage (on the Macs with CRT screens built in).
- Danger, static electricity.

Let's talk about these. They are all disclaimers. They are put onto the packaging of the product—Apple's as well as third-party vendor products—by the legal department for a good reason. These make the particular vendor "squeaky clean" in terms of being liable for any particular damage or injury that happens to an individual or to the product itself through the individual's negligence.

What vendors don't tell you is the actuality of there ever being a problem. While some would argue you only have to be killed once, insurance companies have been made very rich by the statistical laws of averages. There's a similar factor at work here. The likelihood of any harm befalling your Macintosh by opening it and looking around inside, you by working around the high voltage circuitry, or your components by removing them from their plastic shipping bag is fairly remote. Let's examine each one in turn.

Opening your Mac

When you open your Macintosh, you go from a rugged enclosure that you're unlikely to damage in normal operation to an environment containing delicate electronic components that are not designed to be handled a lot. Apple (or any third-party vendor putting a similar disclaimer on its product) has no idea who is opening the Macintosh case—the gorilla depicted in the Samsonite luggage commercials or a trained electronics technician. So the company prepares for the worst in a safe, sane, and legal way by saying if you open the box you void the warranty—that eliminates the whole problem.

After you read this book and know what to look for and be aware of, the likelihood of any harm befalling your Macintosh by you opening the case and looking around inside is pretty remote. Is it possible? Yes. Is it likely? No. So, armed with the light of knowledge, you will no longer have to fear going inside your Mac case because that warning message will really no longer be intended for you. You will be closer to the "experienced technician" end of the spectrum. You will know what you're doing when you go inside the case, and you're not going to do anything dangerous to harm your Macintosh.

High voltage

If you think about the time you stuck your fingers in an electrical wall outlet or came across some wires accidentally, you remember it smarts. The electricity, alternating current, at the U.S. standard of 110 volts and 60 cycles or European standard of 220 volts and 50 cycles, gave you quite a jolt. When you stuck your finger in the wall outlet you were, relative to yourself, connected to an electrical source that was basically inexhaustible—an electrical power plant or a generating station. As long as your finger was in the wall, the source would continue to deliver energy. Your body's resistance—whether you were wet or dry and other factors (you were either a good or bad conductor)—determined how much of an electrical jolt you absorbed.

In immediate contrast, you have to unplug any Macintosh with a CRT in it from the wall in order to open it—otherwise you cannot get the rear cover off. Inside that Macintosh, the voltage you're being asked to worry about is direct current, stored on a small electronic component (a capacitor) in the form of a charge. A capacitor is like a tiny battery, but unlike a battery, its job is only to hold a charge temporarily. This capacitor is not that large, it weighs under one ounce, and it only holds a small amount of charge. The high-voltage source in your Macintosh is the anode lead that goes to the CRT. Later, this book tells you how to discharge the anode properly. The anode derives its charge from this capacitor. If you accidentally brush against it, you "improperly" discharge it with your body providing resistance. Although its potential is thousands of volts, its energy charge is fixed and small. The current it delivers is tiny (measured in microamperes—millionths of an amp) and rapidly declines to zero the instant you touch it.

Unlike a stun-gun, the Mac's high-voltage charge is provided by a capacitor, not a battery. If you can tolerate the discomfort and keep your fingers across the anode lead long enough (a few seconds), you can totally discharge it. So the Mac's internal high voltage is a discomfort as opposed to a lethal threat. Can it harm you? Yes. Is it probable? No. I'm not advocating that you go in and boldly snatch the anode wire off the CRT and touch the middle of your palm with it, but I am saying that should you inadvertently brush against it, you're talking about an uncomfortable experience, not a life-threatening experience. It's not a giant cause for alarm and not even in the same league as sticking your finger accidentally into an electrical outlet. May God and Apple forgive me for telling you this.

On the other hand, a very practical reason to discharge your Mac's CRT anode each time before you work inside of it is the fact that its high-voltage DC is life threatening—to your logic board and all the other components inside your Mac designed to operate on 12 volts or less! Please remember to do this each time. Think of it as if you were saving a life.

Static electricity

With static electricity, you're talking about generating extremely high voltages (50,000 volts or more), much higher than that stored inside your Mac's high voltage area. Static electricity has such extremely low currents that you just feel the barest of pinpricks. Again, your jolt is determined by your personal body resistance—if you are shuffling across the rug in the middle of winter in a dry climate and drawing three-inch static discharge arcs off your doorknobs, you might disagree with me! Although you are not harmed at all by these occurrences, they are literally a bolt of lightning to the one-micron-wide circuit paths on the delicate electronic chips inside your Macintosh. So the vendors protect themselves by putting the appropriate disclaimers on their products.

Is it possible to damage delicate SIMMs and electronic upgrade boards by removing them from their anti-static shipping bags? Yes. Is it probable? Not if you thoroughly discharge yourself first, and/or use a static guard wrist strap, handle these components only by their edges, and set up your working environment to be as static free as possible to begin with.

Power supplies

Now for a real disclaimer—mine. Inside of your other Macintoshes (the Macs that do not have a CRT inside), the NuBus Macs, the Mac LC, the Mac IIsi, you have power supplies with labels on them that say CAUTION—DO NOT OPEN ME. Read these words carefully and pay attention. They are there for a very practical reason—you never have to open them. If anything goes wrong, you return it and get a new one. If you go inside and mess around, you run the very real likelihood of accidentally "adjusting" them to a voltage level that could severely harm your Mac's circuitry—and that could be expensive to you. So just think of your wallet when you look at your power supply, and leave it alone.

Monitors

Another item you never want to open is your monitor. It also has high-voltage and low-voltage power supplies in it, but it is not nearly as well-organized as the Mac's insides. Some monitor innards literally look like a nest of wires going every which way—easy for a casual fiddler to get stuck and burned. If it doesn't work, return it or have it fixed, but pass on messing about inside it. While no more life-threatening to you than your Mac, there is no good reason to go inside of it—you aren't going to upgrade it! Leave repairs to qualified technicians, and turn your curiosity to other areas.

Tools

The tools you need to upgrade your Macintosh are very simple. They are particularly so for the NuBus, LC, IIsi, and Portable Macs—any Mac that does not have a CRT in it.

Two screwdrivers for any Mac without a CRT

The most you're likely to ever need is a medium phillips-head screwdriver. If you're working with SIMM memory boards, a small flat-bladed screwdriver might come in handy, too. That's all you need, and you can do just about any task required. Figure 12-1 tells the whole story.

Two more tools for any Mac with a CRT

On the other Macintoshes (the clip-on Macs, the one-slot Macs, and the Classic), you'll need a spreader tool to open the case and a long-handled Torx-T15 screw-

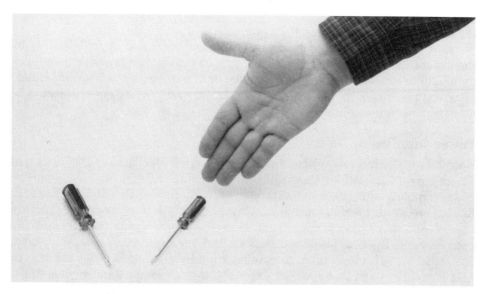

12-1 Two screwdrivers for any Mac without a CRT.

driver. As Fig. 12-2 shows, these come in several varieties:

- *Economy models* (See the right side of the figure.) A simple open wire frame Torx screwdriver long enough to let you get at the deep recessed screws at the top of your Mac case plus a simple spreader bar that looks like an oversized paper clip with a wide mouth. These cost you $10 or so; mail order and some upgrade kits automatically include them.

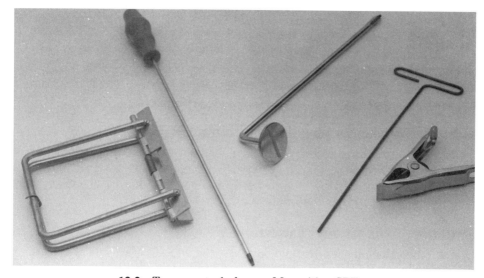

12-2 Two more tools for any Mac with a CRT.

- *Mid-range* (See the middle of the figure.) An ingenious all-in-one tool whose one end becomes a spreader tool with the leverage of the total length of the handle behind it and whose other end is a Torx screwdriver tip—pretty clever. Here you're looking at around $20.
- *Upper end* (See the left side of the figure.) Now you're in the high-rent district; this is what the Apple technicians use. A real Torx-T15 screwdriver and a 6-inch wide spreader bar means that you have very little risk of scratching the case because the leverage is applied over a wide area. In a production environment, you want the best, and for this you pay a little bit more.

Plus your basic toolkit

If you're working on Macs a lot, you probably want to get the small Curtis Tool Kit that goes for around $15 to $20 and has four screwdrivers in it—a medium and a small phillips-head, and a medium and a small flat-bladed. Plus, it has a needle nose pliers and a set of side cutter pliers in it—the small ones. In addition, it has a chip puller that you'll find is real handy for extracting ROM chips from the logic board. It also has a little extractor tool that comes in handy for putting screws in hard to reach places, for example, getting the screws that hold the floppy or the hard disk drive in place inside of an SE started if you don't have a magnetic screwdriver. But you really don't need all the parts in even a small tool kit. Figure 12-3 shows all the tools you need in your basic toolkit.

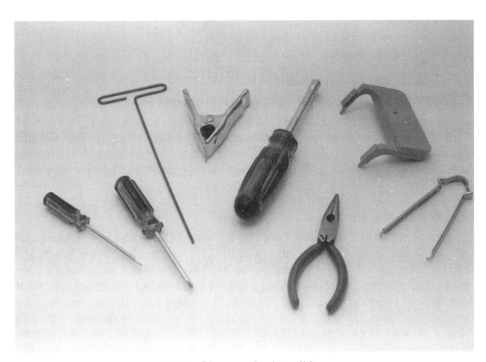

12-3 Plus your basic toolkit.

Plus your protection devices

Figure 12-4 shows the protection devices you need. You have your grounding wrist strap at the bottom that is nothing more than a strap you put around your wrist and the other one plugs into an electrical outlet on your Macintosh that grounds you, or removes the static charge from you to the case and dissipates it. The two long-handled, insulated screwdrivers are very good tools to use to discharge the CRT anode or, alternately, use the cord with the alligator clips at both ends right above them and only one screwdriver.

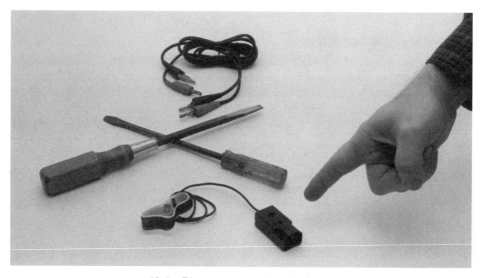

12-4 Plus your protection devices.

A magnetic screwdriver can be a two-edged sword

A magnetic screwdriver with several optional tips and a case barrel that holds them all out of harm's way is also handy, especially for removing the one-slot Mac disk drive screws or in general for any long reach or hard-to-get-at spot. You just have to be extra careful with it when working around your Macintosh and its floppy disks. It's shown in the center of Fig. 12-3.

SIMM removal tool

If you're doing a lot of work with SIMMs, the Amp SIMM removal tool (Amp part number 821987-2) at about $40 shown at the far right in Fig. 12-3 is handy. It is unlikely that you will need this unless you work on Macintosh logic boards every day. Contrary to popular myth, having a SIMM removal tool is not foolproof insurance against breaking SIMM sockets. SIMM sockets are delicate, and they will break if you wrongly apply pressure to them. It doesn't make any difference whether this pressure comes from your fingers, a flat-bladed screwdriver, or a $40 SIMM removal tool.

Sponge my Mac face please

You will also find that a small piece of flat sponge comes in very handy. The sponge, perhaps a foot square or so with the center hollowed out shown as shown in Fig. 12-5, can be cut from packing material if you order a hard disk through the mail, and it should be used to rest your Macintosh face down on while you take it apart. In any event, you want to provide a mat of some sort or a soft work space area (not cardboard or wood) so that when you rest your Mac face down to work on it, it doesn't scratch the front bezel.

12-5   Flat sponge material on which to rest your Mac face down.

What, no soldering iron?

Sorry, you won't need a soldering iron to upgrade your Macintosh. Nor do you need wrenches, socket drivers, drills, hammers, or other tools (darn, and I wanted to go to Sears). As far as tools go, upgrading your Mac is about as simple as it gets.

Dos and don'ts

This next section is just a list of do and don't items you should consider. They are in no particular order and it is not meant to be all-inclusive. A "Preflight checklist" appears at the end.

Work area

Before you do upgrades on your Macintosh, you want to have a work area that is going to give you plenty of room and is well lit. You should think in terms of at least a 30-by-60-inch desk top in an area with plenty of light. It's also ideal if this work area is located on a tiled floor as opposed to a carpeted one for obvious static reasons. It should be physically located in a low traffic area so no one knocks your opened Macintosh onto the floor while answering the doorbell.

Work area tools

Make sure you have all the tools you need before you get started. Keep them near your work area if at all possible. If you have a magnetic screwdriver, you need to be careful where you put it inside your Macintosh and where you lay it down outside of your Macintosh after you're done using it. I just have a special spot for it on the workbench that I return it to each time after using it—that way I enjoy its benefits, and it stays out of harm's way. You'll discover your own technique to keep your eye on it and not put anything else near it.

Handling the merchandise

Handle all upgrade option cards—accelerator, memory, video, PDS, NuBus—and SIMMs by their edges. Never pick up an option card or any other kind of board like you would grab your ham-and-cheese sandwich. You can zap something. Touch a component in the middle of the board inadvertently, and you can break it, short it, or do a myriad of other things to it. Just handle option cards by the edges, and you'll be safe.

Don't use force

Don't force anything when you're opening and closing your Macintosh. If the spreader tool is not opening your Macintosh the way it should, check to see whether you have fully loosened all the screws. If you're putting the cover back on your Macintosh, check to see that one of the edges of the back case is not overhanging the front bezel and preventing it from closing further. The same thing applies on the cover for your NuBus Macs. There's no need to force or jam anything. If something is not fitting easily, chances are it is not fitting right.

Be well grounded

If you're in a high-static environment, use the wrist strap. If you're not sure whether you are or not, use the wrist strap. Other than that, make sure you're on a tile floor, discharge yourself first, pay attention, and handle components by the edges. You can bypass the wrist strap, but you proceed at your own risk.

Unplug your Mac completely

Unplug your Mac, monitors and any other options from the wall electrical outlet before and while you're working on them. This is the most basic rule. The worst thing that could happen is to have your Mac plugged in and be slipping a card into it, accidentally turn it on, and zap the board and your Mac—not a fun thing. Just take away the power cord from the back of your Macintosh—get it up and out of the way—do your upgrading, and then plug it back in.

Don't touch your cables with the power on

Do anything you want to your ADB cables connecting your mouse to the keyboard and your keyboard to your Mac—but not while the power is on! The ADB connection does not like to have its +5 volts shorted to ground. If this is done, you run the risk of ruining both your Mac's logic board and/or those peripherals attached to it—a very expensive mistake. If you're going to remove these connections, do it only with the power off.

While I am talking about not unplugging cables with the power on, the same goes for your SCSI cable. This is always dangerous and just as costly when it's fatal. Here you're talking usually about an expensive hard disk that you've ruined, along with potentially damaging your logic board.

Serial ports on your Mac are a slightly different story, but again just as a matter of good practice, it's not a good idea to unplug and plug anything into your Mac with the power on.

Speaking of good practice, make sure that everything is connected to your Macintosh before you turn the power on. If you have a monitor, hard disk, and printer separate from your Macintosh, make sure all the power cables are plugged in and then turn them on.

Macs don't respond to shock treatment

When your Macintosh is up and running, don't drop your one-pound notebook or beat your fist onto the desk that holds your Mac. Set up your workspace so you don't accidentally drop something and damage your equipment.

Don't turn off power when your Mac is working

When your Macintosh is reading or writing to its hard or floppy disk is a particularly dangerous time—you don't want to turn your power off in the middle of this process. If the drive light is on, don't turn the power off, and just wait till things stop whirring—you'll usually be able to hear it before you shut your Mac down.

Turn off your Mac from the Finder

Always turn off your Mac from the Finder using the Shut Down command on the Special menu as opposed to just flipping the power switch off. Shutting down from the Finder assures you the maximal level of success in bringing everything back on the desktop the way you left it when you start up again.

Listen to the music

Assuming you have a good Macintosh to start with, after you've upgraded your Mac, the first thing you should hear when you turn the Mac's power on, is the familiar "bong" sound or "chord" sound with the newer Macs.

If something is wrong with your Macintosh, when you turn the power on you won't hear the "bong," you'll hear a different "chord" or nothing at all. If you're an Apple technician, you can use Apple diagnostics and loop back connectors to diagnose exactly from the sound what the problem is. In your case, you probably don't have this luxury. If you don't hear the "bong" though, you know there is a problem because it means the Macintosh has failed its power-on self test.

On new SCSI installs, first check the obvious

If everything has been working and all you've done is install a new SCSI peripheral in the chain, then do the obvious SCSI troubleshooting. Is it located at its own device address? Have you terminated the SCSI chain properly, etc.? Are the cables all connected? Look for the obvious things when a new SCSI device does not immediately work, and if you are at all suspicious of some damage, go back to the old setup you had that was working before you introduced the new device into the chain.

If everything else fails, restart

If you've got something that's not working, things lock up or freeze—restart your Mac. This is just the best way to get things going again, and it is painless. On the other hand, if the same thing happens every time you reboot your Mac, then you know you have a problem and must look elsewhere for its solution.

Preflight checklist

Before you can upgrade your Mac you need to:

- Shop for best price/vendor/warranty/return privilege.
- Buy the upgrade part(s).
- Make sure all the pieces you ordered to upgrade your Mac—the hardware and software items you need—are present.
- Find a good work area that is well lighted, has enough space, is low traffic, etc.
- Have all the tools you need.
- Complete pre-upgrade software steps. For example, the software you need to put a new monitor on your Mac is best generated before you put the monitor on so that you have a stable Mac to generate it.

General upgrade checklist

Always, always make sure that you can say you have done these things:

- Do you know what you're doing? Make sure you're familiar with what you're going to do. Whether it's reading this book or reading the instructions that come with every manufacturer's product (except SIMMs!), make sure you read, reread, and reread if necessary until you clearly understand the steps of the process.
- Did you dry run through the process before doing it to familiarize yourself?

- Did you draw up a checklist of what you need to do in your own handwriting—notes—to go down and check off the items with a pencil as you do them?
- It is always prudent to be little more cautious; the extra care you take might save you money.
- Is all the power removed; are all power cords removed from your Mac before you begin the upgrade and not returned until after you completed it?
- Do you know how to take apart your Mac so you don't hurt either yourself or the Mac?
- Have you installed the upgrade as the instructions suggested?
- Are all the cables properly attached, not binding or running into other components or shorting? Are they cinched down tightly?
- Before you "button up" your Macintosh have you performed a "surgeon's check" to see that no tools or sponges are still inside? You want to leave your Mac the way you found it.
- Have you reconnected your Macintosh the way it was before?
- Have you checked out your upgrade first by using the floppy diskette (or a copy of that floppy diskette as is usually recommended) that came with it rather than using your hard disk with your valuable data on it? Isolate any problem at no risk to your good hard disk first. It's just one less thing to worry about.
- If it doesn't work right the first time, do you know how to troubleshoot it?

Troubleshooting

Basic steps in troubleshooting, assuming you've started with a good Mac to begin with, are:

- Can you repeat the problem?
- Can you isolate it to hardware or software?
- Can you then retrace your steps to see where you've gone wrong?

The basic question guiding your troubleshooting process should be: "What have I done, what have I changed since my Macintosh was last working?"

For example, if you have just installed a monitor upgrade, it's highly likely that the monitor is fine, but you're not utilizing the software that came with it to tell your Mac to look at it or to boot to it. If you're not getting an image on the screen, this is probably a software-related problem. If your accelerator board is not working properly, chances are it is a software-related problem and you haven't set it up right and told your Mac to talk to it properly—as opposed to the board itself being at fault, although occasionally it is, maybe less so due to a malfunction or defective component than it is to a jumper setting not having been made correctly.

The two most frequent problems you probably will encounter are the lack of power to a component or it being improperly connected, so if you check your cables and make sure the power cable in particular is attached correctly, this normally nips both of those in the bud.

Troubleshooting checklist

Always remember:

- There's many things that could be the problem, but check the most obvious things first. Usually it's just a cable, jumper, or switch that's not connected or set properly.
- Don't panic. If everything else fails, virtually every vendor will have an 800 or hotline number you can call.
- Before you do call the vendor, write down some notes. Describe your setup, the problem, its symptoms, and what action you have taken.
- If you have to return the equipment to the vendor, always get an RMA number (a return merchandise authorization number) from the vendor before doing it.
- Ship via UPS or some other service that gives you a record of your shipment.
- Extend the same courtesy to your vendor as they extended to you—pack it properly so that it's not damaged in shipping.

In a nutshell

Here are the key points you have seen in this chapter:

- If you have a defective Mac, your best bet is to take it or the defective part to your local Apple dealer or third-party repair specialist.
- Be knowledgeable about the warnings and disclaimers before you upgrade your Mac.
- The tools you need to upgrade your Macintosh are very simple—particularly for the NuBus Macs, LC, IIsi and Portable (any Mac without a CRT in it).
- Organize your work area, your tools, and your parts ordering plan.
- Be familiar with how you're going to do your Mac upgrade installation before you do it, and make written notes to assist you.
- The basic question guiding your troubleshooting process should be: "What have I done, what have I changed since my Macintosh was last working?"
- Have written notes in front of you if you have to call a vendor.

Sources

Some sources for tools are:

Curtis Manufacturing Co.
30 Fitzgerald Dr.
Jaffrey, NH 03452
(603) 532-4123

Jensen Tools
7815 S. 46th St.
Phoenix, AZ 85044-5399
(602) 968-6231

Some parts and repair sources are:

Micromat Computer Systems
7075 Redwood Blvd.
Novato, CA 94945
(800) 829-6227
(415) 898-6227

Microserve
8868 Research #308
Austin, TX 78758
(800) 880-0458

Soft Solutions
907 River Rd., #98
Eugene, OR 97404
(503) 461-1136

Chapter 13
Upgrade your clip-on Mac 128, 512, or Plus

Are you ready to tackle the upgrading of your own Mac? You've come to the right spot.

Whether you've picked this book up off the shelf and have thumbed through it quickly to this point or have read carefully through the preceding 12 chapters, this is the part where the real fun begins—the part where you actually get to go inside your own Macintosh and install the upgrade you've wanted.

In this chapter, you see how to take the cover off your Mac 128, Mac 512, or Mac Plus, and add floppy disk, memory and memory/video card, or accelerator options. As every Macintosh option or upgrade has instructions with it (except SIMMs!), the book will not repeat these except for giving a few guidelines. In the "one picture is worth a thousand words" tradition, I use a photo to make the point wherever possible. Now I invite you to look over my shoulder and see for yourself. Let's get started!

Taking apart your clip-on Mac

As mentioned earlier, the clip-on family is the most difficult to upgrade only because it was never intended to be upgraded. If you can master the art of upgrading your clip-on Mac, you are well on your way to mastering how to upgrade any other Macintosh that has ever been built.

The tools you need

To take apart your clip-on Mac, you need:

- Medium phillips-head screwdriver.
- Small flat-bladed screwdriver.
- Long-handled Torx screwdriver and spreader tool.
- CRT discharging tools.
- Anti-static wrist strap.
- Firm sponge pad to protect your Mac's front bezel when you lay it face down.

Pre-opening steps

Taking the following steps make your life easier:

- Prepare your work area. Make sure a padded mat is available to rest your Mac face down on, and additional space is available away from the main work area to temporarily store your case back and RFI shroud so no harm will come to them.
- Turn off the power, disconnect the power cord, and remove from your work area.
- Disconnect the keyboard and mouse cables, and remove the keyboard and mouse from the work area.

Opening the case

Figure 2-5 in chapter 2 showed you the front on a clip-on Mac Plus. All clip-on Macs look alike from the front except for their color (beige or platinum) and identifying logo. From the rear, you have a different story. Figure 13-1 shows the outside rear of a Mac 512 (also Mac 128) versus a Mac Plus. Different Macs in the clip-on family are distinguishable by their nameplate, rear logo, and rear connector placements. Let's open the case. The example used is a Mac Plus, but the techniques are applicable to the Mac 128 and Mac 512 as well.

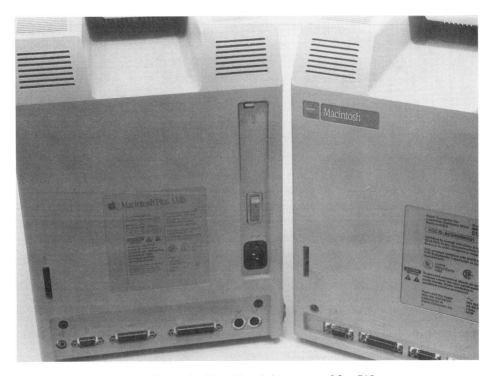

13-1 Rear of a Mac Plus (left) versus a Mac 512.

Remove the reset switch

Remove the reset switch as shown in Fig. 13-2. It is located at the back lower left as you are looking at your Macintosh from the front. A small, flat-bladed screwdriver can be used to gently pry this reset switch out. Be careful not to scratch the plastic when doing it.

Remove the battery door

Remove the battery door as shown in Fig. 13-3. Notice the Torx-head screw.

13-2   Remove the reset switch.

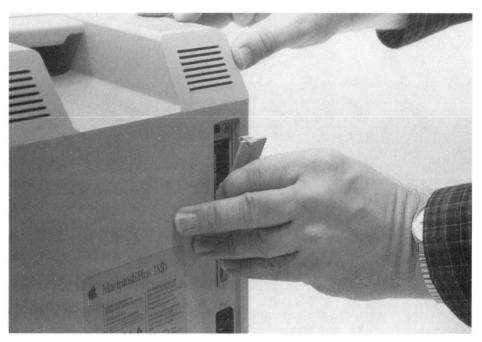

13-3   Remove the battery door.

Remove the top two case screws

Next you need to remove the five screws that hold the clip-on Mac case together. Move your Macintosh to the face down position on a firm rubber or other nonabrasive pad. In Fig. 13-4, I am using the long-handled screwdriver to remove one of the top two screws that are located inside the recess that forms the handle for the

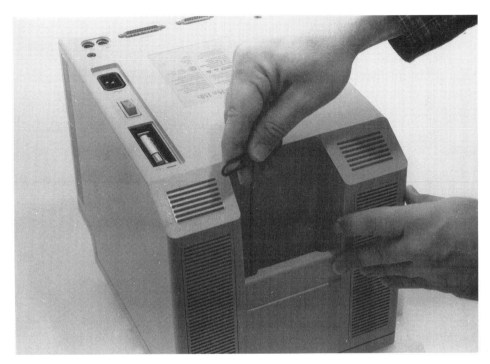

13-4 Remove the top two case screws.

top of the carrying case. If you look down through the recess, you'll see two screws approximately three inches apart, and this is what the long-handled screwdriver is used for as shown in the photograph.

Remove the bottom two case screws

Figure 13-5 shows one of the bottom two screws located at the back of the cover being removed. Notice that these two screws are different from the two screws at the top of the cabinet. The top screws have a coarse thread and are actually holding the case into the plastic bezel. These bottom two screws have a fine thread and hold the back cabinet on through metal clips into the metal chassis, so it's a little bit different type of a screw. Make sure you remember the distinction when you set the screws aside for later reassembly.

Remove the battery door case screw

Figure 13-6 shows removing the screw hidden behind the battery door. The first time I ever attempted to disassemble a clip-on Mac, I didn't have any instructions and had the hardest time figuring out why the case would not come apart. This is the magic screw that caused me the trouble! Because this screw is hidden behind the battery door, you don't see it until you take off the battery door's plastic cover panel. This screw resembles the bottom two screws because it again is attached to metal at the bottom. Set this screw aside with the rest.

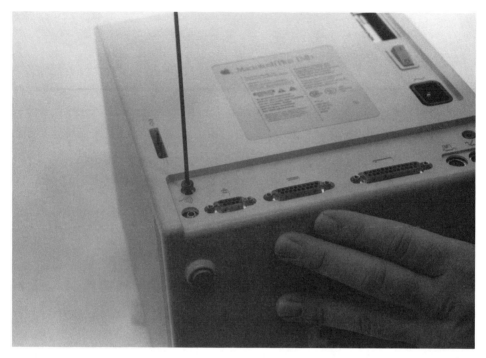

13-5 Remove the bottom two case screws.

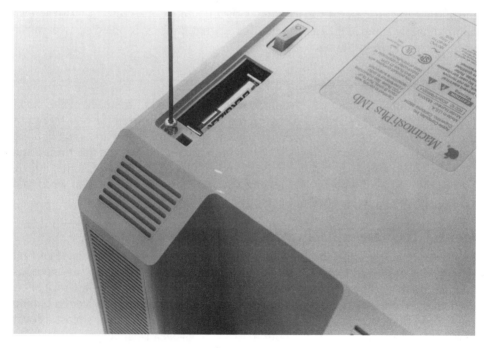

13-6 Remove the battery door case screw.

Remove the case back

Now you are ready to remove the front of the case from the back of the case. The two are separated by a very fine seam that runs all around it. The spreader tool, regardless of the type you have, is used to gently pry these apart in several places so that you can just put your hands around the outside of the case and gently lift it up, letting the weight of the Macintosh do most of the work after getting it pried apart.

So about two or three inches down from the top of the Macintosh if you are looking at it from the front on each side, insert your spreader tool, as shown in Fig. 13-7, and gently pry it apart, about an eighth of an inch or so. When you're through prying at the top, move down to the bottom of the Macintosh on each side and do the same thing so that the case back has been uniformly lifted from the case front about an eighth of an inch, or slightly more, all the way around. When you insert the spreader tool be careful that you don't scratch the plastic; insert the tool deeply enough into the groove so it stays seated while you're exerting the pressure to actually spread the plastic covers apart. If you find any resistance, make sure that you've removed all five screws. It should easily slip off at this point—maybe you will have to work it a little bit—but in most cases, it will easily slide off. Lift it off and put it aside in a safe place away from your work area. Rest it on its front edges, not on the outside back plastic panel, so it is not scratched.

Also remove L-shaped piece of metal with the holes at its back whose purpose is to prevent stray radio frequency interference from coming out of your Mac.

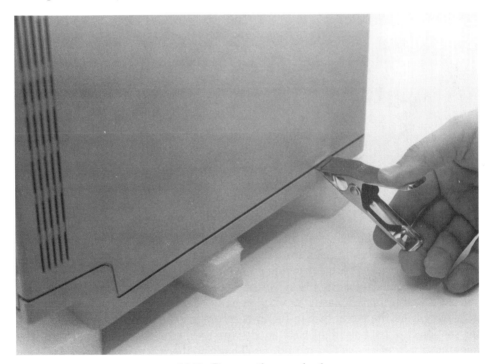

13-7   Remove the case back.

Older versions were just metal foil. New versions are metal and plastic that also protect the bottom of the circuit board from the case. Just slide it gently upwards off the back of your exposed Mac chassis, and set it aside nearby or on top of your cabinet back.

Locate the CRT anode

In Fig. 13-8, my finger points to (without touching!) the high-voltage contact on the CRT tube inside of your Macintosh. This is the part of your Mac that you do not want to touch with your fingers on either side along its extent—neither the tube side nor on the other side.

13-8   Locate the CRT anode.

Discharge the CRT anode

Figure 13-9 shows the wire with an alligator clip on both ends with one end clipped to the CRT grounding lug and the other end to the shaft of a single long-bladed screwdriver. (Go for the CRT grounding lug only because discharging your CRT to other parts of the chassis could inadvertently destroy your logic board!) Make sure you use a well-insulated plastic- or wooden-handled screwdriver, and keep your fingers away from the metal part in this process. Work the screwdriver blade under the suction clip that covers the CRT anode wire until it touches the metal wire. You might hear a brief hiss or tick or nothing. That's all there is to it! Just pay attention to what you are doing because this is high voltage and can bite you and/or the deli-

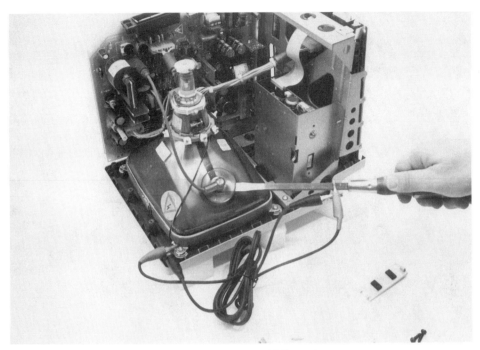

13-9 Discharge the CRT anode.

cate electronics in your Macintosh. Now that you've discharged the high voltage area, it's safe to remove the logic board or perform any other work you need to do inside of your Mac.

Remove the cables

Before you can remove the logic board, you need to remove the two cables that connect it to the Macintosh chassis, the power cable and the floppy drive cable. The finger in Fig. 13-10 points to these cables. Looking down through the top inside of the chassis, you can see that the multi-colored cable is your power cable. A small engaging tab on the logic board holds it in place, and you need to use a little extra effort to pull this connector off. Gently wiggle the connector from side to side until it comes free from the logic board. Next, you'll notice a flat 20-pin, 20-conductor ribbon cable. You can just grab the ribbon cable by its plug near the logic board and, again, gently wiggle it free from the logic board. Now your logic board is ready to be removed from the chassis.

Remove the logic board

Figure 13-11 shows removing the logic board. The removal is done by just pulling the logic board straight up, sliding it up in its metal track after disengaging the two metal clips from their slots in the chassis. Occasionally, you have to wiggle the logic board itself as it slides upward in its chassis channel track to remove it.

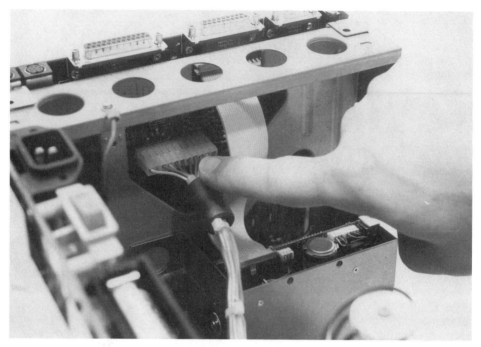

13-10 Remove the cables.

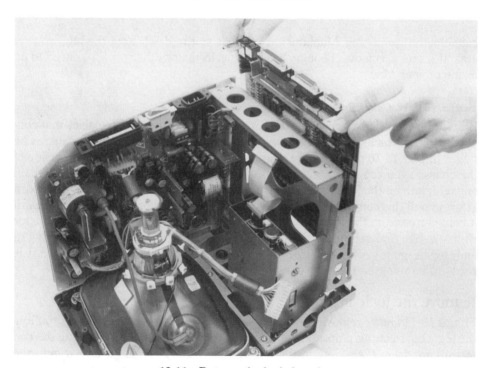

13-11 Remove the logic board.

Mac Plus versus Mac 512 logic board   Figure 13-12 compares Mac Plus and Mac 512 (also Mac 128) logic boards. My finger points to the SIMMs area on the Mac Plus logic board—one of its main differences.

Mac 512 logic board memory area   Figure 13-13 shows the part of the Mac 512 logic board where its memory chips are located. On the 128 and 512 boards, this area differs only in the sizes of the chips used. The 128 board uses 64K memory chips soldered to the board; the 512 board uses soldered-on 256K memory chips plus some additional circuitry.

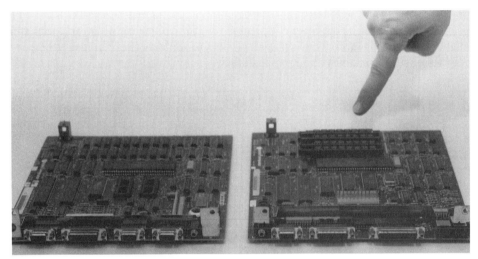

13-12   The Mac 512 (left) versus the Mac Plus logic board.

13-13   Mac 512 logic board memory area.

At this time, it really doesn't make sense to go through the soldering process to change the chips on your 128 logic board, although you can do this. There are many safer and faster ways to get at it and the soldering step is best left to a specialist. To repeat, let me counsel you, in the strongest possible terms, not to do any soldering on your Mac 128 logic board unless you are a glutton for punishment, know exactly what you are doing, and have the time to do it. Oh well, it's only money.

Mac Plus logic board memory area Figure 13-14 shows the layout of the SIMM memory modules along the front of the Mac Plus logic board—a significant improvement over the Mac 512's soldered-on RAM chips! The Mac Plus logic board was the first board in the Macintosh family to use SIMMs, and this step made it much easier for the average person to change the memory chips and SIMMs ensured reliability and expansibility.

13-14 Mac Plus logic board memory area.

Adding upgrades

The most likely upgrades to your clip-on Mac are memory, floppy disk, logic board and daughterboard upgrades.

Adding or removing SIMMs

The most likely upgrade you'll make to your Mac Plus is to add or change SIMMs. Figure 13-15 through Fig. 13-17 show the steps in removing a SIMM. Putting one in is just the reverse, only easier because it just snaps in place. (Are you static-free?)

13-15   The screwdriver points to the plastic finger on the SIMM board.

13-16   The screwdriver points to the plastic finger moved to the edge of the SIMM board.

13-17 The screwdriver points to the edge of the SIMM board now free of the plastic finger.

To remove a SIMM chip, start from the front edge of the board, and work back toward the middle. Notice that the SIMM is held in place by clips at either end. Figure 13-15 shows the corner of the SIMM with the screwdriver pointing to the little black plastic "finger" holding it in place. The plastic "finger" of the SIMM socket is at the edge of the SIMM.

If you carefully use a flat-bladed screwdriver and/or your fingernail, you can in most cases easily remove the SIMM chip. The object of the game is to use either your screwdriver or a fingernail to move the "finger" off to the edge of the SIMM circuit board, working one end at a time. So the process is to pry one edge loose halfway, go back to the other side of the SIMM chip and pry it loose halfway, go back to the other side of the SIMM chip and pry it loose the rest of the way, and finally, go back to the other end of the SIMM chip and pry it loose the rest of the way so that the SIMM chip is just being held at the edges as shown in Fig. 13-16.

Then merely use finger pressure to push the SIMM chip the rest of the way forward out of the socket when the edge connectors no longer restrain it. In Fig. 13-17, the SIMM has been moved forward and is now free of its socket. When removing the SIMM from its socket, be careful to handle the SIMM by its edge only! The most important thing to remember in the care and handling of SIMMs is static. Be sure to thoroughly ground yourself before handling your SIMMs, and, if you feel the least bit unsure, use the anti-static wrist strap.

I have never had a problem using a small, flat-bladed screwdriver to remove SIMMs. The screwdriver is a lot easier to use than my fingers—I am always able to remove the SIMM after a few moments of effort. My secret is I use the screwdriver gently. The process might be a little tedious, but it is quite satisfactory. I have never met anyone who has damaged a SIMM or a socket using this technique if they were careful in what they were doing. Again, the object is never to force anything.

As mentioned in chapter 12, having a SIMM removal tool is not foolproof insurance against breaking SIMM sockets. If you apply the wrong type of pressure, the socket "fingers" will break. It doesn't make any difference whether this pressure comes from your fingers, a flat-bladed screwdriver, or the SIMM removal tool.

One last housekeeping item is to make sure that RAM-size resistors R8 and R9 shown in Fig. 13-18 are set correctly for the amount of memory you have installed per Table 6-3 in chapter 6.

13-18 RAM-size resistors R8 and R9 on the Mac Plus logic board.

400K to 800K floppy disk upgrade

The 400K to 800K floppy drive upgrade is the most likely upgrade you will make to your Mac 128 or Mac 512. Figure 13-19 shows the goodies you get when you unpack your M2516 Apple 800K floppy drive upgrade kit (from right to left) which contains the 800K floppy drive in its bracket with ribbon cable (this drive is shipped with a yellow plastic restrainer inside of the floppy to prevent head move-

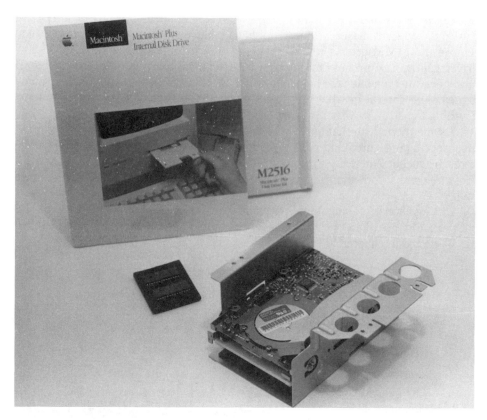

13-19 The Apple 800K Floppy Drive Upgrade Kit.

ment during shipment from damaging it); your software with an instruction manual for your 800K drive; and you get your two new 128K ROM chips.

Removing 400K floppy, installing 800K floppy After you've removed your logic board, look on the bottom of the chassis. Notice four small phillips-head screws with lock washers under their heads that hold the floppy disk bracket to the chassis. Remove them as shown in Fig. 13-20.

Also notice the loose end of the 20-conductor flat ribbon cable still poking down through the chassis opening. Notice this cable is flat and not twisted in any way so that when you reinstall it, it will be in the same way. Make a mental note of whichever way the red conductor is facing now, and replace it the same way when you put the new disk drive with its new ribbon cable back on.

When removing the last screw, hold on to the floppy drive bracket so that the bracket doesn't accidentally bang into the CRT tube and injure either it or the CRT. When you have removed the bracket with the 400K disk drive on it, just set it aside because you will not have a further use for it at this point.

Your new 800K floppy drive bracket is installed into the same spot with the same screw alignment and the same ribbon cable alignment as the 400K floppy drive bracket that you just removed. Put the four phillips-head screws back into

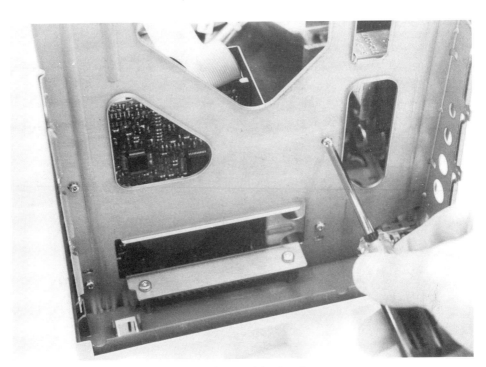

13-20 Remove floppy drive bracket screws.

place, tighten them down at least three-quarters of the way, and while holding the bracket firmly against the inside front bezel tighten the screws the rest of the way. Leave the yellow shipping disk in place during this process because it is automatically ejected later on when you boot up your Mac and it protects your floppy drive until you're ready to use it.

Removing old ROMs, installing new ROMs You will have to remove the two old 64K ROM chips from the logic board before you can put in the two new 128K ROM chips that came with your Apple 800K floppy drive upgrade kit. With the logic board (in this case, a 512 logic board) resting on a smooth, nonconductive surface, use your IC removal tool to gently pry up one of the ROM chips, one end at a time as is shown in Fig. 13-21.

If you don't have a removal tool, you can use a small flat-bladed screwdriver to accomplish the same purpose by just inserting the screwdriver under the ROM chip and then gently prying it upward to work one end free and going then to the other end and repeating the process until you get to the point just described. When you're ready to remove the ROM chip, if you don't have the removal tool, just grasp it firmly between your thumb and index finger, lift it straight up, and set it aside. Before removing them, notice the indentation appearing on one edge (one without pins coming from it) and the orientation of this indentation to the logic board. The new ROMs go in with the exact same orientation. Don't go by the indentation on the ROM sockets. Sometimes they are inadvertently installed backwards! You also should notice that the ROM sockets on the board are labeled High and Low, and

13-21 Remove old 64K ROM chips.

there are numbers on the old ROM chips that you are removing from the board. Here are a few rules involving them:

- Don't mix old and new ROMs.
- Old ROM numbers are 342-0341B High, 342-0342A Low.
- New ROM numbers are 342-0341C High, 342-0342B Low.

Follow the simple step of always putting the high-numbered ROM into the high-numbered ROM socket and the low-numbered ROM into the low-numbered ROM socket. Go ahead and remove the second ROM chip at this point and set it aside. Putting in the two new ROM chips is as straightforward a process as removing them. In this case, you want to be paying attention to the alignment as mentioned. Put one row of the chip legs into the socket, bend the chip slightly so the other legs go into the socket holes on the other side, and push the ROM chip firmly down into the socket holder on the board to seat it. After you have done this, give it a quick visual inspection to make sure all the pins are actually in all the holes and that no pin has accidentally been bent or left out of its socket. The second chip should be inserted in the same way. That's all there is to the 800K floppy upgrade.

Mac 128/512 to Plus logic board swap

If you have an Apple Macintosh Plus Upgrade kit, you are going to be inserting your ROM chips for the 800K upgrade into your new Mac Plus logic board instead of putting them back into your Mac 512 logic board. In this case your steps are as before, up to the point where you came to reinsert your ROM chips. Notice on your

Mac Plus logic board that it too has the High and Low labelled ROM sockets that are empty when you first get the board. To get the proper orientation, notice the way all the other indentations on the board are facing and insert the 128K ROM chips into their sockets on the Mac Plus logic board using the same orientation.

The Mac Plus logic board upgrade kit that you received should have your logic board with 1Mb of 256K SIMMs installed. In other words, you should have four banks, each containing one 256K SIMM in it on your Mac Plus logic board when you receive it. Just make sure visually by inspecting the logic board that these are all firmly seated and in place. Reinstalling the logic board is the reverse of removing it; here you want to make sure the cables, both the power, and floppy drive cable, are out of the way when you push the Mac Plus logic board back into the chassis. If they aren't out of the way, they could accidentally snag on a component and damage it. Make sure these cables are out of the way and gently push your logic board back into the chassis until it is seated again and the two clips near the screw holes on either side are again fully engaged into the chassis.

Adding a daughterboard upgrade

Adding SIMM memory, a SCSI port, and even an external video monitor to your Mac 512 or 128 is a snap these days because of daughterboard option boards by Newbridge Microsystems or Computer Care (introduced in chapter 6) that you merely clip-on to your Mac 512 or 128 logic board.

The key to this process is a little device called a Killy clip shown in Fig. 13-22.

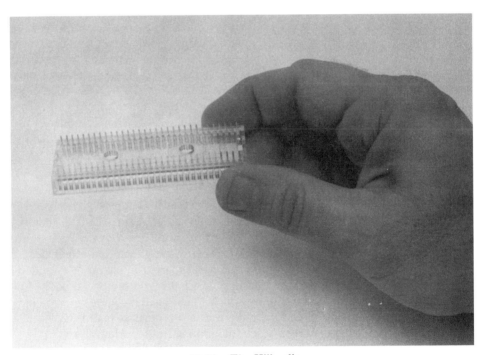

13-22   The Killy clip.

It is a clip that sits over the 68000 CPU chip on your logic board whose upper end connects directly to the daughterboard. The Killy clip will only work with the plastic type of 68000 chips, not the ceramic. If you have a ceramic chip, you'll have to solder an adapter on and you really are, again, best advised to have somebody else do this for you. You attach the Killy by sliding one end of it under the plastic 68000 chip on your logic board as shown in Fig. 13-23, and then go to the other end and hold up the little plastic tab with a small screwdriver just until you can slip it under the chip while pushing down into place with a firm push. Once you've done it, it's like riding a bicycle. Once the Killy clip is in place, you can clip on daughterboards, accelerator boards, video cards, anything to your clip-on Mac.

13-23 The Killy clip being attached to a Mac 512 logic board.

Figure 13-24 shows the Computer Care board being seated on top of a 512 logic board. Figure 13-25 shows the cables and adapters that let you use either external VGA or multisync monitors with this particular Computer Care board.

Although I briefly discussed them earlier under Mac 128/512 memory upgrades, the daughterboards from Computer Care and Newbridge Microsystems more closely resemble accelerator boards in their appearance and attachment. I have used them both. They are easy to install, transparent in operation (you don't even know they are there), reliable, and best of all, easy on the pocketbook. And you get above a 20% improvement over a stock Mac Plus. Of course, you still have to do the Apple 800K floppy/ROM upgrade. Either one of these boards has options that allow you to use larger screen video monitors with your Mac.

13-24 A Computer Care MacRescue memory board being installed on a Mac 512 logic board.

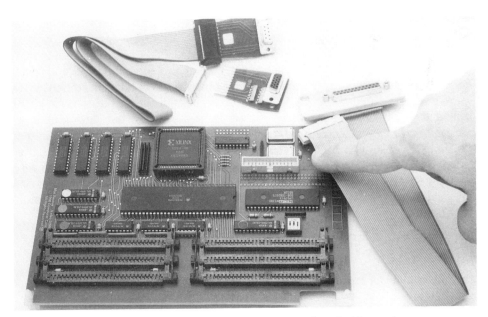

13-25 Computer Care MacRescue memory board video options.

The Newbridge Microsystems board was shown being installed on a 512 logic board in Fig. 6-9 in chapter 6. The main advantage of the Newbridge board, with its eight SIMM sockets, is you can mix and match 256K and 1Mb SIMMs in 512K increments all the way up to the 4Mb Mac Plus limit. This is a handy feature and helps you find a place for all those 256K SIMMs you might have laying around from other upgrades. You can use the memory already on the 512 logic board (but not on the 128 logic board memory) to help you.

The Computer Care board shown in Fig. 13-24, is almost identical to the Newbridge board in appearance, but the Computer Care board has only six SIMMs sockets and uses a DIP switch rather than jumpers for memory settings. You can only use either all 256K or all 1Mb SIMMs at one time with your options being 1Mb, 2Mb, 2.5Mb, or 4Mb. As with Newbridge, the 512 logic board memory is usable, the 128's is not. But the DIP switch makes memory settings a breeze.

Other upgrades

Accelerator board options install on the clip-on Mac family the same way as daughterboards do—via the Killy clip. In all these installations, the only real hitch comes in closing up the Mac after the install. Although all vendor instructions are very explicit, you usually have to install the logic board into one of the chassis grooves, then use your small screwdriver to pry the chassis apart wide enough for the other edge to drop in place. The component height clearances do not permit you to slide the board back into place down the chassis rails as before. Other than the small additional problem of snaking the new SCSI and video cables out the cabinet back, all proceeds quite smoothly.

SCSI hard disks are occasionally installed inside clip-on Macs. I do not recommend you do this unless you buy an adapter kit that also contains an additional internal power supply and fan for providing power and cooling to the hard disk. Many early kits (Rodime, etc.) provided these in addition to the internal SCSI cable and mounting bracket. Today, you are better served by purchasing an inexpensive yet reliable external hard disk drive in a "zero-footprint" enclosure that sits under your clip-on Mac. If you want an internal hard disk, you are better served by going to a one-slot Mac SE or SE 30 or the new Mac Classic. These models have all been specifically designed to accommodate internal hard disks.

That about does it. You have mastered the clip-on Mac family upgrade process. Onward!

In a nutshell

The key points you have seen in this chapter are:

- The tools you need include two screwdrivers, a long-handled Torx screwdriver and spreader, CRT discharge tools, an anti-static wrist strap, and a firm padded rubber mat or equivalent.

- Taking apart a clip-on Mac presents no unusual difficulties once you remember there are five screws to remove—the last one is behind the battery door.
- The four upgrades you are likely to do are all straightforward: memory, 800K floppy disk upgrade, main logic board, and daughterboard/accelerator board.
- Internal SCSI hard disk upgrades are not recommended; use the external type, or go to another model Mac.

Chapter 14
Upgrade your one-slot Mac SE or SE 30

If you've managed any clip-on Mac upgrade described in chapter 13, anything said in this chapter should really be a breeze for you. You have no Killy clips to worry about and only four screws to remove to open the case. See, it's easier already.

The one-slot Macs (the Mac SE and SE 30) were designed by Apple from the very beginning to be upgradable. The result is there are far more upgrades available for them, and the upgrades are much easier to do—just plug a board in a slot or pop in a floppy or hard disk module. Third-party vendors have made numerous provisions (options, brackets, cables, etc.) to accommodate your upgrade whims. Chances are, you will be doing most of your upgrade work on these models and will grow quite familiar with them.

In this chapter you learn how to take the cover off your Macintosh SE or SE 30, then add options such as memory, floppy disk, hard disk, and PDS option cards. Ready?

Taking apart your one-slot Mac

Although one-slot Mac upgrades are much easier to do, they require the same tools as the clip-on Macs for taking them apart.

The tools you need

To take apart your one-slot Mac, you need:

- Medium phillips-head screwdriver.
- Small flat-bladed screwdriver.
- Long-handled Torx screwdriver and spreader tool.
- CRT discharging tools.
- Anti-static wrist strap.
- Firm sponge pad to protect your Mac's front bezel when you lay it face down.

Pre-opening steps

The following steps make your life easier:

- Prepare your work area, make sure a padded mat is available to rest your Mac face down on, and additional space is available away from the main work area to temporarily store your case back and RFI shroud so no harm will come to them.
- Turn off the power, disconnect the power cord, and remove it from your work area.
- Disconnect the keyboard and mouse cables, and remove the keyboard and mouse from the work area.

Opening the case

The case situation with the one-slot Macs is the opposite of the clip-on Macs. One-slot Mac case backs are absolutely identical; only the front bezel is different. Figure 14-1 tells the story. It compares the front of the Mac SE 30 on the left with the SE front bezel I am holding on the right. The SE 30 is only set up for one floppy slot instead of the two slots possible with the SE. When you purchase the Apple SE 30 Upgrade kit, you change the front panel and inside chassis, but keep the case back.

14-1   The front of a Mac SE 30 (left) versus the front of a Mac SE.

Remove the reset switch

Figure 14-2 shows the removal of the reset switch that is on the lower left side of the SE or SE 30 as viewed from the front. This reset switch, although a larger one than on the clip-on Macintoshes, actually comes out a little easier. You pry up the bottom and the switch snaps out. Notice it has two hooks along the top that engage it so that when it's time to put it back in it's relatively easy to do. Also, this reset switch has only one set of slots that accept it and these slots are slightly higher than the ones on both sides of it, so it's pretty hard to put it in the wrong spot when you go to put it back.

Remove the top two case screws

The SE and SE 30 take-apart sequence only involves removing four screws rather than the five screws required to be removed by the clip-on Mac family. Figure 14-3

14-2 Remove the reset switch.

14-3 Remove the top two case screws.

shows the Mac SE in a face-down position on a cushioned pad to protect the front panel bezel and a long-handled screwdriver being used to remove one of the top two screws.

Remove the bottom two case screws

After the top screws are loosened, go back and loosen the bottom two screws as shown in Fig. 14-4. Finally remove all four screws. You will notice that the bottom two screws differ from the top two screws in that they are dark, close-threaded, and designed to hold into metal whereas the top two are bright, coarse-threaded, and designed to hold into plastic. Remember this distinction, and keep the screws separate when you are laying them aside on your work surface.

Remove the case back

Figure 14-5 shows the use of the spreader tool in removing the case back from the SE. Using the same technique as used with the clip-on Macs, you use the spreader around the top of the case and move it up about an eighth of an inch on one side, go to the other side, do the same thing, go to the bottom right, the bottom left, do the

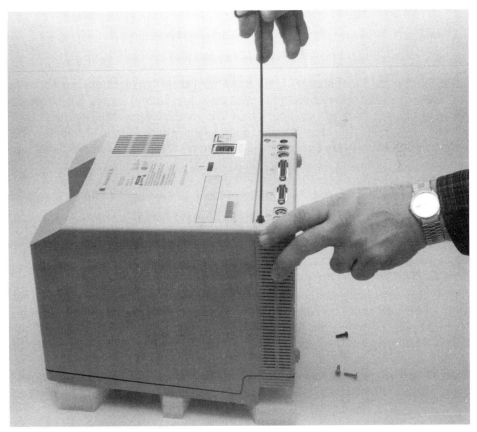

14-4   Remove the bottom two case screws.

14-5 Remove the case back.

same thing until it's about an eighth of an inch or so all away around the case. Then you grab the back of the case with both hands, and let the Mac's weight assist you in removing the case back from the case front attached to the chassis. The slight wiggling or rocking motion is occasionally necessary to accomplish this, but it should slide off very easily. When this is done, temporarily store it away from the work area until you need it. Set the case back on its front edges so that you don't scratch the outside back.

Remove the RFI shroud. It is similar to the one used on the clip-on Macs, but of a different shape to accommodate the different back connector locations. On the SE 30, it actually comes up along the sides as well as covering the back and bottom. Remove this and set it aside, near or on the case back.

Discharge the CRT anode

Figure 14-6 shows the two long-handled screwdriver method of discharging this anode. There are variations of this theme, but in the figure I have two long-handled screwdrivers. Use well insulated plastic- or wooden-handled screwdrivers, and keep your fingers away from the metal part in this process. (Yes, I know my left index finger is on the left screwdriver's metal shaft in Fig. 14-6, but do as I say, not as I do!) In the figure, I'm using the left long-handled screwdriver to work my way under the CRT anode suction cup to reach the lead wire metal part, touching the screwdriver in my right hand to the ground lug (where the black power supply wire is attached under the upper left CRT tie-down screw is the spot as shown in the figure), and holding the two shafts of the screwdrivers together.

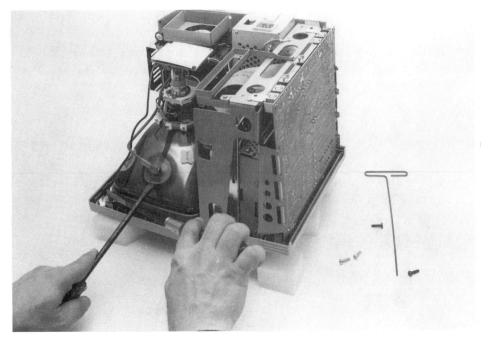

14-6 Discharge the CRT anode.

You should see or hear the spark as you discharge the high-voltage capacitor. Or you might hear nothing. The SE and SE 30 have a bleeder resistor on the anode wire that drains off the charge when the power is off. That's all there is to it! Just as simple as the alligator clip discharging technique discussed in the clip-on Mac chapter. Again, pay attention to what you are doing because this high voltage can bite you and/or the delicate electronics in your Mac. Now that you've discharged the high voltage area, it's safe to remove the logic board or perform any other work you need to do inside of your Mac.

Remove the video card

On the SE and SE 30 (and Mac Classic), the very next thing you want to do is remove the video card from the anode neck as shown in Fig. 14-7. Just lift it straight up and set it off towards the power supply side of the Mac without disconnecting it. If you remove it and get it out of the way, you lessen the chance of either damaging the video card or breaking the neck of your CRT while changing the floppy or hard disk drives or removing the logic board cables.

Remove the expander bracket

Next, again in the interest of making things easier to work on, remove the three phillips-head sheet metal screws holding the expander bracket onto the chassis as shown in Fig. 14-8, and set the bracket aside in a safe place on your work area.

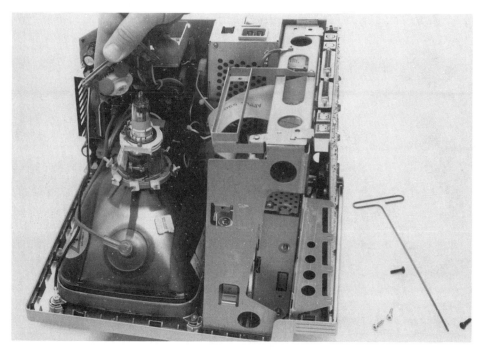

14-7 Remove the video card.

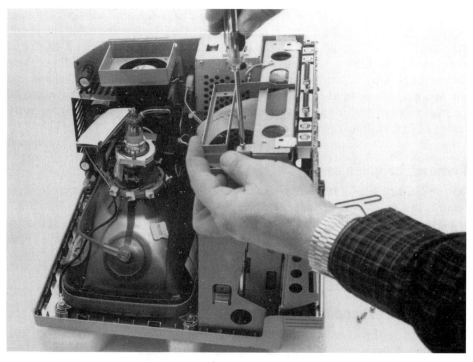

14-8 Remove the expander bracket.

Remove the logic board cables

Now you are ready to remove your logic board. Whether it's an SE or SE 30 logic board, before you can remove it from the chassis, first you need to disconnect the wires from the chassis going to it as shown in Fig. 14-9. For this step, you can either set your Mac upright on your work surface or leave it face down on its front bezel.

Typically, your SE and SE 30 have a hard disk installed inside the chassis, so instead of having two cables to disconnect as with the clip-on Macs, you will actually have four cables to disconnect. (You could have five cables to disconnect if you have a second floppy drive or SCSI hard disk installed.) This time, in addition to the power and the floppy disk cables as you encountered previously, you also have the flat 50-pin SCSI ribbon cable to the hard disk and the two-wire twisted pair speaker cable from the logic board (this wire was in the power cable harness on the clip-on Macs).

Also, and this is very important, notice my hand position in Fig. 14-9. Regardless of how your Mac is oriented, you want to position your hand so that it is holding onto the chassis frame when you are removing the cables. Under no circumstances do you want to pull on a cable and have your hand suddenly come loose and fly up and strike the neck of the CRT.

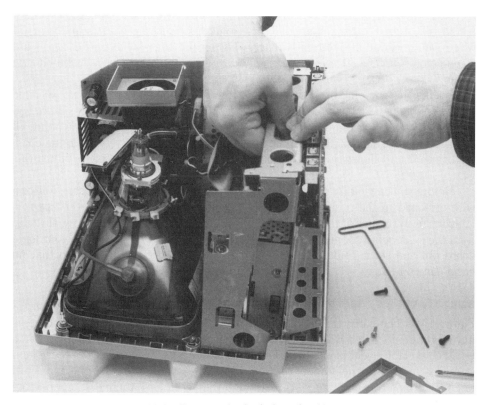

14-9 Remove the logic board cables.

Reach down inside the chassis area and disconnect the multi-colored power cable first. On the SE and the SE 30, it is a Molex-type connector that has a locking tab lever on it. To disengage it, you squeeze this tab lever gently towards the center of the connector shell and at the same time gently lift it up from the Macintosh logic board using a side to side rocking motion. It is a lot easier to do than it is to describe. Do not use force and pull on it—making what I warned you against in the previous paragraph a reality!

Once you have the power cable loose, move it up out of the way. Next, disconnect the SCSI 50-pin flat ribbon cable, which should come out with a gentle tug straight up or you might have to put your fingers around both sides of the connectors and wiggle it free. The 20-pin flat ribbon cable to the floppy disk comes out the same way. Be careful when pulling up on either the SCSI cable or the floppy cable because in certain instances during assembly the top stress relief part of these cables was not put on and pulling these cables (jerking them straight up) could actually pull the backs of these connectors off and pull the cable right off the connector back. You want to avoid this and having to put it back together again, so exercise restraint. Look before you pull, and if you have to pull on the ribbon cable itself, pull gently.

Remove the logic board

Now that you have the cables removed from the top of the board, disengage the two metal tabs from the back that holds the logic board in the chassis at the point where you removed the bottom two screws from the chassis. Once these tabs are disengaged from the chassis, you can slide the logic board upward in the chassis frame.

Unlike the clip-on Macs, the chassis frame holding the SE and SE 30 logic boards is notched. You only need to slide the logic board up a few inches before you can notice its notches match those in the chassis frame holding it. At this point, all you need to do is simply tilt the logic board toward you to remove it from the chassis. Figure 14-10 shows the logic board being removed from the chassis in just this way.

Before you can totally remove the logic board though from the chassis, notice a wire attached to the middle of it. This two-pair twisted wire from the speaker attaches to the center of the logic board via a little clip connector. Remove this clip from the logic board connector, making a note of where it went, and take your logic board out and set it aside face up on a nonconductive, clean surface so that no harm can come to it.

Mac SE Versus Mac SE 30 logic board

Figure 14-11 compares the Mac SE and SE 30 logic boards viewed from the rear (my finger points to the SE logic board's PDS connector). Their rear-facing outside world connector layout is identical. Only two major differences exist between them affecting upgrades. The number of SIMM sockets, layout, and rules on each is different (more on this in a moment). Although they both have their PDS connectors on the left side, the SE 30's PDS connector has 120 pins and is designed to accom-

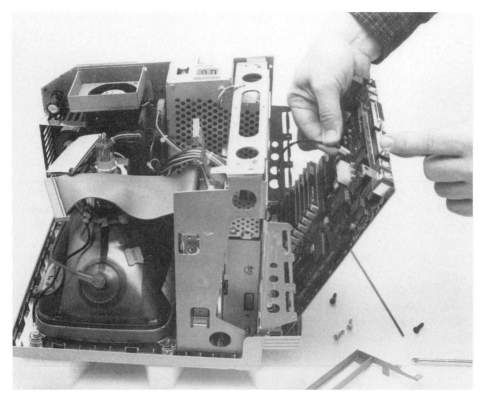

14-10 Remove the logic board.

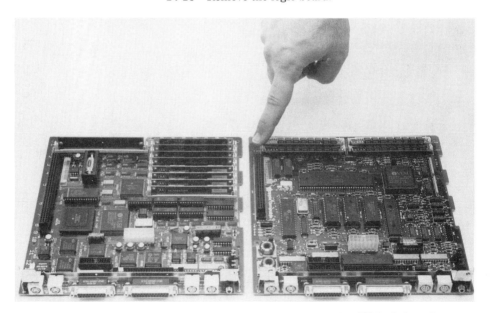

14-11 The Mac SE 30 logic board (left) versus the Mac SE logic board.

modate vertically mounted option cards. The SE's PDS connector has 96 pins and is designed to accommodate horizontally mounted option cards that lay over the top of the logic board.

Adding upgrades

One-slot Mac upgrades you can make include memory, floppy disk, hard disk, logic board, and PDS option cards. Let's take a closer look.

Adding or removing SIMMs

The most likely upgrade you'll make to your one-slot Mac is to add or change SIMMs. You can clearly see the different SIMMs arrangement on the SE 30 (left) versus the SE logic board in Fig. 14-11. The process is exactly the same as that described already in chapter 13, but the rules are different. Mac SE logic boards have four SIMM sockets just like Mac Plus logic boards, but they are arranged in two parallel rows at the front of the board, instead of four in a row as on the Mac Plus. The jumper rule details are again described by Table 6-3 in chapter 6. Figure 14-12 shows details of the SIMM jumper on the new SE logic boards that replace the resistor jumpers on earlier models. On the SE 30, you have eight SIMM sockets in a row with no jumpers to worry about. The rules are described by Table 6-4 in chapter 6. Just load and go!

14-12   SIMM jumpers on the Mac SE logic board.

FDHD floppy upgrade

There are two kinds of Apple SE models. One is the version with two floppy drives; the other is a version with one floppy drive and one 20Mb hard disk. In later SE models, Apple substituted FDHD floppy drives for the 800K drives and changed the SE front bezel logo to show that it was an FDHD version. Depending on the SE you have, you'll either have two floppies, a floppy and a hard drive, or a two-floppy version with a third-party vendor hard drive kit installed for three drives in all.

The most common SE upgrade is to add the Apple FDHD SE Upgrade kit. You wouldn't need to do this upgrade to your SE 30 because it already comes with an FDHD floppy. The FDHD upgrade kit contains three new chips to replace those currently on the SE logic board in addition to the FDHD floppy drive/bracket assembly. Let's upgrade the logic board first.

In Fig. 14-13, my fingers point to the three chips on the SE logic board you have to remove and replace. The logic board on the left already has the new chips installed. From right to left, the new chips you add are:

- High ROM 342-0701 (goes closest to larger chip or under my thumb).
- Low ROM 342-0702.
- SWIM chip 344-0062.

Use your IC extractor or small flat-bladed screwdriver to assist in removal as in chapter 13's ROM chip discussion, and again line up all the chip indentations to face in the same direction as those of the other chips on the board.

When you get your Apple FDHD upgrade kit, the most striking thing about

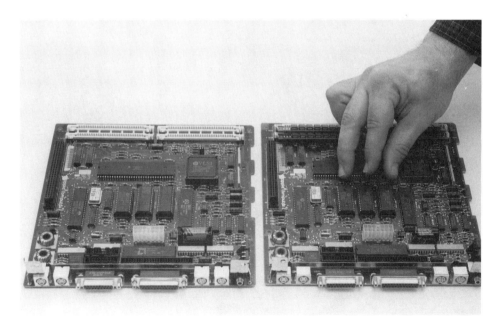

14-13   Replace the SE ROMS and IWM chip.

the floppy drive/bracket assembly is that it looks almost identical to the 800K disk drive and mounting bracket. First appearances are deceiving, however, and you can tell them apart in two ways:

- One way is by turning them upside down as shown in Fig. 14-14 where my finger points to FDHD unit on the right. You'll notice both of them have the words SONY prominently displayed on a label on the flywheel underneath, but one of them indicates it is a SONY 1Mb drive and the other indicates it is a SONY 2Mb drive. The SONY 2Mb drive is what becomes Apple's 1.4Mb FDHD when formatting is completed.
- Another way you can tell them apart is by looking at the front of them as shown in Fig. 14-15. The FDHD unit has three microswitches in the front (one on the left side, two on the right). The 800K drive only has two micro-switches in the front (one on each side). My finger points to the two micro-switches on the right side of the FDHD unit I am holding in my hand (the drive is upside down—it appears on the left in the photo).

Whether you have two or three drives in your SE, you need to first remove your hard disk, the top-most drive. Figure 14-16 shows this being done using a phillips-head screwdriver through one of the chassis access holes to remove one of the two phillips-head screws holding the hard disk bracket to the floppy disk bracket underneath. Figure 14-17 shows the hard disk drive assembly being removed from a two-drive SE. If there is a second, upper floppy drive, remove it in the same

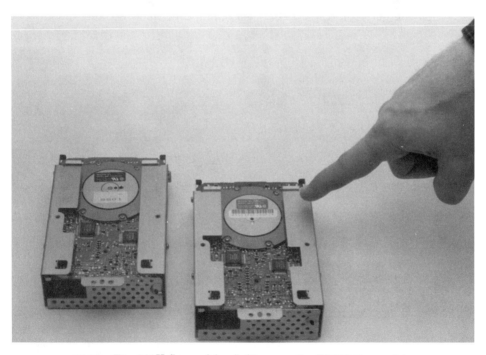

14-14   The 800K floppy drive (left) versus the FDHD floppy drive.

14-15 Three microswitches on the front of the FDHD floppy.

14-16 Remove hard disk assembly mounting screws.

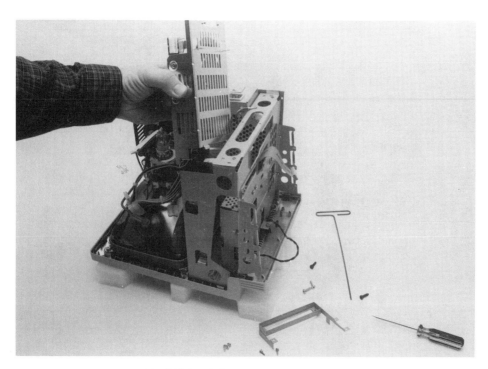

14-17 Lift hard disk assembly out of chassis.

way—it also has two screws facing to the rear attaching it to the floppy drive bracket below it.

Finally, to remove the lower floppy drive bracket, four phillips-head screws hold it to the chassis, just like in the clip-on Macs although the bracket-and-hole pattern is different. You need to get at these screws from the underside of the chassis as shown in Fig. 14-18. Once you have loosened these four screws, remove this floppy drive, and put the FDHD floppy drive back into the chassis in its place. Put the four screws back on. Make sure the FDHD floppy drive is snugly in place against the front bezel—just like the drive you removed—and make sure that it lines up with the opening. After you are sure of its placement, tighten all four screws firmly against their lock washers so that the drive doesn't vibrate loose with use.

The new FDHD drive comes with a pigtail ribbon cable; this is the one you reconnect into the lower drive connector on the SE motherboard. Depending on whether you have the dual floppy version or the SE 20 version, you are either going to be reinstalling your upper floppy or reinstalling your hard disk. With the FDHD floppy, it's really not necessary to have a second floppy drive unless you want the convenience of copying and you do a lot of it. If you do, the FDHD allows you the further flexibility of accommodating either an 800K or another FDHD floppy as the second SE floppy drive. Apple provides you with both decals just in case.

14-18   Remove floppy drive bracket screws.

Hard disk upgrade

The one-slot Mac family has great flexibility for accommodating different $3^{1}/_{2}$-inch form factor hard drives. Figure 14-19 shows the two SE/SE 30 style floppy drives mounted on top of one another just like they would be in the Mac SE chassis and the little U-shaped bracket that holds them together with the help of two screws. To the right is the third-party drive bracket that would mount on top of the two floppy drives in an SE case only. You would use this bracket to mount a third-party hard drive on top of the two floppies to give you three drives inside of your SE. The "offset" in this bracket that moves the third-party hard drives to the rear and outside of the SE case to clear other internal components would not work in an SE 30 that has its PDS card located in the same place.

Figure 14-20 shows how the Apple SE 30 hard disk is removed or installed in its Apple-provided bracket, simply a matter of four phillips-head screws. Figure 14-21 shows the hard disk after removal from the bracket. My finger points to the pigtail lead from the drive indicator LED on the bracket that plugs into the hard disk. Figure 14-22 shows the multitude of choices available to you in SE/SE 30 drive mounting brackets.

Basically, if you are going to put a hard disk in the place of your floppy disk, you are going to do a complete makeover of your dual floppy SE into a hard disk/

14-19 Mounting brackets for two or three drive options in Mac SE.

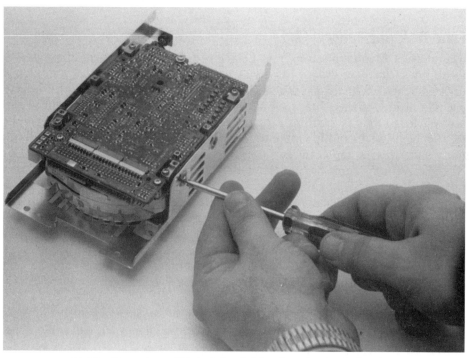

14-20 Removing a 3½-inch hard drive from its Apple bracket.

14-21 A 3½-inch hard drive for one-slot Macs with an Apple bracket.

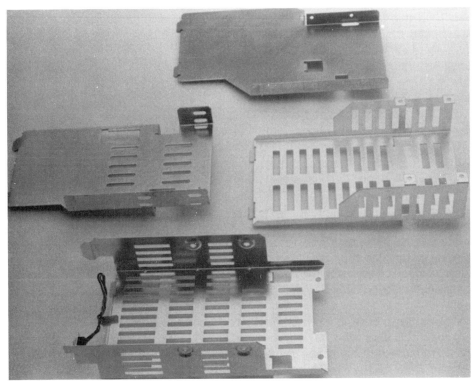

14-22 One-slot Mac hard drive bracket options.

floppy disk version. The small rectangular piece of plastic is provided in most SE hard disk upgrade kits to fill the upper floppy opening in the dual floppy SE version, so merely position this in the upper floppy opening. Notice that the clear window part to accommodate the hard disk drive light goes to the right as you would face the screen just exactly where the hole in the floppy is. Push this down into the opening from the rear until it snaps into place. In some cases, the opening is warped or slightly enlarged from use, and you can facilitate keeping it in place by using a small sliver of tape on either end.

SE to SE 30 upgrade

This Apple SE 30 upgrade kit is almost a complete makeover of your SE. You start with a new chassis and front bezel and put all your SE parts back into it except the logic board, which is replaced by the new SE 30 logic board. The process is best left to a trained technician because it is labor intensive and, whatever the small amount you pay, it's worth it because you get back a working Mac SE 30 with no sweat expenditure, no gray hairs, and no parts "left over" that you can't figure out what to do with.

PDS option card upgrades

SE and SE 30 option cards are not interchangeable. As mentioned earlier, their PDS connector sockets and mounting styles are different; you need to use a separate type of option card to extend the capabilities of each particular model. Many manufacturers, particularly those of video cards, offer their products in flavors to fit both. As a Mac SE or Mac SE 30 owner, the world of opportunities is open to you. Just plug the card of your choice into the PDS slot and go. If you don't have enough slots, plug a card into the one you have that routes you into an expansion chassis. Let's take a look at a few options.

Figure 14-23 shows the Lapis video card being plugged into an SE board. In Fig. 14-24, a Novy Quik 30 accelerator card is plugged into an SE board and Fig. 14-25 shows a Newbridge NewLife SE 25 accelerator card being plugged into an SE board. Notice it has an extension PDS connector on the top of the card so another "thin" card or device can be put on the card. Figure 14-26 shows a Second Wave card plugged into an SE 30 logic board out of its case to give you an idea of the relative positioning of the two. Figure 14-27 shows the same card being plugged into the same SE 30 logic board installed in its SE 30 chassis.

In the SE installations, as with the clip-on Macs, the only real hitch comes in closing up the Mac after the install, although the SE's slotted logic board and chassis make it much easier. In the SE 30, there is no problem. The right-angle method of option board insertion into the SE 30 logic board is positive, foolproof, and reliable.

As opposed to the clip-on Mac method of snaking cables out the back, the Mac SE and SE 30 offer substantial improvements to you here also. Figure 14-28 shows the external end of the connector from an expansion card cable (in this case the Second Wave expansion chassis SE 30 card) being installed in the expander

14-23 This is a Lapis video card being plugged into a Mac SE logic board.

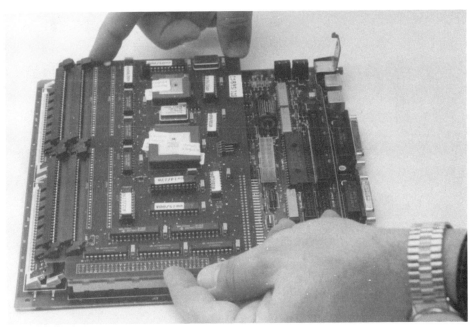

14-24 A Novy Quik 30 accelerator card being plugged into a Mac SE logic board.

14-25   A NewLife SE 25 accelerator card being plugged into a Mac SE logic board.

14-26   A Second Wave option card being plugged into an SE 30 logic board.

14-27 A Second Wave option card being plugged into an SE 30 chassis.

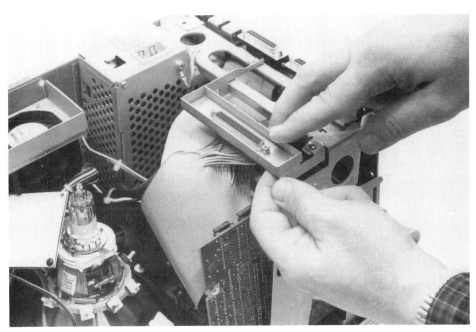

14-28 A Second Wave option card connector being plugged into an SE 30 expander bracket frame.

bracket frame. In Fig. 14-29, the blank plastic panel is removed from the back of the SE 30 case to create the opening for the expansion connector. Figure 14-30 shows the results—a neat, tidy and rugged expansion connector installation ready for business. Expanding your Mac SE or SE 30 via PDS option cards is easy to do and reliably delivers results after installation.

That does it for the one-slot Macs. You have now mastered them. Onward, to your next challenge.

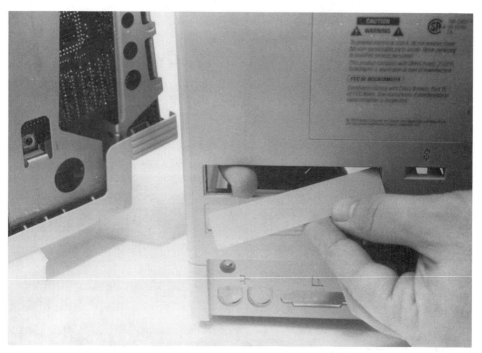

14-29   Removing the blank plastic panel from the back of an SE 30 case.

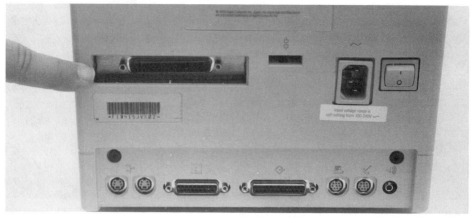

14-30   Completed expansion connector installation in back of an SE 30 case.

In a nutshell

Here are the key points you have seen in this chapter:

- One-slot Macs require the same tools as clip-on Macs: two screwdrivers, plus long-handled Torx screwdriver and spreader, CRT discharge tools, anti-static wrist strap, and a firm padded rubber mat or equivalent.
- Taking apart a one-slot Mac only requires you remove four Torx-head screws; removing a few more phillips-head screws inside the case allows you to take out the floppy and hard disk drives.
- The four upgrades you are likely to do are all straightforward: memory, FDHD floppy disk upgrade, hard disk upgrade, and PDS option cards.
- The one-slot Macs give you a wide range of option choices that are easy to install and, because of their design and attachment method, work reliably once in place.

Chapter 15
Upgrade your NuBus Mac II, IIx, IIfx, IIcx, IIci

Put away that spreader tool.

The only tools you'll need to upgrade your NuBus Macintoshes are two screwdrivers: a phillips-head and a flat-bladed. The NuBus family of Macintoshes, both the six-slot Mac II and its follow-on Macs and the three-slot Mac IIcx and its follow-on counterpart, were designed from the very beginning to be upgradable, flexible, and functional. They deliver in all three areas.

In the Mac II family, all it takes is the removal of one screw and the cover is off; the removal of four more screws takes you down to being able to get at the logic board. In the Mac IIcx family, it's even easier than that. You only remove one screw to take off the cover, and the rest of the IIcx or IIci snaps apart with the exception of a single additional screw to remove later on. You have no CRT or high voltages to worry about—everything is right out there in the open. The NuBus family Macintoshes would be a DOS PC owner's dream to work on—if they only knew.

In this chapter, you learn how to take the cover off your six-slot NuBus Mac, look at upgrades, then do the same for your three-slot NuBus Mac.

On your mark? Go!

Take the cover off your six-slot Mac II, IIx, or IIfx

After working on the clip-on or one-slot Macs, the NuBus Mac family is a real treat. The combination of much more room to work in, plus a greater variety of options to work with, creates an environment that you are not likely to soon outgrow. And if that possibility arises, you have a third-party expansion chassis with another eight slots to rescue you. The NuBus standard, and Apple's and third-party vendors' commitment to it, assures you that your flexibility and functionality will continue to grow in the future to accommodate your upgrade needs.

The tools you need

NuBus Macs only require the following tools:

- Medium phillips-head screwdriver.
- Small flat-bladed screwdriver.
- Anti-static wrist strap.

Pre-opening steps

The following steps make your life easier:

- Prepare your work area as before, but make sure additional space is available away from your work area to store your cover temporarily and near the main work area to store your monitor, video card, keyboard, and mouse.
- Turn off the power, disconnect all power cords, and remove them from your work area.

- Disconnect the keyboard and mouse cables, and remove the keyboard and mouse from the work area.

Opening the case

Figure 15-1 shows the front of a Mac IIfx, but its case is common to every member of the six-slot Mac family—only the logo is different. Figure 15-2 shows the rear of the Mac II case, which is also common to every member of the family. Notice the single screw opening in approximately the center of the top cover and the tabs at opposite ends of the rear of the top cover. With the front of the Mac II facing you, press these tabs gently inward and lift up the back of the top cover as shown in Fig. 15-3.

When you remove the top cover, it is very important to have it tilted up at approximately a 30 degree angle and that you move it slightly backward to disengage it and don't accidentally jerk it directly up. Notice that three little plastic loops at the lower edge of the front of the top cover hold it in place. Lifting the cover directly upwards rather than at an angle will break these little loops. This is the only thing you have to be careful of when removing the cover. And, actually, this is one of the few things you have to be careful of in working around your Mac II. As simple as it is, you can damage your cover, and it is a nuisance to work with a broken one. After you have the cover off, set it aside someplace so that it does not get accidentally scratched or damaged.

The reset switch on the Mac II is identical to the one used on the SE and SE 30, but in this case it is located on the right side of the case toward the rear at the bottom. Unless you're going to be removing the logic board to upgrade it, you'll have no need to do anything to the reset switch.

15-1 The front of a Mac IIfx six-slot NuBus Mac case.

15-2   The rear of a six-slot NuBus Mac case.

15-3   Opening the six-slot NuBus Mac case.

Upgrading your six-slot Mac II, IIx, or IIfx

That was easy, wasn't it? One other item first. Now that you've removed the top cover of your Mac II, IIx, or IIfx, and you're looking down at it from the front, notice the long silver box running the length of the case on the left-hand side. This is the power supply. Don't even think about getting inside of it—leave it alone. The most likely upgrades to your NuBus Mac II are floppy disk, CPU upgrades, memory, hard disk, and NuBus option card upgrades.

FDHD or second 800K floppy upgrade

On the right-hand side of the case is a metal platform whose rear half supports a half-height 5¼-inch (or smaller) hard disk and whose front half supports one or two floppy disks as shown in Fig. 15-4. If you want to add memory to your Mac II, upgrade to an FDHD floppy, or add a PMMU chip, you need to remove this platform.

To remove this platform, the four screws (located two on its left side and two on its right side) that hold it must be removed first. Figure 15-5 shows the platform's left front screw being removed, and Fig. 15-6 shows its left rear screw being removed. Carefully remove all four screws and the lock washers underneath them. If you are removing the platform to add memory or other chips to your logic board, you don't need to take the floppy and hard disks off this platform—merely unplug their cables from the logic board with one hand as you are lifting it off with the other. Notice the 20-pin flat ribbon cable to the right-hand floppy drive goes to the right side floppy connector (marked Lower) on the logic board and the left floppy drive cable goes to left side floppy connector (marked Upper). It's easy enough to remember.

15-4   The disk drive platform inside a six-slot Mac case.

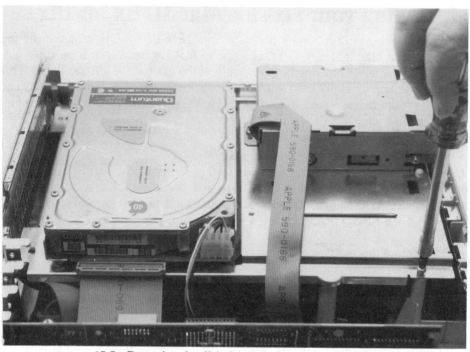

15-5 Removing the disk drive platform's front screw.

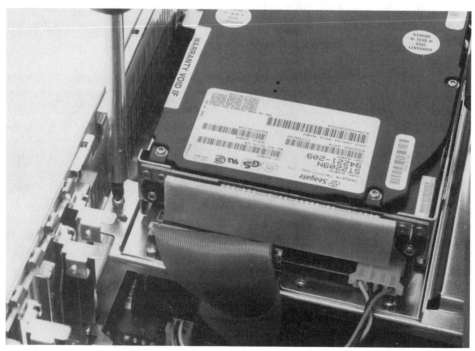

15-6 Removing the disk drive platform's rear screw.

If you are only adding a second floppy of the same type you already have, you don't even have to remove the platform because the floppy drive itself is held to the platform via one screw holding it in place using its bracket's front locking tabs. Just set the new floppy in place next to the existing one as shown in Fig. 15-7, and hook up its floppy drive cable.

Apple's FDHD Mac II Upgrade kit that you would add to an early vintage Mac II (not your Mac IIx or Mac IIfx because they already have one) contains five new chips to replace those currently on the Mac II logic board in addition to the FDHD floppy drive/bracket assembly.

To add the FDHD floppy simply take out the old floppy and put the new FDHD floppy in its place. Your Apple FDHD floppy drive/bracket looks almost identical to the 800K disk drive and mounting bracket. Use the guidelines in chapter 14's FDHD versus 800K drive discussion to distinguish them. You can even use the 800K floppy as a second floppy after the FDHD floppy is installed. If you do install a second floppy drive, be sure to remove the little plastic plate inside the top cover that covers this opening when it's not being used. This is done from the inside of the top cover that you've just taken off and set aside.

Now, you get to upgrade some chips on the logic board. Figure 15-8 shows the SIMMs area of the logic board with the platform removed. It also shows several other chips of interest to you. First, you will be replacing the four ROM chips. They are located directly beneath the SIMMs in Fig. 15-8 and are labeled on the logic board:

- U6—High ROM 342-0639.
- U5—Med High ROM 342-0640.
- U4—Med Low ROM 342-0641.
- U3—Low ROM 342-0642.

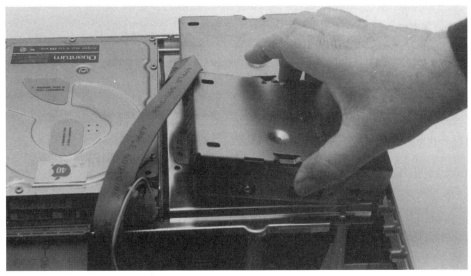

15-7   Adding a second floppy disk to a six-slot Mac.

15-8 A view of a Mac II logic board looking toward the SIMMs area.

Now look again at Fig. 15-8. At a four o'clock direction down from the SIMMs, you see four larger chips arranged in a square pattern. They are the:

- 68020 CPU chip (bright, large chip at upper right closest to speaker).
- 68881 FPU chip (directly beneath CPU chip).
- HMMU chip 343-0002 (directly to left of CPU chip).
- Custom ASIC gate array chip (directly beneath HMMU chip).

This is all very nice, but you haven't gotten to the chip you want yet. Find the support post the screw was being removed from in Fig. 15-5. In Fig. 15-9, my finger points to the IWN chip located directly beneath this same post on the logic board at a location labeled I10; it's also directly in line with the CPU and FPU chips and lies right above the FPU chip. You are going to replace this chip with a SWIM chip (344S0062).

Use your IC extractor or small flat-bladed screwdriver to assist in removal, as in chapter 13's ROM chip discussion. Again use the chip indentations on the chips you remove to guide you in orienting the new chips to face in the same direction. As a further assist, with your Mac II facing you, the beveled edge of the SWIM chip with the indentation or dot is facing the Mac II's power supply—or match the indentation on the chip with the indentation on its socket. Mac II logic board sockets were machine inserted!

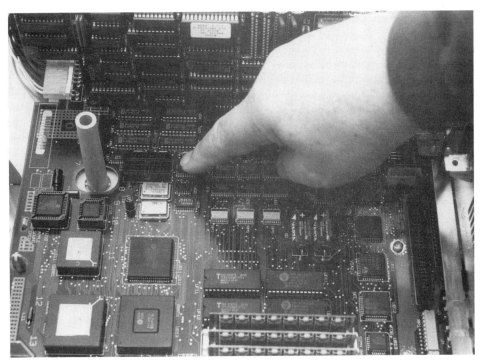

15-9 A view of a Mac II logic board looking away from the SIMMs area.

PMMU upgrade

While you are in this area of your logic board, another chip you are likely to add to your early vintage Mac II is the PMMU chip. This replaces the HMMU chip described earlier, supports both the 24-bit and 32-bit address modes, and lets you run System 7.0 and A/UX software without the expense of going to a 68030 upgrade. Carefully, use your IC extractor or small flat-bladed screwdriver to assist you in removing the HMMU chip. Place the PMMU chip into the socket you just removed the HMMU chip from. Before pushing it into place, with your Mac II facing you, verify that the line on its surface faces the lower right corner of the board, or in other words, towards the speaker.

Mac II CPU upgrade

DayStar's Powercard 030 for the Mac II would also be installed into this area of your logic board. It allows you to upgrade your Mac II to a 68030 Mac in flavors all the way up to a 50 MHz screamer. DayStar's accompanying instructions for its upgrade kit are fantastic, so I'll spare you the details. A few highlights should prove the point that this upgrade is both easy and beneficial.

As part of its kit, DayStar provides the chip puller tool shown in Fig. 15-10 (no, it's not a medieval torture device!). It makes the work of pulling the existing chips

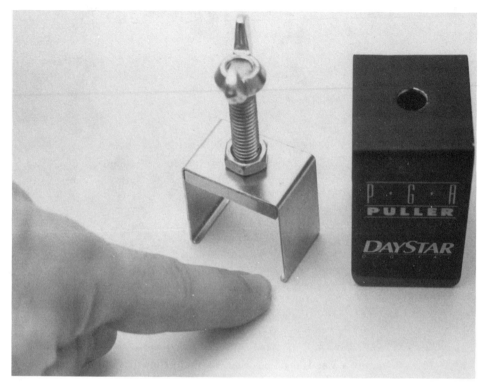

15-10   The DayStar chip puller.

out of their sockets easy and painless—both on you and your chips. It also keeps your delicate 68020 chip from bouncing off the ceiling, which some other chip removal techniques occasionally permit. After removing the 68020 and HMMU chips from the logic board (use the chip puller as shown in Fig. 15-11 and Fig. 15-12 to help you), replace the HMMU chip with DayStar's AMU adapter and insert the DayStar Powercard 030 into the vacant 68020 CPU socket as shown in Fig. 15-13. The DayStar Cache card is then inserted into the Powercard 030's two sockets as shown in Fig. 15-14. That's all there is to it. You boost performance to Mac IIci or IIfx levels, depending on the Powercard option you choose.

Adding or removing SIMMs

While you are in this area of your logic board, you're also able to get at the SIMMs located on your logic board. It's not a good idea to either add or remove SIMMs with the power turned on. It's impossible to do on the CRT-based Macs, because you need to take the logic board out of the case in order to get at the SIMMs. However, it is possible with the NuBus Macs—not that you would do this, of course! Again referring to Fig. 15-8, notice that there are eight SIMMs sockets and these are populated from the rear, working from the outside of the board toward the center of the board. The first SIMM socket you fill should be the one furthest away from the power supply. SIMMs go into the Mac II and Mac IIx exactly the way

15-11 First slide the DayStar chip puller gripper under the chip.

15-12 Then slide the DayStar chip puller frame over the gripper and turn the large wing nut.

15-13 Insert the DayStar Powercard 030 into a vacant 68020 CPU socket.

15-14 Insert the DayStar cache card into the Powercard 030.

they went into the Plus, SE, and SE 30 logic boards. Like the SE 30, the Mac II can accommodate 256K or 1Mb SIMMs, you have no jumpers to worry about, and the rules are described by Table 6-4 in chapter 6. Just load and go!

Piggyback memory cards

Figure 15-15 shows Computer Care's Mac II/IIx Softstep memory card prior to installation of SIMMs on it. This card allows you to utilize your older 256K SIMMs alone (must be faster than 120 ns) or in conjunction with 1Mb SIMMs (must be faster than 120 ns) to build up to 32Mb of memory in your Mac II. If you need to go beyond 8Mb, you need to add Maxima software (or System 7.0). Each Softstep memory card accepts four 256K or four 1Mb SIMMs and, of course, the memory rules follow the standard Mac guidelines. On the down side, the height of these cards extends the SIMM socket heights and does not permit you to use them in a Mac II or IIx at the same time as a full-height 5¼-inch hard drive. You'll have to make a command decision and choose one or the other.

15-15   The Computer Care Mac II/IIx Softstep memory card.

Adding or removing Mac IIfx SIMMs

Figure 15-16 shows the detail of the SIMM socket area of the Mac IIfx logic board. Compared to the Mac II and Mac IIx, they are rotated 90 degrees and now face the back of the Mac so that the first SIMM socket is closest to the rear of the Mac. The 64-pin Mac IIfx SIMMs were described in chapter 6. The metal-clip Mac IIfx SIMM sockets are vastly superior to their plastic counterparts on the Mac II and Mac IIx logic boards. Inserting or removing SIMMs is done much more easily. Your fingernail is about all you need to insert or remove SIMMs. The Mac IIfx follows the memory rules described by Table 6-4 in chapter 6 and, like the Mac II and Mac IIx, can accommodate up to 32Mb of RAM memory by populating each of its SIMM sockets with a 4Mb RAM SIMM. Your dream toy!

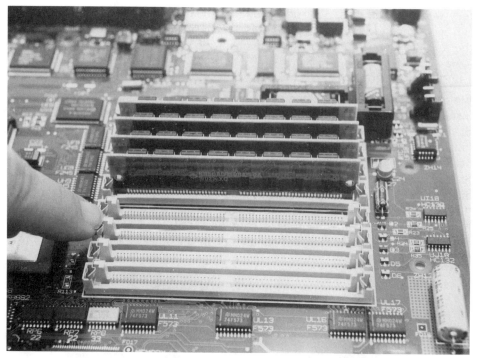

15-16   The Mac IIfx logic board SIMMs area.

Hard disk upgrade

The Mac II family has the greatest flexibility of any Mac model to accommodate a wide variety of hard disk solutions. The original Mac II hard disks were 5¼-inch style Quantum 40Mb or 80Mb models located at the back of your mounting platform, as shown earlier in Fig. 15-4. These were extremely rugged and reliable units and state-of-the-art technology in their time. But one year is a lifetime in hard disks and three years is an eternity, so these disks are no longer cutting-edge, state-of-the-art units, but they are still very usable. What you would most likely be doing in upgrading the hard disk in your Mac II is just getting a larger or faster model.

In my experience, if you're replacing the 40Mb hard drive in your Mac II, you're going with a 105Mb or 170Mb 3½-inch model or a 300Mb 5¼-inch full-height hard disk drive. If you have an 80Mb hard drive, you are replacing it with a 210Mb 3½-inch drive or a 600Mb full-height unit. In either event, the process is basically the same, but the procedure and the parts are different.

If you are replacing your 40Mb or 80Mb unit with a 3½-inch or 5¼-inch half-height unit of the kind that looks identical in size and shape to your 40Mb or 80Mb original-equipment Quantum drive, then you are going to be using the same metal hard disk adapter bracket that came with your present drive. The procedure is very simple.

You disconnect the SCSI drive and power cables from the drive and remove the two screws holding the hard disk adapter bracket to the platform. Then replace your existing hard disk with your new model in this adapter bracket. Then reinstall the adapter bracket with your new disk drive on it on the platform, replace the two screws, and reconnect the cables. That's it, you're done.

If you're installing a 5¹/₄-inch full-height drive in your Mac, the procedure is slightly different. You have to remove both your hard disk and floppy drives from the existing platform and reinstall a new U-shaped mounting platform. This mounting bracket is recessed in the back where the disk drive is located to accommodate the larger vertical clearance required by the 5¹/₄-inch full-height drives. The standard and U-shaped mounting platforms are shown in Fig. 15-17. You install your new 5¹/₄-inch full-height drive in its U-shaped mounting platform, reinstall the floppy disk(s), reattach the cables, and you're done.

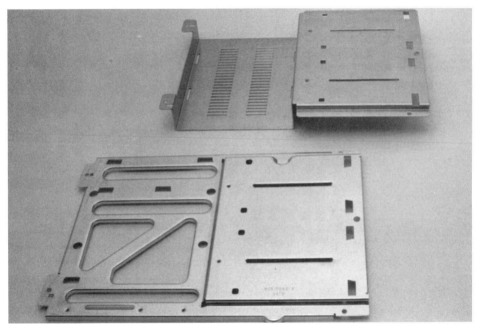

15-17 Standard and U-shaped disk-mounting platforms for six-slot Macs.

Installing NuBus option cards

Compared to having to take apart your one-slot Mac to install a PDS card in it, a NuBus card installation is a snap. For any NuBus Mac all you do is remove the outside plastic cover plate for that NuBus slot on the back of your Mac II, remove the inside metal RFI plate from the inside of your Mac II as shown in Fig. 15-18, and install the NuBus card of your choice into any slot you wish as shown in Fig. 15-19. Notice I am holding the NuBus card by its edges (front and rear) and keeping my fingers away from the chips on the board. Also notice that little tabs inside

15-18 Remove the inside metal RFI cover plate from the six-slot Mac case.

15-19 Installing a NuBus card in a six-slot Mac case.

the case engage the metal front of the NuBus card as you slide the board down to firmly seat it over the NuBus connector on the board. These tabs ensure a good RFI shield. That's all there is to installing a NuBus option card—any NuBus option card.

In most Mac II's I've seen, the NuBus video card is installed next to the power supply. However, you can put any NuBus card in any slot you want. You don't have to worry about where you've put it or setting dip switches. That is one of the beauties of the Mac II family.

Mac IIfx upgrade

Now that you are looking at your Mac II logic board, all that remains if you want to do a complete logic board upgrade, either to the IIx or to the IIfx, is to remove the one you have and replace it with the one you want.

The first step is to remove the reset switch on the rear right-hand side. It is identical to the one used on the one-slot Macs and comes out the same way.

Next, you'll notice two screws just in front of the rear connectors on the logic board. Remove them both as shown in Fig. 15-20.

Next, disconnect the power supply cable from the logic board as shown in Fig. 15-21. This cable is located right near the power supply in the left front of the case.

Next, with the front of the Mac II facing you, remove the logic board from the case by sliding it to the front and upward as shown in Fig. 15-22. And that's all

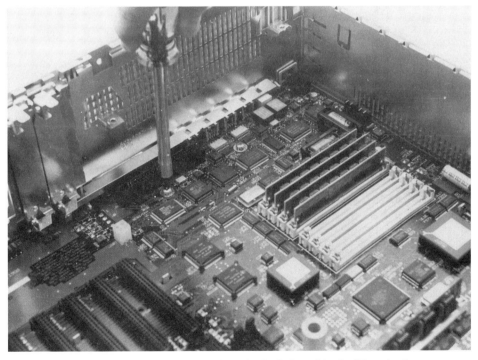

15-20 Remove the two screws holding the logic board in the Mac six-slot case.

15-21 Disconnect the six-slot case power supply cable from the logic board.

15-22 Remove logic board from Mac six-slot case.

there is to it. What you hold in your hands is a Mac II logic board, and what you'll be putting in its place oriented the same way is either a Mac IIx or Mac IIfx logic board. It couldn't be simpler. Just reverse the removal procedure.

Mac IIfx SCSI warning

Unlike the SCSI connector on the Mac II and Mac IIx, the SCSI connector on the Mac IIfx transfers data much faster, so it has its own special SCSI termination needs. The bottom line is pay attention to the rules, or it can cost you money. On the Mac IIfx:

- The internal SCSI connector must be terminated if no internal SCSI drive (or other device) is present.
- More than one SCSI terminator connected on a SCSI daisychain can cause damage to your Mac IIfx.

Taking apart your three-slot Mac IIcx and IIci

As mentioned in chapter 2, the Mac IIcx and IIci introduce a whole new dimension to the Mac II family in terms of technical excellence combined with simplicity. Their construction ensures you will find either model a faithful companion for many years. You can hardly tell them apart from the front. My finger points to the Mac IIci on top in Fig. 15-23 (only the logo is different!), and it only gets a little clearer from the rear, where the IIci on top in Fig. 15-24 is identifiable only by its telltale additional video connector. The only real difference between them is the logic board inside. The tools and pre-opening steps you need to follow are identical to the six-slot Macs.

Opening the case

Unbuttoning your IIcx or IIci Mac couldn't be simpler. Figure 15-25 shows the single phillips-head screw located at the back of the IIcx (or IIci) case being removed. After you've removed the screw in the rear, turn your Mac so that it is facing you. While holding the case back towards its rear, use your index fingers to flip up the two tabs on its top cover and release it from the rest of the cabinet as shown in Fig. 15-26. That's it. You're in.

Upgrading your three-slot Mac IIcx or IIci

Figure 15-27 shows looking down inside the IIcx case from the front. Now that you've removed the top cover, notice the square silver box located at the right rear. This is the power supply. The same message applies as stated for the six-slot Macs: Don't even think about getting inside of it—leave it alone. On the right in front of the power supply is the large plastic disk drive carrier that accommodates a hard disk and a floppy disk. The speaker is located in the center of the front of the case, and you can see the edge of the speaker bracket in this figure. The SIMM slots are located right behind the speaker in the center of the logic board near the

15-23 The front view of a Mac IIci case on top of a Mac IIcx case.

15-24 The rear view of a Mac IIci case on top of a Mac IIcx case.

15-25   Remove the single screw from the rear of the three-slot Mac case.

15-26   Remove the cover from the three-slot Mac case.

15-27   Looking down inside the Mac IIcx case from the front.

front. The slots for three NuBus cards are located on the left. Figure 15-28 shows the first slot (the one closest to the edge of the case on the left) that is typically occupied by a video card as well as a better view of the SIMMs.

Although you have numerous option card possibilities, you would be likely to be doing only a few upgrades to your IIcx or IIci. There is no reason, at this point, to upgrade your IIcx/IIci internal floppy disk located in the lower half of the plastic disk drive carrier. It comes with an FDHD version already. If you want to add a second floppy to make copying easier, an external port is provided on the back to do exactly this. The most likely upgrades to your three-slot Mac IIcx or IIci are memory, CPU upgrades, hard disk, and NuBus card options.

Adding or removing SIMMs

Like the other Mac II models, the Mac IIcx and Mac IIci both have eight SIMM sockets. The number one SIMM socket is closest to the plastic disk drive carrier, or the right side as viewed from the front of your Mac IIcx. SIMMs go into the Mac IIcx and Mac IIci exactly the way they went into the six-slot Macs. Follow the

15-28 Looking down inside the Mac IIcx case from the right showing the NuBus video card in the far left slot.

rules described by Table 6-4 in chapter 6. These SIMMs are easy to get at and work with!

Piggyback memory cards

Figure 15-29 shows Computer Care's Mac IIcx/IIci Softstep memory card prior to installation of SIMMs on it. My finger points to the jumper setting area on it. Like its counterpart card for the II/IIx, this card allows you to utilize your older 256K SIMMs alone (must be faster than 120 ns) or in conjunction with 1Mb SIMMs (must also be faster than 120 ns) to build up to 32Mb of memory in your Mac IIcx/IIci. You need to add Maxima software or Apple's System 7.0 to support this feature. Each Softstep memory card accepts four 256K or four 1Mb SIMMs and, of course, the memory rules then follow the standard Mac guidelines.

Hard disk upgrade

Your hard disk is the one item that you're most likely to be upgrading. Typically, the IIcx came with a Quantum 40Mb or Quantum 80Mb 3¹/₂-inch drive. You will most likely be replacing this with a 105Mb on up to one of the new 400Mb 3¹/₂-inch drives. At least one vendor, Micronet, also makes a "side-saddle" bracket that allows you to mount half-height 5¹/₄-inch drives in your Mac IIcx or Mac IIci. In any event, the procedure is quite similar.

15-29   The Computer Care Mac IIcx/IIci Softstep memory card.

The $3^{1}/_{2}$-inch hard disk drive is held in place in the Mac IIcx by a U-shaped drive bracket that merely clips into place. Grab the bracket's two protruding tabs between your thumb and forefingers as shown in Fig. 15-30, squeeze them together to disengage them from the locking tabs on the plastic disk drive carrier, and lift the hard disk assembly out of your IIcx. Three wires connect to the drive. Figure 15-30 also shows the drive partially removed and the drive indicator lamp wires being disconnected from the front of the hard disk. In Fig. 15-31, my finger points to the SCSI cable connected to the hard disk; the power cable is immediately to its right. Figure 15-32 shows them being disconnected from the rear of the hard disk drive. Depending upon what kind of drive you're installing, these could be in a slightly different orientation, or the cables might be longer or shorter, but these are the three cables involved.

Apple IIci logic board upgrade

This is easily the most major undertaking you'd ever attempt as a Mac IIcx owner—it should take about 15 minutes!

Remove the hard disk as previously described, this time including the SCSI and power cables attached to the logic board.

Next, remove the power supply. Looking at the Mac IIcx case from the top right-hand side as shown in Fig. 15-33, put your left hand under the power supply towards the front (the part that's closest to the drive bracket) and push the tab that

15-30   Removing the Mac IIcx hard drive and the drive indicator lamp wires.

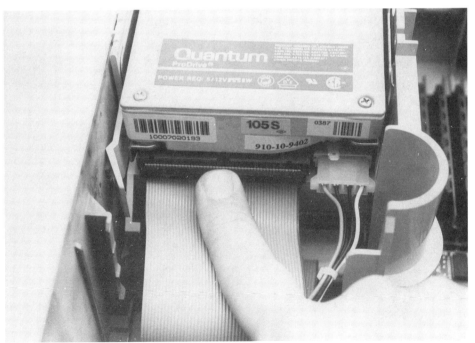

15-31   Detail of the Mac IIcx hard drive SCSI and power cable area.

15-32   Removing the Mac IIcx hard drive SCSI and power cables.

15-33   Release the Mac IIcx power supply locking tab.

extends down from the plastic disk drive carrier and holds the power supply in place toward the drive bracket. You can just barely see my index finger on the tab. This tab releases the power supply so you can slide it up and out of the case as shown in Fig. 15-34.

Next, remove the speaker bracket. After first removing its connecting wire from the logic board, simply tilt the top of the speaker bracket back away from the top of the Mac IIcx case, and it will lift right out as shown in Fig. 15-35.

Next, remove the plastic disk drive carrier. After the power supply is removed, disconnect the floppy disk cable from the logic board under the plastic disk drive carrier near where the hard disk SCSI and power cables were attached. Now that all the cables are out of the way, the large phillips-head screw holding the plastic disk drive carrier to the case should be clearly visible. Remove this screw as shown in Fig. 15-36, and remove the plastic disk drive carrier from the case by disengaging the clip that holds it at its right-hand side by just tilting it out and sliding it back out of the case as shown in Fig. 15-37.

Next, remove the reset and interrupt switch bracket in the left front side of the case. My finger points at it in Fig. 15-23. Remove any NuBus cards still remaining in the case as shown in Fig. 15-38 (the reset switch is clearly visible just under the front edge of the NuBus card). Remember to handle just by the edges please! Now you have full access to the reset switch. The switch is installed in the case from the inside by pushing it forward and then down. To remove it, do the reverse. Inside

15-34   Remove the Mac IIcx power supply.

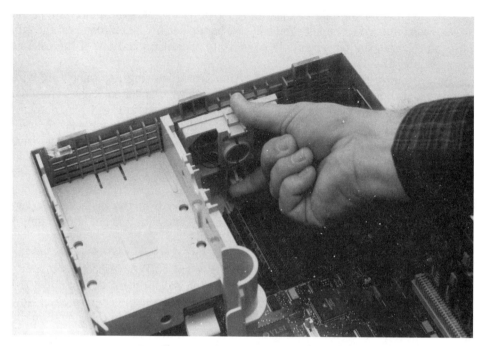

15-35   Remove the Mac IIcx speaker bracket.

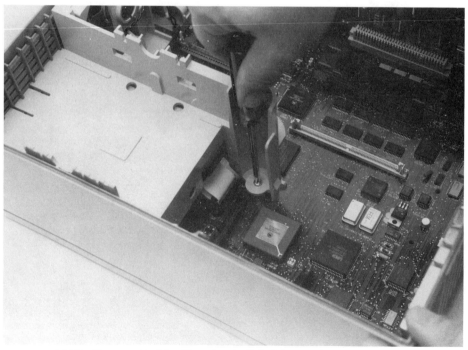

15-36   Remove the Mac IIcx plastic disk drive carrier holding screw.

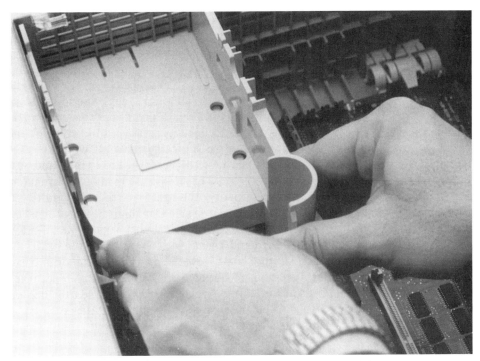

15-37   Remove the Mac IIcx plastic disk drive carrier.

15-38   Removing a Mac IIcx NuBus card.

the IIcx case, disengage the part of the reset switch touching the logic board by pushing it toward the case and lifting it up away from contact with the logic board. Now just push on its buttons outside the case, and it pops right out. Although it's delicate and can be easily broken, if you go slowly and use gentle finger pressure, you will have no problems.

Next remove the logic board itself. This is done by sliding the logic board toward the front of the case and tilting up its front part as it is disengaged from its holding tabs. As you are doing this, notice the location of the button covering the on/off switch at the right rear of the board so you can reinstall it with the same orientation, then continue to slide the board toward the front lifting it up and over the front of the case. That's all there is to it. Elapsed time is about 15 minutes. Reinstalling the IIci board in its place is simply the reverse of this procedure.

While you are looking at the two logic boards side by side from their connector end, the rear as shown in Fig. 15-39, the extra video connector in the rear quickly identifies the IIci board, as does the extra cache slot connector on the board. Of course, a closer examination of the board reveals many physical differences between the IIcx and IIci logic boards, in addition to their internal architecture and performance differences. In PC board layout circles, I am talking the true artisans of the craft here—the SE 30's logic board is a thing of beauty, the IIcx's a thing of beauty with slots, but the IIci's is a true *objet d'art.*

15-39 The Mac IIcx logic board (left) versus the Mac IIci logic board.

Mac IIcx CPU upgrade

DayStar's Powercard 030 for the Mac II is also available for your IIcx logic board. It likewise allows you to upgrade your stock 16 MHz Mac IIcx to a 50 MHz 68030 screamer. To do this upgrade, your IIcx has to be of the vintage that has a socketed 68030 CPU chip. In Fig. 15-40, my finger points to the type of 68030 chip and socket you need. If your chip is soldered on, like the 68030 chip shown in Fig. 15-41, you have to ship your board back to DayStar for them to install the socket. No big deal, just extra time and cost. It's worth whatever they charge. Only one slip of your soldering iron, and you could trash a $1500 multi-layer logic board— believe me you do not want to do this one yourself!

Once you have access to the 68030 socket, the rest of the installation proceeds pretty much as that detailed already for the six-slot version. The installed product

15-40   A Mac IIcx with the socketed 68030 chip.

15-41   A Mac IIci with soldered on 68030 chip.

does not interfere with anything. You have full access to your SIMMs, NuBus slots, and disk drives as before.

Mac IIci CPU upgrade

DayStar's Power Cache 030 installation is a much easier proposition still. This card was discussed in chapter 6 and shown in Fig. 6-24. The installation couldn't be simpler. Take it out of it's box and install it in the Mac IIci's cache slot as shown in Fig. 15-42 (handle by its edges please!). Don't blink, the whole process only takes a few seconds—you might miss it!

15-42   Installing the DayStar IIci Power Cache 030 card.

Installing NuBus option cards

NuBus card installation is a snap, just like the six-slot Macs. The internal metal NuBus bracket and plastic back panel filler clips are of slightly different design, but they function just as reliably and effortlessly. What else is there to say?

That does it for the NuBus Macs. You have now mastered them. Now, there is nothing you cannot handle. Onward.

In a nutshell

Here are the key points you have learned in this chapter:

- NuBus Macs require the simplest tool set: two screwdrivers, one is medium phillips-head and the other is a small flat-bladed screwdriver, plus an anti-static wrist strap.
- Taking apart a six-slot Mac only requires removing one screw. Removing a few more phillips-head screws inside the case allows you to take out the floppy and hard disk drives.
- Taking apart a three-slot Mac is even simpler because you remove one screw, and the rest of the components snap apart. Only one additional screw to remove inside the case takes it completely apart.
- The NuBus upgrades you are likely to do are all straightforward: memory, FDHD floppy disk, CPU, and hard disk. You have a lot more room to work with in the NuBus Macs, and everything is out in the open.
- NuBus option cards are easier to install and remove than their PDS counter-parts used in the other Macs. You are only one screw and one minute away from a complete installation or de-installation.

Chapter 16
Upgrade your new Mac Classic, LC, or IIsi

Take out your spreader tool again, if only briefly. If you've come this far, then upgrading your Classic, LC, or IIsi is easy compared to anything mentioned in the previous upgrade chapters—not that you're likely to be doing that much of it either!

With any of the new Macs, you get at least 2Mb of memory, which is all you really need to run any of today's most popular Mac software programs. There is no floppy disk upgrade. The FDHD floppy drive you get with any one of these models is top-of-the-line as far as today's Macs go. The 40Mb hard disk you get with any of these models makes it unlikely that you'll be adding a hard disk upgrade soon either. About the only thing you'd want to add is an option card, extra memory chips, or something more in the monitor department. Any one of these is small potatoes compared to the process of adding upgrades to the previous Macs discussed.

This chapter starts with upgrading your Mac Classic, then moves to the LC and IIsi in turn. Except for the Classic, which still requires your clip-on Mac toolkit, all you need is a medium phillips-head screwdriver and maybe a small flat-bladed screwdriver. Following the format, you'll first get to take its cover off, then investigate each model's most likely upgrade possibilities. So, let's go!

Taking apart your Mac Classic

Ready to upgrade your Mac Classic? You're in for a big surprise. Although the case is cosmetically similar to both the Mac Plus and the Mac SE family, all similarities (aside from the CRT tube) end once you get inside the case. The tools and many of the steps are similar to other Macs.

The tools you need

To take apart your new Mac Classic, you need the following tools:

- Medium phillips-head screwdriver.
- Small flat-bladed screwdriver.
- Long-handled Torx screwdriver and spreader tool.
- CRT discharging tools.
- Anti-static wrist strap.
- Firm sponge pad to protect your Mac's front bezel when you lay it face down.

Pre-opening steps

The following steps make your life easier:

- Prepare your work area; make sure a padded mat is available to rest your Mac face down on, and additional space is available away from the main work area to store your case back temporarily in safety.
- Turn off the power, disconnect the power cord, and remove from your work area.

- Disconnect the keyboard and mouse cables, and remove the keyboard and mouse from the work area.

Opening the case

As with the one-slot Macs, you only need to remove four screws, two at the bottom (the two black ones) and two at the top (the two silver ones). Use your long-handled Torx screwdriver to loosen each of these as shown in Fig. 16-1 and Fig. 16-2, respectively. Next, use your spreader tool as shown in Fig. 16-3 to open the case, then remove it, and set it aside in a safe place, just as you did previously in opening the Mac Plus and the Mac SE/SE 30 style cases. The Classic has no separate RFI shroud; it is attached to the back of the case itself.

Discharge the CRT anode

Now you're looking at the back of your opened Mac Classic. You want to discharge the Mac Classic's CRT anode exactly as covered previously for the clip-on and one-slot Macs. Whether you use the two-screwdriver method or the screwdriver and alligator clip method, just be sure to ground the CRT's anode wire to its ground lug. (Go for the CRT grounding lug only; discharging your CRT to other parts of the chassis could inadvertently destroy your logic board!) The ground lug is where the black power supply wire is attached under the upper left CRT tie-down screw that is clearly visible in Fig.16-11.

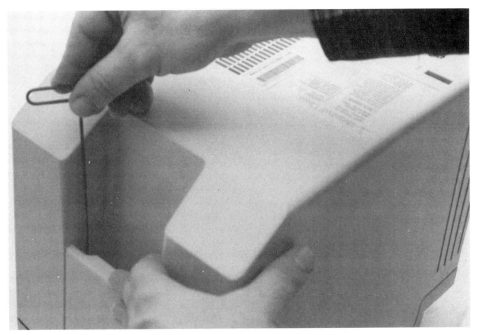

16-1 Remove the top two case screws.

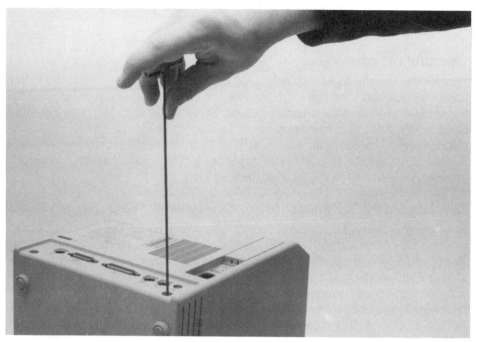

16-2 Remove the bottom two case screws.

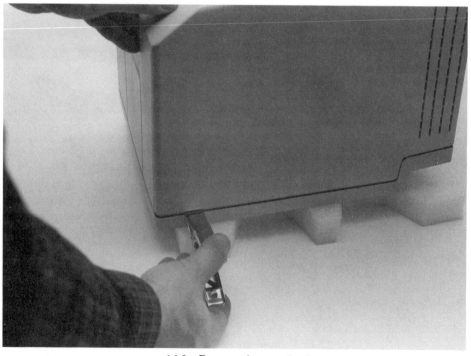

16-3 Remove the case back.

Don't drop or jar your opened Classic

Having a well-padded work area is even more important in the case of the Classic. Apple advocates to be very careful. Don't drop your Classic, particularly a hard disk model, more than one inch to the top of the work surface! The reason becomes obvious after you've opened your Classic. Rather than having a solid, one-piece, integral construction like the Mac Plus and the Mac SE and SE 30 family, the Classic chassis is open-frame construction. That means it's not as rigid or solid inside when the case is removed. In addition, the newer hard drives are smaller, lighter, and themselves less rigid and far less tolerant of bending! So be very careful after you take the case back off.

Removing the memory card

If you have the hard drive model, the first thing you will notice after opening your Classic is the vertical card mounted on the right rear of the chassis in approximately the same location used in the SE 30 for mounting its PDS option cards. This is the Classic's memory card. Remove it as shown in Fig. 16-4 and set it aside in a safe location. The Classic model without a hard disk doesn't have this memory card; its 1Mb of RAM memory is soldered directly to the logic board.

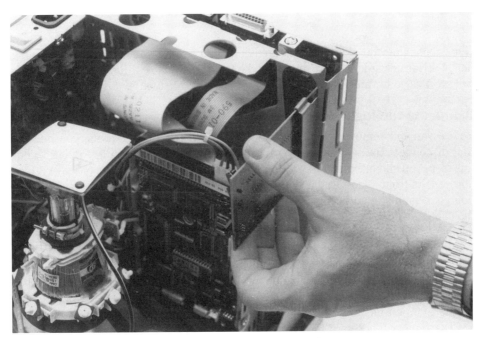

16-4   Remove the memory card.

Removing the video card

The very next thing you want to do with your opened Mac Classic is remove the video card from the anode neck as shown in Fig. 16-5. You should remove it for the same reason you did it after opening your one-slot Mac; removing it lessens the chance of

16-5 Remove the video card.

either damaging the video card or breaking the neck of your CRT while changing floppy drives or hard disks, or removing the logic board cables. Just lift it straight up, and set it aside towards the power supply side of the Mac without disconnecting it.

Removing the logic board cables

Before you can remove your Classic's logic board from the chassis, you need to first disconnect the wires from the chassis going to it as shown in Fig. 16-6. For this step, you can either set your Mac upright on your work surface or leave it face down on its front bezel. Regardless of how your Mac is oriented, you want to position your hand so that it is holding onto the chassis frame when you are removing the cables. Under no circumstances do you want to pull on a cable and have your hand suddenly come loose and fly up and strike the neck of the CRT.

Your Classic probably has a hard disk installed (although it is offered without one), so you have three cables to disconnect, as with the clip-on Macs—the flat 50-pin SCSI ribbon, the flat 20-pin floppy disk ribbon, and the multicolored power cables. The two-wire twisted pair speaker cable is back in the power cable harness for the Classic Mac.

Disconnect the 20-pin flat ribbon cable to the floppy disk first. Next, disconnect the SCSI 50-pin flat ribbon cable. Finally, reach down inside the chassis area to disconnect the multicolored power cable. It has a Molex-type connector, identical to that of the one-slot Macs, that has a locking tab lever on it. To disengage it, you squeeze this tab lever gently towards the center of the connector shell and at the same time lift it up gently from the Classic logic board using a side-to-side rocking motion.

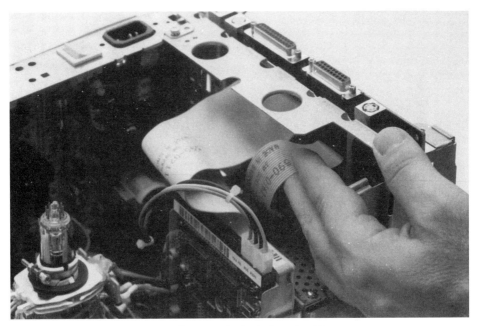

16-6 Remove the logic board cables.

Removing the logic board

Now that you have the cables removed, with your Mac again resting on its front bezel, you can slide the logic board upward in the chassis frame and out from it as shown in Fig. 16-7. Be careful as you do this because the chassis edges are very sharp! Set your logic board aside face up on a nonconductive, clean surface so that no harm will come to it.

Upgrading your Mac Classic

The two most likely upgrades to your Classic Mac are either hard disk or memory card related (combination memory-video expansion cards, etc). A third possibility is via Killy clip attachment to the CPU chip on the logic board.

Hard disk upgrade

Removing the hard disk drive from the Classic is exactly the same as the technique you used in removing the drive from the one-slot models. It is the top-most drive, and two phillips-head screws secure it to the floppy disk drive housing underneath. Before you can remove it, you must first remove the drive power cable as shown in Fig. 16-8 and the 50-pin SCSI ribbon cable as shown in Fig. 16-9. Then remove the two screws securing it to the floppy drive housing as shown in Fig.16-10. Finally, remove the hard disk drive assembly as shown in Fig. 16-11, by tipping it up at the rear and carefully sliding it out.

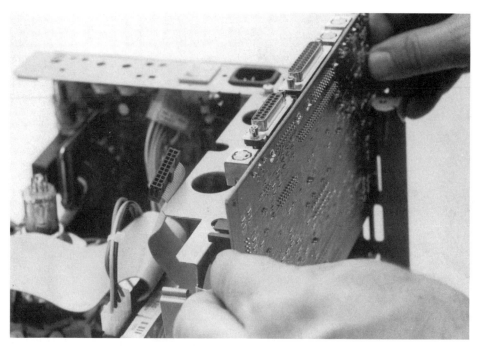

16-7 Remove the logic board.

16-8 Remove the hard drive power cable.

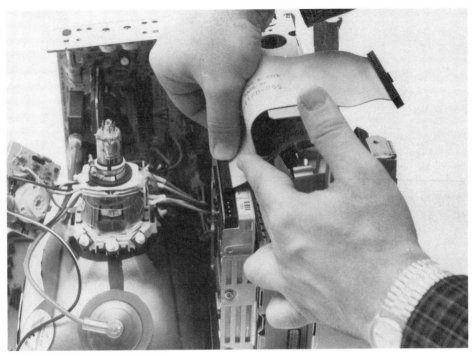

16-9 Remove the hard drive SCSI cable.

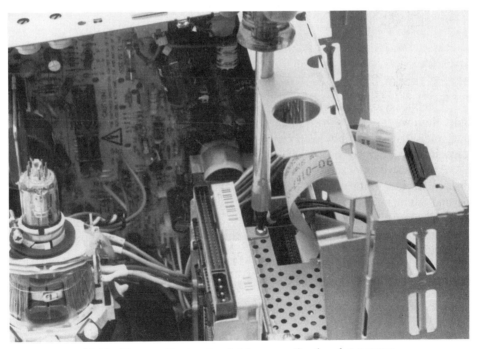

16-10 Remove the two hard drive mounting bracket screws.

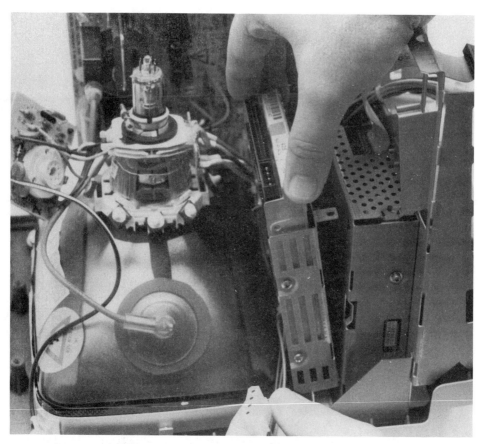

16-11 Remove the hard drive mounting bracket.

The hard disk itself is held in its mounting bracket by four screws, two on each side. Remove these as shown in Fig.16-12 and Fig. 16-13. The fully disassembled hard disk drive assembly is shown in Fig. 16-14, ready for you to install a larger capacity hard disk drive.

Apple also cautions to be careful in tightening up the screws that hold your hard disk in its mounting bracket. It explicitly states not to overtorque these screws beyond 8.0 inch-pounds when reinstalling its hard disks into the bracket. You would be similarly well-advised to heed this caution in installing any third-party vendor hard disks and certainly not to delegate this task to any "gorilla-muscled" friend who had not read this warning first.

Memory card upgrade

The majority of all upgrades you are likely to encounter with your Classic are done via its memory card that attaches to the logic board via a 44-pin connector slot. The memory card slot is the only expansion slot on the Classic, but it's a lot better

16-12 Remove the front screws from hard drive mounting bracket.

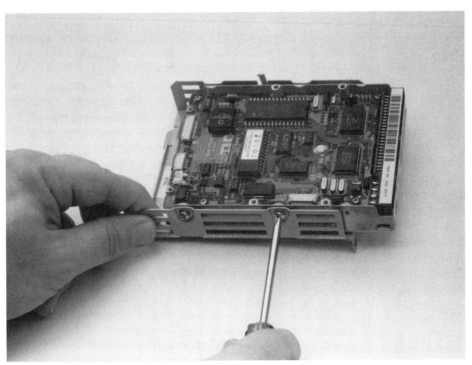

16-13 Remove the rear screws from hard drive mounting bracket.

16-14   Hard drive, mounting bracket, and removal tool.

than whatever is in second place. Figure 16-15 shows Apple's memory card installed in the Classic logic board just to give you an idea of the relative sizes and geometry. The photo also shows the Mac Classic logic board with its memory slot connector at the left and its external connectors to the front.

Figure 16-16 shows one of the many possible memory card options you are likely to encounter called the Computer Care MacStretch Classic Video Card. Typical of what you would encounter on other Classic memory cards, it has 1Mb of RAM soldered onto the board, two SIMM sockets and a jumper (that my finger points to) allowing you to set up the card for different memory configurations. SIMM possibilities follow the rules described by Table 6-5 in chapter 6. Adding 1Mb SIMMs to it brings you up to the Mac Classic's 4Mb memory limit. Unique to the Computer Care card are the pins along the lower right-hand side of the card. This is to attach a video adapter; the Computer Care card has the nifty optional ability to drive a large screen monitor from your Classic.

Many other options are also available for the Classic. Most use this memory card approach. A few, such as the Total Systems Gemini Classic accelerator board option, attach directly to the logic board CPU chip just like in the clip-on Macs to minimize signal path lengths and give you the highest performance.

That about does it for the Classic Mac upgrade discussion.

Take the cover off your Mac LC

Ready to upgrade your Mac LC? Put away that spreader tool again. The Mac LC brings another dimension to the words "ease of access and upgradability," even

16-15 The Mac Classic logic board with a memory card installed.

16-16 Computer Care MacStretch Classic video card.

beyond that enjoyed by the IIcx/IIci models, because it has no extra NuBus slots with cards to worry about and its case is shorter. LC disassembly is really a snap. Apple continued with the IIcx/ci family theme by using snap-apart construction for the LC. Once you get past the cover, all the major components including the power supply, hard disk, floppy disk, logic board, and fan assembly literally snap apart from the main plastic lower chassis and provide easy and instant access to any component for upgrading or removal.

The tools you need

The Mac LC only requires the following tools:

- Medium phillips-head screwdriver.
- Small flat-bladed screwdriver.
- Anti-static wrist strap.

Pre-opening steps

The following steps will make your life easier:

- Prepare your work area as before, but make sure additional space is available away from your work area to store your cover temporarily and near the main work area to store your monitor, keyboard, and mouse.
- Turn off the power, disconnect all power cords, and remove them from your work area.
- Disconnect the keyboard and mouse cables, and remove the keyboard and mouse from the work area.

Opening the case

Unbuttoning your Mac LC couldn't be simpler. Figure 16-17 shows the single phillips-head screw located at the back of the LC case (directly above and to the left of the widest connector—the SCSI 25-pin) along with the two tabs at the top rear of the cover. It also shows the knocked-out opening on the far right (temporarily covered by a plastic plate) that any LC option card connector would emerge from when installed.

To remove the cover, after turning your Mac LC so that it faces you, lift up on these tabs to disengage it from the rest of the case as shown in Fig. 16-18, then lift the cover straight up to remove it and set it aside in a safe place. That's it, you're now looking down at the beautiful inside of your Mac LC.

Upgrading your Mac LC

As you look at the your Mac LC from the front, notice the hard disk on the left front, the floppy disk on the right front, the fan squarely in the middle of the chassis, and the power supply to the right rear. Right next to the power supply notice the two slots for the SIMM memory chips. Directly to the left of that you should see the video RAM SIMM slot and then to the left of that is the 2Mb of built-in RAM already soldered to the board. The three most likely upgrades to your Mac LC are either memory, hard disk, or PDS-card related.

16-17   Rear of the Mac LC case.

16-18   Remove the cover from the Mac LC.

SIMM upgrade

The Mac LC comes with 2Mb of RAM already soldered onto the logic board. This fact makes upgrading your memory in your LC almost trivial. You can put up to 10Mb on the board by using 4Mb SIMMs, or use 1Mb SIMMs to bring it up to 4Mb of RAM total. Either way you do it, you have only two SIMM sockets to fill for upgrades, and it's very straightforward. What could be simpler? The SIMM sockets are very close to the power supply at the right rear of the Mac LC, so it's actually easier to just take the power supply out to install them. The Mac LC logic board is shown in Fig.16-19 with its U-shaped fan cutout in the front. My finger points to the SIMM sockets immediately next to the power supply connector on the far right edge of the board.

The third SIMM socket farthest from the power supply is for the LC's 512K video RAM SIMM upgrade. If you purchase this option to give your LC monitor greater color depth, this is where it goes. If you have it already installed, you might find it more convenient to temporarily remove this video RAM SIMM, and then replace it later after you have finished installing your RAM SIMM upgrade.

The number one SIMM socket is closest to the power supply and you would always install your memory upgrade SIMMs in pairs following the rules described by Table 6-5 in chapter 6. Alternatively, you can take out the entire logic board. The power supply is held in place by two release tabs on either side near its front. Figure 16-20 shows how you just tilt up its front to remove it.

16-19   The Mac LC logic board.

Hard disk upgrade

A Mac LC comes with a 3^1/$_2$-inch 40Mb hard disk that should be more than suitable for all your needs. My first recommendation to upgrade it would be to add an external disk drive in whatever size you need and keep the internal 40Mb one rather than changing anything.

However, should you have the desire for a larger drive inside your LC, you most likely would replace it with a 105Mb and up low-profile (one-third height, or approximately one inch high), low-power consumption hard disk drive. Be careful, because not every drive you can buy is suitable for the Mac LC. You want to make

16-20　Remove the Mac LC power supply.

sure you specify the one-inch height, low-power budget version currently manufactured by Conner, Maxtor, or Quantum, and that the third-party vendor specifically guarantees its drive is designed to work in an LC.

To get at the hard disk, you must first remove the fan/speaker assembly. This is accomplished by disengaging the release tab at the very front of the case and tilting the fan/speaker assembly up and out as shown in Fig. 16-21.

In the Mac LC, both the hard disk drive assembly and the floppy disk drive assembly are held in place by four plastic locking tabs from the chassis. (Mac LC floppy and one hard disk assemblies are interchangeable. An alternate educational-market only version of the Mac LC ships with two FDHD floppy drives instead of the one floppy drive and one hard drive configuration found in the commercial model.) To remove the hard disk, its power and SCSI cables must first be disconnected from the logic board, as shown in Fig. 16-22. In Fig. 16-23, my fingers are on the four tabs that must be released to remove the hard disk from the Mac LC chassis.

Once removed from the chassis, the Mac LC's 3½-inch hard disk drive is held in place in a U-shaped drive bracket almost identical to the Classic's, except for the four phillips-head screws are attached to the drive from underneath. Again, as Apple did for the Mac Classic, Apple cautions exercising care when tightening up the LC drive bracket screws and explicitly states not to overtorque these screws beyond 8.0 inch-pounds when re-installing its hard disks into the bracket. You

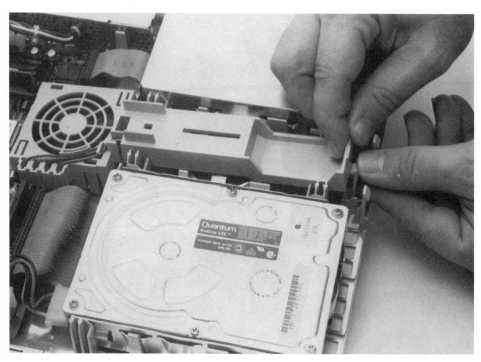

16-21 Remove the Mac LC Fan/speaker assembly.

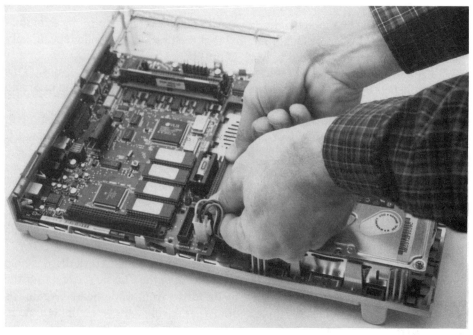

16-22 Disconnect the Mac LC hard disk's SCSI and power cables.

16-23 Remove the Mac LC hard disk.

would be similarly well-advised to heed this caution in installing any third-party vendor hard disks. If you severely overtighten these screws, you could bend the frame and possibly cause damage to your delicate hard disk.

PDS upgrades

The Mac LC logic board has exactly the same 96-pin processor direct slot (PDS) connector on it as Mac SE logic board, but its PDS is totally different. The LC uses a 68020 chip instead of the SE's 68000 chip, and the signals on the connector are different. However, the Mac LC's unique 020 PDS still has the same function of the one-slot Mac PDS in that it is designed to accommodate option upgrade cards.

In Fig. 16-24, my left hand cradles it. Perhaps it is easier to view looking at the extreme left of the LC logic board in Fig. 16-19. In any event, it is over on the left rear of the LC as viewed from the front, and PDS option cards plug into this expansion slot just like they do into the one-slot Macs. Option card external connectors use the port on the left rear of the Mac LC shown in Fig. 16-17 by removing its temporary plastic cover.

Many PDS option possibilities are available—all of them exciting. The most likely ones you will encounter are Apple's Apple II emulator card; the various video cards, some combining that function with optional floating point chip capability like DynaMac's flat screen display card; accelerator boards, such as the Total Systems Enterprise LC; and all kinds of networking and connectivity cards.

16-24   LC 020 PDS at the left side of Mac LC logic board.

The process of putting a PDS card into an LC is much simpler than putting a PDS card into a one-slot Mac. The LC PDS card installation is just like a NuBus card. All you do is remove the plastic plug from the connector opening, put the LC PDS card in the slot, and hook up a cable to the board's external connector output. That's all there is to it for any expansion card you're likely to use on the LC.

Here again, power is a concern, and you want to make sure that the expansion card you get from the manufacturer has been specifically designed with the LC's power budget in mind and that the third-party vendor specifically guarantees its card is designed to work in the LC.

There now, that about does it for the Mac LC upgrade discussion.

Take the cover off your Mac IIsi

Ready to upgrade your Mac IIsi? No need to use that spreader tool here either. The Mac IIsi features the identical snap-apart construction benefits offered by the LC combined with the increased functionality of a faster, more powerful 68030 CPU chip and the increased flexibility of offering either SE 30-style PDS or NuBus-style expansion options, with many option cards already available. Once you get past the cover, like the LC, all the IIsi's major components (power supply, hard disk, floppy disk, logic board, fan assembly) literally snap apart from the main plastic lower chassis and provide easy and instant access to any component for upgrading or removal. The tools and pre-opening steps you need to follow are identical to those for the Mac LC.

Opening the case

Do you want to open your Mac IIsi? You remove a single phillips-head screw from just to the left of the fan opening of the rear of the chassis, as shown in Fig. 16-25. Also notice the two sets of rear tabs with two in the top cover and two on the case back. Then turn your Mac IIsi so that its front is facing you, and lift up its cover by pushing down on the center two rear tabs with your thumbs and pulling up on the outer two rear tabs with your fingers as shown in Fig. 16-26. Once you elevate the

16-25   The rear of the Mac IIsi case.

16-26   Put your fingers on the tabs to start the Mac IIsi top cover removal.

cover an inch or two as shown in Fig. 16-27, you just pull it slightly forward to clear the front case lip and then straight up. After you take it off, set it aside in a safe place. Then look at the IIsi in all its glory.

16-27　To remove the Mac IIsi cover completely, tilt at a slight angle and lift it straight off.

Upgrading your Mac IIsi

Figure 16-28 shows you what I mean. Here you are looking at your Mac IIsi case from the top viewed from its left side; rotate yourself 90 degrees and use your imagination to view it from the front. In Fig. 16-28, my finger points to the SIMMs area. You can see the main parts. The floppy disk is at the right front side of the IIsi case; the hard disk on the left front side; the power supply at the right rear side; and the adapter card slot at the right rear side. The SIMMs module sockets are directly next to the IIsi's PDS option connector separated by the ROM upgrade slot.

In the case of the Mac IIsi, like the Mac LC, its three most likely upgrades are either memory, hard disk, or PDS-card related.

SIMM upgrade

Upgrading your SIMMs in the IIsi is exactly the same as upgrading your LC and almost as trivial. In the Mac IIsi, only 1Mb of RAM is soldered-on and four on board SIMM sockets are available for expansion. You can upgrade to 17Mb total on the board by using 4Mb SIMMs and 5Mb total using 1Mb SIMMs following the rules described by Table 6-5 in chapter 6.

16-28   Looking down inside Mac IIsi case from the left side; my finger points to the SIMM area.

Hard disk upgrade

The Mac IIsi comes with a 3^1/$_2$-inch 40Mb hard disk, just as the Mac LC does, and it should be more than suitable for your needs. Here again, my first upgrade recommendation would be to add an external disk drive in whatever size you need and keep the internal 40Mb one rather than changing anything.

Should you desire a larger drive inside your IIsi, you most likely would replace it with a 105Mb and up low-profile (one-third height or approximately one inch high), low-power consumption hard disk drive. The same rules of the game apply as in the LC's case; because of the IIsi's strict power budget make sure the hard disk you purchase is suitable for your Mac IIsi. Make sure you specify a one-inch height, low-power budget version currently manufactured by Conner, Maxtor, or Quantum, and that the third-party vendor specifically guarantees its drive is designed to work in a Mac IIsi.

The hard disk and floppy disk drive assemblies in the Mac IIsi are held in place by two wider plastic locking tabs from the chassis, unlike their four narrower tab counterparts in the Mac LC. Figure 16-29 shows my thumbs resting just beneath these two tabs on the Mac IIsi's hard disk. To remove the hard disk, detach its power and SCSI cables from the logic board and snap it out. What could be easier?

Once removed from the chassis, the Mac IIsi's 3^1/$_2$-inch hard disk drive is held in a U-shaped drive bracket with four phillips-head screws holding the drive in the

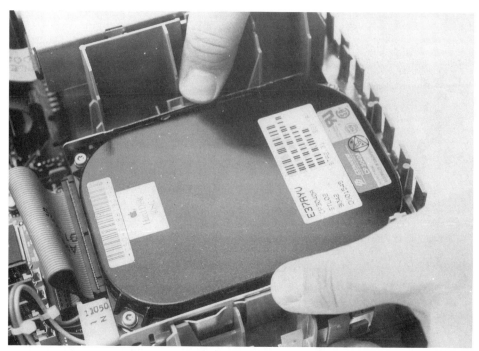

16-29   Removing the Mac IIsi hard disk.

bracket from underneath; this arrangement is identical to the bracket arrangement of the Mac LC. The same Apple caution also applies here. Be careful not to over-torque the IIsi's drive bracket screws beyond 8.0 inch-pounds when reinstalling Apple or third-party hard disks into the bracket, or you could bend the frame and possibly cause damage to your delicate hard disk.

PDS upgrades

The Mac IIsi has a very clever answer to the question of what expansion card can you can use. Either SE 30 compatible PDS or NuBus option cards can be used as long as you buy the right adapter. With the Apple-provided adapters you get a bonus. Either adapter also contains a 68882 FPU and associated chips to speed up your floating point operations.

The addition of the option adapter is very straightforward. The items you get with the Apple NuBus card adapter kit are show in Fig. 16-30. You install the NuBus directly into this adapter as shown in Fig. 16-31. Then this adapter assembly (with NuBus card attached) fits directly into the adapter card slot on the IIsi logic board as shown in Fig. 16-32. Taking out the plastic plug in the opening at the rear of the IIsi allows normal access to any NuBus card's connectors. If you're just using the adapter card for its 68882 value or if your NuBus card is of the type that has no external connector, just install the new plastic plug with the two screws that hold the adapter card firmly in place at the rear of the Mac IIsi as shown in Fig. 16-33. The SE 30 PDS adapter kit is equally equipped.

16-30 Here's what you get with the Mac IIsi NuBus adapter.

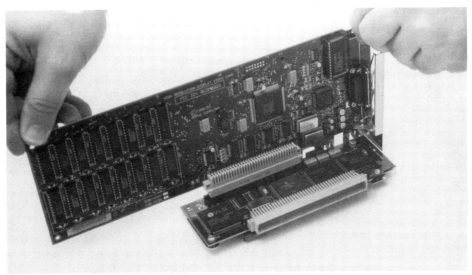

16-31 Installing a NuBus card into Mac IIsi NuBus adapter.

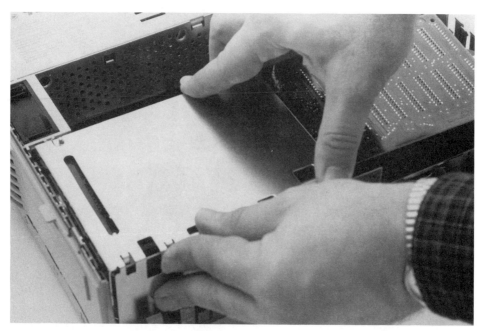

16-32 Install IIsi adapter with NuBus card into Mac IIsi.

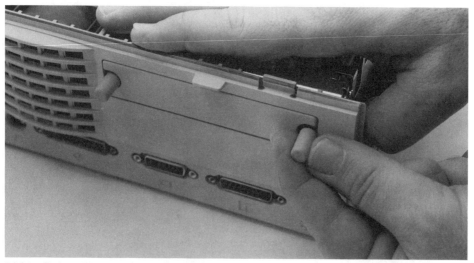

16-33 Reinstalling new Mac IIsi option cover so that the screws hold the adapter firmly in place.

The option adapter, whether you have the NuBus or the PDS kind, works smoothly and permits you to use any SE 30 style or NuBus style expansion card as you normally would. The only restriction is, again, in the power budget area. Although many SE 30 PDS and NuBus option cards are available, not all of them will work in the IIsi. Be careful, as with your hard disk selection, that the expansion card you get from the manufacturer has been specifically designed with the IIsi's power budget in mind and that the third-party vendor specifically guarantees its card is designed to work in the Mac IIsi.

That about does it for the Mac IIsi and the other new Macs. Now, that you have mastered them, the world is your oyster. Onward, only one small hurdle remains—and it's portable.

In a nutshell

Here are the key points you have seen in this chapter:

- Mac Classic disassembly reverts to the tradition and tools of the clip-on and one-slot Macs. Once inside, upgrade options are a breeze. Only the hard disk, memory card, and clip-on upgrades face you; everything else you are likely to need already came with your purchase—2Mb RAM, FDHD floppy, and 40Mb hard disk.
- Opening the Mac LC reverts to the far easier tradition of the NuBus Macs where removing one screw does it all, followed by snap-apart disassembly of the rest of the components. Hard disk and option card power budgets are a concern, but many exciting cards are available for the LC's 020 PDS slot.
- Opening the Mac IIsi follows the Mac LC's path, so removing one screw does it all, and is followed by snap-apart disassembly of the rest of the components. Hard disk and option card power budgets are also a concern, but once dealt with, the world of SE 30 and NuBus card options are available for the Mac IIsi's PDS slot.

Chapter 17
Upgrade your Mac Portable

The Mac Portable upgrading is the simplest of any of the Macs. You can probably delegate it to your six-year-old child if you trust him or her with your $3000 toy. You're not likely to be doing that much upgrading to the Mac Portable in its current incarnation either! It already comes with backlit LCD display, 2Mb of memory, FDHD floppy disk, and a 40Mb hard disk. While you'd want to upgrade and can do so to your earlier Mac Portable, about the only things you'd want to add to the current model is a modem, more memory, and an option card that allows you to attach a larger monitor or other accessory while at your "home" base.

This chapter shows you the basics of upgrading your Mac Portable. It is quite simple, so you require the minimum of tools, words, and photographs to accomplish your mission. Go for it!

Opening your portable Mac

Notice that in this instance, I said "opening" rather than "taking apart." What you are about to do here is really no more difficult than replacing the batteries in your electronic camera, portable tape recorder, or radio. So the pre-opening steps are also minimal. You really don't need any tools at all. What you are working on is totally in your hands in front of you. After all, it's portable!

You do need to worry about one thing after you open the case, but I'll get to that.

The tools you might need

To open your Mac Portable, these might be handy:

- Small flat-bladed screwdriver.
- Anti-static wrist strap.

Pre-opening step

Prepare your work area, and make sure additional space is available nearby to store temporarily any parts you remove.

Opening the case

Start with your Mac Portable closed in the locked position. The screen is latched to the keyboard, and it's facing away from you. Figure 17-1 shows the back of the Portable case. Notice the two plastic squares on the left and right sides. These are the cover release latches.

Now turn your Portable around so it is facing you. Press both the back cover release latches in and lift the back cover up from the rear as shown in Fig. 17-2. After you have released the cover and are lifting it up, you wind up at a point where you have it at a certain angle—say about 45 degrees—as shown in Fig. 17-3. Once you reach this angle, the cover can then be lifted the rest of the way up and off.

17-1   Rear of Mac Portable.

17-2   Opening Mac Portable case.

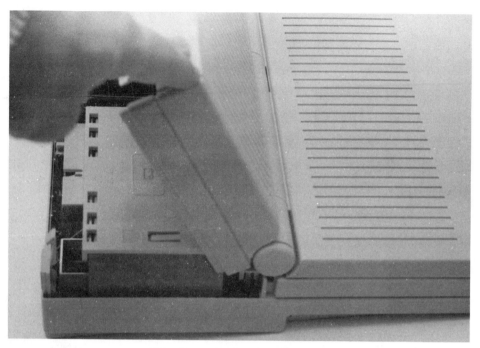

17-3 Removing the Portable cover.

Figure 17-4 shows the Mac Portable from its left side. The rear of the Portable is to the left in the figure, the battery cover is at the left rear of the Portable, the expansion slots are in the rear middle, and the floppy and the hard disks are at the right rear of the Portable. That's it. You're in.

Upgrading your portable Mac

The first step before proceeding any further is to learn about the battery cover. This is the one item I want you to worry about and to be aware of. Here is the big rule:

- After you've taken the main battery out, replacing the battery cover disconnects the backup battery. Leaving the battery cover off keeps power connected to the Mac Portable's logic board. Removing and replacing a module with the power connected could damage the module.

Here is the big rule in short form:

- Always replace the battery cover after you've taken the main battery out. (The only exception to this rule is if you have also removed the backup battery.)

Figure 17-5 shows how to remove the battery cover. Removing the main battery is shown in Fig. 17-6. Next, either replace the battery cover or remove the backup

17-4   The Portable with cover removed showing battery and hard disk.

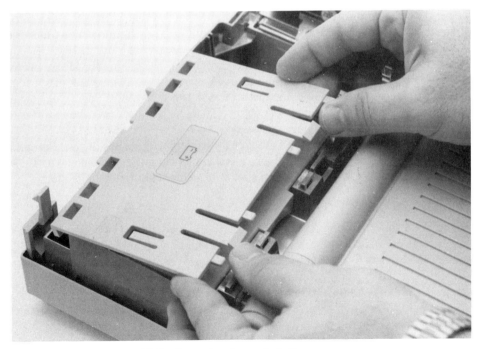

17-5   Removing the main battery cover.

17-6 Removing the main battery.

battery. The backup battery is a 9 volt unit located at the rear of the chassis behind the main battery location and is clearly visible in Fig. 17-7. Remove it just like you would the 9 volt battery in your portable radio or garage door opener. If you remove the backup battery, you erase the contents of parameter RAM. So before beginning this procedure, you should probably note all the control panel settings so they can be restored upon completion of your work. If you're unsure of how to use the control panel desk accessory to modify these settings, you should refer to your Macintosh Portable owner's guide.

Looking at Fig. 17-7, you see four slots available for you to use in your Portable. From left to right they are the PDS (processor direct slot), the RAM slot, the ROM slot, and, on the far right, the modem slot. Your choices are really quite simple.

Modem upgrade

Figure 17-8 shows putting a modem card into the modem slot (Applied Engineering's DataLink Mac Portable). Notice the modem and other slots have card edge guides on both sides, and the trick is to get the card seated into both guides at the same time and then slide it down and push it into the slot. This slot is the smallest of any of the slots and the modem is the most bulky of any of the boards in terms of components sticking up from it. Everything else you need to do is in the software or just cabling up to the modem port. The modem port is the square slot visible in the middle of the rear of your Portable in Fig. 17-1. Use a piece of phone wire with an RJ11 plug on it.

17-7 The slots inside the Portable case viewed from the rear.

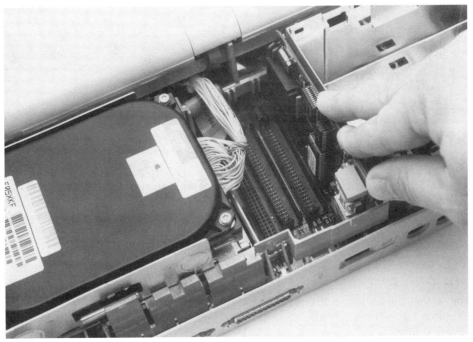

17-8 Installing the modem card.

Memory upgrade

Figure 17-9 shows putting a RAM card into the slot positioned one slot over from the modem card (the ROM slot is next to the modem slot). Numerous vendors provide this option card. This is installed the same way as the modem card, except this card is typically thinner, unless it's populated with a very large amount of RAM, as are some of the third-party vendor's 8Mb RAM Portable option cards. Engage both the edges and slide it in place. Once it is all the way down and connecting to the socket, push it firmly into the slot.

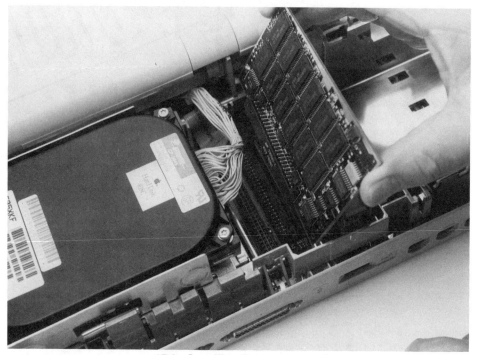

17-9 Installing the memory card.

Screen upgrade

Up until recently when Apple's new backlit Portable model became available, the ROM slot right next to the modem slot had no options available. Now, the backlit Portable screen option plugs into this ROM slot and utilizes it. Finally, there is a use for all the Portable's slots!

PDS upgrades

PDS upgrades install into the largest slot just as the other option cards do. This is the one on the far left in Fig. 17-7. A number of PDS options are available for the Portable today. Probably the most popular Portable options are those for larger external monitors (Computer Care's Video Mac Pac Card) or expansion chassis to put extra cards into your "home" system (Second Wave's ExpanSE Home BaSE).

SCSI upgrade

It's also possible to upgrade the Mac Portable without going inside the case at all. Aura Systems makes a dandy upgrade, the ScuzzyGraph Portable Large Screen Display shown in Fig. 17-10, that allows you to use a color monitor with your Mac Portable while at your "home" station. Obviously, you could also use other external SCSI devices such as hard disks, etc.

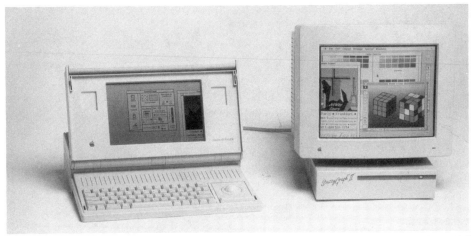

Aura Systems (17-10)

17-10   ScuzzyGraph Portable Large-Screen Display.

Hard drive upgrade

This is a little trickier. If you want an Apple drive, my recommendation is that you have a local Apple dealer do the upgrade for you. Apple ships its Portable hard drive units with the cable as an integral part of the drive assembly. The removal process requires you first remove the cover from the Portable's keyboard:

- Remove the two plastic feet from under the front of the Portable.
- Insert a small screwdriver through the center hole vacated by the removed plastic foot and disengage the corner latch by pushing down and out until it snaps free. Do this at each front corner underneath the Portable.
- Once both front corners are free, lift the keyboard cover from the front.
- Remove the keyboard and trackball assembly.
- Remove the drive cable and display cable from connectors J18 and J19 on the Mac Portable's logic board.

In Fig. 17-11, my finger points to this cable entering the hard drive assembly. To remove the hard drive assembly, press the two latches in the center of its drive bracket outward (just like on the IIsi), and lift it up and out as shown in Fig. 17-12. (The floppy disk drive in the Portable sits directly under the hard drive. If you need to remove it for any reason, disconnect its floppy cable from the Portable, and lift the floppy disk drive assembly up and out as you did the hard drive.) Remove your hard drive carefully. When you have the hard drive in your hands, imagine holding

17-11   Mac Portable hard drive cable assembly.

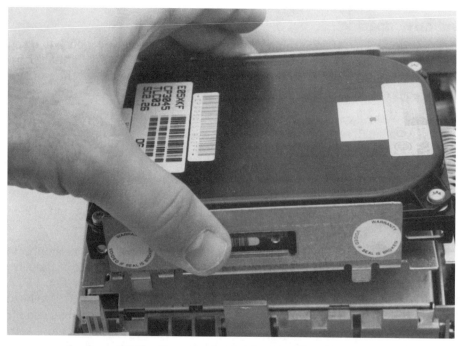

17-12   Removing hard drive from Portable.

a $1000 egg and treat it accordingly. Don't drop it, shake it, move it, or rattle it in any way.

You can upgrade your hard drive at this point, subject to the power and weight restrictions of the Mac Portable. As with the other new Macs, thoroughly check with the third-party vendor to verify its product is designed for, and will work in, your Mac Portable. Remember Apple's caution for the drives that go into the new Macs also applies to the Portable. Go extra easy on tightening down the screws holding your upgraded disk drive in its Portable bracket.

You've done it. You've opened your Macintosh Portable and upgraded it. Enjoy, enjoy, this is your journey's end.

In a nutshell

- The Mac Portable is by far the easiest of the Macs to open and to upgrade. Disassembly is far too severe a term and does not apply.
- In its newest vintage, the Mac Portable is a very powerful package from the beginning. Its upgradability makes it even more powerful and flexible.
- The earliest Mac Portable can easily be upgraded to the latest Apple version—and beyond—just as the newest models.

Chapter 18
The end of the beginning

You made it all the way through the book. Every day, third-party vendors are developing new and innovative options that will enable you to enhance your Mac even more. Of course, Apple is quietly working on next year's models that continue to push to the outside of the envelope. I called this chapter, "the end of the beginning" because upgrading your Macintosh is a never-ending process, and as Darwin Gross said in several of his books, "There's always another step to take."

This chapter tidies up a few remaining areas such as software, housekeeping, and the future. This book has focused on hardware. I haven't said much about software, so I say it here. While everyone has their own work habits, that is, how you operate your Macintosh, you can improve your housekeeping efficiency by backing up and using a UPS. For your own future growth, I'll direct you to sources that can help you continue to grow and to expand your Macintosh knowledge base.

A few words about software

Although you use your System software every day, most of the time you don't even think about it. Your System software works whenever your Mac is turned on. That's the ultimate endorsement and kudo to Apple's software gurus and architects whose marching orders were to "make the Macintosh software transparent to the user."

When you do think about it, either you're consciously making a change, or something has gone wrong. Despite the increasing sophistication of the Macintosh and number of Apple and third-party upgrade options, successive generations of Macintosh System software have proven to be ever more trouble free, with only occasional lapses.

As with other areas of life, we bring most of the problems upon ourselves. You have a perfectly good, stable, working Macintosh hardware and software setup. Then you introduce a new piece of hardware. This hardware says it requires this new version of System software to run. You add the System software and, all of a sudden, your problems begin. Some of your applications that ran perfectly before the new System software was installed now crash for no apparent reason. You get random system bombs when doing nothing at all, and on and on. You make phone calls. You find the problems and make the fixes. After days, weeks, or months, all your problems are cleared up and you're back to where you were before. Then you introduce another new piece of hardware and the process starts anew. Sound familiar?

The problem is caused by incompatibility across older and newer generations of hardware and software products, assuming you're using defect-free hardware and software. It's like when you grow up and go back to your old neighborhood, the vacant lot that you used to walk across on your way to the store now has a building on it. The shortcuts taken by earlier hardware/software designers were invalidated by the rules Apple ever more stringently followed in designing new System software and putting massive amounts of its software code into ROM to make things run swifter. The example that most easily comes to mind is Apple's introduction of its 512K ROMs on the Mac IIci and later Macs. Many respectable and well established third-party vendors' products crashed. The analogy of what happened from a third-party vendor's viewpoint, "It's as if the automobile seat belt laws were suddenly strictly enforced in your home state one day without warning."

What do you do? Make haste slowly, don't fix it if it ain't broke, don't be an early innovator or early adopter—especially not on your Macs being used in a production environment.

System 6.0x software

Much has changed in system software since the early days of Macintosh. As mentioned earlier, your hardware goal is to at least bring your earlier Macs up to 2Mb and the Mac Plus logic board standard. The reason for this is so you can run Apple System 6.0x or later software with MultiFinder. Table 18-1 shows Apple's recommended latest System software versions.[1] Available as an upgrade kit from your friendly, local Apple dealer, this software in its latest form simplifies whatever you might want to do, and does so with fewer bugs or hitches than earlier versions.

You might have heard of the virtues of MultiFinder and its benefits. The Apple 6.0x System package brings them to you. You just choose MultiFinder from the desktop menu and reset. Now you are working in the MultiFinder rather than the Finder environment. Your ability to switch back and forth between multiple applications is limited only by the amount of memory you have. My experience has shown you really need at least 2Mb to be happy with its performance. Enjoy.

Table 18-1. Recommended Macintosh System software.

CPU	System software	Reason
Classic	6.07 required	Software brightness control
Mac LC	6.07 required	Sound-input support
Mac IIsi	6.07 required	Sound-input support
Mac IIfx	6.05 required	Hardware support
Mac IIci	6.05 recommended	Improves compatibility
Mac Portable	6.05 recommended	Fixes serial and power problems
Mac IIcx	6.04 recommended	Fixes bugs
Mac SE 30	6.04 recommended	Fixes bugs
Mac IIx	6.04 recommended	Fixes bugs
Mac II	6.04 recommended	Fixes 800K floppy drive eject problem
Mac SE	6.04 recommended	Fixes 800K floppy drive eject problem
Mac Plus	6.04 recommended	Fixes 800K floppy drive eject problem
Mac 512	System 3.2, Finder 5.3	Recommend upgrade to Mac Plus
Mac 128	System 2.0, Finder 4.1	Recommend upgrade to Mac Plus

---

[1] Raines Cohen, "System 6.07 upgrade not for all Mac models," *MacWEEK*, 11/6/90, p. 1.

System 7.0 software

You have heard of Apple's new 7.0 System software throughout the book and the fact that it will run on your Mac Plus or later Mac with 2Mb of memory or more. To take full advantage of its features, you need a 68030 Macintosh or a 68020 with a PMMU chip. Other than the fact that Apple is betting its company on it, as mentioned in chapter 2, what is it and what does it do for you? The answer is mucho.

While nearly all of its components and features are available in other products today, in System 7.0 Apple ties it all together in a neat, integrated package that works.[2] Here's a preview:

- *32-bit addressing and virtual memory*   This is the feature of System 7.0 I've talked about the most. While chapter 6 talked about 32-bit 68030 CPU chips being able to directly address 232 bits or 4 gigabytes, this is the software that supports it. Virtual memory lets you set aside a portion of your hard disk as an extension of your Mac's memory. You can run larger, slicker programs because program parts are swapped in and out of memory from the hard disk as you need them.
- *More powerful Finder*   Imagine your Finder more intuitive with auto-scrolling, auto-sizing, windows but with a manual trash can that you have to empty deliberately; MultiFinder permanently turned on; powerful file search features; aliases that allow you to open the original "target" file from another location, and customizable Apple and tear-off menus.
- *True Type*   Apple's own technology for outline fonts, which are smooth representations of characters generated by a Font Manager, is now resident in System software. (Adobe had this playing field all to itself before Apple's announcement created a furor in the industry. The combatants have now declared a state of Peristroyka exists.)
- *IAC (Interapplication Communication)*   This is the slickest feature of System 7.0 in my opinion. Imagine that the clipboard sharing data between applications was a dynamic one instead of a static cut, copy, and paste. Apple calls this dynamic data sharing "publish and subscribe." Any user can "publish" information and "subscribers" receive a new version of the data each time the original is updated.
- *AppleTalk Fileshare*   AppleTalk Fileshare incorporates the features of Sitka (formerly TOPS) software into every Mac system; users can share files over a network without a dedicated server.
- *Data Access Manager*   The Data Access Manager allows any user application to access remote databases without having to deal with the particulars of their software query languages. These queries to the host database language are done transparently.

These are some, but not all, of the goodies you get. You also get additional utility applications, 32-bit QuickDraw, communications toolbox, sound-system improve-

[2] Eric Lach, "Applications Now Offer Features in System 7.0," *Infoworld*, 9/24/90, p. 47; Lon Poole, "Here Comes System 7.0," *Macworld*, August 1989, p. 124.

ments, and the list goes on—all as part of System 7.0. Having all these capabilities on your Macintosh puts an enormous amount of computer power on the top of your desk.

Apple Unix software (A/UX)

While Apple has developed a world-class System software product for its Macintosh, a lot of the rest of the world is doing its work on a Unix-based software machine. So Apple astutely covered its bet by developing for this platform also. Apple's highly touted virtual memory and multi-programming features of System 7.0 have always been available on Unix. In its latest incarnation, A/UX 2.0 gives Unix capabilities that it can't get anywhere else.[3] The A/UX 2.0 software developers had their work cut out for them, and it is hard to think of two more "opposite" environments. Unix is almost all "left-brained"—sequential, logical, textual. Macintosh is almost all "right-brained"—random, subjective, graphic. In A/UX 2.0, you get the best of both worlds, and you give up very little. Unix programmers will be at home with the three flavors of Unix available for the Macintosh on their desktop: Berkeley (default version), System 5, and Network File System. Mac users will appreciate the Mac-like command shell interface when accessing the power of Unix programs. Here you are looking at a non-trivial Macintosh. My recommendation is at least put it on a 68030 Mac with a fast 80Mb hard disk and 4Mb of memory. A 300Mb hard disk and 8Mb is probably a more useful size.

A few words about good housekeeping

Let me give you just two tips to maximize your enjoyment of your newly upgraded Macintosh. If you are already a Macintosh owner, you can perhaps empathize with me in one area or the other.

To go forward, you must back up

Dantz Development Corp, developers of "Retrospect" archiving and backup software, used "To go forward, you must back up" as a lead line in some of their ads (*MacWEEK*, 5/1/90, p. 20 is one). Its truth and simplicity in the backup area gave me a chuckle when I first saw it.

The analogy I would make here is: Before you've experienced death, you don't know what you're talking about. After you've experienced death, it's difficult to talk about it or hard to find anyone who will listen! If you've never lost part of or all of your data, nothing I say here really means anything to you. On the other hand, . . . you get the message.

For just pennies a day, you can avoid disaster. Whether self-inflicted, done by a well-meaning friend or by Mother Nature, you can never be sure that an accident will not happen to you. Your insurance policy—backup copies in any form—protects you. Even the simplest backup, such as copying via the Finder onto a floppy

---

[3] Dan Magorian, "A/UX 2.0: A Mac Unix that is smooth, superb," *MacWEEK*, 8/7/90, p. 104.

disk is better than nothing. Backup software (Fastback, Retrospect, etc.) is available from numerous sources. The backup utility of your choice and 800K floppy diskettes are great for simplicity and low cost. Beyond that, your choices are hard disk, removable hard disks, optical read-write disks, WORMs, cartridge tapes, even reel-to-reel tape might be a good solution for you. How many and what kind of (full, partial) backups you need are determined by how important your data is. The simplest technique is just to have two sets and alternate them. Reams of magazines articles and books are available to help you decide how. Just do it!

Don't interrupt me

For a city dweller, a blackout can either be a fun party or a disaster. For a Macintosh owner, it's always the latter. Whatever you were doing when the lights went out, Murphy's law says that it was probably important.

A small uninterruptible power supply (UPS) can save the day for you. Think of it as a surge protector with a battery attached plus some minor switching electronics. You are talking about a $200 to $400 investment here. When the ac power goes away, it quickly switches over to an inverter that provides replacement ac power uninterrupted, as if nothing had happened. Without a UPS, your safest course of action is to turn off your Mac after a power hit. Sometimes the power surges a few times before the power company fixes the problem. None of these surges does your Mac any good.

I was minding my own business, working at my Mac one sunny day, when in the middle of the day, the power went out. When it came back on, my Mac came on, but I got that sickening feeling in the pit of my stomach as the screen sat there with the dreaded blinking question mark icon. No hard disk. The power hit knocked out my hard disk—it still rotated, but some of the data was scrambled. Luckily, the data was backed up, but I still had to go through all the steps to restore it. Cut to the same scene six months later, this time at night. The power went out, the UPS came on and I resumed working, but in the dark. Not exactly. By the light of my Macintosh screen. My next step was to save what I had been doing. If nothing else, you will sleep better at night. In my case, the UPS paid for itself in only one power outage.

More for your money

Yes, I know I said two tips. These next two are on the house:

- *Cleanliness*   Wherever you locate your Mac, just keep it in a clean, dust-free environment. Ever since one of my friends, who works in airline maintenance, showed me the "gunk" that came out of an airliner's air filter system, I have been a believer. Hey, closer to home, just look at your furnace filter. Excessive dust, dirt, or cigarette smoke will eventually work its way into your Mac and create problems for you.
- *Static*   Some people are just naturally highly charged individuals—seriously. While others have no problems with their computers ever, some peo-

ple constantly encounter strange error messages and system bombs and lose data on their floppies and hard disks. For these people, I recommend a three step solution: An anti-static mat on your desktop under your computer; another anti-static mat on the floor under your chair in front of your desk (use anti-static mats of the type that come with a wire that attaches to the ground wire of the wall electrical outlet); and then make two backups of everything. If this doesn't work, I have more drastic measures I have used.

A few words about the future

No, you have not accidentally just picked up your larger copy of *Omni* magazine. Whatever Macintosh you are now using or plan to use, it is certain that a slicker, faster, cheaper, or lighter one will be developed in the future. The same statement, only more strongly, can be made for Macintosh software. Yet the avalanche of new products coming regularly from Apple and third-party software and hardware manufacturers requires that you adopt some sort of procedure, tailored to your own set of circumstances, ensuring your Macintosh setup is reasonably up to date. How do you do it? Keeping up is easy. Read. Talk with others. Visit shows. Then formulate your own opinions and procedures.

The Macintosh world is unique. The Macintosh user benefits from a combination of dedicated and focused media, events, distribution methods, and user groups unlike those found in any other industry. A wide variety of information sources are available to assist you. This list is not intended to be all-inclusive. I can only touch on the highlights here. Many other excellent sources are not included, but you will undoubtedly find them in your search.

Mail order

Some geographic areas have an unusual concentration of good dealers to assist you and that you assist in return by buying from them. However, you can benefit from the mail order channel regardless of where you are located. Virtually anything can be purchased through the mail. You can buy books, magazines, software, hardware, accessories, up through complete systems.

How do you deal with this channel? I have found a very simple process works for me. If I am buying a commodity item and I am not already buying that item from a vendor I know, I stick with one of the major mail order suppliers who advertises in the pages of the Macintosh magazines. If it's a new item on the market or a new item for me to buy, I go directly to the manufacturer or supplier, large or small, and place a small order for it. If the product, their service, and the price measure up, I favor them with a larger order. If not, I buy from another source, or even return the product.

The mail order sources for the specific products mentioned in this book have already been listed at the end of each chapter so they will not be repeated here.

However, here are some Macintosh add-on hardware and software mail order sources:

Alliance Peripheral Systems
2900 S. 291 Hwy., Lower H
Independence, MO 64057
(800) 233-7550
(816) 478-8300

Axone Computer Systems
60 Chestnut Ave., #207
Devon, PA 19333
(800) 955-0388
(215) 341-8608

Beverly Hills Computer
279 S. Beverly Dr., #1200
Beverly Hills, CA 90212
(800) 426-8166

Club Mac
7 Musick
Irvine, CA 92718
(800) 258-2622
(714) 768-8130

Dr Mac
14542 Ventura Blvd., #200
Sherman Oaks, CA 91403
(800) 825-6227

DMA Technologies
601 Pine Ave.
Goleta, CA 93117
(800) 233-9443

Hard Drives International
1912 W. 4th St.
Tempe, AZ 85281
(800) 234-3475
(602) 967-5128

Mac and More
11266 W. Hillsborough Ave.
Tampa, FL 33635
(800) 622-0052
(813) 888-9535

Mac Connection
14 Mill St.
Marlow, NH 03456
(800) 334-4444

Mac Direct
60 East Chestnut, #145
Chicago, IL 60611
(800) 621-8461

Mac Sale International
(800) 729-7031

MacCenter
(800) 950-3726
(512) 476-7466

MacLand
5006 S. Ash Ave., #101
Tempe, AZ 85282
(800) 333-3353

MacOutlet
48860 Milmont Dr.
Fremont, CA 94537
(800) 622-6885
(415) 623-8890

MacProducts USA
8303 Mopac Expwy., #218
Austin, TX 78759
(800) 622-3475

MacSystems
Broadway Plaza
Altus, OK 73521
(800) 942-6227
(405) 477-3777

MacTel Technology
3007 N. Lamar
Austin, TX 78705
(800) 950-8411
(512) 451-2600

MacWarehouse
1690 Oak St.
Lakewood, NJ 08701
(800) 255-6227

MacZone
6825 176th St. NE , #100
Redmond, WA 98052
(800) 248-0800

Mass Microsystems
810 W. Maude Ave.
Sunnyvale, CA 94086
(800) 522-7979
(408) 522-1200

Peripheral Vision
2333 Fairmount Ave.
Philadelphia, PA 19130
(800) 800-7868
(215) 232-9800

QMS Technical Systems
9370 G Court
Omaha, NE 68127
(800) 878-2881
(402) 331-2881

Quadmation
(800) 733-7887
(408) 733-5557

Relax Technology
3101 Whipple Rd.
Union City, CA 94587
(415) 471-6112

Software And Hardware That Fits
610 South Frazier
Conroe, TX 77301
(800) 972-3018
(409) 760-2400

Third Wave Computing
1826B Kramer Ln.
Austin, TX 78758
(800) 284-0486
(512) 832-8282

US Computer Merchants
4747 E. Elliot Rd., #29-461
Phoenix, AZ 85044
(800) 888-8779

VCP
(800) 447-6350
(714) 779-7478

Warehouse 54
520 S. 52nd St., #204
Tempe, AZ 85281
(800) 955-0054

Magazines

The Macintosh community is blessed with an amazing selection of outstanding weekly and monthly magazines to suit every palette. They, as much as the enthusiasm of the Macintosh users themselves, are responsible for the spread and absorption of the Macintosh into the mainstream of computer culture.

I have referenced the monthly magazines *Macworld* and *MacUser* repeatedly in the text. I cannot say enough about them. From the beginning they were a cut above any other computer periodicals I have ever received.

MacWEEK is another outstanding publication, perhaps the best weekly I have ever received. They are legendary in the Mac community for reporting the facts just as they happen straight off the cuff—even if they absorb a little heat in the process from Apple and others for being a little too soon and a little too accurate in their reporting.

As a minimum, you should be subscribing to:

Macworld
P.O. Box 51666
Boulder, CO 80321-1666
(800) 234-1038

MacUser
P.O. Box 56986
Boulder, CO 80321-6986
(800) 627-2247

MacWEEK
P.O. Box 5821
Cherry Hill, NJ 08034
(609) 428-5000

Although they are not Macintosh specific, three other magazines you should subscribe to will make you a well rounded individual. These magazines are:

Byte
P.O. Box 555
Hightstown, NJ 08520
(800) 257-9402

Computer Shopper
P.O. Box 52568
Boulder, CO 80321
(800) 274-6384

Infoworld
P.O. Box 5994
Pasadena, CA 91107
(818) 577-7233

Two shoppers guides are available to assist you quarterly and annually:

Macintosh Buyer's Guide
5615 W. Cermak Rd.
Cicero, IL 60650-2290
(800) 826-9553

Macintosh Product Registry
660 Beachland Blvd.
Vero Beach, FL 32963-1794
(407) 231-6904

There are many other magazines serving niches in the Macintosh market and other aspects of the personal computer field from which you might benefit, but these should get you started.

Computer shows

Again the Macintosh community is blessed. No other industry has a dedicated user event that you can attend once a year and actually see and hear it all. The Macworld Exposition, held in the Spring in San Francisco and in the Fall in Boston is the one event every Macintosh user should plan to attend at least once, if not annually. It normally attracts around 50,000 people and, unlike other trade shows, caters specifically to Macintosh products and, except for one industry day, specifically to the Macintosh end user. To learn more about it, contact:

Mitch Hall Associates
P.O. Box 4010
Dedham, MA 02026
(617) 361-3941

User groups

Although every industry has its user groups, the Macintosh community has raised this phenomena to an art form. Nothing else that can give you as high a return on, and as much benefit from, your low annual dues investment. Only minutes of networking at a monthly general or special interest group meeting can save you hours, if not days, of time. Later on, when you have established relationships within the group, you can accomplish the same over the telephone.

The user groups are a marketing force to be reckoned with also. The monthly meetings of the larger user groups such as Berkeley, Boston, and Portland (OR), regularly attract industry leaders who know this fact very well. An auditorium full of experienced, opinionated, and intelligent Macintosh users is also a force with which to be reckoned. It is a two-way street, and the industry leaders go back with much useful marketing feedback.

A simple phone call to Apple Computer gets you the number of the Macintosh user group nearest to you. Call (800) 538-9696, ext. 500.

Local dealers

Hey, how about that, even the local dealers made the list. This is another resource you might consider, and it's right underneath your nose. Where I live (Portland, Oregon), there are five Apple dealers—Alpha Computers, The Computer Store, ComputerLand, Heath/Zenith, and BusinessLand. Plus one very Mac-knowledgable independent dealer, Computer Friends. I hope you are similarly blessed in your area.

Ah, but there are rules to obey here. When you use the resources of your local computer store, remember it's a two-way street. The person on the other side of the counter from you is being compensated for his or her time in assisting you. So, use these resources wisely. If someone has just pulled 50 monitors off the shelf for you to take a look at before making your selection, do not go and buy your monitor from a mail order source after giving that person a polite thank you. They will not be excited about working with you again. You've probably heard, "What goes around comes around."

If you're getting good assistance from a store and from a sales person, it's just good manners and taste on your part to compensate them for their efforts by bringing them your business. Sure, you might pay more. But it will certainly pay dividends to you over the long haul.

Consultants

Remember the movie, *The Good, The Bad, and The Ugly*? That's the whole book on consultants in short form. My best advice is find one who:

- You can trust.
- Is empathetic to your needs.
- Knows what he or she is talking about.
- Is reasonably priced.
- Is there for you when you need him or her.

They are out there, believe me. A good Macintosh consultant will make you feel like you have just died and gone to heaven. Treat yourself.

Books

History   Books on the history of the Macintosh include:

Jeffery S. Young, *Steve Jobs: The Journey Is the Reward*, Scott, Foresman and Co., 1987.
John Sculley with John A. Byrne, *Odyssey*, Harper and Row, 1987.
Frank Rose, *West of Eden: The End of Innocence at Apple Computer*, Penguin Books, 1989.
Guy Kawasaki, *The Macintosh Way*, Scott, Foresman and Co., 1990.
Jean-Louis Gassee, *The Third Apple*, Harcourt Brace Jovanovich, 1987.

Hardware   In addition to this book, you might find these books helpful:

Apple Computer, *Macintosh Family Hardware Reference*, Addison-Wesley Publishing, 1988.
Michael Brown, *Desktop Video Production*, Windcrest Books, 1991.
Horace W. LaBadie, Jr., *Build Your Own PostScript Laser Printer and Save a Bundle*, Windcrest Books, 1991.
Peter Norton and Robert Jourdain, *The Hard Disk Companion*, Simon and Schuster, 1988.
Aubrey Pilgrim, *Build Your Own 80486 and Save a Bundle* and *Upgrade Your IBM Compatible and Save a Bundle*, Windcrest Books, 1990 and 1991, respectively.
Larry Pina, *Macintosh Repair & Upgrade Secrets*, Howard W. Sams & Co., 1990
Charles Rubin and Bencion Calica, *Macintosh Hard Disk Management*, Hayden Books, 1988.
Gene B. Williams, *Macintosh Repair and Maintenance*, Chilton Book Company, 1986.

Software   A list of Macintosh software books could itself fill a chapter. A visit to your favorite local bookseller or reseller that stocks software products and books gets you started. Enjoy.

Glossary

A/UX Apple's version of Unix, the near industry standard multiprogramming, virtual memory operating system. Apple's advantage is their Unix version has a front end of a Macintosh interface making it more user friendly and easier to use while retaining all its powerful features.

access time, average The amount of time it takes the computer to find and read data from a disk or from memory. For a hard disk it is defined as seek time (time to find the track) plus settling time (time to stabilize over the track) plus latency time (time to bring the sector data on the track under the head). Some manufacturers ignore both the average consideration and the latency factor to publish better times.

ADB Apple Desktop Bus is now the Apple standard serial communication bus that allows you to connect up to 15 input devices such as keyboard, mouse, joystick, puck, other pointing/motion devices, and graphics tablets to your SE and newer Macintosh. It allows the devices to be connected in daisychain fashion. The bottom line is increased flexibility at minimal increase in cost.

alphanumeric Data that has both numerals and letters.

analog data Data varying smoothly and continuously over a range, rather than changing in discrete jumps as with digital data.

ANSI Stands for American National Standard Institute, which sets standards for devices such as computer terminals.

Apple menu The menu farthest to the left in the menu bar, indicated by an Apple symbol, from which you choose desk accessories.

AppleTalk The system of network software and hardware used in various implementations of Apple's communications network.

application   Short for application program.

ASCII   Abbreviation for American Standard Code for Information Interchange. Binary numbers from 0 to 127 that represent the upper- and lowercase letters of the alphabet, the numbers 0 to 9, and the several symbols found on a keyboard. A block of eight 0s and 1s are used to represent all of these characters. The first 32 characters, 0 to 31, are reserved for noncharacter functions of a keyboard, modem, printer, or other device. Number 32, or 0010 0000, represents the space, which is a character. The numeral 1 is represented by the binary number for 49, which is 00110001. Text written in ASCII is displayed on the computer screen as standard text. Text written in other systems, such as WordStar, has several other characters added and is very difficult to read. Another 128 character representations have been added to the original 128 for graphics and programming purposes.

ASIC   Stands for application specific integrated circuit.

assembly language   A low-level machine language, made up of 0s and 1s.

asynchronous   A serial type of communication where one bit at a time is transmitted. The bits are usually sent in blocks of eight 0s and 1s.

backup   A copy of a disk or of a file on a disk. Backing up your files and disks ensures that you won't lose data if the original is lost or damaged.

baud   A measurement of the speed or data transfer rate of a communications line between the computer and printer, modem, or another computer. Most present day modems operate at 1200 baud. This is 1200 bits per second or about 120 characters per second.

benchmark   A standard type program against which similar programs can be compared.

bezel   The plastic or metal plate typically covering the front of a floppy or hard disk mounted in a computer case or chassis.

bidirectional   Of or relating to both directions. Most printers print in both directions, thereby saving the time it takes to return to the other end of a line.

binary numbers   Computers "think" in binary language, or in 1s or 0s. The circuit is either "on" or "off." In computer terms, each individual 1 or 0 is called a bit. In mathematical terms, the number 2 raised to a power is a binary number. If I had three bits in a row, 111, that represented binary numbers with values of 2^0, 2^1, 2^2, then their base ten values (the numbers we think in) would be 1, 2, 4. The binary number 111 would then represent the decimal number 7. By changing the 1s and 0s pattern, the sum of their digits could represent any number from 0 to 7, or eight different values. In this way, computer values are changed to those we understand and vice versa.

bits   A contraction of *binary* and *digits*. The smallest unit of information that a computer can hold. The value of a bit (1 or 0) represents a simple two-way choice such as yes or no, on or off, positive or negative.

boot or bootstrap or reset   The process of the Macintosh turning on, checking its memory is okay, checking its stored parameters are set as they should be, and turning over control to the user. A small amount of the program to do this is stored in ROM. Using this the computer pulls itself up by its bootstraps. A reset is sometimes necessary to get the computer out of an error message or bomb dialog box if it is hung up for some reason.

buffer   A buffer is usually some discrete amount of memory that is used to hold data. A computer can send data thousands of times faster than a printer or modem can utilize it. But in many cases, the computer can do nothing else until all of the data has been transferred. The data can be input to a buffer, which can then feed the data into the printer as needed. The computer is then freed to do other tasks.

bug   The early computers were made with high voltage vacuum tubes. It took rooms full of hot tubes to do the job that a credit card calculator can do today. One of the large systems went down one day. After several hours of trouble-shooting, the technicians found a large bug that had crawled into the high voltage wiring. It had been electrocuted, but had shorted out the whole system. Since that time, any type of trouble in a piece of software or hardware is called a bug. To *debug* it, of course, is to try to find all of the errors or defects.

bulletin boards   Usually a computer with a hard disk that can be accessed with modem. Software and programs can be uploaded or left on the bulletin board by a caller, or a caller can scan the software that has been left there by others and download any that he likes. A great source of help for a beginner.

bus   Wires or circuits that connect a number of devices together or a path over which signals travel. Typically refers to the input and output paths to the Macintosh such as the Nubus cards in the Mac II family and the expansion bus slot in the Mac SE.

byte   The smallest computer word or character consists of 8 bits and is called a byte. These 8 bits can be arranged in 256 different ways. This is $2 \times 2 \times 2 \times 2 \times 2 \times 2 \times 2 \times 2 = 256$, or 2^8. Therefore, one byte can be made to represent any one of the 256 characters in the ASCII character set. It takes one byte to make a single character.

cache memory   High-speed memory in front of regular processor memory to speed up the computer. When the computer writes data in main memory, it leaves a copy of it in cache memory too. When the computer goes to read data, it looks first in cache memory. If it finds the data there, it doesn't bother with looking in main memory. If the cache and program loops are of the right size, the computer hardly ever looks in main memory. The result is that everything runs a lot faster.

capacity   This refers to the amount of binary data in 8 bit bytes that can be stored on the hard disk's multiple surfaces. Be aware that not all hard disk capacities are stated equally. It is difficult to state accurately until after the disk is installed in the computer and formatted as different computer types, controllers, formatting software, and disk drives produce different results.

Cat Mac   The book *Build Your Own Macintosh and Save a Bundle* is about building your own Macintosh from catalog parts. Catalog Macintosh has been shortened to Cat Mac throughout the book.

CD ROM   Stands for compact disk read-only memory. A convenient and compact way of storing and distributing large volumes of data.

character   A letter, a number, or an eight-bit piece of data.

chip   An integrated circuit, usually made from a silicon wafer. It is microscopically etched and has thousands of transistors and semiconductors in a very small area. The 80286 CPU used in the AT has an internal main surface of about one-half-inch-square. It has 120,000 transistors on it.

clipboard   A holding place for temporarily storing text or graphics.

clock speed   The operations of a computer are based on very critical timing, so they use a crystal to control their internal clocks.

clone   Computer slang for a copy of another manufacturer's computer. IBM defined the DOS personal computer with their model in 1981. All the copies of it today are clones, they copy its ROM and other features. In contrast, no Apple Macintosh clones exist because Apple has not licensed its ROM therefore it is illegal to copy. A "build-it-yourself" Macintosh is not a clone, it is just a Macintosh logic board typically mounted in a DOS PC-style case.

CPU   Stands for central processing unit. Today the engine or chip that drives your Macintosh.

consultant   Someone who is supposed to be an expert who can advise and help you determine what your computer needs are. Similar to an analyst. There are no standard requirements or qualifications that must be met. So anyone can call claim to be an analyst or consultant.

coprocessor   Usually an 8087 or 80287 that works in conjunction with the CPU and vastly speeds up some operations.

cursor   The blinking spot on the screen that indicates where next character will be.

database   A collection of data, usually related in some way.

desktop   The screen or environment that the Apple Macintosh initially presents to the user, just like working at a real desk.

dialog box   A window or full-screen display that pops up in response to a command.

DIP   Stands for dual inline package, a type of packaging for a chip.

DMA   Stands for direct memory access. Some parts of the computer, such as the disk drives, can exchange data directly with the RAM without having to go through the CPU.

DOS   Stands for disk operating system. Also shorthand for MS-DOS and PC-DOS, the software engines that drive the majority of the IBM-compatible clone computers. Totally transparent to the user in the Macintosh environment.

DOS PC   Denotes a personal computer which utilizes the IBM DOS operating system as opposed to utilizing the Macintosh operating system, Unix, or something else.

double density   Original Mac diskettes were 400K capacity single-sided diskettes, then 800K double-density was introduced, then today's highest density standard the 1.4Mb capacity drive used by Apple's FDHD SuperDrive.

dot matrix printer   A printer which represents each character using a series of dots in a closely spaced matrix. The Apple ImageWriter printer is an example.

DRAM Stands for dynamic random access memory. A type of memory that must constantly be refreshed, or recharged. Primary type of memory used in PCs.

emulation mode A manner of operating in which one system imitates another. For example, a Macintosh computer in emulation mode can imitate the operation of a DOS PC, Apple II, or other computer.

Ethernet A high-speed local area network, developed by Xerox, which consists of a cable technology and a series of communication protocols. Interconnecting cable can be either thin, thick, or twisted pair.

expansion boards Boards that can be plugged into one of the eight slots on the motherboard to add memory or other functions.

FDHD Stands for floppy disk high-density, Apple's latest floppy drive 1.4Mb standard.

Finder Stands for the part of the Apple Macintosh software that creates and maintains the user environment, which keeps track of files on the desktop, etc.

floppy disk A disk made of flexible plastic, as opposed to a hard disk, which is made of rigid material. The term floppy was formerly applied to disks with thin, flexible disk jackets, such as $5^1/4$-inch floppy disks. With $3^1/2$-inch floppy disks, the disk media itself is still flexible, but the jacket is made of hard plastic.

fonts The different types of print letters such as Gothic, Courier, Roman, Italic, and others.

formatting The formatting step puts specific track and sector "pockets" into the hard disk. Formatting builds exact locations where you can later find data. To quickly move data on and off the disk, it identifies certain tracks as "directory" tracks. These contain information tags, or flags or pointers, which point to or identify the location of data on the disk.

FPU Stands for floating point unit. An additional chip working in parallel that speeds up processing time for numerical calculations.

fragmentation If a diskette has several records that have been changed several times, bits of the files can be on several different tracks and sectors. This slows down writing and reading of the files because the head has to move back and forth to the various tracks. If these files are copied to a newly formatted diskette, each file will be written to clean tracks that are contiguous. This will decrease the access time to the diskette or hard disk.

gigabyte One billion bytes.

glitch An unexpected electrical spike or static disturbance that can cause loss of data.

gray market The practice of dealers selling their product to other dealers without adding value in order to meet their manufacturer's delivery quotas and keep their discount levels.

grayscale Each pixel can display up to 256 shades of gray as opposed to just black or white available in a standard monitor. Many monitors can be converted into grayscale just by changing the interface card driving them. This is useful for working with scanned photographs; you can see much more of the tonal range.

handshaking   A protocol between systems, usually the printer and the computer, to indicate readiness to communicate with each other.

hard disk cylinders, tracks, sectors   Like a phonograph record, floppy and hard disk platters have information stored on each side. Unlike a phonograph record's spiral, a computer disk's platter is recorded in concentric areas. Each side of a platter is called a *cylinder*. *Tracks* are the pattern of concentric circles or rings on the disk's surfaces established by the formatting software onto which the data is written. Frequently, cylinders and tracks are interchanged in usage. *Sectors* are the subdivided portions of the tracks. They are also called *blocks* and refer to a specific location on a given track onto which data is written. A Mac disk might be formatted with 512 bytes of data in a sector or block. The interface reads or writes one sector at a time regardless of the amount of data actually being read from or written into the sector.

hard disk platters   Also called the media. This is the flexible disk medium in a floppy diskette, typically of thin plastic with an even thinner magnetic coating on both sides of it, or rigid disk medium in a hard disk of a metallic alloy or glass, again magnetically coated.

hard disk size, height   Size refers to the diameter of the disk inside the enclosure or its width, $5^1/_4$ inch and increasingly $3^1/_2$ inch today. Height is a carry over from early IBM DOS PC days. Full-height refers to a disk that takes up the entire height of the original PC front bezel opening designed to fit $5^1/_4$-inch wide disk cases. Half-height means half that dimension, or two drives in the same space. Today, new Mac's feature one-third height (approximately one inch high) $3^1/_2$-inch disk drives.

hard disk heads   Like the tone arm to the phonograph record, the hard disk read/write heads go to any spot on the disk instantly and transfer information at a very high rate once there. Hard disk heads float on a cushion of air and never touch the platter's surface. On a floppy drive, heads on opposite sides of the media press it between them and tiny electromagnets at the tip of the heads either read or write data.

hertz (Hz)   A unit of frequency of vibration or oscillation expressed in cycles per second. For example, the Mac 68000 CPU operates at 8 megahertz (MHz).

hi-res   Stands for high resolution. A 640 × 480 or greater capacity monitor as opposed to Apple's standard 9-inch 512 × 342 display.

IC   Stands for integrated circuit. Virtually all the components on today will soon be in IC form to improve efficiencies and achieve manufacturing economies.

icon   A graphical representation of an application program, program file, or a file folder (to hold either) on the Apple Macintosh desktop. A mouse can be pointed to an icon and double clicked on the application or file. A key feature of the easy to use Macintosh graphical interface.

initialize   To place system software information on hard drive after formatting. Frequently, "format" and "initialize" are used interchangeably.

input/output (I/0)   The process by which information is transferred between the computer's memory and its keyboard or peripheral devices.

interface   A piece of hardware or software that follows a distinct set of rules and allows communications between two systems.

interface card   A peripheral card that implements a particular interface (such as a parallel or serial interface) by which the computer can communicate with a peripheral device such as a printer or modem.

interleave   Depending on the speed of the computer attached to the hard disk, it might not be fast enough to read all the data from one sector transferred by the disk interface or to write it in one rotation of the disk. To avoid this problem, disks initially being formatted to work with slower Macintoshes have their sectors "interleaved." A "slow" Mac Plus requires a 3:1 interleave. That means the next "logical" sector from which the controller reads or writes data actually skips two sectors over from the last "physical" sector located on the disk. A "faster" Mac SE requires a 2:1 interleave. The next logical sector read or written actually skips one sector over from the last physical sector located on the disk. Mac II's, Mac SE 30's, and up use a 1:1 interleave. The next logical sector read or written by the controller is identical with the physical sector located on the disk.

Killy clip   A clip type device useful for its special ability to securely attach a ribbon cable to a 68000 or 5380 IC chip.

K, kilobyte   1024 bytes or 2^{10} bytes. Two multiplied by itself ten times equals 1024.

LaserWriter   The Apple proprietary laser printer with the intelligent 68000 based Postscript engine.

LAN   Stands for local area network; a system in which several computers are tied together or to a central server.

LCD   Stands for liquid crystal display.

logic board   A large circuit board that holds RAM, ROM, the microprocessor, custom-integrated circuits, and other components that make the computer a computer.

Mb, meg, megabyte   Stands for one million bytes—1,048,576 bytes to be precise. A measurement of disk or memory storage capacity.

mainframe   A large computer that might serve several users.

megahertz (MHz)   Stands for one million cycles per second—a measurement of frequency.

memory   A high-speed temporary storage area next to the main computer used to store data and its location information.

memory, RAM   Stands for random access memory. Today's semiconductor computer memory, like the processor chips, is very fast but volatile. Memory is erased when power is turned off. RAM memory only temporarily stores data. No power, no data.

memory, DRAM   Stands for dynamic RAM because it has to constantly be refreshed.

memory, SRAM   Stands for static RAM, because it does not need constant refreshing.

memory, PRAM   Stands for parameter RAM. A small amount of RAM powered by the Mac's internal battery is set aside to store a few user-definable settings and so they are not lost each time the Mac is turned off.

memory, ROM   Stands for read-only memory. This is a permanent storage medium that is uniquely "programmed" with data. Think of it as a chip with thousands and thousands of tiny fuses on it that are either blown or intact, in accordance with the instructions. It gives any computer its unique personality by telling it how it will execute certain instructions.

menu   A list of choices or options. The menu-driven Apple Macintosh system makes it very easy for persons new to computers to learn how to use it.

microsecond   Stands for one millionth of a second, or 10^{-6} seconds in math notation.

modem   A device that converts digital signals to analog form for transmission over a phone line and reverses the process on the other end.

Molex   A type of electrical connector useful for it properties of being able to be keyed, polarized, or locked.

monitor   A device to look at a picture (video monitor) or listen to a sound (audio monitor).

monitor, full-page   Also called a *portrait monitor*. Reproduces the vertical format $8^{1}/_{2}$-x-11-inch (or A4 European) page on the screen. Good for heavy word processing work where it is helpful to see the entire page at a glance.

monitor resolution   The amount of information displayed or the number of pixels, the pixel dimensions, across and down. The 9-inch Mac screen paints a picture that has a resolution of 512 pixels across by 342 pixels down, for a total of 175,104 pixels.

monitor size   Sometimes called viewing area. Measured diagonally from corner to corner. The 9-inch Mac screen is actually $7^{1}/_{2}$ inches wide by $5^{1}/_{2}$ inches high.

monitor, two-page   Also called a *landscape monitor*. Reproduces two full side-by-side pages and is useful for doing page layout work. It is also useful for working with spreadsheets. It can either show many cells of a spreadsheet at one time or enlarge a few cells at a time for better viewing in group presentations.

mono   Stands for one. A monochrome monitor has one-color capability.

mouse   A pointing device that controls the movement of a cursor on the screen.

MTBF   Stands for mean time before failure. An average of the time between failures, usually used in describing a hard disk or other components. An MTBF rating of 50,000 hours does not mean each hard disk will last that long before needing repair. It means that in a population of 50,000 hard disks, one will fail every hour, 24 hours per day. This means that about 18% of the drives will have to be repaired before year's end. Over a three-year period, over one half (54%) of the original 50,000 hard disks will require some amount of service.

multisync   The ability of a more expensive than regular TTL monitor to adjust itself to a wide range of video input signal frequencies and thus be usable for a large variety of applications implemented over numerous computer platforms.

nanosecond (ns)   Stands for one-thousandth of a microsecond, or in math notation 10^{-9} seconds—a very short time. Used to measure speeds of SIMM memory chips, i.e., a 80 nanosecond SIMM is capable of operating faster than a 120 nanosecond SIMM.

network, networking The ability to connect two devices together, similar or dissimilar, or the resultant product after it has been done.

PC Stands for personal computer.

peripheral card A removable printed-circuit board that plugs into one of the computer's expansion slots, allowing the computer to use a peripheral device or to perform some subsidiary or peripheral function.

peripheral device A piece of hardware (such as a video monitor, disk drive, printer, or modem) used in conjunction with a computer and under the computer's control. Peripheral devices are often (but not necessarily) physically separate from the computer and connected to it by wires, cables, or some other form of interface. Such devices often require peripheral cards.

pixel Short for "picture element." It's the smallest dot that a monitor can display.

pixel density The number of dots per inch (dpi) on the monitor screen.

ports Access connections to gain entry to the Macintosh to instruct it what to do a give or receive data from it—usually serial, SCSI, or ADB but can be via direct attachment to the CPU chip or a special connector interface.

PMMU Stands for paged memory management unit. Used with A/UX and Apple system 7.0 software to give multiprogramming and virtual capabilities.

price performance A measure of efficiency when one factor is divided by the other. Also enables different types of objects to be compared easily by setting up a standard of price and performance.

RAM Stands for random access memory. A volatile memory. Any data stored in it is lost when the power is turned off.

RGB For red, green, and blue, the three primary colors that are used in color monitors and TVs. Each color has its own electron gun that shoots streams of electrons to the back of the monitor display and causes it to light up in the various colors.

ribbon cable A type of cable with multiple conductors bonded together to lay flat.

ROM Stands for read-only memory. It does not change when the power is turned off.

SCSI Stands for small computer system interface. A fast parallel hard disk interface system developed by Shugart Associates and adopted by the American National Standards Institute (ANSI). The high-speed SCSI bus allows up to seven devices (disk drives, CD-ROM drives, tape drives, scanners, printers, etc.) to be connected, each generating its own input and output traffic on the bus.

scanner A device that converts printed information to electronic. It works similar to a copier machine except the information is stored electronically.

sector A section of a track on a disk or diskette.

serial The transmission of one bit at a time over a single line.

SIMM Stands for single in-line memory module. A SIMM typically consists of two to eight individual RAM chips attached to a small printed circuit card. Some IIci and IIfx SIMMs use nine chips; the extra one is for parity, a quick way of checking your memory's health. Memory was revolutionized by use of

SIMMs. First introduced with the Mac Plus in 1986, SIMMs made it possible to easily add additional memory to the Macintosh Plus logic board and to any Macintosh developed since then.

slots Refers to the connectors or connections used for additional boards to be added to a SE, SE 30, or Mac II family computer.

SOJ Refers to surface mount, a method of attaching chips or components to a circuit board without having to make holes. The chips are soldered onto the surface of the board.

SRAM Stands for static random access memory. It is made up of transistors that remain in whatever state they are placed in, either on or off, until changed or power is removed. SRAM can be very fast and does not need to be refreshed.

static Refers for an electrical charge picked up by a user that can be very damaging to delicate electronic computer circuitry, and magnetic media. Precautions need to be taken against it.

submin D A connector type typically used with the logic boards of Macintosh computers for SCSI, floppy, and video monitor connections.

SWIM Stands for super Wozniak integrated machine and is the latest in the family (following the IWM) of chips that reduce complex floppy disk controller circuitry onto a single chip.

synchronous Able to perform two or more processes at the same time, such as sending and receiving data, by means of a mutual timing signal or clock.

System, System icon, System software Apple's Macintosh operating system software, totally transparent to the user, that is merely an icon in a folder which resides on a graphical desktop. The user doesn't even know of its presence, but just utilizes its features.

System 7.0 The latest in the family of Apple systems and the first one to introduce multi-programming and virtual capabilities to the Macintosh environment.

throughput The amount of data input a device is able to handle. It is a measure of capacity.

tracks The pattern of concentric circles or rings on the hard disk's surfaces, established by the formatting software, onto which the data is written.

trash icon The icon which is part of the process that allows the Macintosh user to delete a file by pointing to it on the screen and performing a simple operation rather than a command as in the DOS world.

TTL Stands for transistor to transistor logic. An electrical interface definition but also applies to the simplest, lowest cost class of monitors.

Unix The industry standard, multiprogramming, virtual operating system developed and supported by AT&T.

user groups Usually a club or a group of people who use computers. Often the club will be devoted to users of a certain type of computer. Usually anyone is welcome to join.

video Stands for visual or screen or picture-oriented data.

virtual memory A feature that allows certain operating systems to designate a portion of the disk space as a part of memory in a manner totally transparent to the user so that larger programs are apparently memory-resident all the time.

volatile   Refers to memory units that lose stored information when power is lost. Nonvolatile memory would be that of a hard disk or tape.

wait state   Slower devices on the bus might not be able to respond at the same speed as the CPU. For instance, if a memory access by the CPU requires more than one clock cycle, then the CPU is slowed down by having the CPU sit idle for one or more cycles while the procedure is accomplished.

word length   Earlier computers and chips "thought" in word lengths of 8, 12, 16, and 24 bits. They defined and moved data in chunks of that size. Two raised to that number defined the limit of memory they could directly address. Most of today's computers and chips use 32 bits and are able to directly address four billion address locations, or more precisely, 2^{32} or four gigabytes.

WYSIWYG   Pronounced "wizzywig." Stands for what you see is what you get. One of the benefits of the Mac interface is what you see on the screen is reproduced faithfully by the printed output. Apple specified that Mac compatible displays have a one-to-one ratio between the 72 dots per inch on the display and the 72 dots per inch at which the Apple ImageWriter prints. This feature, used by many software applications, produces high-quality output in less time because intermediate steps are saved when the layout for the final print product is done on the screen.

Index

Macintosh upgrade checklists

Before you upgrade checklist

- ☐ Shop for best price/vendor/warranty/return privilege.
- ☐ Buy the upgrade part(s).
- ☐ Make sure all the pieces you ordered to upgrade your Mac (the hardware and software items you need) are present.
- ☐ Find a good work area—well lighted, enough space, low traffic, etc.
- ☐ Get all the tools you need.
- ☐ Complete pre-upgrade software steps. For example, the software you need to put a new monitor on your Mac is best generated before you put the monitor on so that you have a stable Mac to generate it.

General upgrade checklist

- ☐ Make sure you're familiar with what you're going to do, whether it's reading this book or reading the instructions that come with every manufacturer's product (except SIMMs!). Make sure you read, reread, and reread if necessary until you clearly understand the steps of the process.
- ☐ Did you dry run through the process before doing it to familiarize yourself?
- ☐ Did you draw up a checklist of what you need to do in your own handwriting (notes) to go down and check off the items with a pencil as you do them?
- ☐ It is always prudent to be a little more cautious, the extra care you take may save you money.
- ☐ Is all the power removed; are all power cords removed from your Mac before you begin the upgrade and not returned until after you completed it?
- ☐ Do you know how to take apart your Mac so you don't hurt either yourself or the Mac?
- ☐ Have you installed the upgrade as the instructions suggested?
- ☐ Are all the cables properly attached, not binding or running into other components or shorting? Are they cinched down tightly?
- ☐ Before you "button up" your Macintosh have you performed a "surgeon's check" to see that no tools or sponges are still inside? You want to leave your Mac the way you found it.
- ☐ Have you reconnected your Macintosh the way it was before?
- ☐ Have you checked out your upgrade first by using the floppy diskette (or a copy of that floppy diskette as is usually recommended) that came with it rather than using your hard disk with your valuable data on it? Isolate any problem at no risk to your good hard disk first. It's just one less thing to worry about.
- ☐ If it doesn't work right the first time, do you know how to troubleshoot it?